PRENTICE HALL PTR SERIES O

MFC Programming in C++ with the Standard Template Libraries

William H. Murray

Chris H. Pappas

Prentice Hall PTR, Upper Saddle River, NJ 07458
www.phptr.com

Library of Congress Cataloging-in-Publication Data

Murray, William H., 1943-
    MFC programming in C++ with the standard template libraries. / William H. Murray, Chris H.
Pappas.
        p. cm. -- (Prentice Hall PTR Microsoft technologies series)
    ISBN 0-13-016111-X
        1. C++ (computer program language).   2. Microsoft foundation class library.   I. Pappas, Chris
H., 1953-   II. Title.   III. Series

    QA76.73.C153 M865 2000
    005.13'3--dc21

                                                                    00-037306

Editorial/Production Supervision: Wil Mara
Acquisitions Editor: Paul Petralia
Editorial Assistant: Justin Somma
Marketing Manager: Bryan Gambrel
Manufacturing Manager: Alexis R. Heydt
Cover Design: Talar Agasyan
Cover Design Direction: Jerry Votta
Art Director: Gail Cocker-Bogusz

Prentice Hall books are widely used by corporations and government agencies for training, marketing, and
resale. The publisher offers discounts on this book when ordered in bulk quantities. For more information,
contact Prentice Hall's Corporate Sales Department—phone: 1-800-382-3419; fax: 1-201-236-7141;
email: corpsales@prenhall.com; address: Corp. Sales Dept., Prentice Hall PTR, 1 Lake Street, Upper
Saddle River, NJ 07458.

Printed in the United States of America
10   9   8   7   6   5   4   3   2   1

ISBN 0-13-016111-X

Prentice-Hall International (UK) Limited, *London*
Prentice-Hall of Australia Pty. Limited, *Sydney*
Prentice-Hall Canada Inc., *Toronto*
Prentice-Hall Hispanoamericana, S.A., *Mexico*
Prentice-Hall of India Private Limited, *New Delhi*
Prentice-Hall of Japan, Inc., *Tokyo*
Pearson Education Asia P.T.E., Ltd.
Editora Prentice-Hall do Brasil, Ltda., *Rio de Janeiro*

MFC Programming in C++ with the Standard Template Libraries

ISBN 0-13-016111-X

90000

9 780130 161116

- Supporting Windows NT and 2000 Workstation and Server
  Mohr

- Zero Administration Kit for Windows
  McInerney

- Tuning and Sizing NT Server
  Aubley

- Windows NT 4.0 Server Security Guide
  Goncalves

- Windows NT Security
  McInerney

- Windows NT Device Driver Book
  Baker

CERTIFICATION

- Core MCSE: Windows 2000 Edition
  Dell

- Core MCSE
  Dell

- Core MCSE: Networking Essentials
  Keogh

- MCSE: Administering Microsoft SQL Server 7
  Byrne

- MCSE: Implementing and Supporting Microsoft Exchange Server 5.5
  Goncalves

- MCSE: Internetworking with Microsoft TCP/IP
  Ryvkin, Houde, Hoffman

- MCSE: Implementing and Supporting Microsoft Proxy Server 2.0
  Ryvkin, Hoffman

- MCSE: Implementing and Supporting Microsoft SNA Server 4.0
  Mariscal

- MCSE: Implementing and Supporting Microsoft Internet Information Server 4
  Dell

- MCSE: Implementing and Supporting Web Sites Using Microsoft Site Server 3
  Goncalves

- MCSE: Microsoft System Management Server 2
  Jewett

- MCSE: Implementing and Supporting Internet Explorer 5
  Dell

- Core MCSD: Designing and Implementing Desktop Applications with Microsoft Visual Basic 6
  Holzner

- Core MCSD: Designing and Implementing Distributed Applications with Microsoft Visual Basic 6
  Houlette, Klander

- MCSD: Planning and Implementing SQL Server 7
  Vacca

- MCSD: Designing and Implementing Web Sites with Microsoft FrontPage 98
  Karlins

Dedicated to Richard Hernandez

What a success story!

ABOUT THE FTP SITE

For your convenience, Prentice Hall PTR and the authors have provided a file transfer protocol (FTP) site containing all the source codes for this book. The URL is as follows—

ftp://ftp.prenhall.com/pub/ptr/computer_science_reference.w-021/murray_pappas.mfc_programming.sourcecodes

CONTENTS

PREFACE

In order to take full advantage of the features of this book, you should have a basic programming familiarity with developing both procedure-oriented and object-oriented C++ applications for both the command line and Windows environments. Our role will then be to introduce you to key STL and MFC components. You'll then learn how to combine these components into working MFC Windows applications using the STL.

The Standard Template Library brings robust programming power to the Visual C++ programmer. This book is divided into three basic sections. In the first section you'll learn the fundamentals of using the STL in command-line applications. The second section introduces you to the world of object-oriented MFC Windows programming. The third section shows you how the STL and MFC libraries can be combined to produce powerful new Windows applications for both Windows 98 and 2000.

Join Pappas and Murray for a practical look at the power of combining the STL and MFC libraries in simple straightforward programming applications. You'll then be able to add your own programming expertise to build robust applications of your own.

Before Jumping into MFC with STL Programming . . .

The ANSI/ISO C++ Standard Template Library, or STL, promises to deliver to algorithm design what the Microsoft Foundation Class library, or MFC, provides Windows programmers, mainly application code that is easy to generate, use, modify, and maintain, and is portable across architectures! STL is a standalone library of routines that does not have to be used in a multitasking, object-oriented Windows application. MFC has functioned well for years on its own prior to the development of STL. This text is undoubtedly the first book you will read that combines the tremendous power of these two technologies. MFC with STL brings to the Windows developer the closest, to date, they can come to a robust, off-the-shelf problem solutions.

C++, MFC, and STL, however, are moving targets—meaning that as you read this, all three technologies are evolving. This is good in that they continue to provide today's programmers with the necessary tools to get the job done, but they demand a programmer's continual retraining. This book is not only designed to teach you how to combine MFC with STL, but will update your skills in C++ along the way. This chapter begins by reviewing a few C++ fundamentals heavily employed by the STL technology, and will probably introduce experienced C++ programmers to some very recent "moving target" C++ language updates.

From BASIC, to Object-Oriented Programming, Now STL—WHY?

From a programming point of view, today's development environment is a hundred times more complex than a decade ago. Instead of PC application development targeting a standalone DOS text-mode environment, it must

1

now deal with hundreds of PC clones and other popular competing platforms.

Not All PCs are Alike

These new architectures have their own evolving operating systems and multi-tasking, multimedia capabilities—plus the typical Internet presence. In other words, today's programming environment, programmed by a single developer, was once the domain of systems, communications, security, networking, utility, etc. specialists all working as a team to keep the "mother ship," or mainframe, up and running!

Something had to come along to enable application developers to keep pace with this ever-increasing resource management nightmare. Voila, enter C++. These new languages incorporated brand new programming capabilities to melt through this hidden iceberg of programming demands.

C++ Is Not For Children

The biggest stumbling block to accessing these incredibly powerful C++ features is ignorance of their existence. In the real world, most experienced FORTRAN, COBOL, Pascal, PL/I, and assembly language programmers, when asked by their bosses to use a new language, taught themselves the new language! Why? Because of course, the company wouldn't give them the time off to learn them. They diligently studied nights and weekends, on their own, and mapped their understanding of whatever language they knew well to the new language's syntax.

This approach worked for decades as long as a programmer went from one "older high-level language" to the next. Unfortunately, this approach, when it comes to C++, leaves the diligent, self-motivated, learn-on-their-own employee FIRED and wondering what went wrong *this time?*

Here's a very small example to illustrate the point. In COBOL, for instance, to increment a variable by 1, you would write:

```
accumulator = accumulator + 1;
```

Then one day, the boss says you need to write the program in FORTRAN. You learn FORTRAN and rewrite the statement:

```
accumulator = accumulator + 1;
```

No problem. Then your company migrates to Pascal and once again you teach yourself the new syntax:

```
accumulator := accumulator + 1;
```

Ta da! Then your boss says that your million dollar code needs to be ported over to Microsoft Windows in C++. After a divorce, heart attack, and alcohol addiction, you emerge feeling you have mastered Microsoft Windows/C++ logic and syntax and finally rewrite the statement:

```
iaccumulator = iaccumulator + 1; //i for integer in Hungarian Notation
```

and you get fired! The senior programmer, hired from a local two-year college, looks at your code and scoffs at your inept translation. Oh, sure you got the idea behind Hungarian Notation (a C++ naming convention that precedes every variable's name with an abbreviation of its data type), but you created a literal statement *translation* instead of incorporating the efficiency alternatives available in C++.

Your senior programmer, green, 20 years younger than you, only knowing Microsoft Windows and C++ syntax, knew the statement should have been written:

```
iaccumulator++;
```

This statement, using the C++ increment operator, efficiently instructs the compiler to delete the double fetch/decode of the incorrectly written *translation*, and to treat the variable *iaccumulator* as its name implies, as an accumulator within a register, a much more efficient machine language encoding.

This extremely simple code example is only the beginning of hundreds of C++ language features waiting, like quicksand, to catch the unwary programmer. Because of these C++ peculiarities, this chapter highlights the STL-related C++ topics necessary to fully understand and use STL. The chapter only assumes a minimum comfort level with C++.

The first half of the chapter introduces you to STL philosophy. The last half of the chapter reviews the pivotal fundamentals provided by C++ that make the STL possible, and ends with the highest level C++ syntax that actually creates STL's generic algorithms. While you may think you are an experienced enough C++ programmer to skip this chapter and begin immediately using STL, you may be surprised to find out just how much C++ has evolved. Even if you had introductory and advanced C++ courses, you may again be surprised to find out just how much your professor *didn't* know or tell you. Or even worse, the C++ you currently know, well quite frankly, is just plain incorrect. For all of these reasons, it is strongly suggested that you sit down with a nice cup of coffee and read this chapter, and the *next chapter*, all the way through.

STL, An Alternative to Data Structures—Really?

In a programmer's formal educational path, there stands a course typically called Data Structures, which statistically has an attrition rate of 50%. Why? Because it deals with two extremely efficient concepts, pointers and dynamic memory allocation/deallocation, which when combined generate a geometric complexity in program development and debugging requirements. These concepts typically present such a steep learning curve that many programmers either avoid the course altogether, or lop along getting by, and then *never* use the concepts in the real world. This is unfortunate since pointers and dynamic memory allocation present some of the most powerful and efficient algorithms available to a programmer. Enter the Standard Template Library!

STL—A First Look

In a nutshell, the STL encapsulates the pure, raw horsepower of the C++ language, plus the advanced efficient algorithms engendered within a good Data Structures course, all bundled into a simple-to-use form! It is similar in a way to having struggled with years of pre-Calc and Calculus courses only to be given an advanced portable calculator that does all the work for you.

You may view the STL as an extensible framework, which contains components for language support, diagnostics, general utilities, strings, locales, the STL itself (containers, iterators, algorithms, numerics), and input/output.

Who Invented STL?

With the ever-increasing popularity of C++ and Microsoft Windows-controlled environments, many third-party vendors evolved into extremely profitable commodities by providing libraries of routines designed to handle the storage and processing of data. In an ever-ongoing attempt to maintain C++'s viability as a programming language of choice, and to keep the ball rolling by maintaining a strict control of the language's formal definition, the ANSI/ISO C++ committee added a new approach to defining these libraries called the Standard Template Library, or STL.

STL was developed by Alexander Stepanov and Meng Lee of Hewlett Packard (HP). STL is expected to become the standard approach to storing and processing data. Major compiler vendors are beginning to incorporate the STL into their products. The STL is more than just a minor addition to the world's most popular programming language; it represents a revolutionary new capability. The STL brings a surprisingly mature set of generic containers and algorithms to the C++ programming language, adding a dimension to the language that simply did not exist before.

Is STL Only For Experienced Programmers?

You have all you need to know right now, simply by picking up this book. Unlike many other STL books which simply enumerate endless lists of STL template names, functions, constants, etc., this book will begin by first teaching you the advanced C++ language fundamentals that make the STL syntactically possible.

Along the way, this instructional section will show you the syntax that allows an algorithm to be generic, in other words, how C++ syntactically separates *what* a program does from the *data type(s)* it uses. You will learn about the generic **void *** pointer's strengths and weaknesses, "a better way" with generic types, "an even better way" using templates, and finally, the "best way" with cross-platform, portable standard templates!

The section on template development begins with simple C++ structures used syntactically to create *objects* (yes, you can create an object with this keyword; however, it is a very bad idea—you'll have to wait until the next chapter to see why)! The **struct** object definition is then evolved over, logically and syntactically, into the C++ **class.** Finally, the **class** object is mutated into a generic **template.** This progressive approach allows you to easily assimilate the new features of C++ and paves the way to technically correct use of the STL. With this under your belt, you will both logically and syntactically understand how the STL works and begin to immediately incorporate this technology into your application development.

Generic programming is going to provide you with the power and expressiveness of languages like SmallTalk while retaining the efficiency and compatibility of C++. STL is guaranteed to increase the productivity of any programmer who uses it.

STL—The "Big Picture"

Although the STL is large and its syntax can be initially intimidating, it is actually quite easy to use once you understand how it is constructed and what elements it employs. At the core of the STL are three foundational items called *containers, algorithms*, and *iterators*. These libraries work together, allowing you to generate, in a portable format, frequently employed algorithmic solutions such as array creation, element insertion/deletion, sorting, and element output. But, the STL goes even further by providing internally clean, seamless, and efficient integration of iostreams and exception handling.

STL Standardization Breeds Industry Acceptance

Multi-vendor implementations of C/C++ compilers would have long ago died on the vine were it not for the ANSI C/C++ Committees. They are responsible for giving us *portable* C and C++ code by filling in the *missing* details for the formal language descriptions of both C and C++ as presented by their authors, Dennis Ritchie and Bjarne Stroustrup, respectively. And to this day, it is the ANSI/ISO C++ Committee that continues to guarantee C++'s portability into the next millennium.

While on the subject of language authorship, it is Alexander Stepanov and Meng Lee of HP who developed the concept and coding behind the STL. The industry anticipates that STL will become *the* standard approach to storing and processing data.

The ANSI/ISO C++ Committee's current standards exceed its past recommendations, which historically decided only to codify existing practice and resolve ambiguities and contradictions among existing translator implementations. The C++ Committee's changes are innovations. In most cases, the changes implement features that committee members admired in other languages, features that they viewed as deficiencies in traditional C++, or simply features that they always wanted in a programming language. A *great* deal of thought and discussion were invested in each change, and consequently, the committee feels that the new C++ definition, along with the evolutionary definition of STL, is the best definition of C++ possible today.

Most of these recommended changes consist of language additions that should not affect existing code. Old programs should still compile with newer compilers as long as the old code does not coincidentally use any of the new keywords as identifiers. However, even experienced C++ programmers may be surprised as to how much of C++ has evolved without even discussing STL; for example, the use of namespaces, new-style type casting, and run-time type information (discussed in detail in Chapter 2) are markedly different.

The Three Components of STL

Conceptually, STL encompasses three separate algorithmic problem-solvers: containers, algorithms, and iterators. A *container* is a way that stored data is organized in memory, for example, an array, stack, queue, linked list, or binary tree. However, there are many other kinds of containers, and the STL includes the most useful. STL containers are implemented by template classes so they can be easily customized to hold different data types.

All the containers have common management member functions defined in their template definitions: `insert()`, `erase()`, `begin()`, `end()`, `size()`, `capacity()`, and so on. Individual containers have member functions that support their unique requirements.

Algorithms are behaviors or functionality applied to containers to process their contents in various ways. For example, there are algorithms to sort, copy, search, and merge container contents. In the STL, algorithms are represented by template functions. These functions are not member functions of the container classes. Instead, they are standalone functions. Indeed, one of the surprising characteristics of the STL is that its algorithms are so general. You can use them not only on STL containers, but also on ordinary C++ arrays or any other application-specific container.

A standard suite of algorithms provides for searching, copying, reordering, transforming, and performing numeric operations on objects in containers. The same algorithms are used to perform operations for all containers of all object types!

Once you have decided on a container type and data behaviors, the only thing left is to connect the two with *iterators*. You can think of iterators as generalized pointers that point to elements within containers. You can increment an iterator, as you can a pointer, so it points in turn to each successive element in the container. Iterators are a key part of the STL because they connect algorithms with containers.

What Is a Container?

All STL library syntax incorporates the full use of C++ templates (data type-independent syntax). As we discuss container types, remember that they are implemented as templates; the types of objects they contain are determined by the template arguments given when the program instantiates the containers. There are three major types of containers: vectors (or dynamic arrays), deques (or double-ended queues), and linear lists (bitsets, maps, and multimaps).

Sequence containers store finite sets of objects of the same type in a linear organization. An array of names is a sequence. You use one of the sequence types, vector, list, or deque, for a particular application, depending on its retrieval requirements.

VECTOR CLASS

Vector sequences allow random data access. A vector is an array of contiguous homogeneous objects with an instance counter or pointer to indicate the end of the vector sequence. Random access is facilitated through the use of a subscript operation. Vector sequences allow you to append entries to and remove entries from the end of the dynamic structure without undue overhead. Inserts and deletes from the middle, however, naturally take longer due to the time involved in shifting the remaining entries to make room for the new or deleted item.

LIST CLASS

A list sequence provides bidirectional access; it allows you to perform inserts and deletes anywhere without undue performance penalties. Random access is simulated by forward or backward iteration to the target object. A list consists of noncontiguous objects linked with forward and backward pointers.

DEQUE CLASS

A deque sequence is similar to a vector sequence except that a deque sequence allows fast inserts and deletes at the beginning as well as at the end of the container. Random inserts and deletes are less efficient.

BITSET CLASS

The bitset class supports operations on a set of bits, such as `flip()`, `reset()`, `set()`, `size()`, `to_string`, etc.

MAP CLASS

The map class provides associative containers with unique keys mapped to specific values.

MULTIMAP CLASS

The multimap class is very similar to the map class in raw horsepower except for one minor difference, the availability of a non-unique key mapped to specific values.

What Is an Adapter?

STL supports three adapter containers that you can combine with one of the sequence containers listed above. The scenario goes like this: First, you select the appropriate application-specific container; then, you instantiate a container adapter class by naming the existing container in the declaration:

```
queue< list< bank_customer_struct > >TellerOneQueue;
```

The example instantiates a queue container, one of the three adapter containers supported by STL, by using the list container as the underlying data structure built around a hypothetical bank customer waiting for an available teller.

Container adapters hide the public interface of the underlying container and implement their own. A queue data structure, for example, resembles a list, but has its own requirements for its user interface. STL incorporates three standard adapter containers: stack, queue, and priority_queue.

STACK CLASS

The stack adapter provides the logical operations of push() and pop(), enabling the standard Last In First Out, or LIFO, solution. Stacks are great for certain types of problem solutions like evaluating an Infix arithmetic expression that has been translated into Postfix for the purposes of unambiguous evaluation.

QUEUE CLASS

Regardless of whether or not the storage sequence container is a vector or linked list, the queue adapter uses this underlying scheme to add items to the end of the list using the push() method, and to delete or remove items from the front of the list using pop(). The acronym for a queue algorithm is First In First Out, or FIFO.

PRIORITY_QUEUE CLASS

A priority_queue is similar to a queue adapter in that all items added to the queue are at the end of the list. However, unlike a queue adapter, which *only* removes items from the front of the list, a priority_queue adapter removes the highest priority item within the list first!

What Are Algorithms?

Similar to container adapters, algorithms also act on containers. Algorithms provide for container initializations, sorting, searching, and data transformations. Interestingly, algorithms are *not* implemented as class methods, but instead standalone template functions. For this reason, they not only work on STL containers, but on standard C++ arrays or with container classes you create yourself.

Typical algorithmic behaviors include find(), to locate a specific item, count(), to let you know how many items are in the list, equal(), for comparisons, and search(), copy(), swap(), fill(), sort(), and so on.

What Is an Iterator?

Whenever an application needs to move through the elements of a container, it uses an iterator. Iterators are similar to pointers used to access individual data items. In the STL, an iterator is represented by an object of an iterator class. You can increment an iterator with the C++ increment operator, ++, moving it to the address of the next element. You can also use the dereference operator, *, to access individual members within the selected item. Special iterators are capable of remembering the location of specific container elements.

There are different classes of iterators which must be used with specific container types. The three major classes of iterators are: forward, bidirectional, and random access.

- Forward iterators can only advance forward through the container one item at a time. They cannot move backward, and they cannot be updated to point to any location in the middle of the container.
- Backward iterators work like their forward iterator counterparts, except backward.
- Bidirectional iterators can move forward as well as backward and cannot be assigned or updated to point to any element in the middle of the container.
- Random access iterators go one step further than bidirectional iterators in that they allow the application to perform arbitrary location jumps within the container.

In addition, STL defines two specialized categories known as input and output iterators. Input and output iterators can point to specific devices; for example, an input iterator may point to a user-defined input file, or cin, and it may be used to perform sequential reads into the container. Likewise, an output iterator may point to a user-defined output file, or cout, performing the logical inverse operation of sequentially outputting container elements.

Unlike forward, backward, bidirectional, and random access iterators, input and output iterators cannot store their current values. The first four iterators must hold their values for them to know where they are within the container. The last two, input and output, since they are pointers to devices, do not structurally represent the same type of information and therefore have no memory capabilities.

Are There Any More STL Components?

Beyond containers, algorithms, and iterators, STL defines:

- *Allocators* for managing memory allocation for individual containers.
- *Predicates,* which are unary or binary in nature, meaning they work on either one operand or two, and always return either TRUE or FALSE.

- *Comparison functions,* unique binary predicates comparing two elements and returning TRUE only if the first argument is less than the second.
- *Function objects,* including plus, minus, multiply, divide, modulus, negate, equal_to, not_equal_to, greater, greater_equal, less, less_equal, logical_and, logical_or, logical_not, and so on.

The Complete STL Package

The following review is included to help you formalize the structural components of the STL. You can logically divide the STL into the following categories:

A) STL headers can be grouped into three major organizing concepts.
   1) Containers are template classes that support common ways to organize data: <deque>, <list>, <map>, <multimap>, <queue>, <set>, <stack>, and <vector>.
   2) Algorithms are template functions for performing common operations on sequences of objects, including <algorithm>, <functional>, and <numeric>.
   3) Iterators are the glue that pastes together algorithms and containers, and include <iterator>, <memory>, and <utility>.
B) Input output includes components for:
   1) Forward declarations of iostreams, <iosfwd>.
   2) Predefined iostreams objects, <iostream>.
   3) Base iostreams classes, <ios>.
   4) Stream buffering, <streambuf>.
   5) Stream formatting and manipulators: <iosmanip>, <istream>, and <ostream>.
   6) String streams, <sstream>.
   7) File streams, <fstream>.
C) Other standard C++ headers include:
   1) Language support includes:
      a) Components for common type definitions used throughout the library, <cstddef>.
      b) Characteristics of the predefined types <limits>, <cfloat>, and <climits>.
      c) Functions supporting the start and termination of a C++ program, <cstdlib>.
      d) Support for dynamic memory management, <new>.
      e) Support for dynamic type identification, <typeinfo>.

      f) Support for exception processing, `<exception>`.

      g) Other run-time support: `<cst.darg>`, `<ctime>`, `<csetlmp>`, and `<csignal>`.

  2) Diagnostics include components for:

      a) Reporting several kinds of exceptional conditions, `<stdexcept>`.

      b) Documenting program assertions, `<cassert>`.

      c) A global variable for error number codes, `<cerrno>`.

  3) Strings include components for:

      a) String classes, `<string>`.

      b) Null-terminated sequence utilities: `<cctype>`, `<cwctype>`, and `<cwchar>`.

  4) Cultural language components include:

      a) Internationalization support for character classification and string collation, numeric, monetary, and date/time formatting and parsing, and message retrieval using `<locale>` and `<clocale>`.

Historic C, ANSI C, C++, ANSI C++—HELP!

Chaos! The world of C++ programming is a mess. There's "Historic C," ANSI C, C++, ANSI C++, ANSI/ISO C++, Borland International's C++, Microsoft's C++, your senior programmer's version of C++, maybe even a version of C++ created by an ego-centric, self-taught university professor, not to mention next year's state-of-the-art C++ bell'n whistle standard.

The biggest problem to learning C++ is finding a reputable source. With few exceptions, many programmers taught themselves C++. They were professionally degreed programmers with many years of experience who progressed from using some institutional training language to whatever language was in vogue that day. So, typically their learning curve went from COBOL, to FORTRAN, to PL/I, to Pascal, to Modula-2, and on and on.

This scenario actually worked out quite well *in the past*, because all of the older high-level languages had basically the same features, just different syntax. Now take this previously successful self-taught, highly motivated programmer and thrust them into the world of multi-tasking application development, in a GUI (graphical user interface) environment, using C++ and object-oriented technology. Result? Chaos!

C++ provides so many new language features, design philosophies, and sophisticated syntax that mapping over your understanding from some other language just will not do. This book is all about you learning to fly a stealth bomber called STL, even if the only thing you've ever gotten off the ground was a Piper Cub.

The great news is that with a few instructional tips, you *can* take what you currently know about any programming language and get up to speed on this latest technology. That is what this chapter is all about. So, let's get started.

Data Structures—A Review

The code contained within the STL is extremely efficient. One reason for this efficiency is that the objects created use dynamically allocated memory, tracked by pointers. This section reviews the C++ building blocks that make this possible.

Static vs. Dynamic

First, it is important to understand that the word "static" used in this section is *not* the C++ keyword **static.** Instead, static is used to describe a category of memory allocation. Since most programmers understand code more clearly than verbiage, here's an example:

```
void main( void )
{
   int ivalue; // i(nt)value
   .
   .
   .
}
```

This code segment declares an integer variable *ivalue*. Now if you think about it, *ivalue*'s storage location is allocated when the program loads, and this memory allocation persists until the program exits. This is an example of static memory allocation.

Static memory allocation is *not* under the control of the programmer at run-time, but instead is under load-time control. The programmer cannot get more *ivalues*, nor can the programmer delete *ivalue*'s memory allocation at run-time. And that is the downfall to this storage class.

Dynamic memory allocation has the advantage of being under run-time control. Unfortunately, its syntax is not as straightforward and entails the use of pointers. (Note: This example only highlights the difference between static and dynamic memory allocation and is not intended as a real-world example:)

```
void main( void )

   int *pivalue;        // p(ointer to)i(nt)value;
   int iLoopControl, iAsManyAsUserWants;
```

```
cout << "How many integer's would you like to create at run-time?";
cin >> iAsManyAsUserWants;
for( iLoopControl = 0, iLoopControl < iAsManyAsUserWants, iLoopControl++)
   pivalue = new int; // pivalue set to address of
                              // run-time dynamically allocated RAM
```

In this example, the variable *pivalue* is not an integer, but instead is a *pointer variable* that can hold the address to a RAM location big enough to store an integer. Actual integer-sized RAM allocation is accomplished with the C++ **new** keyword. C programmers might recognize the equivalent to **new** as **malloc()** or **calloc()**.

Most importantly, notice that the end-user, at run-time, can select just how many integers they would like to store. Also, at run-time, the user can choose how many to delete by simply using the C++ keyword **delete,** as in:

```
delete pivalue;
```

It is simple to see that run-time control of memory allocation/deallocation has tremendous efficiency benefits. Your program is never grabbing system resources beyond its current needs. The STL makes heavy use of this fundamental.

Typed Pointers

Unlike normal variables of the type **int**, **float**, **char**, etc., pointer variables do not hold data per se; instead they hold addresses to data. In the last section, you saw just how efficient this concept could be when combined with dynamic memory allocation. There is, however, one problem generated by these sibling concepts: type-checking!

By design, C++ is not a strongly typed language. This means that compilers will accept statements like:

```
char cvalue = 65; // initializing a character variable with an integer
```

and

```
int ivalue = 'A'; // initializing an integer variable with a character
```

However, when it comes to pointers, C++ becomes a strongly typed language. So, for example, a float-sized dynamically allocated memory location's address may not be assigned to a pointer of type int, as in:

```
int *pivalue;                    // p(ointer to) i(nt)value;
pivalue = new float;             // illegal attempt to
                                 // assign a float address to int pointer
```

From its inception, C++ has had a syntatical way around type-checking by using the standard type **void**.

Void Pointers

The C++ void data type, when combined with pointer variable definitions, tells the compilers that the defined variable does not hold data per se, but an address. And, it does *not* tell the compilers the data type! This can lead to very powerful code solutions.

In the following example, one subroutine is used to output one of three dynamically allocated data types:

```cpp
#include <iostream>
using namespace std;
void printit ( void *pData, char cRunTimeChoice );

void main ( void )
{
  char  *pchar, cRunTimeChoice;
  int   *pivalue;
  float *pfvalue;

  cout << "Please enter the dynamic data type you want to create\n"
       << " press c for char, i for int, or f for float: ";

  cin  >> cRunTimeChoice;

  switch ( cRunTimeChoice ) {

    case 'c': pchar = new char;
            cout << "\nEnter a character: ";
                  cin  >> *pchar;
                  printit ( pchar, cRunTimeChoice );
                  break;

    case 'i': pivalue = new int;
                  cout << "\nEnter an integer: ";
                  cin  >> *pivalue;
                  printit ( pivalue, cRunTimeChoice );
                  break;

    default:  pfvalue = new float;
                  cout << "\nEnter a float: ";
                  cin  >> *pfvalue;
                  printit ( pfvalue, cRunTimeChoice );

  }
}

void printit ( void *pData, char cRunTimeChoice )
{
  cout << "\nThe Dynamic Data type entered was ";
```

```
switch ( cRunTimeChoice ) {

   case 'c': cout << "char and a value of: "
                  << *(char *)pData;
                  break;

   case 'i': cout << "int and a value of: "
                  << *(int *)pData;
                  break;
   default:  cout << "float and a value of: "
                  << *(float *)pData;

}
delete pData;
}
```

The key statement to understanding void pointers is the *printit()*
prototype:

```
void printit ( void *pData, char cRunTimeChoice );
```

and the three calls to *printit():*

```
printit ( pchar,   cRunTimeChoice );
printit ( pivalue, cRunTimeChoice );
printit ( pfvalue, cRunTimeChoice );
```

Notice how, officially, you have told the compiler that *printit()*'s
first formal argument type is a **void** pointer (**void ***). This suspends normal
type-checking between a function's formal argument list and the calling statement's actual arguments—the only reason the program works.

However, unlike **int ***, definitions, or **float *** syntax, using:

```
void * pToWhoKnowsWhat;
```

doesn't specify *what* the address points to. This is both good and bad. It's
good because the compiler can't do any type-checking when an actual address is assigned, and bad because the compiler can't do any type-checking!
Even worse, a program cannot point with a **void *** type. This explains the
three cast statements within *printit()*'s **switch-case** statement, converting
a pointer to nothing (**void ***) to a specific pointer type:

```
*(char *)pData;
*(int *)pData;
*(float *)pData;
```

Without type-checking, if your code accidentally assigns the wrong address type, the code compiles.

```
void * pivalue;         // variable name indicates it will hold an int type 61
                           address
...
pivalue = new float;    // incorrect assignment of RAM float precision!
```

The previous code section declares *pivalue* as a **void *** pointer; however, the variable's name implies that it will hold the address to integer
p(ointer to)*i*(nt). The pointer is then initialized to the address of a float-sized
memory location. This is still perfectly legal code, maybe even logically okay
for some applications, but look at these next two statements:

```
some_function( pivalue ); // call to some function
...
void some_function( int * pivalue ); // function prototype
```

First, the code will not compile because the compiler (C++) recognizes
that *pivalue*'s formal declaration, **void *,** does not match the function's
first formal argument, which has a type of **int ***. Remember, by default,
pointers are typed, and the compiler, at compile-time, recognizes the mis-
match. But a clever C++ programmer could rewrite the call statement to:

```
some_function( (int *) pivalue );    // working call statement!
...
void some_function( int * pivalue )
{
 //    sample function body code...
cout << "The integer value is: " << *pivalue;     // outputs garbage
```

Executing a program of this nature causes *some_function()* to output
garbage since the memory location contains an IEEE floating-point encrypted
value and the function instructs the compiler to decode a four-byte integer!
The sad news is that the code compiles without warnings and errors.
The point is (no pun intended) **void** pointers can create debugging and run-
time nightmares. The solution is the C++ template.

Hungarian Notation

Test question: Is there anything wrong with the following code segment?

```
int operandA = 1, operandB = 2;
float result;
...
result = operandA / operandB
```

If you answered yes, great! However, if you think the equation is fine, well let's just say it's a good thing there's Hungarian Notation, invented by Charles Simony.

The initial problem begins with the C++ divide operator, /, which is overloaded for different data types. In many other programming languages, there are two separate operators to distinguish integral division from floating-point division. Pascal, for example, uses the divide operator for floating-point precision and the **div** operator for integral results. Obviously, a Pascal programmer can easily see which operator an equation employs. Unfortunately, for unwary C++ programmers, there are no visual clue similarities. Instead, the C++ divide operator itself examines each operand's formal data type and then decides whether or not to perform integer/integer division with an integer result, or floating-point/floating-point with a floating-point result. The previous equation assigns a 0 to the variable *result* instead of the logically intended 0.5 (since *result*'s type is float) because *operandA* and *operandB*'s data types are integer.

Now, imagine that the equation is nested in a large program that is miscalculating values and you, *not* the author of the code, must track down the problem. Enter Hungarian Notation. In Hungarian Notation, each identifier's name (your name for variables, constants, etc.) begins with an abbreviation of its data type. Here are some examples:

```
char            cMenuSelection;
int             iValue;
float           fValue;
char            szLastName[ MAX_LETTERS + NULL_STRING_TERMINATOR ];
int             *piValue;
float           *pfValue;
char            *pszLastName = szLastName;
double          dValue, *pdValue = &pValue;
long double     ldValue, *pldValue = &pldValue;
```

Now imagine the rewrite of the original code segment:

```
int iOperandA = 1, iOperandB = 2;
float fResult;
...
fResult = iOperandA / iOperandB
```

In this version, an experienced C++ programmer, seeing the divide operator employed on two *i*(nt tagged) variable names, and then an *f*(loat tagged)*Result* storage precision, would immediately suspect the equation as possibly generating the beginnings of a numeric miscalculation.

With the hundreds of thousands of lines of code given to you in the Microsoft Windows' objects, or IBM's OS/2 objects, etc., Hungarian Notation goes a long way to helping a programmer intimately understand the data types involved in an algorithm. This directly translates into time savings, whether in digesting a program's logic or in flagging starting points for a de-bugging session.

Overloading Functions

Many C++ object-oriented concepts have procedural underpinnings. Function overloading is a procedural concept that allows a programmer to define several functions by the same name. The syntax only requires that each function's formal argument list be unique. Unique is defined by the number of formal arguments and/or their order and/or their data type(s). Look at the following example function prototypes:

```
int averageArray(int iarray[]);
float averageArray(float farray[]);
double averageArray(double darray[]);
```

Beyond the straightforward syntax, there is the proper logical use of function overloading. Typically, this involves a repetition of function body algorithms that do the same thing, but very often on different data types. A case in point is the averaging of array elements. One subroutine performs this array element processing on integer array elements, another on float array elements, and a third on double array elements. However, all three functions *average array elements!*

Note: An overloaded function's return type does not play any role in defining uniqueness. For this reason, the following overloaded function prototypes are illegal:

```
void averageArray(int iarray[]);
int averageArray(int iarray[]);
float averageArray(int iarray[]);
```

While function overloading is a powerful procedural problem-solving tool, it is also the building block concept behind overloaded class member functions (classes are reviewed later in this chapter).

Function Pointers

All the examples so far have shown you how various items of data can be referenced by a pointer. As it turns out, you can also access *portions of code* by using a pointer to a function. Pointers to functions serve the same purpose as do pointers to data; that is, they allow the function to be referenced indirectly, just as a pointer to a data item allows the data item to be referenced indirectly.

A pointer to a function can have a number of important uses. For example, consider the qsort( ) function. The qsort( ) function has as one of its parameters a pointer to a function. The referenced function contains the necessary comparison that is to be performed between the array elements being sorted. qsort( ) has been written to require a function pointer because the comparison between two elements can be a complex process beyond the scope of a single control flag. It is not possible to pass a function by value, that is, pass the code itself. C++, however, supports passing a pointer to the code, or a pointer to the function.

The concept of function pointers is frequently illustrated by using the qsort( ) function supplied with the compiler. Unfortunately, in many cases, the function pointer is declared to be of a type that points to other built-in functions. The following C and C++ programs demonstrate how to define a pointer to a function and how to "roll your own" function to be passed to the STD library function qsort( ). Here is the C program:

```
/*
 *   fncptr.c
 *   A C program illustrating how to declare your own
 *   function and function pointer to be used with qsort( )
 *   Chris H. Pappas and William H. Murray, 1999
 */

#include <stdio>
#include <stdlib>
using namespace std;

#define IMAXVALUES 10

int icompare_funct(const void *iresult_a, const void *iresult_b);
int (*ifunct_ptr)(const void *, const void *);

void main( )
{
  int i;
  int iarray[IMAXVALUES]={0,5,3,2,8,7,9,1,4,6};

  ifunct_ptr=icompare_funct;
  qsort(iarray,IMAXVALUES,sizeof(int),ifunct_ptr);
  for(i = 0; i < IMAXVALUES; i++)
    printf("%d ",iarray[i]);
}

int icompare_funct(const void *iresult_a, const void *iresult_b)
{
  return((*(int *)iresult_a)-(*(int *) iresult_b));
}
```

The function `icompare_funct( )` (which will be called the *reference function*) was prototyped to match the requirements for the fourth parameter to the function `qsort( )` (which will be called the *invoking function*). To digress slightly, the fourth parameter to the function `qsort( )` must be a function pointer. This reference function must be passed two `const void *` parameters and it must return a type `int`. (Note: Remember that the position of the `const` keyword in the formal parameter list *locks* the data pointed to, not the address used to point. This means that even if you write your compare routine so that it *does not* sort properly, it can in *no way* destroy the contents of your array!) This is because `qsort( )` uses the reference function for the `sort` comparison algorithm. Now that you understand the prototype of the reference function `icompare_funct( )`, take a minute to study the body of the reference function.

If the reference function returns a value < 0, then the reference function's first parameter value is less than the second parameter's value. A return value of zero indicates parameter value equality, with a return value > 0 indicating that the second parameter's value was greater than the first's. All of this is accomplished by the single statement in `icompare_funct( )`:

```
return((*(int *)iresult_a)-(*(int *) iresult_b));
```

Since both of the pointers were passed as type `void *`, they were cast to their appropriate pointer type `int *` and then dereferenced (`*`). The result of the subtraction of the two values pointed to returns an appropriate value to satisfy `qsort( )`'s comparison criterion.

While the prototype requirements for `icompare_funct( )` are interesting, the meat of the program begins with the pointer function declaration below the `icompare_funct( )` function prototype:

```
int icompare_funct(const void *iresult_a, const void *iresult_b);
int (*ifunct_ptr)(const void *, const void *);
```

A function's type is determined by its return value and argument list signature. A pointer to `icompare_funct( )` must specify the same signature and return type. You might therefore think the following statement would accomplish this:

```
int *ifunct_ptr(const void *, const void *);
```

That is almost correct. The problem is that the compiler interprets the statement as the definition of a function `ifunct_ptr( )`, taking two arguments and returning a pointer of type `int *`. The dereference operator unfortunately is associated with the type specifier, not `ifunct_ptr( )`.

Parentheses are necessary to associate the dereference operator with ifunct_ptr( ).

The corrected statement declares ifunct_ptr( ) to be a pointer to a function taking two arguments with a return type int—that is, a pointer of the same type required by the fourth parameter to qsort( ).

In the body of main( ), the only thing left to do is to initialize ifunct_ptr( ) to the address of the function icompare_funct( ). The parameters to qsort( ) are the address to the base or zeroth element of the table to be sorted (*iarray*), the number of entries in the table (*IMAXVALUES*), the size of each table element (*sizeof(int)*), and a function pointer to the comparison function (*ifunct_ptr( )*).

The C++ equivalent follows:

```
//  quicksrt.cpp
//  A C program illustrating how to declare your own
//  function and function pointer to be used with qsort( )
//  Chris H. Pappas and William H. Murray, 1999

#include <iostream>
#include <stdlib>

#define IMAXVALUES 10

int icompare_funct(const void *iresult_a, const void *iresult_b);
int (*ifunct_ptr)(const void *,const void *);

void main( )
{
  int i;
  int iarray[IMAXVALUES]={0,5,3,2,8,7,9,1,4,6};

  ifunct_ptr=icompare_funct;
  qsort(iarray,IMAXVALUES,sizeof(int),ifunct_ptr);
  for(i = 0; i < IMAXVALUES; i++)
    cout <<[{|"|}]" << iarray[i];
}

int icompare_funct(const void *iresult_a, const void *iresult_b)
{
  return((*(int *)iresult_a)-(*(int *)iresult_b));
}
```

Learning to understand the syntax of a function pointer can be challenging. Let's look at just a few examples. Here is the first one:

```
int *(*(*ifunct_ptr)(int))[5];
float (*(*ffunct_ptr)(int,int))(float);
typedef double (*(*(*dfunct_ptr)( ))[5])( );
```

```
dfunct_ptr A_dfunct_ptr;
(*(*function_ary_ptrs( ))[5])( );
```

The first statement defines ifunct_ptr( ) to be a function pointer to a function that is passed an integer argument and returns a pointer to an array of five int pointers. The second statement defines ffunct_ptr( ) to be a function pointer to a function that takes two integer arguments and returns a pointer to a function taking a float argument and returning a float.

By using the typedef declaration, you can avoid the unnecessary repetition of complicated declarations. The typedef declaration is read as follows: dfunct_ptr( ) is defined as a pointer to a function that is passed nothing and returns a pointer to an array of five pointers that point to functions that are passed nothing and return a double.

The last statement is a function declaration, not a variable declaration. The statement defines function_ary_ptrs( ) to be a function taking no arguments and returning a pointer to an array of five pointers that point to functions taking no arguments and returning integers. The outer functions return the default C++ type int.

The good news is that you will rarely encounter complicated declarations and definitions like these. However, by making certain you understand these declarations, you will be able to confidently parse the everyday variety.

Objects Using the C++ *Struct* Keyword

Many C++ programmers are surprised to discover that the C++ **class** type is an extension of the standard type **struct.** In this section, you will learn how you can use the **struct** type in C++ to form a primitive class, complete with data and members. Next, you will examine the formal syntax for defining a class and see several simple examples of its implementation. This section discusses the differences between a primitive **struct** class type and an actual C++ class and presents several simple examples to illustrate class concepts.

A Structure as a Primitive Class

In many respects, the structure in C++ is an elementary form of a class. You use the keyword **struct** to define a structure. Examine the following code:

```
//  squarrt.cpp
//  C++ program using the keyword "struct" to illustrate a
```

```
//   primitive form of class. Here several member functions
//   are defined within the structure.
//   Chris H. Pappas and William H. Murray, 1999

#include <iostream>
#include <math>
using namespace std;

struct math_operations {
  double data_value;

  void set_value(double ang) {data_value=ang;}
  double get_square(void) {double answer;
                           answer=data_value*data_value;
                           return (answer);}
  double get_square_root(void) {double answer;
                           answer=sqrt(data_value);
                           return (answer);}
} math;

main()
{
  // set numeric value to 35.63
  math.set_value(35.63);

  cout << "The square of the number is: "
       << math.get_square() << endl;
  cout << "The square root of the number is: "
       << math.get_square_root() << endl;
  return (0);
}
```

The first thing to notice in this code is that the structure definition contains member data and functions. While you are used to seeing data declarations as part of a structure, this is probably the first time you have seen member functions defined within the structure definition. These member functions can act upon the data contained in the structure (or class) itself.

Recall that a class can contain member data and functions. By default, in a **struct** declaration in C++, member data and functions are public. (A public section is one in which the data and functions are available outside the structure.)

In this example, the structure definition contains a single data value:

```
double data_value;
```

Next, three member functions are defined. Actually, the code for each function is contained within the structure:

```
void set_value(double ang) {data_value=ang;}
double get_square(void) {double answer;
                         answer=data_value*data_value;
                         return (answer);}
double get_square_root(void) {double answer;
                              answer=sqrt(data_value);
                              return (answer);}
```

The first member function is responsible for initializing the variable *data_value*. The remaining two member functions return the square and square root of *data_value*. Notice that the member functions are not passed a value; *data_value* is available to them as members of the structure. Both member functions return a **double.**

The program's **main()** function sets the value of *data_value* to 35.63 with a call to the member function *set_value()*:

```
math.set_value(35.63);
```

Notice that the name *math* has been associated with the structure *math_operations*.

The remaining two member functions return values to the **cout** stream:

```
cout << "The square of the number is: "
     << math.get_square() << endl;
cout << "The square root of the number is: "
     << math.get_square_root() << endl;
```

This example contains a structure with member data and functions. The functions are contained within the structure definition. You won't find an example simpler than this one.

In the next program, the **struct** keyword is still used to develop a primitive class, but this time the member functions are written outside the structure. This is the way you will most commonly see structures and classes defined.

This example contains a structure definition with one data member, *data_value,* and seven member functions. The member functions return information for various trigonometric values.

```
//  structur.cpp
//  C++ program using the keyword "struct" to illustrate a
//  primitive form of class. This program uses a structure
//  to obtain trigonometric values for an angle.
//  Chris H. Pappas and William H. Murray, 1999

#include <iostream>
#include <math>
using namespace std;

const double DEG_TO_RAD=0.0174532925;
```

```
struct degree {
  double data_value;

  void set_value(double);
  double get_sine(void);
  double get_cosine(void);
  double get_tangent(void);
  double get_secant(void);
  double get_cosecant(void);
  double get_cotangent(void);
} deg;

void degree::set_value(double ang)
{
  data_value=ang;
}

double degree::get_sine(void)
{
  double answer;

  answer=sin(DEG_TO_RAD*data_value);
  return (answer);
}

double degree::get_cosine(void)
{
  double answer;

  answer=cos(DEG_TO_RAD*data_value);
  return (answer);
}

double degree::get_tangent(void)
{
  double answer;

  answer=tan(DEG_TO_RAD*data_value);
  return (answer);
}

double degree::get_secant(void)
{
  double answer;

  answer=1.0/sin(DEG_TO_RAD*data_value);
  return (answer);
}

double degree::get_cosecant(void)
```

```
{
  double answer;

  answer=1.0/cos(DEG_TO_RAD*data_value);
  return (answer);
}

double degree::get_cotangent(void)
{
  double answer;

  answer=1.0/tan(DEG_TO_RAD*data_value);
  return (answer);
}

main()
{
  // set angle to 25.0 degrees
  deg.set_value(25.0);

  cout << "The sine of the angle is: "
       << deg.get_sine() << endl;
  cout << "The cosine of the angle is: "
       << deg.get_cosine() << endl;
  cout << "The tangent of the angle is: "
       << deg.get_tangent() << endl;
  cout << "The secant of the angle is: "
       << deg.get_secant() << endl;
  cout << "The cosecant of the angle is: "
       << deg.get_cosecant() << endl;
  cout << "The cotangent of the angle is: "
       << deg.get_cotangent() << endl;
  return (0);
}
```

Notice that the structure definition contains the prototypes for the member functions. The variable *deg* is associated with the *degree* structure type.

```
struct degree {
  double data_value;

  void set_value(double);
  double get_sine(void);
  double get_cosine(void);
  double get_tangent(void);
  double get_secant(void);
  double get_cosecant(void);
  double get_cotangent(void);
} deg;
```

Immediately after the structure is defined, the various member functions are developed and listed. The member functions are associated with the structure or class by means of the scope operator (::). Other than the use of the scope operator, the member functions take on the appearance of normal functions.

Examine the first part of the **main()** function:

```
// set angle to 25.0 degrees
deg.set_data(25.0);
```

Here, the value 25.0 is being passed as an argument to the *set_value()* function. Observe the syntax for this operation. The *set_value()* function itself is very simple:

```
void degree::set_value(double ang)
  {
   data_value=ang;
  }
```

The function accepts the argument and assigns the value to the class variable *data_value*. This is one way of initializing class variables. From this point forward, in the class, *data_value* is accessible by each of the six member functions. The job of the member functions is to calculate the sine, cosine, tangent, secant, cosecant, and cotangent of the given angle. The respective values are printed to the screen from the **main()** function with statements similar to the following:

```
cout << "The sine of the angle is: "
     << deg.get_sine() << endl;
```

You can use the dot notation commonly used for structures to access the member functions. Pointer variables can also be assigned to a structure or class, in which case, the arrow operator is used.

The Syntax and Rules for C++ Classes

The definition of a C++ class begins with the keyword class. The class name (tag type) immediately follows the keyword. The framework of the class is very similar to the **struct** type definition you have already seen.

```
class type {
   type var1
   type var2
   type var3
      .
      .
      .
  public:
   member function 1
```

```
member function 2
member function 3
member function 4
        .
        .
        .

} name associated with class type;
```

Member variables immediately follow the class declaration. These variables are, by default, private to the class and can be accessed only by the member functions that follow. Member functions typically follow a public declaration. This allows access to the member functions from calling routines external to the class. All class member functions have access to public, private, and protected parts of a class.

The following is an example of a class that is used in the next programming example:

```
class degree {
  double data_value;

public:
  void set_value(double);
  double get_sine(void);
  double get_cosine(void);
  double get_tangent(void);
  double get_secant(void);
  double get_cosecant(void);
  double get_cotangent(void);
} deg;
```

This class has a type (tag name) of *degree*. A private variable, *data_value*, will share *degree* values among the various member functions. Seven functions make up the function members of the class. They are *set_value()*, *get_sine()*, *get_cosine()*, *get_tangent()*, *get_secant()*, *get_cosecant()*, and *get_cotangent()*. The name that is associated with this class type is *deg*. Unlike this example, the association of a variable name with the class name is most frequently made in the **main()** function.

Does this class definition look familiar? It is basically the structure definition from the previous example converted to a true class.

A Simple C++ Class

In a C++ class, the visibility of class members is private by default. That is, member variables are accessible only to member functions of the class. If the member functions are to have visibility beyond the class, you must explicitly specify that visibility.

The conversion of the last program's structure to a true C++ class is simple and straightforward. First, the **struct** keyword is replaced by the **class** keyword. Second, the member functions that are to have public visibility are separated from the private variable of the class with the use of a public declaration. Examine the complete program:

```
//  class.cpp
//  C++ program illustrates a simple but true class and
//  introduces the concept of private and public.
//  This program uses a class to obtain the trigonometric
//  value for given angle.
//  Chris H. Pappas and William H. Murray, 1999

#include <iostream>
#include <math>
using namespace std;

const double DEG_TO_RAD=0.0174532925;

class degree {
  double data_value;

public:
  void set_value(double);
  double get_sine(void);
  double get_cosine(void);
  double get_tangent(void);
  double get_secant(void);
  double get_cosecant(void);
  double get_cotangent(void);
} deg;

void degree::set_value(double ang)
{
  data_value=ang;
}

double degree::get_sine(void)
{
  double answer;

  answer=sin(DEG_TO_RAD*data_value);
  return (answer);
}

double degree::get_cosine(void)
{
  double answer;

  answer=cos(DEG_TO_RAD*data_value);
```

```
  return (answer);
}

double degree::get_tangent(void)
{
  double answer;

  answer=tan(DEG_TO_RAD*data_value);
  return (answer);
}

double degree::get_secant(void)
{
  double answer;

  answer=1.0/sin(DEG_TO_RAD*data_value);
  return (answer);
}

double degree::get_cosecant(void)
{
  double answer;

  answer=1.0/cos(DEG_TO_RAD*data_value);
  return (answer);
}

double degree::get_cotangent(void)
{
  double answer;

  answer=1.0/tan(DEG_TO_RAD*data_value);
  return (answer);
}

main()
{
  // set angle to 25.0 degrees
  deg.set_value(25.0);

  cout << "The sine of the angle is: "
       << deg.get_sine() << endl;
  cout << "The cosine of the angle is: "
       << deg.get_cosine() << endl;
  cout << "The tangent of the angle is: "
       << deg.get_tangent() << endl;
  cout << "The secant of the angle is: "
       << deg.get_secant() << endl;
  cout << "The cosecant of the angle is: "
       << deg.get_cosecant() << endl;
```

```
   cout << "The cotangent of the angle is: "
       << deg.get_cotangent() << endl;
   return (0);
}
```

In this example, the body of the program remains the same. The structure definition has been converted to a true, but elementary, class definition with **private** and **public** parts.

Note that the variable *data_value* is private to the class (by default) and as a result is accessible only by the member functions of the class. The member functions themselves have been declared public in visibility and are accessible from outside the class. Each class member, however, whether public or private, has access to all other class members, public or private.

Again, class member functions are usually defined immediately after the class has been defined and before the **main()** function of the program. Non-member class functions are still defined after the function **main()** and are prototyped in the normal fashion.

Objects Using the C++ *Class* Keyword

From the previous discussion, you learned that you could create a primitive C++ class by using the **struct** keyword. Next, several elementary C++ classes were created by using the **class** keyword. Both types of examples illustrated the simple fact that classes can contain member data and member functions that act on that data. In this section, you will learn more details about C++ classes. This section details the nesting of classes and structures, the use of constructors and destructors, overloading member functions, friend functions, operator overloading, derived classes, virtual functions, and other miscellaneous topics. These class structures create objects that form the foundation of object-oriented programs.

Much of the programming flexibility offered to the C++ programmer is a result of the various data types discussed in earlier sections. The C++ class gives you another advantage: the benefits of a structure along with the ability to limit access to specific data to functions that are also members of the class. As a result, classes are one of the greatest contributions made by C++ to programming. The added features of the class over earlier structures include the ability to initialize and protect sensitive functions and data.

In studying C++ programming, consider the increase in programming power you have gained with each new data type. Vectors or one-dimensional arrays allow a group of like data types to be held together. Next, structures allow related items of different data types to be combined in a group. Finally, the C++ class concept takes you one step further with abstract data types. A class allows you to implement a member data type and associate member functions with the data. Using classes gives you the storage concept associated with a structure along with the member functions to operate on the member variables.

Class Features

In the previous discussions, you learned the syntax for creating an elementary C++ class. Classes have extended capabilities that go far beyond this simple syntax. This section is devoted to exploring these capabilities with an eye toward object-oriented programming.

YOUR FIRST CLASS

Remember that a class starts with the keyword **class** followed by a class name (tag). In the following example, the class tag name is *car*. If the class contains member variables, they are defined at the start of the class. Their declaration type is private, by default. This example defines three member variables: *mileage, tire_pressure*, and *speed*. Class member functions follow the member variable list. Typically, the member functions are declared public. A private declaration limits the member variables to member functions within the class. This is often referred to as *data hiding.* A public declaration makes the member functions available outside of the class.

```
class car {
   int    mileage;
   int    tire_pressure;
   float speed;

public:
   int maintenance(int);
   int wear_record(int);
   int air_resistance(float);
} mycar;
```

Here, three member functions are prototyped within the class definition. They are *maintenance()*, *wear_record()*, and *air_resistance()*. All three return an **int** type. Typically, however, the contents of the member functions are defined outside the class definition—usually, immediately after the class itself.

Let's continue the study of classes with a look at additional class features.

Classes within Classes

Recall from an earlier discussion that structures can be nested. This also turns out to be true for C++ classes. When using nested classes, you must take care not to make the resulting declaration more complicated than necessary. The following examples illustrate the nesting concept.

STRUCTURES WITHIN CLASSES

The following is a simple example of how two structures can be nested within a class definition. Using nesting in this fashion is both common and practical. You can also use the **class** keyword in this manner.

```
//   nestclas.cpp
//   C++ program illustrates the use of nesting concepts
//   in classes. This program calculates the wages for
//   the named employee.
//   Chris H. Pappas and William H. Murray, 1999

#include <iostream>
using namespace std;

char newline;

class employee {
  struct emp_name {
    char firstname[20];
    char middlename[20];
    char lastname[20];
  } name;
  struct emp_hours {
    double hours;
    double base_sal;
    double overtime_sal;
  } hours;

public:
  void emp_input(void);
  void emp_output(void);
};

void employee::emp_input()
{
  cout << "Enter first name of employee: ";
  cin >> name.firstname;
  cin.get(newline);    // flush carriage return
  cout << "Enter middle name of employee: ";
  cin >> name.middlename;
```

```
      cin.get(newline);
      cout << "Enter last name of employee:   ";
      cin >> name.lastname;
      cin.get(newline);

      cout << "Enter total hours worked:   ";
      cin >> hours.hours;
      cout << "Enter hourly wage (base rate):    ";
      cin >> hours.base_sal;
      cout << "Enter overtime wage (overtime rate): ";
      cin >> hours.overtime_sal;
      cout << "\n\n";
}

void employee::emp_output()
{
      cout << name.firstname << " " << name.middlename
           << " " << name.lastname << endl;
      if (hours.hours <= 40)
        cout << "Base Pay:   $"
             << hours.hours * hours.base_sal << endl;
        else {
          cout << "Base Pay:   $"
               << 40 * hours.base_sal << endl;
          cout << "Overtime Pay: $"
               << (hours.hours-40) * hours.overtime_sal
               << endl;
      }
}

main()
{
      employee acme_corp;      // associate acme_corp with class

      acme_corp.emp_input();
      acme_corp.emp_output();
      return (0);
}
```

In the next example, two classes are nested within the *employee* class definition. As you can see, the use of nesting can be quite straightforward.

```
class employee {
  class emp_name {
    char firstname[20];
  char middlename[20];
  char lastname[20];
  } name;
  class emp_hours {
    double hours;
```

```
    double base_salary;
    double overtime_sal;
  } hours;

public:
  void emp_input(void);
  void emp_output(void);
};
```

The *employee* class includes two nested classes, *emp_name* and *emp_hours*. The nested classes, while part of the private section of the *employee* class, are actually available outside the class. In other words, the visibility of the nested classes is the same as if they were defined outside the *employee* class. The individual member variables, for this example, are accessed through the member functions (public, by default) *emp_input()* and *emp_output()*.

Both member functions *emp_input()* and *emp_output()* are of type **void** and do not accept arguments. The *emp_input()* function prompts the user for employee data that will be passed to the nested structures (classes). The data collected include the employee's full name, the total hours worked, the regular pay rate, and the overtime pay rate. Output is generated when the *emp_output()* function is called. The employee's name, base pay, and overtime pay will be printed to the screen.

The **main()** function in this program is fairly short. This is because most of the work is being done by the member functions of the class.

```
employee acme_corp;     // associate acme_corp with class

acme_corp.emp_input();
acme_corp.emp_output();
```

First, the variable *acme_corp*, representing the Acme Computer Corporation, is associated with the *employee* class. To request a member function, the dot operator is used. Next, *acme_corp.emp_input()* is called to collect the employee information, and then *acme_corp.emp_output()* is used to calculate and print the payroll results.

OTHER NESTING STYLES

The following form of nesting is also considered acceptable syntax:

```
class cars {
  int mileage;
public:
  void trip(int t);
  int speed(float s);
};

class contents {
```

```
    int count;
public:
  cars mileage;
  void rating(void);
{
```

Here, `cars` becomes nested within the `contents` class. Nested classes, whether inside or outside, have the same scope.

Object Initialization and Destruction

A *constructor* is a class member function. Constructors are useful for initializing class variables or allocating memory storage. A constructor always has the same name as the class it is defined within. Constructors have additional versatility: they can accept arguments and be overloaded. A constructor is executed automatically when an object of the **class** type is created. *Free store objects* are objects created with the **new** operator and serve to allocate memory for the objects created. Constructors are generated by Microsoft's Visual C++ compiler if they are not explicitly defined.

A *destructor* is a class member function typically used to return memory allocated from free store memory. A destructor, like a constructor, has the same name as the class it is defined in, preceded by the tilde character (~). Destructors complement their constructor counterparts. A destructor is automatically called when the **delete** operator is applied to a class pointer or when a program passes beyond the scope of a class object. Destructors, unlike their constructor counterparts, cannot accept an argument and may not be overloaded. Destructors are also generated by Microsoft's Visual C++ compiler if they are not explicitly defined.

YOUR FIRST CONSTRUCTOR AND DESTRUCTOR

In this first example involving the use of constructors and destructors, a constructor and destructor are used to signal the start and end of a coin conversion. This program illustrates that constructors and destructors are called automatically:

```
//  convert.cpp
//  C++ program illustrates the use of constructors and
//  destructors in a simple program.
//  This program converts cents into appropriate coins:
//  (quarters, dimes, nickels, and pennies).
//  Chris H. Pappas and William H. Murray, 1999
//

#include <iostream.h>
using namespace std;

const int QUARTER=25;
```

```
const int DIME=10;
const int NICKEL=5;

class coins {
  int number;

public:
  coins() {cout << "Begin Conversion!\n";}      // constructor
  ~coins() {cout << "\nFinished Conversion!";}  // destructor
  void get_cents(int);
  int quarter_conversion(void);
  int dime_conversion(int);
  int nickel_conversion(int);
};

void coins::get_cents(int cents)
{
  number=cents;
  cout << number << " cents, converts to:"
       << endl;
}

int coins::quarter_conversion()
{
  cout << number/QUARTER << " quarter(s), ";
  return(number%QUARTER);
}

int coins::dime_conversion(int d)
{
  cout << d/DIME << " dime(s), ";
  return(d%DIME);
}

int coins::nickel_conversion(int n)
{
  cout << n/NICKEL << " nickel(s), and ";
  return(n%NICKEL);
}

main()
{
  int c,d,n,p;

  cout << "Enter the cash, in cents, to convert: ";
  cin >> c;

  // associate cash_in_cents with coins class.
  coins cash_in_cents;
```

```
      cash_in_cents.get_cents(c);
      d=cash_in_cents.quarter_conversion();
      n=cash_in_cents.dime_conversion(d);
      p=cash_in_cents.nickel_conversion(n);
      cout << p << " penny(ies).";
      return (0);
    }
```

This program uses four member functions. The first function passes the number of pennies to the private class variable *number*. The remaining three functions convert cash, given in cents, to the equivalent cash in quarters, dimes, nickels, and pennies. Notice in particular the placement of the constructor and destructor in the class definition. The constructor and destructor function descriptions contain nothing more than a message that will be printed to the screen. Constructors are not specifically called by a program. Their appearance on the screen is your key that the constructor and destructor were automatically called when the object was created and destroyed.

```
class coins {
  int number;

public:
  coins() {cout << "Begin Conversion!\n";}       // constructor
  ~coins() {cout << "\nFinished Conversion!";}   // destructor
  void get_cents(int);
  int quarter_conversion(void);
  int dime_conversion(int);
  int nickel_conversion(int);
};
```

Here is an example of the output from this program:

```
Enter the cash, in cents, to convert: 157
Begin Conversion!
157 cents, converts to:
6 quarter(s), 0 dime(s), 1 nickel(s), and 2 penny(ies).
Finished Conversion!
```

In this example, the function definition is actually included within the constructor and destructor. When the function definition is included with member functions, it is said to be *implicitly defined*. Member functions can be defined in the typical manner or declared explicitly as inline functions.

You can expand this example to include dollars and half-dollars.

INITIALIZING MEMBER VARIABLES WITH CONSTRUCTORS

Another practical use for constructors is for the initialization of private class variables. In the previous examples, class variables were set by utilizing separate member functions. In the next example, the original class of the previous program is modified slightly to eliminate the need for user input. In this case, the variable *number* will be initialized to 431 pennies.

```
class coins {
  int number;

public:
  coins() {number=431;}                        // constructor
  ~coins() {cout << "\nFinished Conversion!";}  // destructor
  int quarter_conversion(void);
  int dime_conversion(int);
  int nickel_conversion(int);
};
```

The route to class variables is always through class member functions. Remember that the constructor is considered a member function.

CREATING AND DELETING FREE STORE MEMORY WITH CONSTRUCTORS AND DESTRUCTORS

Perhaps the most significant reason for using a constructor is to utilize free store memory. In the next example, a constructor is used to allocate memory for the *string1* pointer with the **new** operator. A destructor is also used to release the allocated memory back to the system when the object is destroyed. This is accomplished with the use of the **delete** operator.

```
class string_operation {
  char *string1;
  int  string_len;

public:
  string_operation(char *) {string1=new char[string_len];}
  ~string_operation() {delete string1;}
  void input_data(char *);
  void output_data(char *);
};
```

The memory allocated by **new** to the pointer *string1* can only be deallocated with a subsequent call to **delete.** For this reason, you will usually see memory allocated to pointers in constructors and deallocated in destructors. This also ensures that if the variable assigned to the class passes out of its scope, the allocated memory will be returned to the system. These operations make memory allocation dynamic and are useful in programs that utilize linked lists.

The memory used by data types such as **int** and **float** is automatically restored to the system.

Member Function Overloading

Class member functions, like ordinary C++ functions, can be overloaded. *Overloading* functions means that more than one function can have the same function name in the current scope. It becomes the compiler's responsibility to select the correct function based upon the number and type of arguments used during the function call. The first example in this section illustrates the overloading of a class function named *number()*. This overloaded function will return the absolute value of an integer or double with the use of the math functions **abs()**, which accepts and returns integer values, and **fabs()**, which accepts and returns double values. With an overloaded function, the argument types determine which member function will actually be used.

```
//   abs.cpp
//   C++ program illustrates member function overloading.
//   Program determines the absolute value of an integer
//   and a double.
//   Chris H. Pappas and William H. Murray, 1999

#include <iostream>
#include <math>
#include <stdlib>
using namespace std;

class absolute_value {
public:
  int number(int);
  double number(double);
};

int absolute_value::number(int test_data)
{
  int answer;

  answer=abs(test_data);
  return (answer);
}

double absolute_value::number(double test_data)
{
  double answer;

  answer=fabs(test_data);
  return (answer);
```

```
}

main()
{
  absolute_value neg_number;

  cout << "The absolute value is "
       << neg_number.number(-583) 8<< endl;
  cout << "The absolute value is "
       << neg_number.number(-583.1749) << endl;
   return (0);
 }
```

Notice that the dot operator is used in conjunction with the member function name to pass a negative integer and negative double values. The program selects the proper member function based upon the type (int or double) of argument passed along with the function name. The positive value returned by each function is printed to the screen:

```
the absolute value is 583
the absolute value is 583.1749
```

In another example, angle information is passed to member functions in one of two formats: a double or a string. With member function overloading, it is possible to process both types.

```
//  ovrld.cpp
//  C++ program illustrates overloading two class member
//  functions. The program allows an angle to be entered
//  in decimal or deg/min/sec format. One member function
//  accepts data as a double, the other as a string. The
//  program returns the sine, cosine, and tangent.
//  Chris H. Pappas and William H. Murray, 1999

#include <iostream>
#include <math>
#include <string>
using namespace std;

const double DEG_TO_RAD=0.0174532925;

class trigonometric {
  double angle;
  double answer_sine;
  double answer_cosine;
  double answer_tangent;

public:
  void trig_calc(double);
  void trig_calc(char *);
```

```
      };

      void trigonometric::trig_calc(double degrees)
       {
        angle=degrees;
        answer_sine=sin(angle * DEG_TO_RAD);
        answer_cosine=cos(angle * DEG_TO_RAD);
        answer_tangent=tan(angle * DEG_TO_RAD);
        cout << "\nFor an angle of " << angle
             << " degrees." << endl;
        cout << "The sine is " << answer_sine << endl;
        cout << "The cosine is " << answer_cosine << endl;
        cout << "The tangent is " << answer_tangent << endl;
       }

      void trigonometric::trig_calc(char *dat)
      {
        char *deg,*min,*sec;

        deg=strtok(dat,"ó ");   //make ó with alt-248
        min=strtok(0,"' ");
        sec=strtok(0,"\"");
        angle=atof(deg)+((atof(min))/60.0)+((atof(sec))/360.0);
        answer_sine=sin(angle * DEG_TO_RAD);
        answer_cosine=cos(angle * DEG_TO_RAD);
        answer_tangent=tan(angle * DEG_TO_RAD);
        cout << "\nFor an angle of " << angle
             << " degrees." << endl;
        cout << "The sine is " << answer_sine << endl;
        cout << "The cosine is " << answer_cosine << endl;
        cout << "The tangent is " << answer_tangent << endl;
       }

      main()
      {
        trigonometric data;

        data.trig_calc(75.0);
        data.trig_calc("35° 75' 20\"");
        data.trig_calc(145.72);
        data.trig_calc("65° 45' 30\"");
        return (0);
      }
```

This program makes use of a very powerful built-in function, **strtok()**, prototyped in string. The syntax for using **strtok**() is straightforward:

```
char *strtok(string10,string20);  //locates token in string1
char *string10;                   //string that has token(s)
const char *string20;             //string with delimiter chars
```

The **strtok()** function will scan the first string, *string1,* looking for a series of character tokens. For this example, the tokens representing degrees, minutes, and seconds are used. The actual length of the tokens can vary. The second string, *string2,* contains a set of delimiters. Spaces, commas, or other special characters can be used for delimiters. The tokens in *string1* are separated by the delimiters in *string2.* Because of this, all of the tokens in *string1* can be retrieved with a series of calls to the **strtok()** function. **strtok()** alters *string1* by inserting a null character after each token is retrieved. The function returns a pointer to the first token the first time it is called. Subsequent calls return a pointer to the next token, and so on. When there are no more tokens in the string, a null pointer is returned.

This example permits angle readings formatted as decimal values, or in degrees, minutes, and seconds of arc. For the latter case, **strtok()** uses the degree symbol (ó) to find the first token. For minutes, a minute symbol (') will pull out the token containing the number of minutes. Finally, the \" symbol is used to retrieve seconds. The last delimiter uses two symbols because the double quote by itself is used for terminating strings.

Class member function overloading gives programs and programmers flexibility when dealing with different data formats. If you are not into math or engineering programs, can you think of any applications that interest you where this feature might be helpful? Consider this possibility: If you are the cook in your household, you could develop an application that modifies recipes. You could write a program that would accept data as a decimal value or in mixed units. For example, the program might allow you to enter "3.75 cups, 1 pint 1.75 cups" or "1 pint 1 cup 12 tbs".

What Is the C++ *friend* Keyword?

One important feature of classes is their ability to hide data. Recall that member data is private by default in classes—that is, sharable only with member functions of the class. It is almost ironic, then, that there is a category of functions specifically designed to override this feature. Functions of this type are called *friend functions.* Friend functions allow the sharing of private class information with nonmember functions. Friend functions, not defined in the class itself, can share the same class resources as member functions.

Friend functions offer the advantage that they are external to the class definition, as shown here:

```
//  friendfn.cpp
//  C++ program illustrates the use of friend functions.
//  Program will collect a string of date and time
//  information from system. Time information will
//  be processed and converted into seconds.
```

```
//  Chris H. Pappas and William H. Murray, 1999

#include <iostream>
#include <time>     // for tm & time_t structure
#include <string>   // for strtok function prototype
#include <stdlib>   // for atol function prototype
using namespace std;

class time_class {
  long secs;
  friend char * present_time(time_class);  //friend
public:
  time_class(char *);
};

time_class::time_class(char *tm)
{
  char *hours,*minutes,*seconds;

  // data returned in the following string format:
  // (day month date hours:minutes:seconds year
  // Thus, need to skip over three tokens, ie.
  // skip day, month and date
  hours=strtok(tm," ");
  hours=strtok(0," ");
  hours=strtok(0," ");

  // collect time information from string
  hours=strtok(0,":");
  minutes=strtok(0,":");
  seconds=strtok(0," ");

  // convert data to long type and accumulate seconds.
  secs=atol(hours)*3600;
  secs+=atol(minutes)*60;
  secs+=atol(seconds);
}

char * present_time(time_class);  // prototype

main()
{  // get the string of time & date information
  struct tm *ptr;
  time_t ltime;
  ltime=time(NULL);
  ptr=localtime(&ltime);

  time_class tz(asctime(ptr));

  cout << "The date/time string information: "
```

```
             << asctime(ptr) << endl;
     cout << "The time converted to seconds: "
             << present_time(tz) << endl;
     return (0);
}

char * present_time(time_class tz)
{
  char *ctbuf;
  ctbuf=new char[40];
  long int seconds_total;

  seconds_total=tz.secs;
  ltoa(seconds_total,ctbuf,10);
  return (ctbuf);
}
```

Notice the use of the keyword **friend** along with the description of the *present_time()* function in the class definition. When you examine the program listing, you will notice that this function, external to the class, appears after the **main()** function description. In other words, it is written as a traditional C++ function, external to member functions of the defined class.

This program has a number of additional interesting features. In the function **main()**, the system's time is obtained with the use of *time_t* and its associated structure *tm*. In this program, *ltime* is the name of the variable associated with *time_t*. Local time is initialized and retrieved into the pointer *ptr* with the next two lines of code. By using *asctime(ptr)*, the pointer will point to an ASCII string of date and time information.

```
struct tm *ptr;
time_t ltime;
ltime=time(NULL);
ptr=localtime(&ltime);

time_class tz(asctime(ptr));
```

The date and time string is formatted in this manner:

day month date hours:minutes:seconds year \n \0

For example:

```
Mon Sep 17  13:12:21 1999
```

Below is a more detailed discussion of built-in functions, including those prototyped in *time*.

The string information that is retrieved is sent to the class by associating *tz* with the class **time_class:**

```
time_class tz(asctime(ptr));
```

A constructor, **time_class(char *)**, is used to define the code required to convert the string information into integer data. This is accomplished by using the **strtok()** function.

Date/time information is returned in a rather strange format. To process this information, **strtok()** must use a space as the delimiter to skip over the day, month, and date information in the string. In this program, the variable *hours* initially serves as a junk collector for unwanted tokens. The next delimiter is a colon (:), which is used in collecting both hour and minute tokens from the string. Finally, the number of seconds can be retrieved by reading the string until another space is encountered. The string information is then converted to a **long** type and converted to the appropriate number of seconds. The variable *secs* is private to the class, but accessible to the friend function.

The friend function takes the number of accumulated seconds, *tz.seconds,* and converts it back to a character string. The memory for storing the string is allocated with the **new** operator. This newly created string is a result of using the friend function.

The program prints two pieces of information:

```
The date/time string information: Mon May 25 16:01:55 1992

The time converted to seconds: 57715
```

First, **cout** sends the string produced by **asctime()** to the screen. This information is obtainable from the **time_t()** function and is available to the **main()** function. Second, the system time is printed by passing *present_time* to the **cout** stream.

While friend functions offer some interesting programming possibilities when programming with C++ classes, they should be used with caution.

The Hidden *this* Pointer

The keyword **this** is used to identify a self-referential pointer that is implicitly declared in C++ as follows:

```
class_name *this;    //class_name is class type.
```

The **this** pointer is used to point to the object for which the member function is invoked. Here is an example, used in a class definition:

```
class class_name {
  char chr;
```

```
public:
  void begin_conv(char k) {chr=k;}
  char conv_chr(void) {return (this -> chr);}
};
```

In this case, the pointer **this** is used to access the private class variable member *20chr*.

There are additional uses for the **this** pointer. You can use it to include a link on a doubly linked list or when writing constructors and destructors involving memory allocations. Examine the following example:

```
class class_name {
  int x,y,z;
  char chr;

 public:
  class_name(size) {this=new(size);}
  ~class_name(void) {delete(this);}
};
```

Overloading Operators

Earlier in this chapter, you learned that it is possible to overload member functions in a class. In this section, you will learn that it is also possible to overload C++ operators. In C++, new definitions can be applied to such familiar operators as +, -, *, and / in a given class.

The idea of operator overloading is common in numerous programming languages, even if it is not specifically implemented. For example, all compiled languages make it possible to add two integers, two floats, or two doubles (or their equivalent types) with the + operator. This is the essence of operator overloading—using the same operator on different data types. In C++, it is possible to extend this simple concept even further. In most compiled languages, it is not possible, for example, to take a complex number, matrix, or character string and add them together with the + operator.

These operations are valid in all programming languages:

3 + 8

3.3 + 7.2

These operations are typically not valid operations:

(4–j4) + (5 + j10)

(15° 20' 15") + (53° 57' 40")

"combine" + "strings"

If the last three operations were possible with the + operator, the workload of the programmer would be greatly reduced when designing new applications. The good news is that in C++, the + operator can be overloaded and the previous three operations can be made valid. Many additional operators can also be overloaded. Operator overloading is used extensively in C++. You will find examples throughout the various Microsoft C++ libraries.

OVERLOADED OPERATORS AND FUNCTION CALLS

In C++, the following operators can be overloaded:

+	-	*	/	=	<	>	+=	-=
*=	/=	<<	>>	>>=	<<=	= =	!=	<=
>=	++	- -	%	&	^^	!	|	~
&=	^=	|=	&&	||	%=	[ ]	( )	new

```
delete
```

The main restrictions are that the syntax and precedence of the operator must remain unchanged from their originally defined meanings. Another important point is that operator overloading is valid only within the scope of the class in which overloading occurs.

WRITING YOUR OWN OVERLOADED OPERATORS

To overload an operator, the **operator** keyword is followed by the operator itself:

```
type operator opr(param list)
```

For example:

```
angle_value operator +(angle_argument);
```

Here, *angle_value* is the name of the class type, followed by the **operator** keyword, the operator itself (+), and a parameter to be passed to the overloaded operator.

Within the scope of a properly defined class, several angles specified in degrees/minutes/seconds can be directly added together:

```
angle_value angle1("37°15' 56\"");
angle_value angle2("10° 44' 44\"");
angle_value angle3("75° 17' 59\"");
angle_value angle4("130° 32' 54\"");
angle_value sum_of_angles;

sum_of_angles=angle1+angle2+angle3+angle4;
```

As you know from earlier examples, the symbol for seconds is the double quote mark ("). This symbol is also used to signal the beginning and ending of a character string. The quote symbol can be printed to the screen if it is preceded with a backslash. This book uses this format for data input.

There is another problem that must be taken into account in programs such as this: the carry information from seconds to minutes and from minutes to hours must be handled properly. A carry occurs in both cases when the total number of seconds or minutes exceeds 59. This doesn't have anything to do with operator overloading directly, but the program must take this fact into account if a correct total is to be produced, as shown here:

```
//  operver1.cpp
//  C++ program illustrates operator overloading.
//  Program will overload the "+" operator so that
//  several angles, in the format degrees minutes seconds,
//  can be added directly.
//  Chris H. Pappas and William H. Murray, 1999


#include <strstrea>
#include <stdlib>
#include <string>
using namespace std;

class angle_value {
  int degrees,minutes,seconds;

  public:
  angle_value() {degrees=0,
                 minutes=0,
                 seconds=0;}   // constructor
  angle_value(char *);
  angle_value operator +(angle_value);
  char * info_display(void);
};

angle_value::angle_value(char *angle_sum)
{
  degrees=atoi(strtok(angle_sum,"6"));
  minutes=atoi(strtok(0,"' "));
  seconds=atoi(strtok(0,"\""));
}

angle_value angle_value::operator+(angle_value angle_sum)
{
  angle_value ang;
  ang.seconds=(seconds+angle_sum.seconds)%60;
  ang.minutes=((seconds+angle_sum.seconds)/60+
               minutes+angle_sum.minutes)%60;
  ang.degrees=((seconds+angle_sum.seconds)/60+
               minutes+angle_sum.minutes)/60;
```

```
    ang.degrees+=degrees+angle_sum.degrees;
    return ang;
}

char * angle_value::info_display()
{
    char *ang[15];
    // strstream required for incore formatting
    ostrstream(*ang,sizeof(ang)) << degrees << "°"
                                 << minutes << "' "
                                 << seconds << "\""
                                 << ends;
    return *ang;
}

main()
{
    angle_value angle1("37° 15' 56\"");     //make with alt-248
    angle_value angle2("10° 44' 44\"");
    angle_value angle3("75° 17' 59\"");
    angle_value angle4("130° 32' 54\"");
    angle_value sum_of_angles;

    sum_of_angles=angle1+angle2+angle3+angle4;
    cout << "the sum of the angles is "
         << sum_of_angles.info_display() << endl;
    return (0);
}
```

The details of how the mixed units are added together are included in the small piece of code that declares that the + operator is to be overloaded:

```
angle_value angle_value::operator+(angle_value angle_sum)
{
    angle_value ang;
    ang.seconds=(seconds+angle_sum.seconds)%60;
    ang.minutes=((seconds+angle_sum.seconds)/60+
                minutes+angle_sum.minutes)%60;
    ang.degrees=((seconds+angle_sum.seconds)/60+
                minutes+angle_sum.minutes)/60;
    ang.degrees+=degrees+angle_sum.degrees;
    return ang;
}
```

Here, divide and modulus operations are performed on the sums to ensure correct carry information.

Further details of the program's operation are omitted since you have seen most of the functions and modules in earlier examples. However, it is important to remember that when you overload operators, proper operator syntax and precedence must be maintained.

The output from this program shows the sum of the four angles to be as follows:

```
the sum of the angles is 253° 51' 33"
```

Is this answer correct?

Class Inheritance

A derived class can be considered an extension, or inheritance, of an existing class. The original class is known as the *base,* or *parent, class* and the derived class as the *subclass,* or *child class.* As such, a derived class provides a simple means for expanding or customizing the capabilities of a parent class, without the need for re-creating the parent class itself. With a parent class in place, a common interface is possible to one or more of the derived classes.

Any C++ class can serve as a parent class, and any derived class will reflect its description. The derived class can add additional features to those of the parent class. For example, the derived class can modify access privileges, add new members, or overload existing ones. When a derived class overloads a function declared in the parent class, it is said to be a *virtual member function.* You will see that virtual member functions are very important to the concept of object-oriented programming.

DERIVED CLASS SYNTAX

You describe a derived class by using the following syntax:

```
class derived-class-type :(public/private/protected)...
        parent-class-type { . . . .};
```

For example, in creating a derived class, you might write:

```
class retirement:public consumer { . . . .};
```

In this case, the derived class tag is **retirement.** The parent class has public visibility, and its tag is **consumer.**

A third visibility specifier is often used with derived classes—*protected.* A protected specifier is the same as a private specifier with the added feature that class member functions and friends of derived classes are given access to the class.

YOUR FIRST DERIVED CLASS

The next program depicts the concept of a derived class. The parent class collects and reports information on a consumer's name, address, city, state, and ZIP code. Two similar child classes are derived. One child class maintains information on a consumer's accumulated airline mileage, while the second derived child class reports information on a consumer's accumulated rental car mileage. Both derived child classes inherit information from the parent class. Study the listing and see what you can discern about these derived classes.

```cpp
//   subclass.cpp
//   C++ program illustrates derived classes.
//   The parent class contains name, street, city,
//   state, and zip information. Derived classes add
//   either airline or rental car mileage information
//   to parent class information.
//   Chris H. Pappas and William H. Murray, 1999

#include <iostream>
#include <string>
using namespace std;

char newline;

class consumer {
  char name[60],
       street[60],
       city[20],
       state[15],
       zip[10];
public:
  void data_output(void);
  void data_input(void);
};

void consumer::data_output()
{
  cout << "Name: " << name << endl;
  cout << "Street: " << street << endl;
  cout << "City: " << city << endl;
  cout << "State: " << state << endl;
  cout << "Zip: " << zip << endl;
}

void consumer::data_input()
{
  cout << "Enter The Consumer's Full Name: ";
  cin.get(name,59,'\n');
  cin.get(newline);       //flush carriage return
  cout << "Enter The Street Address: ";
  cin.get(street,59,'\n');
  cin.get(newline);
  cout << "Enter The City: ";
  cin.get(city,19,'\n');
```

```
  cin.get(newline);
  cout << "Enter The State: ";
  cin.get(state,14,'\n');
  cin.get(newline);
  cout << "Enter The Five Digit Zip Code: ";
  cin.get(zip,9,'\n');
  cin.get(newline);
}

class airline:public consumer {
  char airline_type[20];
  float acc_air_miles;
public:
  void airline_consumer();
  void disp_air_mileage();
};

void airline::airline_consumer()
{
  data_input();
  cout << "Enter Airline Type: ";
  cin.get(airline_type,19,'\n');
  cin.get(newline);
  cout << "Enter Accumulated Air Mileage: ";
  cin >> acc_air_miles;
  cin.get(newline);          //flush carriage return
}

void airline::disp_air_mileage()
{
  data_output();

  cout << "Airline Type: " << airline_type
       << endl;
  cout << "Accumulated Air Mileage: "
       << acc_air_miles << endl;
}

class rental_car:public consumer {
  char rental_car_type[20];
  float acc_road_miles;
public:
  void rental_car_consumer();
  void disp_road_mileage();
};

void rental_car::rental_car_consumer()
{
  data_input();
  cout << "Enter Rental_car Type: ";
```

```
  cin.get(rental_car_type,19,'\n');
  cin.get(newline);       //flush carriage return
  cout << "Enter Accumulated Road Mileage: ";
  cin >> acc_road_miles;
  cin.get(newline);
}

void rental_car::disp_road_mileage()
{
  data_output();

  cout << "Rental Car Type: "
       << rental_car_type << endl;
  cout << "Accumulated Mileage: "
       << acc_road_miles << endl;
}

main()
{
  //associate variable names with classes
  airline jetaway;
  rental_car varooom;

  //get airline information
  cout << "\n—Airline Consumer—\n";
  jetaway.airline_consumer();


  //get rental_car information
  cout << "\n—Rental Car Consumer—\n";
  varooom.rental_car_consumer();

  //now display all consumer information
  cout << "\n—Airline Consumer—\n";
  jetaway.disp_air_mileage();
  cout << "\n—Rental Car Consumer—\n";
  varooom.disp_road_mileage();

  return (0);
}
```

In the example, the parent class is type *consumer*. The private part of this class accepts consumer information for name, address, city, state, and ZIP code. The public part describes two functions, *data_output()* and *data_input()*. You have seen functions similar to these gather class information in earlier programs. The first derived child class is *airline*.

```
class airline:public consumer {
  char airline_type[20];
  float acc_air_miles;
```

```
public:
  void airline_consumer(void);
  void disp_air_mileage(void);
};
```

This derived child class contains two functions: *airline_consumer()* and *disp_air_mileage()*. The first function, *airline_consumer()*, uses the parent class to obtain name, address, city, state, and ZIP code, and *attaches* the airline type and accumulated mileage.

```
void airline::airline_consumer()
{
  data_input();
  cout << "Enter Airline Type: ";
  cin.get(airline_type,19,'\n');
  cin.get(newline);
  cout << "Enter Accumulated Air Mileage: ";
  cin >> acc_air_miles;
  cin.get(newline);        //flush carriage return
}
```

Do you understand how the derived class is being used? A call to the function *data_input()* is a call to a member function that is part of the parent class. The remainder of the derived class is involved with obtaining the additional airline type and accumulated mileage.

The information on accumulated air mileage can be displayed for a consumer in a similar manner. The parent class function *data_output()* prints the information gathered by the parent class (name, address, and so on), while *disp_air_mileage()* attaches the derived child class information (airline type and mileage) to the output. The process is repeated for the rental car consumer. Thus, one parent class serves as the data-gathering base for two derived child classes, each obtaining its own specific information.

Experiment with this program by entering your own database of information. You might also consider adding additional member functions to the *consumer* class.

I Thought Templates Were Just for C++!

Once again, C++'s flexible and extensible language constructs allowed clever programmers to generate very esoteric code solutions. These advanced code solutions got the job done with three downsides. First, the average programmer got lost in deciphering the code. Second, debugging was like trying do your first recursive call trace. Third, the solutions were not necessarily as portable as today's environments demand.

Templates out of Structures

Take, for example, the following C code section that uses the **#define** and concatenation (**##**) preprocessor statements to define a binary tree node:

```
C Example
#define BINARY_TREE( t )
typedef struct _tree_##t {
  t data;
  struct _tree_##t *left;
  struct _tree_##t *right;
} BINARY_TREE_##;
```

Notice how the preprocessor would substitute the argument *t* with whichever data type the user chose, as in:

```
BINARY_TREE( int );
BINARY_TREE( float );
BINARY_TREE( my_structure );
```

and then totally redefine the node. For example, for int data types, the binary tree node's definition would look like:

```
typedef struct _tree_int {
  int data;
  struct _tree_int *left;
  struct _tree_int *right;
} BINARY_TREE_int;
```

Now, *this* is just a minor example of the inherited sophistication and modularity provided by the C/C++ languages. Remember, the previous examples are all legal in C and require no additional C++ syntax and sophistication!

However, for as slick as this example is, there is one inherent problem: Unlike **inline** functions, which can also be used to generate macros, **#define**-defined macros have no error-checking capabilities. They are strictly string search-and-replace operations that pass one of C/C++'s two pass compiles. Obviously, to generate reliable and portable code, some other means was necessary—enter the C++ **template**.

The *Template* Keyword

Templates were one of the last features added to C++ before the ANSI/ISO C++ standardization process began. As Bjarne Stroustrup (author of C++) states, "Templates were considered essential for the design of proper container classes . . . For many people, the largest single problem with C++ is the lack of an extensive standard library. A major problem in producing such a library is that C++ does not provide a sufficiently general facility for defining 'container classes' such as lists, vectors, and associative arrays."

It is the incorporation of templates into the C++ language that led directly to the development of the STL, a standardized library of container classes and algorithms using template classes and functions.

Template Syntax

As a programmer, you undoubtedly understand the concepts of functions and function calls. A function contains a modularly designed, reusable, single problem-solving algorithm; a function call passes the actual values needed by a function at a particular instance in the execution of the calling routine's algorithm.

C++ templates use parameters in an entirely new way: to create new functions and classes. And, unlike parameters passing to functions, templates create these new functions and classes at *compile-time* rather than at run-time.

The straightforward syntax for templates looks like:

```
template <argument_list> declaration
```

After the **template** keyword and *argument_list,* you supply the template declaration, where you define the parameterized version of a class or function. It's up to the C++ compiler to generate different versions of the class or function based on the arguments passed to the template when it is used.

Template Functions!

To understand how templates function in the STL, you need to understand that there are two types of templates: class templates and function templates. Function templates generate functions, while class templates generate classes.

The following example defines a function template that squares any data type:

```
template <class Type>
Type squareIt( Type x ) { return x * x; } //function tem-
plate
```

The function template *squareIt()* can be passed any appropriate data *Type.* For example:

```
void main( void )
{

  cout << "The square of the integer 9 is: " << squareIt( 9 );
  cout << "The square of the unsigned int 255 is: " << squareIt( 255U );
```

```
cout << "The square of the float 10.0: " << squareIt( 10.0 );
//...
}
```

These three statements cause the compiler to generate, at compile-time, three unique function bodies: one instance for integer data, another for unsigned integer data, and a third for floating-point values.

```
int square(int x) { return x * x; }
unsigned int square(unsigned int x) { return x * x; }
double square(double x) { return x * x; }
```

Template Classes

Class templates comprise the second category of templates. The following example defines a simple array container class template:

```
template < class Type, int MAX_ELEMENTS >
class Array {
  protected:
    Type *pTypeArray;
  public:
    Array()  { pTypeArray  = new Type[ MAX_ELEMENTS ]; }
//constructor
    ~Array() { delete[] pTypeArray; } //destructor
    // ...
  };
```

The template class definition creates an array container class of any *Type*. The first argument to the template defines what type of elements the array will hold, while the second argument defines how many rows, or number of elements, the array will hold. The array's *Type* can be anything from a simple standard C++ data type such as int to a complex application-specific structure or complex object.

A program instantiates an actual, tangible instance of the template class definition with almost a function-like syntax:

```
void main( void )
{
  Array < float, 10 >  fArray;
  Array < int, 25 > iArray;
  Array < MY_STRUCTURE_DEFINITION, MAX_RECORDS > strucArray;
  Array < MY_CLASS_DEFINITION, iRunTimeUsersChoice > classArray;
  //...
}
```

For each instantiation, the compiler generates a brand new version of the *Array* class for every different combination of types passed to it. It does this at compile-time by performing a substitution of the arguments wherever they appear in the formal template definition.

Why STL Is Better Than Templates

In theory, C++ templates fill the need for easy-to-use container classes. But in real life, it wasn't always that simple, because several obstacles got in the way. First, depending on the implementation of template container classes, either from compiler or third-party vendors, template-based containers could be noticeably slower than their C counterparts. For instance, many template-based container classes relied on inheritance to do their jobs, and certain kinds of inheritance could measurably slow down a program.

Another problem with templates was compatibility. If you happened to use templates from two different vendors, there could be compatibility conflicts between them since there was no standard. But, this was a lesser problem than customization, to some extent; customizing code is a normal part of working with templates. Take a class called *VehicleSalesRecord*, for instance. For this class to work with a linked list template, you would have to define operations like less-than (<), the equivalence operator (==), and possibly a greater-than operator (>). Providing these operations or requirements for every class was part of the overhead of working with any template.

Traditionally, to work with container templates, a programmer needed to customize the objects in the container, not the container template itself. A problem came into play when you needed to modify the way a template worked. For example, imagine wanting to customize the way items were sorted. With most template-based classes, you needed to decipher someone else's code, modify the template source code, and re-compile your program—assuming you had access to the original template definition.

With the inherent slowness in template-based container classes, along with their being historically nonstandard and not easy to customize, there needed to be a better way. Welcome to STL!

Summary

This chapter presented the nuts and bolts of the newest addition to C++, the ANSI/ISO Standard Template Library. You now know:

- What the STL concept entails.
- How it evolved into existence.
- Who is credited for inventing it.
- What it gives you as an application developer.
- Its underlying data structures.

This chapter highlighted the fact that even "experienced" C++ programmers, wishing to dive directly into the later chapters, might be surprised to see just how much C++ has changed within this past year, even without the topic of STL. By design, this chapter has taken you from an introductory understanding of STL and strategically highlighted those components of C++ that are fundamental STL building blocks.

The next chapter takes these concepts and combines them with a high-level overview of STL features and syntax. It is this next chapter that will highlight the structure of the STL, show you how to interpret the various libraries' contents, tellyou any mandatory steps needed to use STL, and include a few code examples. Once you have digested the information presented in this chapter and the next, you will be fully empowered to maximize the use of any STL definition you choose!

Understanding the Difference Between the Standard C++ Library and STL

Assuming you have never used the STL before, Chapter 2 stands as a bridge between the history of non-STL C++ language syntax and Chapter 3, which begins defining and using specific STL templates.

Note   When reading this chapter, pay close attention to the two different libraries, the standard C++ library, which is different from, though used in conjunction with, the STL.

This chapter begins with a discussion of the latest ANSI/ISO language concept updates. Many of these innovations are used within the standard C++ library and the STL. The chapter finishes with an overview of the standard C++ library, as implemented in Microsoft Visual C++, and the STL. By the end of the chapter, you will be able to:

1. Understand namespaces.
2. Understand and use the "new-style" casts.
3. Understand and use run-time type information (RTTI).
4. Name the different components of the standard C++ library.
5. Write simple programs that use STL components using Visual C++.
6. In addition, skillfully use standard C++ library exception handling and language support.

This chapter assumes that you understand basic C++ programming and have a good understanding of C++ templates (discussed in the last chapter).

What's New in the Latest ANSI/ISO C++ Standard?

While the ANSI/ISO Committee was busy incorporating STL, they took the opportunity to introduce modifications to the C++ language definition. These modifications, in most cases, implement features that the committee members admired in other languages, features that they viewed as deficiencies in traditional C++. These new changes, which consist of language additions, should not affect any previously written code.

An Introduction to Namespaces

We'll look at the definition for *namespace* from a bottom-up point of view. Namespaces control scope, or identifier (constants, variables, functions, classes, etc.) visibility. The tightest scope is local—the identifiers declared within a function, and associated at this level, would be member functions, or method declarations. Higher up on the scale would be class scope.

There are visibility issues associated with file scope, for example, when 1.cpp, 2.cpp, and 3.cpp are combined to generate 123.exe. Identifiers declared in 1.cpp, for example, are not visible (by default) in 2.cpp and 3.cpp.

At the highest level is program or workspace scope. Historically, this worked fine until the advent of today's complex programming environment, where source files are coming at you from all directions. Today's programs are a combination of source files you write, those supplied by the compiler(s), some from the operating system itself, and some from third-party vendors. Under these circumstances, program scope is not sufficient to prevent identifier collisions between categories. Namespaces allow you to lock down all program identifiers, successfully preventing these types of collisions.

Collisions usually fall under the category of external, global identifiers used throughout a program. They are visible to all object modules in the application program, in third-party class and function libraries, and in the compiler's system libraries. When two variables in global scope have the same identifier, the linker generates an error.

Many compiler manufacturers initially solved this problem by assigning unique identifiers to each variable. For example, under standard C, the compiler system prefixes its internal global identifiers with underscore characters, and programmers are told to avoid that usage to avoid conflicts.

Third-party vendors prepended unique mnemonic prefixes to global identifiers in an attempt to prevent collisions. However, even this failed whenever two developers chose the same prefix. The problem is that the language had no built-in mechanism with which a library publisher could stake out a so-called namespace of their own—one that would insulate its global identifiers from those of other libraries being linked into the same application.

Traditionally a programmer had three choices for eliminating collisions: they could get the source code, modify it, and rebuild all; have the authors of the offending code change *their* declarations; or select an alternate code source containing the same functionality. These were not very pleasant alternatives!

The C++ **namespace** keyword limits an identifier's scope to the namespace identifier. All references from outside the block to the global identifiers declared in the block must, in one way or another, qualify the global identifier's reference with the namespace identifier. In actuality, this is logically similar to prepending prefixes; however, namespace identifers tend to be longer than the typical two- or three-character prefixes and stand a better chance of working.

Coding Namespaces

To define a **namespace,** you encapsulate your declarations within a namespace block, as in:

```
namespace your_namespace_name {
  int ivalue;
  class my_class {/*....*/};
  // more declarations;
}
```

In the above example, any code statements within `your_namespace_name` have direct access to the namespace's declarations. However, any code statements outside of `your_namespace_name` must use a qualifying syntax. For example, from the `main()` function, accessing `ivalue` would look like:

```
void main ( void )
{
  your_namespace_name::ivalue++;
}
```

The `using` Statement

If you do not like the idea of always having to qualify an identifier with its namespace every time you access it, you can use the **using** statement, as in:

```
using namespace your_namespace_name;
void main ( void )
{
  ivalue++;
}
```

This approach can, however, be like giving a hotel guest the key to the entire hotel instead of a single room—inviting trouble! The **using name-space** syntax provides access to all of the namespace's declarations. Each application will benefit from the best selection of these two approaches.

The Selective `using` Statement

Somewhere between a fully-qualified namespace identifier (*your_name-space_name::ivalue1++;*) and the **using namespace *your_name-space_name*** syntax, there's the simpler **using** statement. The **using** directive tells the compiler that you intend to use specific identifiers within a namespace. Using the previous examples, this would look like:

```
using your_namespace_name::ivalue;
void main ( void )
{
   ivalue++;
}
```

Just as a programmer would not choose to always use **for** loops when there are **while** and **do-while** alternatives, so too a programmer should carefully select the best, application-specific approach to namespace identifier access.

Renaming Namespaces

Sometimes, third-party namespace names can get in your way because of their length; for example, *your_namespace_name* is quite long. For this reason, the namespace feature allows a programmer to associate a new name with the namespace identifier, as in:

```
namespace YNN = your_namespace_name;
void main ( void )
{
   YNN::ivalue++;
}
```

`static` File Scope vs. Unnamed Namespaces

One way to enforce file scope is with the keyword **static.** For example, if 1.cpp, 2.cpp, and 3.cpp all have the external variable declaration int ivalue, and you do not want internal linkage (meaning all three identifiers *share* the same storage location), you precede all three declarations with the keyword **static:**

```
// 1.cpp              // 2.cpp                   // 3.cpp
static int ivalue;    static int ivalue;         static int ivalue;
void main ( void )    void some_funcs( void );   void more_funcs( void );
```

Unnamed namespaces provide the same capability, just with a slightly different syntax:

```
// 1.cpp
namespace {
   int ivalue;
}
void main ( void )
{
   ivalue++;
}
```

To create an unnamed namespace, you simply omit a namespace identifier. The compiler then generates an internal identifier that is unique throughout the program. All identifiers declared within an unnamed namespace are available only within the defining file. Functions in other files, within the program's workspace, cannot reference the declarations.

Updated ANSI/ISO C++ Casting Operations

With traditional-style casting proving to be unsafe, error-prone, and difficult to spot when reading programs, and even more challenging when searching in large bodies of source code, the newer-style casting is a huge improvement. There are four new types of casts. The general syntax looks like:

```
cast_operator <castType> (objectToCast)
```

Dynamic Casting

You use a *dynamic_cast* whenever you need to convert a base class pointer or reference to a derived class pointer or reference. The one restriction is that the base, parent, or root class must have a least one **virtual** function. The syntax for a *dynamic_cast* looks like:

```
dynamic_cast < castType > ( objectToCast );
```

This type of cast allows a program, at run-time, to determine whether a base class pointer or reference points to an object of a specific derived class, or to an object of a class derived from the specified class.

You also use *dynamic_cast* to upcast a pointer or reference to a derived class to a pointer or reference to one of the base, parent, or root classes in the same hierarchy. Upcasting allows a program to determine, at runtime, whether or not a pointer to a derived class really contains the address of an object of that class and, at the same time, if you want to force the address into a pointer of one of the object's ancestor classes.

Static Casting

A *static_cast* implicitly converts between types that are not in the same class hierarchy. The type-checking is static, where the compiler checks to ensure that the conversion is valid as opposed to the dynamic run-time type-checking that is used with *dynamic_cast*s. The syntax for a *static_cast* looks like:

```
static_cast < castType > ( objectToCast );
```

The *static_cast* operator can be used for operations such as converting a pointer to a base class to a pointer to a derived class. Such conversions are not always safe. For example:

```
class typeA { ... };

class typeB : public typeA { ... };

void someFunction(typeA* ptypeA, typeB* ptypeB)
{
    typeB* ptypeB2 = static_cast<typeB*>(ptypeA);   // not safe, ptypeB may
                                                    // point to just typeB

    typeA* ptypeA2 = static_cast<typeA*>(ptypeB);   // BETTER—this is a safe
                                                    //        conversion
    ...
}
```

In this code segment, the object pointed to by *ptypeA* may not be an object of type *typeB,* in which case, the use of **ptypeB2* could be disastrous. For instance, calling a function that is a member of the *typeB* class, but not the *typeA* class, could result in an access violation.

C-type Cast

The *reinterpret_cast* operator replaces many of the older C-type casts, except those removing an identifier **const** restriction. The *reinterpret _cast* is capable of converting one pointer type into another, numbers into pointers, and vice versa, pointers into numbers. The syntax looks like:

```
reinterpret_cast < castType > ( objectToCast );
```

The *reinterpret_cast* operator can be used for conversions such as **char*** to **int*** and *Base_class** to *anyOtherNONrelated_class**, which are inherently unsafe.

The result of a *reinterpret_cast* cannot safely be used for anything other than being cast back to its original type. Other uses are, at best, non-portable. The following code segment demonstrates a pointer type cast in C, C++, and C++ using the *reinterpret_cast* syntax:

```
void main ( void )
{
  int * pointer_to_int;
  /* in C */
  pointer_to_int = malloc(100); /* implicit void * cast to int *,
                                   with warning */
  pointer_to_int = (int *) new int[100]; // C++ required cast of void *
                                            to int *
  pointer_to_int = reinterpret_cast<int *>( new int[100]); // new style cast
}
```

Constant Cast

The *const_cast*, operator can be used to remove the **const, volatile,** and **__unaligned** attribute(s) from a class. The general syntax looks like:

```
const_cast < castType > ( objectToCast )
```

With a *const_cast*, your program can cast a pointer to any object type or a pointer to a data member to a type that is identical except for the **const**, **volatile**, and **__unaligned** qualifiers. For pointers and references, the result will refer to the original object. For pointers to data members, the result will refer to the same member as the original (uncast) pointer to a data member.

What is RTTI?

The *typeid* operator found in <typeinfo> supports the new C++ run-time type information (RTTI) feature. The operator returns a reference to a system-maintained object of the type *type_info,* which identifies the type of the argument. RTTI was added to the C++ language because many vendors of class libraries were implementing this functionality themselves. This caused incompatibilities between libraries. Thus, it became obvious that support for RTTI was needed at the language level.

The following code segment demonstrates straightforward syntax and logical use:

```
#include <typeinfo>
#include <iostream>
using namespace std;
// ...
class someClassType { };
// ...
  someClassType sCTinstance;
  int ivalue;
  cout << "object type = " << typeid(sCTinstance).name(); // type's name
  if ( typeid ( ivalue ) == typeid ( sCTinstance ) ) // type comparisons
    cout << "I DON'T BELIEVE IT!";
```

Had this code section defined, and then dynamically created, a plethora of object types and instances, knowing which dynamically allocated type is in use at any point within an algorithm can be an extremely useful piece of runtime logic control.

The ANSI/ISO C++ Standard Library

No matter how sophisiticated your procedural or object-oriented standalone or Windows application is—using every available feature of C++—as a programmer you must invariably resort to tried and true data structures algorithms for creating linked lists, stacks, queues, binary trees, etc. By necessity, you will re-invent the wheel for each application's unique user-defined data types. Along with this application-specific proprietary code comes the developer's nighmare—design changes that are not easily added in such cases, and code maintenance.

Unlike many other object-oriented languages, such as SmallTalk, had these common programming components been part of the C++ language, you could have avoided re-inventing data-specific algorithms. In a nutshell, that is what STL is all about. Finally, the C++ language provides you with general-purpose components for common programming tasks through the standard C++ library.

Some of the more interesting reusable components of the standard C++ library include powerful and flexible containers, and programmable algorithms. The facilities provided by the standard C++ library are as follows:

- **C++ language support** includes common type definitions used throughout the library such as predefined types, C++ program start and termination function support, support for dynamic memory allocation, support for dynamic type identification, and support for exception processing.

- **Diagnostic tools** provide components for reporting several kinds of exceptional conditions, components for documenting program assertions, and a global variable for error number codes.
- **General C/C++ utilities** provide components used by other elements of the standard C++ library. This category also includes components used by the STL and function objects, dynamic memory management utilities, and date/time utilities. These components may also be used by any C++ program. The general C/C++ utilities also include memory management components derived from the C library.
- **Strings** include components for manipulating sequences of characters, where the characters may be of type *char*, *w_char* (used in UNICODE applications), or of a type defined in a C++ program. UNICODE uses a two-byte value to represent every known written language's symbol set versus the limiting one-byte ASCII code.
- **Cultural formatting support** provides numeric, monetary, and date/time formatting, plus parsing and support for character classification and string collation.
- **STL (Standard Template Library)** includes the most widely used algorithms and data structures in data-independent format. STL headers can be grouped into three major organizing concepts: containers, iterators, and algorithms. *Containers* are template classes that provide powerful and flexible ways to organize data, for example, vectors, lists, sets, and maps. *Iterators* are the glue that pastes together algorithms and containers.
- **Advanced numerical computation** includes semi-numerical operations and components for complex number types, numeric arrays, and generalized numeric algorithms.
- **Input/output** includes components for forward declarations of iostreams, predefined iostream objects, base iostream classes, stream buffering, stream formatting and manipulators, string streams, and file streams.
- The standard C++ library also incorporates the standard C library.

A Look at the Libraries

An application accesses Microsoft's standard C++ library facilities by using appropriate include files and associated static and dynamic libraries. Tables 2.1 and 2.2 list the standard C++ library headers and the associated static and dynamic libraries provided by Visual C++, respectively.

Table 2.1	The Standard C++ Library Headers		
algorithm	bitset	cassert	cctype
cerrno	cfloat	ciso646	climits
clocale	cmath	complex	csetjmp
csignal	cstdarg	cstddef	cstdio
cstdlib	cstring	ctime	cwchar
cwctype	deque	exception	fstream
functional	iomanip	ios	iosfwd
iostream	istream	iterator	limits
list	locale	map	memory
new	numeric	ostream	queue
set	sstream	stack	stdexcept
streambuf	string	strstream	utility
valarray	vector		

Note: Remember, the standard C++ library headers have no `.h` file extension in accordance with the latest ANSI/ISO C++ standard.

Microsoft also provides the following static and dynamic libraries:

Table 2.2	Static and Dynamic Libraries Included with Microsoft Visual C++		
Library Types	**C Run-Time Library**	**Standard C++ Library**	**Old iostream Library**
Single-threaded	LIBC.LIB	LIBCP.LIB	LIBCI.LIB
Multi-threaded	LIBCMT.LIB	LIBCPMT.LIB	LIBCIMT.LIB
Multi-threaded DLL version	MSVCRT.LIB (uses MSVCRT.DLL)	MSVCPRT.LIB (uses MSVCRT.DLL)	MSVCIRT.LIB (uses MSVCIRT.DLL)
Debug Single-threaded	LIBCD.LIB	LIBCPD.LIB	LIBCID.LIB
Debug Multi-threaded	LIBCMTD.LIB	LIBCPMTD.LIB	LIBCIMTD.LIB
Debug Multi-threaded	MSVCRTD.LIB (uses MSVCRTD.DLL)	MSVCPRTD.LIB (uses MSVCRTD.DLL)	MSVCIRTD.LIB (uses MSVCIRTD.DLL)

Practice With the ANSI/ISO C++ Standard Library

To make you feel right at home, the following C++ program uses the standard C++ library iostream to print "Hello World!"

```
#include <iostream>
void main( void )
{
    cout << "Hello World!";
}
```

The code segment uses the standard C++ library input/output component to print "Hello World!" by simply including the standard C++ library header **<iostream>**. It is important to remember that starting with Visual C++ 4.0, a C++ program, depending on the run-time library compiler option specified (/ML[d],/MT[d], or /MD[d]), will always link with one basic C run-time library and, depending on headers included, will link with either a standard C++ library (as in the example program above) or the old iostream library (as in the following coded example):

```
#include <iostream.h>
void main( void )
{
  cout << "Hello World!";
}
```

Designing a Template

Frequently, a C++ program uses common data structures such as stacks, queues, and linked lists. Imagine a program that requires a queue of customers and a queue of messages. You could easily implement a queue of customers, and then take the existing code and implement a queue of messages.

If the program grows and there is a need for a queue of orders, you could take the queue of messages and convert it to a queue of orders. But, what if you then needed to make some changes to the queue implementation? This would not be a very easy task because the code has been duplicated in many places. Re-inventing source code is not an intelligent approach in an object-oriented environment that encourages reusability. It seems to make more sense to implement a queue that can contain any arbitrary type rather than duplicating code. How does one do that? The answer is to use *type parameterization*, more commonly referred to as *templates*.

Templates are very useful when implementing generic constructs such as vectors, stacks, lists, and queues that can be used with any arbitrary type. C++ templates provide a way to reuse source code, as opposed to inheritance and composition, which provide ways to reuse object code.

C++ provides two types of templates: *class templates* and *function templates*. Use function templates to write generic functions, for example, searching and sorting routines that can be used with arbitrary types. The STL generic algorithms have been implemented as function templates, and the containers have been implemented as class templates.

The Class Template

The good news is that a class template definition looks very similar to a regular class definition, except for the prefix keyword **template.** The following example defines a stack class template, independent from any stack element type definitions:

```
template <class T>

class genericStack

{
public:
        genericStack( sizeOfStack = 25);
        ~genericStack() { delete[] stackPtr; }
        int pushElement(const T&);
        int popElement(T&) ;
        int isStackEmpty()const { return stackTop == -1 ; }
        int isStackFull() const { return stackTop == sizeOfStack-1 ; }
private:
        int sizeOfStack ;   // number of stack elements
        int stackTop ;
        T* stackPtr ;
} ;
```

T represents any data type. It is important to note that *T* does not have to be a class type as implied by the keyword class. *T* can be anything from a simple data type like int, to a complex data structure like pToArrayOf-Structures *.

The Function Template

Implementing template member functions is somewhat different than implementing regular class member functions. The declarations and definitions of the class template member functions should all be in the same header file. Why do the declarations and definitions need to be in the same header file? Consider the following:

```
//sample.h
template <class t>      //sample.cpp           //main.cpp
class sample            #include "sample.h"    #include "sample.h"
{                       template <class t>     void main( void )
```

```
public:                 sample<t>::sample()    {
    sample() ;          {                          sample<int> si ;
    ~sample() ;         }                          sample<float> sf ;
} ;                     template <class t>     }
                        sample<t>::~sample()
                        {
                        }
```

When compiling sample.cpp, the compiler has both the declarations and the definitions available. At this point, the compiler does not need to generate any definitions for template classes, since there are no instantiations. When the compiler compiles main.cpp, there are two instantiations: template classes sample<int> and sample<float>. At this point, the compiler has the declarations, but no definitions!

Implementing Class Templates

Using a class template is very easy—create the required classes by plugging in the actual type for the type parameters. This process is commonly known as *instantiating* a class. Here is a sample class that uses the genericStack class template:

```
#include <iostream>
#include "stack.h"
using namespace std;
void main( void )
{
   typedef genericStack<float> floatStack;
   typedef genericStack<int> intStack;
   FloatStack actualFloatStackInstance( 10 );
```

In the above example, we defined a class template genericStack. In the program, we instantiated a genericStack of type float (floatStack) and a genericStack of type int(intStack). Once the template classes are instantiated, you can instantiate objects of that type (for example, *actual FloatStackInstance*).

It is good programming practice to use **typedef** while instantiating template classes. Then, throughout the program, one can use the **typedef** name. There are two advantages. First, **typedef**s are helpful when nesting template definitions. For example, when instantiating an int STL vector, you could use:

```
typedef vector<int, allocator<int> > intVECTOR ;
```

Second, should the template definition change, simply change the **typedef** definition. This practice is especially helpful when using STL components.

Class Template Parameters

The *genericStack* class template, described in the previous section, used only type parameters in the template header. It is also possible to use non-type parameters. For example, the template header could be modified to take an *int number_of_elements* parameter as follows:

```
#define MAX_ELEMENTS 32
template <class T, int number_of_elements>
class genericStack ;
```

Then, a declaration such as:

```
genericStack<float, MAX_ELEMENTS> currentStackSize;
```

could instantiate (at compile-time) a *MAX_ELEMENTS* genericStack template class named *currentStackSize* (of float values); this template class would be of type *genericStack<float, 32>*.

Default Template Parameters

Let us look at the genericStack class template again:

```
template <class T, int number_of_elements> genericStack { ....};
```

C++ allows you to specify a *default template parameter*, so the definition could now look like:

```
template <class T = float, int number_of_elements = 10> genericStack { ....};
```

Then a declaration such as:

```
genericStack<> defaultStackSize;
```

would instantiate (at compile-time) a 10-element *genericStack* template class named *defaultStackSize* (of float values); this template class would be of type *genericStack<float, 10>*.

If you specify a default template parameter for any formal parameter, the rules are the same as for functions and default parameters. Once you begin supplying a default parameter, all subsequent parameters must have defaults.

The Standard Template Library

The STL is a part of the standard C++ library. Every C++ programmer at one time or another has implemented a common data structure such as a vector, list or queue, and a common algorithm such as a binary search, sort, and so on. Through STL, C++ gives programmers a set of carefully designed generic data structures and algorithms.

These generic data structures and algorithms are parameterized types (templates) that only require you to plug in actual types to be ready for use. Finally, STL brings to C++ the long-promised goal of reusable software components. More importantly, the STL substructure generates extremely efficient code in terms of size and performance.

Components of STL

- **Containers** are objects that store other objects.
  Sequential containers include:
  - Vectors.
  - Lists.
  - Deques.
  Associative containers include:
  - Maps.
  - Multimaps.
  - Sets.
  - Multisets.
- **Algorithms** include generic functions that handle common tasks such as searching, sorting, comparing, and editing.
- **Iterators** are generic pointers used to interface containers and algorithms. STL algorithms are written in terms of iterator parameters, and STL containers provide iterators that can be plugged into algorithms. Iterators include:
  - Input.
  - Output.
  - Forward.
  - Bidirectional.
  - Random access.
  - Istream_iterator.
  - Ostream_iterator.
- **Function** templates are objects of any class or struct that overload the function call **operator()**. Most STL algorithms accept a function object as a parameter that can change the default behavior of the algorithm. Function template argument types include:
  - Plus.
  - Minus.
  - Times.
  - Divide.

The unary, logical, bitwise, and comparison operator object types include:
- Modulus.
- Negate.
- Equal_to.
- Not_equal_to.
- Greater.
- Less.
- Greater_equal.
- Less_equal.
- Logical_and.
- Logical_or.
- Logical_not.
- **Adapter**s modify the interface of other components. There are three kinds of STL adaptors:
  - Container adapters: stack, queue, priority_queue.
  - Iterator adapters: reverse_bidirectional_iterator, back_insert_iterator, front_insert_iterator, and insert_iterator.
  - Function adapters: not1, not2, bind1st, and bind2nd.

The individual STL libraries and glue components are designed to work together in useful ways to produce the kind of larger and more specialized algorithms needed in today's applications.

Standard Template Library Rules

The following sections highlight fundamental principles employed by the C++ compiler when using STL components. For example, when an object is used with an STL container, it is first copied with a call to the copy constructor, and the copy is what is actually inserted into the container. This means an object held by an STL container must have a copy constructor. If the application removes an STL container object, the object is destroyed with a call to the destructor. If an STL container is destroyed, it destroys all objects it currently holds.

Frequently, STL components use compare container objects with a complete set of logical tests such as **<**, **<=**, **>**, **>=**, **==**, and **!=**. This means the comparison operators must be defined for objects used with an STL component. Of course, some STL components modify the value of an object. This is accomplished using the assignment operator. This means the assignment operator, **=**, must be defined for objects used with an STL component. Your application can use the <utility> definitions of the **<=**, **>**, **>=**, and **!=** operators, which are all defined in terms of the **<** and **==**.

The simplest way for you to guarantee that your objects will sucessfully interact with STL containers is to make certain your objects contain:

1. A copy constructor.
2. An assignment operator, =.
3. An equality comparison operator, ==.
4. A less than comparison operator, < .

Standard Template Library Function Objects

Function objects are relatively new to the C++ programming language. Their usage may seem odd at first glance, and the syntax may appear to be confusing. A function object is an object of a class or struct type that includes an `operator()` member function. An `operator()` member function allows the creation of an object that behaves like a function. For example, a two-dimensional `Array2D` class could overload `operator()` to access an element whose row and column indexes are specified as arguments to `operator()`.

```
class Array2D
{
  public:
    Array2D(int, int);
    int operator(int, int) const;
  private:
    Array<int> Array2Def;
    int rowOffset;
    int colOffset;
} ;
int Array2D::operator(int currentRow, int currentCol) const
{
  if ( currentRow > 0 && currentRow <= rowOffset && currentCol > 0 &&
       currentCol <= colOffset)
    return Array2Def[currentRow, currentCol];
  else
    return (0);
}
Array2D intArray2D(10, 10);
int  intArray2D_element = intArray(5, 5);
```

It is important to note that function objects are objects that behave like functions; as such, they can be created and must always return a value.

Function Objects

The STL provides function objects for standard math operations such as addition, subtraction, multiplication, and division. STL also provides function objects for unary operations, logical operations, bitwise operations, and comparison operations. The next chapter lists all the function objects defined in the STL header file **\<functional\>**.

The following example program demonstrates how these function objects can be used with STL algorithms to change their default behavior. The STL sort algorithm, by default, sorts in ascending order. However, by using the greater(T) function object, you can "trick" the sort algorithm to work in descending order:

```
#include <iostream>
#include <vector>
#include <functional>
#include <algorithm>
using namespace std;

void main( void )
{
   typedef vector<int, allocator<int> > iVECTOR;
   int iArray[5] = {10, 15, 22, 31, 18, 5};
   iVECTOR iVectorInstance(iArray, iArray + 5) ;

// default ascending sort
   copy(iVectorInstance.begin(), iVectorInstance.end(), out) ;
   sort(iVectorInstance.begin(), iVectorInstance.end()) ;
// use of function object to reverse sort to descending

   copy(iVectorInstance.begin(), iVectorInstance.end(), out) ;
   sort(iVectorInstance.begin(), iVectorInstance.end(), greater<int>()) ;
 }
```

Basically, it is the *greater\<int\>()* function object passed to *sort()* that inverts the comparison logic used by *sort()*, thereby tricking it into a descending algorithm. You can also use STL function objects directly in a C++ program, as in the following two statements:

```
float floatCalculation = (times<float>())(1.1, 2.2); // assigns 2.42
int intCalculation = (minus<int>())(15, 5); // assigns 10
```

Function Adapters

Function adapters help to construct a wider variety of function objects using existing function objects. Using function adapters is often easier than directly constructing a new function object type with a struct or class definition. STL provides three categories of function adapters: *negators*, *binders*, and *adapters for pointers to functions*.

Binders are function adapters that convert binary function objects into unary function objects by binding an argument to some particular value. STL provides two types of binder function objects: **binder1st<Operation>** and **binder2nd<Operation>**. A binder function object takes only a single argument. STL provides two template functions, **bind1st** and **bind2nd,** to create binder function objects.

The functions **bind1st** and **bind2nd** each take as arguments a binary function object *f* and a value *x*. **bind1st** returns a function object of type **binder1st<Operation>**, and **bind2nd** returns a function object of type **binder2nd<Operation>**. Here are the function prototypes for the **bind1st** and **bind2nd** functions:

```
template <class Operation, class T>
binder1st<Operation> bind1st(const Operation& f, const T& x) ;
template <class Operation, class T>
binder2nd<Operation> bind2nd(const Operation& f, const T& x) ;
```

Look at this first example:

```
int iGreater = (bind2nd(greater<int>(), 15))(actual_int_value)
```

Assume *actual_int_value* is defined as type **int.** The above statement could have been rewritten as:

```
int iGreater = (greater<int>())(actual_int_value, 15)
```

Negators are the second type of function adaptor. Negators are used to return the complement of a result obtained by applying a provided unary or binary operation. STL provides two types of negator function objects: **unary_negate<Operation>** and **binary_negate<Operation>**. A negator function object takes only a single argument.

The two template functions, **not1** and **not2,** create negator function objects. The function **not1** takes a unary function object *f* as its argument and returns a function object of type **unary_negate<Operation>**. The function **not2** takes a binary function object *f* as its argument and returns a function object of type **binary_negate<Operation>**. Here are the function prototypes for the **not1** and **not2** functions:

```
template <class Operation>
unary_negate<Operation> not1(const Operation& f) ;
template <class Operation>
binary_negate<Operation> not2(const Operation& f) ;
```

The following code segment demonstrates **find_if()** used with the **not1** function used to locate the first element in the array that is not greater than 15:

```
int iArray[25] = {/* your initialization code here */};
int* offset = find_if(iArray, iArray+25, not1(bind2nd(greater<int>(), 15)));
```

The function **bind2nd** creates a unary function object which returns the result of the comparison int > 15. The function **not1** takes the unary function object as an argument and creates another function object. This function object merely negates the results of the comparison int > 15. This next statement uses the **not2** function in a game-playing match by causing the **greater** function object to trigger an ascending **sort** order:

```
sort(iVectorInstance.begin(), iVectorInstance.end(), not2(greater<int>())) ;
```

Pointer-to-Function Adapters

STL provides two types of pointer-to-function objects: pointer_to_unary_function<Arg, Result> and pointer_to_binary_function <Arg1, Arg2, Result>. An application can use adapters for pointers to functions to convert existing binary or unary functions to function objects. Adapters for pointers to functions allow the programmer to utilize the existing code to uniquely extend the library.

The pointer_to_unary_function function object takes one argument of type Arg, and pointer_to_binary_function takes two arguments of type Arg1 and Arg2. STL provides two versions of the template function ptr_fun to create pointer-to-function function objects.

The first version of ptr_fun takes a unary function f as its argument and returns a function object of type pointer_to_unary_function<Arg, Result>. The second version of ptr_fun takes a binary function f as its argument and returns a function object of type pointer_to_binary_function<Arg1, Arg2, Result>. Here are the function prototypes for the ptr_fun functions:

```
template<class Arg, class Result>
    class pointer_to_unary_function
        : public unary_function<Arg, Result> {
public:
    explicit pointer_to_unary_function(Result (*pf)(Arg));
    Result operator()(const Arg x) const;
};
```

The template class stores a copy of pf. It defines its member function operator() as returning (*pf)(x).

Standard Template Library Algorithms

This section serves to introduce STL algorithm fundamentals and present some examples. Remembering some basic rules will help you to understand the algorithms and how to use them. STL provides generic, parameterized, iterator-based functions (a fancy description for template functions). These functions implement some common array-based utilities, including searching, sorting, comparing, and editing. The STL algorithms are user-programmable. What this means is that you can modify the default behavior of an algorithm to suit your needs. An example of this is the sort algorithm:

```
sort(first, last) ; //sorts elements of a sequence
                    //in ascending order by default.
```

In this case, the STL algorithm assumes that an operator == or operator < exists, and uses it to compare elements. The default behavior of the STL algorithms can be changed by specifying a predicate. The predicate function could be a C++ function. For example, sort_descending is a C++ function that compares two elements. In this case, the sort algorithm takes a function pointer as follows:

```
sort(first, last, sort_descending);
```

Or, the predicate function could be a function object. Either define a function object, or use the function objects provided by STL. For example (as seen earlier):

```
sort(first, last, greater<int>());
```

Every algorithm operates on a range of sequence. A sequence is a range of elements in an array or container, or user-defined data structures delimited by a pair of iterators. The identifier *first* points to the first element in the sequence. The identifier *last* points one element beyond the end of the region you want the algorithm to process. A common notation used to represent a sequence is [*first, last*). This is a notation for an open interval. The notation [*first, last*) implies that the sequence ranges from *first* to *last,* including *first* but not including *last.* The algorithm will increment an internal iterator with the ++ operator until it equals *last.* The element pointed to by *last* will not be processed by the algorithm.

STL algorithms do not perform range or validity checking on the iterator or pointer values. Many algorithms work with two sequences. For example, the copy algorithm takes three parameters, as follows:

```
copy(firstValue1, lastValue1, firstValue2);
```

If the second sequence is shorter than the first, copy will blindly continue writing into unconnected areas of memory. Some STL algorithms also create an in-place version and a copying version. For example:

```
reverse(first, last); // places results in original container
reverse_copy(firstValue1, lastValue1, firstValue1); // results in du-
plicate location
```

The STL generic algorithms can be divided into the following four main categories: nonmutating-sequence algorithms operate on containers without, in general, modifying the contents of the container; mutating-sequence algorithms typically modify the containers on which they operate; sorting-related algorithms include sorting and merging algorithms, binary searching algorithms, and set operations on sorted sequences; and a small collection of generalized numeric algorithms are defined in the files <algorithm>, <functional>, and <numeric>.

ANSI/ISO C++ Standard Library Language Support

The language support section of the standard C++ library provides common type definitions used throughout the library, characteristics of pre-defined types, functions supporting the start and termination of C++ programs, support for dynamic memory allocation, support for dynamic type identification, support for exception processing, and other run-time support.

A Look at <cstddef>

This header file basically includes stddef.h. There are two macros, NULL and offsetof, and two types, ptrdiff_t and size_t, specifically listed in this section of the standard. To determine the distance (or the number of elements) between two elements, you can use the distance() function. If you pass it an iterator pointing to the first element and one pointing to the third element, it will return a 2. The distance() function is in the utility header file and it takes two iterators as parameters and returns a number of type difference_type. Difference_type maps is an int.

Architecture-specific Headers: <limits>, <climits>, and <cfloat>

The numeric_limits component provides information about properties of fundamental types. Specializations are provided for each fundamental type such as int, floating point, and bool. The member is_specialized returns true for the specializations of numeric_limits for the fundamental types. The numeric_limits class is defined in the limits header file:

```
template<class T>  class numeric_limits {
public:
static const bool has_denorm;
static const bool has_denorm_loss;
static const bool has_infinity;
static const bool has_quiet_NaN;
static const bool has_signaling_NaN;
static const bool is_bounded;
static const bool is_exact;
static const bool is_iec559;
static const bool is_integer;
static const bool is_modulo;
static const bool is_signed;
static const bool is_specialized;
static const bool tinyness_before;
static const bool traps;
static const float_round_style round_style;
static const int digits;
static const int digits10;
static const int max_exponent;
static const int max_exponent10;
static const int min_exponent;
static const int min_exponent10;
static const int radix;
static T denorm_min() throw();
static T epsilon() throw();
static T infinity() throw();
static T max() throw();
static T min() throw();
static T quiet_NaN() throw();
static T round_error() throw();
static T signaling_NaN() throw();
};
```

Catching Exceptions

The C++ standard library exception class defines the base class for the types of objects thrown as exceptions. The exception header file defines the exception class that is the base class for all exceptions thrown by the C++ standard library. The following code would catch any exceptions thrown by classes and functions in the standard C++ library:

```
try {
    // your code here
```

```
}
catch ( const exception &ex)
{
    cout << "exception: " << ex.what();
}
```

The exception class is defined in the header file exception as follows:

```
class exception {
public:
    exception() throw();
    exception(const exception& rhs) throw();
    exception& operator=(const exception& rhs) throw();
    virtual ~exception() throw();
    virtual const char *what() const throw();
private:
// ...
};
```

Additional ANSI/ISO C++ Standard Library Headers

Each of these header files, cstdarg, csetjmp, ctime, csignal, and cstdlib, includes the corresponding C header files stdarg.h, setjmp.h, time.h, signal.h, and stdlib.h. Macros, types, and functions listed for each of these in the standard C++ library are as follows:

File	Macros	Types	Functions
cstdarg	va_arg, va_end,va_start	va_list	
csetjmp	Macro: setjmp	jmp_buf	longjmp
ctime	CLOCKS_PER_SEC	clock_t	clock
csignal	SIGABRT, SIGILL, SIGSEGV, SIG_DFL, SIG_IGN, SIGFPE, SIGINT, SIGTERM, SIG_ERR	sig_atomic_t	raise, signal
cstdlib	getenv, system		

Summary

These first two chapters may have clouded the goal of STL—*simplicity*. Unfortunately, this kind of generic, bulletproof, robust code capability does not come easy. From the confusing library names, to the standard C++ library and

STL, to the interactions between templates, algorithms, iterators, binders, and beyond, STL intimidates.

Chapters 1 and 2 served to reverse-engineer STL components down to their simpler C++ and even C underpinnings. With a little persistence and initially some patience, you should be able to now start using the simpler STL routines. The next chapter uses the syntax and logic explained in Chapters 1 and 2 to enumerate and use, by example, the STL <utility> and <functional> support libraries.

STL <utility>, <functional>, <algorithm>, and <iterator> Templates

Just as every solid building starts with proper footers and a strong foundation, so too do C++ applications need the correct building blocks for an entire structure to stand. Before discussing the structural requirements for applications using the STL, you need to recognize the syntax evolution behind the new standard C++ libraries. These are separate library routines used by most C/C++ applications and have nothing directly to do with STL.

The <utility> template defines global versions of the <=, >, >=, and != operators, which are all defined in terms of the < and ==. Both the <utility> and <functional> templates are viewed as support libraries. You use the <functional> STL for defining several templates that help construct predicates for the templates defined in <algorithm> and <numeric>.

The <algorithm> template functions and classes work on containers. Although each individual container provides support for its own basic operations, the standard algorithms provide more extended or complex actions. They also allow you to work with two different types of containers at the same time.

The STL <iterator> template is an extremely important component of STL. While many of the other STL templates, such as container types, are easier to digest and use, in actuality STL is composed of many interrelated components. Iterators are every bit as important as containers, algorithms, and allocators.

Note   The standard C++ library is a separate entity from the STL.

The standard C++ library encompasses all the latest ANSI C++, including the STL and a new iostream library. The standard C++ library provides new functionality, such as numerous algorithms that manipulate C++ objects, and a migration path for developers who want to move to the standard iostream.

The standard C++ library is a set of 51 header files. The new header files do *not* have the .h extension. The standard C++ library also has 18 standard C headers with the .h extension, for example, errno.h and stdio.h.

The main difference between the standard C++ library and previous run-time libraries is in the iostream library. Details of the iostream implementation have changed, and you cannot mix calls to the old iostream library and to the new standard C++ library.

From iostream.h to <iostream>

Traditional C++ applications have always accessed library routines with the straightforward **#include <filename.h>** syntax, as in:

```
#include <fstream.h>
#include <iomanip.h>
#include <ios.h>
#include <iostream.h>
#include <istream.h>
#include <ostream.h>
#include <strstrea.h>
```

Under the new ANSI C/C++/ISO standard, to use the new standard C++ library, you include one or more of the standard C++ library header files in your code, with a different syntax, as in:

```
#include <iostream>
```

The new header files do not have the .h extension. You should *not* use the old iostream header files (fstream.h, iomanip.h, ios.h, iostream.h, istream.h, ostream.h, streamb.h, and strstrea.h). You cannot mix calls to the old iostream library and the new standard C++ library.

The good news is that many of the new standard C++ iostream header files, fstream, iomanip, ios, iosfwd, iostream, istream, ostream, sstream, streambuf, and strstream, have names that are the same as or similar to the old iostream header files, but without the .h extension. If you include the new standard C++ header files, the run-time library files that contain the standard C++ library will be the default libraries.

Many of the underlying details of the iostream implementation have changed. For some applications, you may have to rewrite parts of your code that use iostream if you want to link with the Standard C++ library by removing any old iostream headers, such as `fstream.h`, `iomanip.h`, `ios.h`, `iostream.h`, `istream.h`, `ostream.h`, `streamb.h`, and `strstrea.h`, included in your code. They are replaced with one or more of the new standard C++ iostream headers, `fstream`, `iomanip`, `ios`, `iosfwd`, `iostream`, `istream`, `ostream`, `sstream`, `streambuf`, and `strstream`, all without the `.h` extension.

One option for older applications making heavy use of iostream is to simply link with the new standard C++ library. In this case, leave the old iostream headers in your code and the old iostream library will automatically be linked. However, you cannot include any of the new standard C++ library headers. You cannot mix calls to the old iostream library and the new standard C++ library.

The following section explains the differences in the new standard C++ iostream library and the old iostream library. In the new standard C++ iostream library:

- Open functions no longer have a third protection parameter.
- You can no longer create streams from file handles.
- There are no open ofstream objects with the ios::out flag by itself; instcad, you combine the flag with another ios enumerator in a logical AND, for example, with `ios::in` or `ios::nocreate`.
- `ios::unsetf` returns void instead of the previous value.
- `istream::get( char& rchar )` does not assign to `rchar` if there is an error.
- `istream::get( char* pchar, int nCount, char cdelim )` is different in three ways:
  - When nothing is read, the failbit is set.
  - `istream::seekg` with an invalid parameter does not set the failbit.
  - The return type `streampos` is a class with overloaded operators. In functions that return a `streampos` value (such as `istream::tellg`, `ostream::tellp`, `strstreambuf::seekoff`, and `strstreambuf::seekpos`), you should cast the return value to the type required: `streamoff`, `fpos_t`, or `mbstate_t`.
- The first function parameter `falloc`, in `strstreambuf::strstreambuf`, takes a `size_t` argument, not the older type long.
- The following list enumerates elements of the old iostream library that are not elements of the new iostream library:
  - Attach member function of `filebuf`, `fstream` `ifstream`, and `ofstream`..
  - `filebuf::openprot` and `filebuf::setmode`.

- `ios::bitalloc, ios::nocreate, ios::noreplace,` and `ios::sync_with_stdio`
- `streambuf::out_waiting,` and `streambuf::setbuf.`

STL Syntax

Microsoft Visual C++ ships with a complete set of tools to help the STL beginner. Should you wish to view the formal definitions of any of the individual template libraries, follow these simple steps:

1. Click on the Visual C++ `Help` menu.
2. Choose the `Search` option.
3. When the `Help` window opens, make certain that the `Index` tab is selected.
4. Type in an STL name. For example, to find the definition for the `<utility>` template, type `utility` without the angle brackets.
5. Once the search has narrowed down to words close to your selection, search for the entry that uses the template's name, i.e., `utility` followed by the words `header file`.
6. Click on that entry and you'll launch yourself off into the template's formal syntax definition.
7. From there, hot-links can take you to any necessary related definitions and sample code.

STL <utility> and <functional> Templates

The `<utility>` and `<functional>` templates are very rarely used by themselves. Instead, they can be viewed as adding additional functionality to the other STLs. Since they are such a frequent component of mainstream STL applications, it is worthwhile to view their definitions and capabilities.

<utility> Template Syntax

The header file `<utility>` defines global versions of the `<=`, `>`, `>=`, and `!=` operators, which are all defined in terms of the `<` and `==`. In principle, STL assumes that all object containers have at least the following:

- An assignment operator (`=`).
- An equality comparison operator (`==`).
- A less than comparison operator (`<`).
- A copy constructor.

Include the STL standard header <utility> to define several templates of general use throughout the STL. Four template operators, operator!=, operator<=, operator>, and operator>=, define a total ordering on pairs of operands of the same type, given definitions of operator== and operator<. If an implementation supports namespaces, these template operators are defined in the rel_ops namespace, nested within the std namespace.

To use the <utility> template operators, you use the following syntax:

```
using namespace std::rel_ops;
```

which promotes the template operators into the current namespace.

Those familiar to C/C++ programming know that frequently, to understand a particular definition, declaration, or statement, it is necessary to nest backwards through many levels of predefined identifiers (constants, variables, functions, and classes). The same holds true with the STL library. The following section saves you the time of doing this for all related support definitions.

STRUCT PAIR

```
template<class T, class U>
    struct pair {
    typedef T first_type;
    typedef U second_type
    T first;
    U second;
    pair();
    pair(const T& x, const U& y);
    template<class V, class W>
        pair(const pair<V, W>& pr);
    };
```

You use the pair template class to store pairs of objects. *first* is assigned the type *T*, and *second* type *U*. The type definition *first_type* is the same as the template parameter *T*, while *second_type* is the same as the template parameter *U*. The first (default) constructor initializes *first* to *T()* and second to *U()*. The second constructor initializes first to x and second to y. The third (template) constructor initializes first to pr.first and second to pr.second. T and U each need to supply only a single argument constructor and a destructor.

MAKE_PAIR

```
template<class T, class U>
    pair<T, U> make_pair(const T& x, const U& y);
```

The template function returns pair<T, U>(x, y).

THE PAIRDATA.CPP APPLICATION

The first example application, `pairdata.cpp`, shows how the `<utility>` `make_pair()` method is used to create and use a pair of data types:

```
// pairdata.cpp
// Testing <utility>
// make_pair()
// Chris H. Pappas and William H. Murray, 1999


#include <utility>
#include <iostream>

using namespace std;

// STL id_PAIR, struct pair typedef using int and char
member types

typedef struct pair<int,char> ic_PAIR;

void main(void){

  // create storage for and initialize
  // an_int_char_pair using make_pair()

  ic_PAIR an_int_char_pair = make_pair(15,'c');


  // output the individual members
  cout << an_int_char_pair.first
       << "   "
       << an_int_char_pair.second
       << endl;


  // assign new member values
  an_int_char_pair.first  = 20;
  an_int_char_pair.second = 'a';


  // output the new values
  cout << an_int_char_pair.first
       << "   "
       << an_int_char_pair.second
       << endl;
}
```

The straightforward output from the program looks like:

```
15   c
20   a
```

THE UTILITY.CPP APPLICATION

This next example uses an int, double *pair* to test the overloaded <utility> operators:

```cpp
// utility.cpp
// Testing <utility>
// ==, !=, <, <=, >, >=
// Chris H. Pappas and William H. Murray, 1999


#include <iostream>
#include <utility>

using namespace std ;

// STL id_PAIR, struct pair typedef usingint and double member types

typedef struct pair<int, double> id_PAIR;

void main(void)
{
  id_PAIR pair33_56a(33,5.6);
  id_PAIR pair22_56 (22,5.6);
  id_PAIR pair33_95 (33,9.5);
  id_PAIR pair33_56b(33,5.6);

// output original values

  cout << "pair33_56a = ( " << pair33_56a.first << " , " <<
pair33_56a.second << " )" << endl;
  cout << "pair22_56  = ( " << pair22_56.first  << " , " <<
pair22_56.second  << " )" << endl;
  cout << "pair33_95  = ( " << pair33_95.first  << " , " <<
pair33_95.second  << " )" << endl;
  cout << "pair33_56b = ( " << pair33_56b.first << " , " <<
pair33_56b.second << " )" << endl;

  cout << "\n\n\n";

// test for equality ==

  cout << ((pair33_56a == pair33_56b) ?
      "pair33_56a and pair33_56b are     equal \n" :
      "pair33_56a and pair33_56b are not equal \n");

// test for non-equality !=
```

```
    cout << ((pair22_56 != pair33_95) ?
        "pair22_56  and pair33_95  are not equal \n" :
        "pair22_56  and pair33_95  are      equal \n");

    cout << "\n\n";

// test for greater than >

    cout << ((pair33_56a > pair33_95) ?
        "pair33_56a is     greater than pair33_95 \n" :
        "pair33_56a is not greater than pair33_95 \n");

// test for greater than or equal >=

    cout << ((pair33_56a >= pair33_95) ?
        "pair33_56a is     greater than or equal to pair33_95 \n" :
        "pair33_56a is not greater than or equal to pair33_95 \n");

    cout << "\n\n";

// test for less than <

    cout << ((pair33_95 < pair33_56a) ?
        "pair33_95  is     less    than pair33_56a \n" :
        "pair33_95  is not less    than pair33_56a \n");

// test for less than or equal <=

    cout << ((pair33_95 < pair33_56a) ?
        "pair33_95  is     less    than or equal to pair33_56a \n" :
        "pair33_95  is not less    than or equal to pair33_56a \n");
}
```

The output from the program looks like:

```
        pair33_56a = ( 33 , 5.6 )
        pair22_56  = ( 22 , 5.6 )
        pair33_95  = ( 33 , 9.5 )
        pair33_56b = ( 33 , 5.6 )

        pair33_56a and pair33_56b are      equal
        pair22_56  and pair33_95  are not equal

        pair33_56a is not greater than pair33_95
        pair33_56a is not greater than or equal to pair33_95

        pair33_95  is not less    than pair33_56a
        pair33_95  is not less    than or equal to pair33_56
```

<functional> Template Syntax

As mentioned earlier, both the <utility> and <functional> templates are viewed as support libraries. You use the <functional> STL for defining several templates that help construct predicates for the templates defined in <algorithm> and <numeric>.

When you include the STL standard header <functional>, you gain access to several templates that help construct function objects. These are objects of a class that defines operator(). Later chapters will demonstrate how function objects behave much like function pointers, except that the objects can store additional information that can be used during a function call.

THE ITEMPLAT.CPP APPLICATION

The following program instantiates the plus, minus, multiplies, and divides templates for the standard C/C++ integer data type:

```
// itemplat.cpp
// Testing <functional>
// plus<>, minus<>, multiplies<>, divides<>
// Chris H. Pappas and William H. Murray, 1999

#include <iostream>
#include <functional>

using namespace std ;

class functional_tmplts :   public plus<int>, public minus<int>,
               public multiplies<int>, public divides<int>
{
public:

   int iValue1;

   // Overloaded constructors
   functional_tmplts()            {iValue1 = 0       ;}
   functional_tmplts(int aValue1 ){iValue1 = aValue1;}

   // Overloaded operators
   result_type operator+(second_argument_type iValue2_to_add)
                              {return iValue1 + iValue2_to_add;}
   result_type operator-(second_argument_type iValue2_to_sub)
                              {return iValue1—iValue2_to_sub;}
   result_type operator*(second_argument_type iValue2_to_mul)
                              {return iValue1 * iValue2_to_mul;}
   result_type operator/(second_argument_type iValue2_to_divby)
                              {return iValue1 / iValue2_to_divby;}
```

```
} ;

ostream& operator<<(ostream& os, const functional_tmplts& obj )
{
        os << obj.iValue1 ;
        return os ;
}

void main(void)
{
   functional_tmplts iFirstResult,iSecondResult,
                   iThirdResult,iFourthResult,iFifthResult;

   cout << "Testing <functional> STL library \n\n";

   iFirstResult = 10;
   cout << "iFirstResult   = "
        <<  iFirstResult << endl ;

   iSecondResult = iFirstResult + 10;
   cout << "iSecondResult = iFirstResult  + 10 = "
        <<  iSecondResult << endl ;

   iThirdResult = iSecondResult-5;
   cout << "iThirdResult  = iSecondResult -  5 = "
        <<  iThirdResult << endl ;

   iFourthResult = iThirdResult * 2;
   cout << "iFourthResult = iThirdResult  *  2 = "
        <<  iFourthResult << endl ;

   iFifthResult = iFourthResult / 15;
   cout << "iFifthResult  = iFourthResult / 15 =  "
        <<  iFifthResult << endl ;
}
```

STL <algorithm> Template

The <algorithm> template functions and classes work on containers. Although each individual container provides support for its own basic operations, the standard algorithms provide more extended or complex actions.
They also allow you to work with two different types of containers at the
same time.

The <algorithm> template functions allow you to sort, compare,
merge, insert, delete, swap, copy, fill, and do many other container element

manipulations. This section is used to introduce STL <algorithm> fundamentals and present several examples you can use to model additional applications. With over sixty <algorithm> template functions available, remembering some basic rules will help you to understand the algorithms themselves and how to use them.

The C++ STL provides generic, parameterized, iterator-based functions that implement some common array-based utilities, including searching, sorting, comparing, and editing. The default behavior of the STL algorithms can be changed by specifying a predicate, or modifying a function template. For example, the sort algorithm has a formal third argument specifying the sort type, as in `sort_descending`, or an STL template function like `greater< ... >()`.

Every <algorithm> template function operates on a sequence. A sequence is a range of elements in an array or container, or user-defined data structures delimited by a pair of iterators. The identifier *first* points to the first element in the sequence. The identifier *last* points one element beyond the end of the region you want the algorithm to process.

Many <algorithm> function templates use the (...*first,last*) sequence. This syntax implies that the sequence ranges from *first* to *last*, including *first* but not including *last*. <algorithm> template funtions use the increment operator until it equals `last`. The element pointed to by *last* will not be processed by the algorithm.

Certain STL algorithms will create an instance copy of a container. For example, the `reverse(first, last)` template function call adjusts container contents in the original container, while `reverse_copy (first, last)` generates a copy of the container with the adjusted element contents.

Sample Code

The following four programs, `algorth1.cpp`, `algorth2.cpp`, `algorth3. cpp`, and `algorth4.cpp`, demonstrate several of the <algorithm> template functions. These examples lay down the fundamental syntax requirements for using the <algorithm> template functions and STL iterators (see below).

THE ALGORTH1.CPP APPLICATION

The first example application, `algorth1.cpp`, shows how the `find()` function template can be used to locate the first occurrence of a matching element within a sequence. The syntax for `find()` looks like:

```
template<class InIt, class T>
    InIt find(InIt first, InIt last, const T& val);
```

find() expects two input iterators (discussed later in the chapter) and the address of the comparison value. It returns an input iterator. The program looks like:

```
// algorth1.cpp
// Testing <algorithm>
// find()
// Chris H. Pappas and William H. Murray, 1999

#include <iostream>
#include <algorithm>

using namespace std;

#define MAX_ELEMENTS 5

void main( void )
{
  // simple character array declaration and initialization
  char cArray[MAX_ELEMENTS] = { 'A', 'E', 'I', 'O', 'U' }
;

  char *pToMatchingChar, charToFind = 'I';

  // find() passed the array to search, length +1, and
charToFind ptr
  pToMatchingChar = find(cArray, cArray + MAX_ELEMENTS,
charToFind);

  if( pToMatchingChar!= cArray + MAX_ELEMENTS )
    cout << "The first occurrence of " << charToFind
         << " was at offset " << pToMatchingChar—cArray;
  else
    cout << "Match NOT found!";
};
```

Remember, all you need to do to use any STL template function is use the proper include statement:

```
#include <algorithm> // for this chapter
```

and a using statement:

```
using namespace std;
```

The program first defines the character array cArray and initializes it to uppercase vowels. The program then searches the array, using the find() function template for the letter 'I', and reports its offset into the cArray if found. The output from the program looks like:

```
The first occurrence of I was at offset 2
```

THE ALGORTH2.CPP APPLICATION

Randomization of data is an extremely important component of many applications, whether it's the random shuffle of a deck of electronic poker cards or truly random test data. The following application uses the `random_shuffle()` template function to randomize the contents of an array of characters. This simple example can be easily modified to work on any container element type.

Several of the applications use additional STL templates. Each chapter will emphasize, in the discussion, only those code segments relating to that chapter's STL template. Without this approach, each chapter would endlessly digress. With patience and practice, you will soon understand how the support STL templates work together, in much the same way someone learning to speak a new language may know *how* to use a verb without really knowing the details of sentence construction.

The syntax for `random_shuffle()` looks like:

```
template<class RanIt>
    void random_shuffle(RanIt first, RanIt last);
```

random_shuffle requires two random access iterator formal arguments (discussed below). The program looks like:

```
// algorth2.cpp
// Testing <algorithm>
// random_shuffle()
// Chris H. Pappas and William H. Murray, 1999

#include <iostream>
#include <algorithm>
#include <vector>

using namespace std;

#define MAX_ELEMENTS 5

void main( void )
{
  // typedef for char vector class and iterator
  typedef vector<char> cVectorClass;
  typedef cVectorClass::iterator cVectorClassIt;

  //instantiation of character vector
  cVectorClass cVowels(MAX_ELEMENTS);

  // additional iterators
  cVectorClassIt start, end, pToCurrentcVowels;

  cVowels[0] = 'A';
  cVowels[1] = 'E';
```

```
cVowels[2] = 'I';
cVowels[3] = 'O';
cVowels[4] = 'U';

start = cVowels.begin();    // location of first cVowels
end = cVowels.end();        // one past the last cVowels

cout << "Original order looks like: ";
cout << "{ ";
for(pToCurrentcVowels = start; pToCurrentcVowels != end;
    pToCurrentcVowels++)
        cout << *pToCurrentcVowels << " ";
  cout << "}\n" << endl;

  random_shuffle(start, end); // <algorithm> template function

  cout << "Shuffled order looks like: ";
  cout << "{ " ;
  for(pToCurrentcVowels = start; pToCurrentcVowels != end;
        pToCurrentcVowels++)
    cout << *pToCurrentcVowels << " ";
  cout << "}" << endl;
}
```

Notice that the application incorporates the STL templates <vector> and <algorithm>. The STL <vector> template provides the definitions necessary to create the character vector container, while <algorithm> defines the random_shuffle() template function. The application uses the <vector> templates begin() and end() to locate the front and back offset addresses into the *cVowels* container. These two parameters are then passed to the random_shuffle() template function so the algorithm knows where the container starts and ends in memory. The output from the program looks like:

```
Original order looks like: { A E I O U }

Shuffled order looks like: { U O A I E }
```

THE ALGORTH3.CPP APPLICATION

This next application uses the remove_if() template function along with the <functional> less_equal() template to remove any container elements matching the test value. The syntax for remove_if() looks like:

```
FwdIt remove_if(FwdIt first, FwdIt last, Pred pr);
template<class InIt, class OutIt, class T>
```

remove_if() is passed two forward iterators and a predicate telling remove_if() what comparison test to perform. The program looks like:

```cpp
// algorth3.cpp
// Testing <algorithm>
// remove_if()
// Chris H. Pappas and William H. Murray, 1999

#include <iostream>
#include <algorithm>
#include <vector>
#include <functional>

using namespace std;

#define MAX_ELEMENTS 10

void main( void )
{
  typedef vector<int> cVectorClass ;
  typedef cVectorClass::iterator cVectorClassIt;

  cVectorClass iVector(MAX_ELEMENTS);

  cVectorClassIt start, end, pToCurrentint, last;

  start = iVector.begin();    // location of first iVector
  end = iVector.end();        // location of one past last iVector

  iVector[0] =  7;
  iVector[1] = 16;
  iVector[2] = 11;
  iVector[3] = 10;
  iVector[4] = 17;
  iVector[5] = 12;
  iVector[6] = 11;
  iVector[7] =  6;
  iVector[8] = 13;
  iVector[9] = 11;

  cout << "Original order: {";

  for(pToCurrentint = start; pToCurrentint != end;
      pToCurrentint++)
    cout << *pToCurrentint << " " ;
  cout << " }\n" << endl ;

  // call to remove all values less-than-or-equal to the value 11
  last = remove_if(start, end, bind2nd(less_equal<int>(), 11) ) ;

  cout << end-last << " elements were removed.\n" << endl;
```

```
cout << "The " << MAX_ELEMENTS-(end-last)
    << " valid remaining elements are: { " ;
for(pToCurrentint = start; pToCurrentint != last;
    pToCurrentint++)
  cout << *pToCurrentint << " " ;
  cout << " }\n" << endl ;

}
```

While many components of this application are similar to the two previous examples, this program uses the <functional> template function bind2nd() along with the less_equal template class, as the second argument to remove_if(), to find all occurrences with values less than or equal to the integer value 11. The output from the program looks like:

```
Original order: { 7 16 11 10 17 12 11 6 13 11 }
6 elements were removed.
The 4 valid remaining elements are: { 16 17 12 13 }
```

Notice that the values 7, 11, 10, 11, 6, and 11 were removed, respectively.

THE ALGORTH4.CPP APPLICATION

This last application uses the <algorithm> sort() and set_union() template functions. First, the program instantiates two integer vectors, iVector1 and iVector2, and a third iUnionedVector twice the length of the first two. Sorting is necessary for the set_union() template function to correctly locate and eliminate all duplicate values. The syntax for set_union() looks like:

```
template<class InIt1, class InIt2, class OutIt>
    OutIt set_union(InIt1 first1, InIt1 last1,
        InIt2 first2, InIt2 last2, OutIt x);
```

set_union() uses four input iterators and one output iterator to point to the comparison containers and output the results, respectively. The program looks like:

```
// algorth4.cpp
// Testing <algorithm>
// set_union()
// Chris H. Pappas and William H. Murray, 1999

#include <iostream>
#include <algorithm>
#include <vector>
```

```
#include <functional>

using namespace std;

#define MAX_ELEMENTS 10

void main( void )
{
  typedef vector<int> cVectorClass ;
  typedef cVectorClass::iterator cVectorClassIt;


  cVectorClass iVector1(MAX_ELEMENTS), iVector2(MAX_ELEMENTS),
               iUnionedVector(2 * MAX_ELEMENTS) ;

  cVectorClassIt start1, end1,
                 start2, end2,
                        pToCurrentint, unionStart;

  start1 = iVector1.begin();   // location of first iVector1
  end1 = iVector1.end();       // location of one past last iVector1

  start2 = iVector2.begin();   // location of first iVector2
  end2 = iVector2.end();       // location of one past last iVector2

  // locating the first element address of result union container
  unionStart = iUnionedVector.begin();

  iVector1[0]  =  7; iVector2[0]  = 14;
  iVector1[1]  = 16; iVector2[1]  = 11;
  iVector1[2]  = 11; iVector2[2]  =  2;
  iVector1[3]  = 10; iVector2[3]  = 19;
  iVector1[4]  = 17; iVector2[4]  = 20;
  iVector1[5]  = 12; iVector2[5]  =  7;
  iVector1[6]  = 11; iVector2[6]  =  1;
  iVector1[7]  =  6; iVector2[7]  =  0;
  iVector1[8]  = 13; iVector2[8]  = 22;
  iVector1[9]  = 11; iVector2[9]  = 18;

  cout << "iVector1 as is : { ";

  for(pToCurrentint = start1; pToCurrentint != end1;
      pToCurrentint++)
    cout << *pToCurrentint << " " ;
  cout << "}\n" << endl ;

  cout << "iVector2 as is : { ";

  for(pToCurrentint = start2; pToCurrentint != end2;
      pToCurrentint++)
```

```
   cout << *pToCurrentint << " " ;
cout << "}\n" << endl ;

// sort of both containers necessary for correct union
sort(start1,end1);
sort(start2,end2);

cout << "\niVector1 sorted: { ";

for(pToCurrentint = start1; pToCurrentint != end1;
    pToCurrentint++)
  cout << *pToCurrentint << " " ;
  cout << "}\n" << endl ;

cout << "\niVector2 sorted: { ";

for(pToCurrentint = start2; pToCurrentint != end2;
    pToCurrentint++)
  cout << *pToCurrentint << " " ;
  cout << "}\n" << endl;

// call to set_union() with all necessary pointers
set_union(start1,end1,start2,end2,unionStart);

cout << "After calling set_union()\n" << endl ;

cout << "iUnionedVector { " ;
for(pToCurrentint = iUnionedVector.begin();
    pToCurrentint != iUnionedVector.end(); pToCurrentint++)
  cout << *pToCurrentint << " " ;
cout << "}\n" << endl ;
}
```

The output from the program looks like:

```
iVector1 as is : { 7 16 11 10 17 12 11 6 13 11 }
iVector2 as is: { 14 11 2 19 20 7 1 0 22 18 }
iVector1 sorted: { 6 7 10 11 11 11 12 13 16 17 }
ivector2 sorted: { 0 1 2 7 11 14 18 19 20 22 }
After calling set_union():
iUnionedVector { 0 1 2 6 7 10 11 11 11 12 13 14 16 17 18 19 20 22 0 0 }
```

Notice that the union of ivector1's and iVector2's value of 11 removes their duplicate occurrences, explaining the last two 0s' in iUnioned-Vector, indicating null elements.

STL <iterator> Template

The STL <iterator> template is an extremely important component of STL. While many of the other STL templates, such as container types, are easier to digest and use, in actuality STL is composed of many interrelated components. Iterators are every bit as important as containers, algorithms, and allocators.

The ANSI/ISO Committee defines an iterator as a generalized pointer that allows a programmer to work with different data structures (or containers) in a uniform manner. Structurally, an iterator is a pointer data type with a few surprising subtleties of its own. Like all pointers, for example:

```
int * pi, or float * pf, or MYCLASS* pmyclass
```

iterators are defined in terms of what they point to. Their syntax:

```
container<Type>::iterator iterator_instance;
```

begins with the type of container they are associated with. The syntax looks slightly different than your standard pointer syntax because it is associated with a template type instead of a simple data type. In the example above, iterator_instance is going to be a pointer to elements in a container that holds objects of type Type. Dereferencing iterator_instance yields a reference to an object of type Type.

Since iterators allow algorithms to access the elements of any container type in a uniform way, you can generate code solutions that are easily ported to different application needs. For example, the following example uses the iterators InIt and OutIt to copy the elements of one container to another:

```
template <class InIt, class OutIt>
OutIt copy(InIt first, InIt last, OutIt copiedContainer)
   {
    while( first != last ) *copiedContainer++ = *first++;
    return copiedContainer;
   }
```

Here, the copy() template function works by using the iterator interface. It expects the input and output iterators to provide the basic set of three operations: operator*(), which returns a reference to the container's content_type; operator!=(), a template function that determines when it's time to exit the main loop; and operarator++(), which is used to move to the next container element in both the source and destination containers.

Since all the different iterator types used in the STL support these basic operations, the `<algorithm>` `copy()` template function can work on *any* container type. With iterators not caring about a container's type or element's type, you do not have to write custom versions of your algorithm for each container class.

Iterator Precedence

The following list of iterators begins with the simplest and most straightforward and progresses to iterators with the most capabilities. At the bottom of the tree are input and output iterators, followed by forward and bidirectional, and finally, at the top of the tree, random access iterators.

INPUT AND OUTPUT ITERATORS

Both input and output iterators are pointers to container elements. The only operations allowed on these iterators are pointer dereferencing and incrementing. Each specific location can only be dereferenced *once* to reference or store an individual container element.

FORWARD ITERATORS

Unlike input and output iterators, forward iterators return a true reference when the pointer is dereferenced so it can be read and written to multiple times.

BIDIRECTIONAL ITERATORS

Bidirectional iterators go forward iterators one better by allowing the pointer to be decremented, not just incremented. Any container that uses this iterator is no longer limited to single-pass algorithms.

RANDOM ITERATORS

As their name implies, random iterators behave most closely to true pointer variables in that they can be both incremented and decremented, or have a constant value added to or subtracted from them.

Iterator Range

If you have had a Data Structures course sometime during your software engineering career, you should be intimately aware of the debugging nightmare pointer variables can introduce into a program. Iterators are no exception.

The biggest problem associated with pointer variables is pointing with a garbage address. To avoid this disaster when you start working with iterators, you need to adopt the STL philosophy of using an interator's range. Most STL template functions that work on a container do so over the range of the container. A container's range is defined by the `begin()` and `end()` template functions, for example:

```
for( vector<float>::iterator pElement = ctr.begin(); pElementlll !=
  ctr.end(); pElement++ )
```

constructs a well-formed **for** loop with the iterator pElement always within a valid range.

One important concept to grasp when dealing with iterators, which remember are most closely related to pointer variable types, is that you do *not* compare their values with the standard pointer value NULL, or ask if one iterator is greater than or less than another. Instead, you use iterators in pairs to define the range over which the algorithm operates.

Important Naming Conventions

Not all algorithms support all iterator types. This could present a problem to you, the user of STL, were it not for certain naming conventions. For example, the `sort()` template function needs a random access iterator, not just one starting at `crt.begin()` and ending at `crt.end()`. In an attempt to avoid this type of confusion, the STL uses a standardized naming of the class arguments used to parameterize template functions.

Microsoft uses a very consistent naming convention that you will soon pick up on as you continue through the examples in this chapter and the remainder of the book. For example, look at the following STL definition for the `<algorithm>` `sort()`:

```
template<class RanIt> void sort(RanIt first, RanIt last);
```

In this definition, `first` and `last` are defined by a random iterator, `RanIt`. The name of an iterator type indicates the category of iterators required for that type. In order of increasing power, the categories are summarized here as:

- `OutIt`—An output iterator X can only have a value V stored indirectly on it, after which it must be incremented before the next reference.
- `InIt`—An input iterator X can represent a singular value that indicates end-of-sequence. If such an iterator does not compare

equal to its end-of-sequence value, it can have a value V accessed indirectly on it any number of times. To progress to the next value, or end-of-sequence, you increment it, as in ++X, X++. Once you increment any copy of an input iterator, none of the other copies can safely be compared, dereferenced, or incremented.

- FwdIt—A forward iterator X can take the place of an output iterator or an input iterator. You can read what you just wrote through a forward iterator. And, you can make multiple copies of a forward iterator, each of which can be dereferenced and incremented independently.
- BidIt—A bidirectional iterator X can take the place of a forward iterator. You can, however, also decrement a bidirectional iterator, as in – –X, X– –.
- RanIt—A random access iterator X can take the place of a bidirectional iterator. You can also perform much the same integer arithmetic on a random access iterator that you can on an object pointer.

Table 3.1 lists the iterators you can use to perform read, write, or read/write container element access.

Table 3.1	Read, Write, and Read/Write Iterators
Mode	**Legal Iterator Type(s)**
Write-only Iterators	Output Iterator
	(**FwdIt**) forward iterator
	(**BidIt**) bidirectional iterator
	(**RanIt**) random access iterator
Read-only Iterators	Input Iterator
	(**FwdIt**) forward iterator
	(**BidIt**) bidirectional iterator
	(**RanIt**) random access iterator
Read/Write Iterators	Forward Iterator
	(**BidIt**) bidirectional iterator
	(**RanIt**) random access iterator

The vectorit.cpp Application

The following application uses three iterators: **vector::begin**, which returns an iterator to start the traversal of the vector; **vector::end**, which returns an iterator for the last element of the vector; and **vector::traverse,** which traverses the vector. The program first creates a vector instance named **iVectorInstance**, then initializes the vector's contents with the offset address into the vector.

```
// vectorit.cpp
// Testing <iterator>
// ::iterator
// Chris H. Pappas and Willliam H. Murray, 1999

#include <iostream>
#include <vector>


using namespace std ;

#define MAX_ELEMENTS 10

typedef vector<int> iVector;

void ShowVector(iVector &iVectorInstance);

void main( void )
{
  iVector iVectorInstance;

  // Initialize vector elements with
  // the offset's value
  for (int offsetAndValue = 0; offsetAndValue < MAX_ELEMENTS;
       offsetAndValue++)
         iVectorInstance.push_back(offsetAndValue);

  // Iterator used to traverse vector elements
  iVector::iterator actualIterator;

  // Output original contents of iVectorInstance.
  cout << "iVectorInstance with the last element: ";
  for (actualIterator  = iVectorInstance.begin();
       actualIterator != iVectorInstance.end();
       actualIterator++)
         cout << *actualIterator << " ";

  cout << "\n\n";
```

```
    // Use <vector> erase() to delete last value
    iVectorInstance.erase(iVectorInstance.end() -1);

    // Output contents of iVectorInstance.minus last element
    cout << "iVectorInstance minus the last element: ";
    for (actualIterator = iVectorInstance.begin();
         actualIterator != iVectorInstance.end();
         actualIterator++)
            cout << *actualIterator << " ";
}
```

The program finishes by first printing the original vector's contents, then deleting the last element, and finally printing the modified container. The output from the program looks like:

```
iVectoInstance with the last element: 0 1 2 3 4 5 6 7 8 9
iVectorInstance minus the last element 0 1 2 3 4 5 6 7 8
```

The listit.cpp Application

For a change, the following application uses a \<list\> instead of a \<vector\> container to hold a series of words. The program uses a list::iterator, a list::difference_type (holding the type of element pointers it will be subtracting), and the advance() template function, which moves the input iterator *n* elements.

```
// listit.cpp
// Testing <iterator>
// ::iterator
// Chris H. Pappas and William H. Murray, 1999

#include <list>
#include <string>
#include <iostream>

using namespace std ;

typedef list<string> strClassList;

void main( void ) {

  strClassList List;

  // iterator used to traverse list of strings
  strClassList::iterator iteratorForListElements;
```

```
// list::difference_type describes an object that represents
// the difference between the addresses of any two elements.

strClassList::difference_type distance_between;

List.push_back("Sun,");
List.push_back("Sand,");
List.push_back("Ocean,");
List.push_back("Beach,");
List.push_back("Lotion,");
List.push_back("equals ");
List.push_back("Ahhhhhh!");

// output the list
iteratorForListElements = List.begin();
cout << "The vacation begins: ";
for( int i = 0; i < 7 ; i++, iteratorForListElements++ )
  cout << *iteratorForListElements  << "   ";

// Find the first element
iteratorForListElements=List.begin();

cout << "\n\nUsing advance() to locate the KEY word :) \n";

advance(iteratorForListElements,2); // move iterator two elements

cout << "\nThe magic word is " << *iteratorForListElements << endl;

// calculating the distance between first and third elements
distance_between = distance( List.begin(), iteratorForListElements);

// Output difference
cout << "\nThe distance between the elements is : " << distance_between;
}
```

Notice that both programs declare container iterators using the identical syntax, just different container types:

```
iVector::iterator actualIterator;
strClassList::iterator iteratorForListElements;
```

The following statement defines what container element type distance_between will need to subtract:

```
strClassList::difference_type distance_between;
```

Next, the program uses the `list::push_back()` method to insert an element with the current string constant at the end of the list container. At this point, the list iterator needs the address to the first container element:

```
iteratorForListElements = List.begin();
```

before it can begin traversing the list and outputting its contents. Once the for loop executes, the iterator needs to be reset back to the beginning of the list container so that it may be advanced *n* elements from the beginning.

The advance() template function moves the list pointer two elements forward:

```
advance(iteratorForListElements,2); // move iterator two elements
```

The distance() template function uses the advanced iterator's address and compares it with the beginning of the list:

```
distance_between = distance( List.begin(), iteratorForListElements);
```

The output from listit.cpp looks like:

```
The vacation begins: Sun, Sand, Ocean, Beach, Lotion, equals Ahhhhhh!
Using advance() to locate the KEY word :)
The magic word is Ocean,
The distance between the elements is: 2
```

Summary

In this chapter, you learned to separate the standard C++ library from the C++ STL. You saw how to facilitate STL—basically, certain components of historic C++ need updating, in particular iostream.h. You also looked at the two "support" templates, <utility> and <functional>, which are frequently combined with additional templates to increase their usability.

You also explored several of the STL <algorithm> template functions as used on integer <vector> classes. The applications demonstrated how to find a container element, randomly shuffle container contents, scan a container for certain comparison conditions (less-than-or-equal-to), and perform a union.

Finally, you looked at the similarities and differences between standard C/C++ pointers and STL iterators. The advantage of iterators involves their generic syntax that allows them to work on any container type/element type. You also discovered that when using template functions with iterator arguments, you must pay close attention to the required iterator type (input, output, random, etc.) and Microsoft's naming conventions for each category.

The good news is that with `<utility>`, `<functional>`, `<algorithm>`, and `<iterator>` STL routines behind you, you are ready to knowledgeably understand how the remaining STL definitions (`<vector>`, `<stack>`, `<queue>`, `<list>`, etc.) interface, providing extremely powerful, portable, and generic code solutions for today's applications.

STL Containers

Any STL data structure that can hold information is called a container. Just about every program ever written stores data in some form of list or container. Regardless of how the internal coding implements this storage, additional functionality is always included to insert, delete, sort, and search data items, to find out if the list exists, and to discern how many items the container holds.

Modifications on this functionality include where the data items are inserted and removed and how efficiently internal container coding can retrieve information (remember the Big O function, or Order of Magnitude algorithm efficiency ratings). This chapter introduces you to several of the most frequently used STL containers, namely vectors, stacks, queues, and deques (not as in removing an item from a queue, but as in d(ouble)-e(nded)-que(ue).

Question: If <vector> containers are arrays, then are arrays <vector> containers? Answer: No! Okay, here's the good news: Using <vector> containers is logically and syntactically very similar to using simple C/C++ arrays. The great news is that unlike statically allocated arrays, <vector> containers are dynamic—dynamic in the sense of linked list technology, meaning that a <vector> container can grow and shrink its size to maximize the use of RAM.

The <stack> and <queue> data types in the STL are interesting because they are not provided as true standalone data types, but rather are constructed as adaptors placed on top of other containers. The <queue> template, like the <stack> template, is implemented as an adaptor that wraps around an underlying container. As with the <stack> template, the <queue> adaptor does not actually provide any new functionality, but simply modifies the interface. Operations are provided with their conventional queue-like names, but are actually performed using operations on the underlying containers.

Containers in the standard library that implement the necessary operations for the <queue> adaptor include the <list> and <deque> data structures that we will introduce later in the chapter. Unlike the <stack> template, the <queue> class in STL provides the ability to access both the front and back elements of the queue, while the conventional description of the queue data abstraction only permits access to the front.

Dynamic Arrays

The term *"vector"* is commonly used to mean an indexed collection of similarly typed values. In C++, we can represent this abstract concept as a one-dimensional array. Recall that an array is a fixed-size collection of values of homogeneous data types, indexed by integer keys. The number of elements held by the array is provided as part of the declaration. The following, for example, creates an array of ten float values:

```
float fArray[10];
```

Legal index values range from zero to one less than the size of the collection. Values are accessed using the subscript operator. A programmer can think of the elements of an array as being placed end to end in memory. The underlying C++ language provides only a primitive mechanism for the support of one-dimensional arrays, and this mechanism provides few safeguards. Most importantly, index values are *not* checked against declared bounds at run-time.

The problem is compounded by the fact that there is no way to determine from the value of a simple C++ array the extent, or number of elements, it should contain. Furthermore, there are even fewer high-level operations defined for the array type than there are for character strings. By adding a new abstraction layer on top of the basic language framework, we can correct many of these deficiencies.

Making Vectors Data Type-specific

A vector viewed as a data abstraction is different in one very important respect from the data types we have previously investigated. As an abstract concept, the idea of a vector describes an incomplete data type. The solution of any particular problem might require a vector of integers, a vector of floating-point values, or even a vector of strings. To abstract the concept of a vector out of these more concrete realizations, we need a facility to parameterize a type description with another type. That is, we need some way to describe the idea of a vector of type T, where T represents an unknown type.

Within a vector class description, the unknown parameter type T can be used in any situation requiring the use of a type name. This allows you to declare an instance variable as a pointer to T, and we can declare an operator as returning a T reference. In the copy constructor, we need to refer to an object of the same type as the receiver. Although only the keyword vector is used, it is implicitly assumed to mean vector of T.

How to Instantiate a Vector

To use a template class as a type, you have to provide bindings for the unknown argument types. This is accomplished by providing the element type in a list, again surrounded by angle brackets. For example, the following declares a vector of five integer values, each entry initialized to 0, a vector consisting of 20 uninitialized, float-precision values, and a vector of ten strings, all initialized to the string "abc":

```
// overloaded <vector> constructors
vector<int> iVector(5,0);
vector<float> fVector(20);
vector<string> szVector(10,"abc");
```

An Example Using Vector Template Functions

The following template function max(), which appears in the STL, is used to compute the maximum of two arguments. This functionality is parameterized using the template syntax:

```
template <class T> max(T a, T b)
{
  if( a < b )
    return b;
  return a:
}
```

The template function will work as long as the arguments are of a type that can be compared. Thus, the function will work with integers, floating-point precision, and strings. Many of the template functions used by the <vector> template library use this data-independent syntax.

Referencing Single Elements

Accessing an individual <vector> element is no more difficult than accessing a simple array element. The syntax looks identical:

```
standardArrayElementReference[ 1 ];
myVectorInstanceElementReference[ 1 ];
```

The syntax changes slightly when traversing an entire `<vector>` versus an array. Look at the two equivalent statements that follow:

```
// traversing a simple array
for( int offset = 0; offset < MAX_ELEMENTS; offset++)...
// traversing a <vector> instance
vector<int>::iterator iteratorOffset;
for( iteratorOffset = myVector.front(); iteratorOffset != myVector.end();
     iteratorOffset++)...
```

Similar to the `<string>` template, the `<vector>` template contains a type definition for the name iterator. This permits an iterator to be easily declared for any particular type of vector value. The template functions `begin()` and `end()` yield random access iterators for the vector. Again, note that the iterators yielded by these operations can become invalidated after the insertion or removal of elements.

Adding and Deleting Elements

You use the `<vector>` template functions `push_back()`, `insert()`, `pop_back()`, and `erase()` to insert and remove `<vector>` elements. The template function `push_back()` takes a new value as an argument, and inserts the element at the end of the vector, increasing the size of the vector by one. The more general template function `insert()` takes as arguments an iterator and a value, and inserts the new element preceding the position specified by the iterator. Again, the size of the vector is increased by one.

The `<vector>` template function `pop_back()` removes the last element of the vector, reducing the size of the vector by one. The more general template function `erase()` is overloaded. In the easier form, a single location is specified using an iterator, and the value denoted by the iterator is removed from the vector. Again the size of the vector is reduced by one. The more general form of `erase()` takes two iterator arguments, which specify a range of values within the vector. All elements within this range are removed, regardless of the number of elements being removed.

The template function `swap()` takes as an argument another vector that holds the same type of elements. The values of the two vectors are then exchanged; after the operation, all values from the argument will be held by the receiving vector, and all elements in the current vector will be held by the argument.

Determining the Size of a Vector Container

Unlike a standard C++ array, which has a fixed size determined by the declaring statement, `<vector>` vectors are dynamic in size, growing and shrinking as needed. However, vectors have two different sizes associated with them. The first is the number of elements currently in the vector; the second is the maximum size to which the vector can grow, without actually allocating that new storage. The <vector> template function size() fulfills the first category, returning the actual number of vector elements, while capacity() returns your "wish list" for the total number of elements to be stored.

It therefore follows that inserting and deleting vector elements always changes the vector's size, but may or may not change its capacity. An insertion that causes the size to exceed the capacity generally results in a new block of memory being allocated to hold the vector elements. Values are then copied into this new memory using the assignment operator appropriate to the element type, and the old memory is deleted. This can generate a significant performance hit on your algorithm should the vector be large in size.

The <vector> template function reserve() is a directive to the vector, indicating that the vector is expected to grow to at least the given size. If the argument used with reserve() is larger than the current capacity, then a reallocation occurs and the argument value becomes the new capacity. If subsequent inserts cause the vector to grow even larger than this new value, the vector can grow even larger. The reserved value is not a fixed delimiter, but an application's best guess at the maximum vector size. When the capacity is already in excess of the reserved size request, no reallocation takes place. Remember, calling reserve() does *not* change the actual size of the vector, nor the element values themselves.

Caution is the word when dealing with pointers to vectors as a reallocation invalidates *all* references, pointers, and iterators denoting elements being held by a vector. This means that it is dangerous to lock onto an iterator's address thinking that the address associated with the pointer will *never* change.

```
vector<double>::iterator FrontOfVectorConstant;
FrontOfVectorConstant = myVector.begin();
// code using FrontOfVectorConstant instead of myVector.begin()...
```

Using the <algorithm> Template with Vectors

While the <vector> template does not directly provide any template function that can be used to determine if a specific value is contained in the collection, the generic <algorithm> template functions find() and count() can be used for these purposes.

<vector> Example Programs

The following sample applications demonstrate many of the more frequently used <vector> template functions, overloaded operators, and areas of caution when using this template library.

THE IVECTOR.CPP APPLICATION

This first application demonstrates the dimensioning of vector containers, from the initial instantiation of the vector, to a dynamically allocated "guess" length, to actually increasing the size of the container.

```cpp
// ivector.cpp
// Testing <vector>
// push_back(), size(), capacity(), max_size(), reserve(), resize()
// Chris H. Pappas and William H. Murray, 1999


// When symbols are longer than 255 characters, the warning is disabled.
#pragma warning(disable:4786)

#include <vector>
#include <iomanip>
#include <iostream>

using namespace std ;

typedef vector<int> iVector;

void main( void )
{
    // Instantiation of 0 element integer vector.
    iVector iVectorInstance;

    // Inserting a 5, at the end of the vector
    iVectorInstance.push_back(5);

    // Current vector statistics.
    cout << "Current statistics:" << endl;
    cout << "iVectorInstance's current size: "
        <<  setw(10) << iVectorInstance.size() << endl;
    cout << "iVectorInstance's maximum size: "
        <<  iVectorInstance.max_size() << endl;
    cout << "iVectorInstance's capacity    : "
        <<  setw(10) << iVectorInstance.capacity() << endl;

    // See if there is room for a total of 15 elements
    iVectorInstance.reserve(15);
    cout << "\nReserving storage for 15 elements:" << endl;
    cout << "iVectorInstance's size is     : "
        <<  setw(10) << iVectorInstance.size() << endl;
    cout << "iVectorInstance's maximum size: "
        <<  setw(10) << iVectorInstance.max_size() << endl;
    cout << "iVectorInstance's capacity is : "
        <<  setw(10) << iVectorInstance.capacity() << endl;

    // Demanding room for at least 25 elements.
    iVectorInstance.resize(25);
    cout << "\nAfter resizing storage for 25 elements:" << endl;
    cout << "iVectorInstance's size is     : "
        <<  setw(10) << iVectorInstance.size() << endl;
    cout << "iVectorInstance's maximum size: "
```

```
        <<  iVectorInstance.max_size() << endl;
    cout << "iVectorInstance's capacity is : "
        <<  setw(10) << iVectorInstance.capacity() << endl;
}
```

The program begins with the following typedef:

```
typedef vector<int> iVector;
```

that defines *iVector* as an integer vector type. Next, the *iVectorInstance* is instantiated:

```
iVector iVectorInstance;
```

Notice that the container does *not* specify any fixed length. The first action on the vector is to insert the integer value *5* into the container using the push_back() template function:

```
iVectorInstance.push_back(5);
```

The next series of statements output the containers size(), max_size(), and capacity(), all with template functions:

```
cout << "Current statistics:" << endl;
    cout << "iVectorInstance's current size: "
        <<  setw(10) << iVectorInstance.size() << endl;
    cout << "iVectorInstance's maximum size: "
        <<  iVectorInstance.max_size() << endl;
    cout << "iVectorInstance's capacity    : "
        <<  setw(10) << iVectorInstance.capacity() << endl;
```

This series of statements repeats the same statistics based on two container size-changing statements. The first looks like:

```
iVectorInstance.reserve(15);
```

Remember that reserve() only checks to see if the requested size could indeed fit in available RAM, but does *not* actually increase the actual size of the container. The second dimension change comes from the following statement:

```
iVectorInstance.resize(25);
```

Unlike reserve(), resize() physically increases the maximum number of elements. Look at the output from the program and notice the effect on the various container statistics:

```
Current statistics:
iVectorInstance's current size:          1
iVectorInstance's maximum size: 1073741823
iVectorInstance's capacity    :          1
```

```
Reserving storage for 15 elements:
iVectorInstance's size is      :              1
iVectorInstance's maximum size: 1073741823
iVectorInstance's capacity is :             15

After resizing storage for 25 elements:
iVectorInstance's size is      :             25
iVectorInstance's maximum size: 1073741823
iVectorInstance's capacity is :             25
```

Notice that the `reserve()` request did *not* change the number of elements from *1* to *15*, but *did* change the capacity to *15*. However, `resize()` changed both the *size* and *capacity*. Also notice that the `maximum_size()`, which returns the length of the longest sequence that the object can control, remains constant.

THE CVECTOR.CPP APPLICATION

This next example demonstrates how to access vector elements using iterators and various `insert()` and `erase()` operations. Pay particular attention to how you syntactically and logically access vector elements:

```cpp
// cvector.cpp
// Testing <vector>
// push_back(), insert(), delete(), begin(), end()
// Chris H. Pappas and William H. Murray, 1999


// When symbols are longer than 255 characters, the warning is disabled.
#pragma warning(disable:4786)

#include <vector>
#include <iostream>

using namespace std ;

typedef vector<char> cVector;

void main( void )
{
    // Instantiation of 0 element integer vector.
    cVector cVectorInstance;

    // Inserting five vowels
    cVectorInstance.push_back('A');
    cVectorInstance.push_back('E');
    cVectorInstance.push_back('I');
    cVectorInstance.push_back('O');
    cVectorInstance.push_back('Y');
```

```
// Accessing vector elements using array syntax—DANGEROUS
for(int i = 0; i < 5; i++)
  cout << cVectorInstance[i];
cout << endl;

// Accessing vector elements using iterators—BEST APPROACH
vector<char>::iterator p = cVectorInstance.begin();
while(p != cVectorInstance.end()) {
  cout << *p;
  p++;
}
cout << endl;

// Inserting a NEW fifth element extending the vector's size
p = cVectorInstance.begin();
p += 4; // moves pointer to fifth element's address
cVectorInstance.insert(p,'U');

// Accessing the NEW list
p = cVectorInstance.begin();
while(p != cVectorInstance.end()) {
  cout << *p;
  p++;
}
cout << endl;

// Deleting the sixth element 'Y'
p = cVectorInstance.end();
cVectorInstance.erase(--p);

// Printing the modified container
p = cVectorInstance.begin();
while(p != cVectorInstance.end()) {
  cout << *p;
  p++;
}
}
```

Most of the initial program statements should now look familiar to you, so the discussion begins with the two methods for accessing container elements:

```
// Accessing vector elements using array syntax—DANGEROUS
for(int i = 0; i < 5; i++)
  cout << cVectorInstance[i];
cout << endl;
```

While this for loop works, it is not the most generalized approach and breaks many of the STL rules. In particular, it is hardwired to the element cout. The better, standard STL approach below uses the begin() and end() template functions, along with the iterator *p* to perform the task:

```
// Accessing vector elements using iterators—BEST APPROACH
vector<char>::iterator p = cVectorInstance.begin();
while(p != cVectorInstance.end()) {
  cout << *p;
  p++;
}
```

The next three statements insert a new fifth vowel into the container, preceding the current fifth element of *Y*:

```
p = cVectorInstance.begin();
p += 4; // moves pointer to fifth element's address
cVectorInstance.insert(p,'U');
```

The re-initialization of *p* is necessary since the previous loop moved the pointer beyond the end of the vector container. Pointer arithmetic is next employed to move *p* to the address of the fifth element, followed by a call to the insert() template function. This function accepts an iterator *p* and valid element type *U*.

To output the updated container, iterator *p* needs to be reset:

```
p = cVectorInstance.begin();
while(p != cVectorInstance.end()) {
  cout << *p;
  p++;
}
```

The final two statements:

```
p = cVectorInstance.end();
cVectorInstance.erase(--p);
```

reset *p* one more time, only this time to the end of the container. Use caution as the template function end() returns an interator *one beyond the end* of the container. This explains the prefix decrement of *p* in the template function call statement (--*p*). Lastly, the template function erase() removes the element at the specified location. The template function could have removed a range of values with just a slightly different syntax:

```
cVectorInstance.erase(initializedIterator, initializedIterator + n);
```

The output from the program looks like:

```
AEIOY
AEIOY
AEIOUY
AEIOU
```

Implementing Stacks with STL Technology

This section details the concepts of a stack as they apply to the STL `<stack>` template. The `<stack>` and `<queue>` data types in the STL are interesting because they are not provided as true stand alone data types, but rather are constructed as adaptors placed on top of other containers. This section illustrates the use of these abstractions in the solution of several programming problems.

Many everyday objects provide most people with a good intuitive understanding of the stack and queue data abstractions. An excellent example of a stack is a pile of papers on a desk (not segued); an even better example is a stack of dishes in a cupboard. The pivotal characteristic for both is that the item on the top is most easily accessed, with new items being added to the collection by placing them above all the current items in the stack. Items removed from a stack are those most recently added, or last-in-first-out (LIFO).

Stacks are used by compilers (internal coding) and programmers to solve an array of problems. For example, compilers use stacks to allocate space for parameters and local variables. Each function call made by a program translates into machine code that increments a memory stack to create space for the parameters and local variables associated with the function. This use of a stack to perform memory allocation has many advantages. It allows recursive procedures that possess, in each iteration, a unique data area for local variables. The release of memory simply means decrementing the stack and invoking destructors for any values that define destructors. This construct allows the maximum use of memory, since no more memory is required for the stack than what is absolutely necessary for the parameters and local variables in use at any one instance.

C++ uses a stack to implement the input stream mechanism. The stream data structure maintains two data areas. It must hold a pointer to the file from which the raw characters are obtained. It also maintains a stack of characters that have been pushed back into the input. This allows the method `putback()` to return a character to an input stream. A subsequent character read operation will first yield the pushed-back character, before continuing with the remainder of input from the file.

STL Defines Stacks, Queues, and Deques as Adaptors

STL implements both stacks and queues as adaptors. This means they do not directly implement the structures that hold the data values, but are instead built on top of other containers. In other words, they adapt the interface to these containers, providing names for the operations that make sense in the context of their use.

Any container that defines the internal type *T* and implements the operations empty(), size(), back(), push_back(), and pop_back() can be used as a container for a stack. Both the <vector> and <list> templates support these operations, as well as the STL <deque>.

Care is needed when selecting the container type. Remember, vectors grow dynamically, but seldom shrink. On the other hand, space for a list both grows and shrinks as elements are added and removed from the collection. But, for a given size collection, a vector will use less overall memory space than will a list. For this reason, a vector, queue, or deque is a good candidate container if the size of the collection being maintained by a stack will remain relatively stable in size. You should select a list container when the collection will vary widely in size during program execution.

To appreciate these differences, consider the underlying container in response to stack operations. The capacity of a vector is given by the largest number of elements it has been asked to hold up to a specific point in time, whereas the size of a vector represents the number of elements the vector currently holds. A push_back() will simply increase the size, unless the size reaches the capacity, in which case a memory reallocation is performed, creating a larger buffer. However, in a list container, only the elements currently in the collection are maintained. Each push() operation causes a new memory allocation, and each pop() returns the memory location to the pool of available memory.

<stack> Example Program

The following example uses the <stack> STL template to convert an Infix expression to Postfix. Infix expressions are the way most people think of numeric calculations, such as 4 * (16 + 2 * 8) + 22. However, considering all of the arithmetic operators available in mathematics, writing a compiler to correctly translate an infinite combination would require a very inefficient, time-consuming algorithm. Instead, compilers first take an Infix expression, translate it into Postfix, and then translate the Postfix equation into machine code (Postfix notation places the operators *after* the operands, for example, A B + instead of the Infix A + B). What looks like unnecessary overprocessing on the surface ends up saving execution time. While the program that follows may initially look quite complicated, in essence it is a fraction of the code that would be necessary for a compiler to decipher an arithmetic equation using Infix notation.

THE PUSHPOP.CPP APPLICATION

The following <stack> template application is based on a user-defined stack element type of *OPERATORS*. This enumerated type arranges the arithmetic operators from lowest precedence (ordinal value of 0) to highest (in this case, *divideop*, or 4):

```
// pushpop.cpp
// Testing <stack>
// push(), pop() top(), empty()
// Chris H. Pappas and William H. Murray, 1999

#pragma warning(disable:4786)
#include <stack>
#include <list>
#include <string>
#include <iostream>
#include <cctype>    // isdigit()

using namespace std ;

typedef enum tagOPERATORS{ leftparenthesis, plusop,
                            minusop, multiplyop,
                            divideop } OPERATORS;

typedef stack<OPERATORS> CONVERSIONSTACK;


string ConvertOpToString(OPERATORS CurrentOperator);
void processOperator(OPERATORS currentOperator,
                     stack<OPERATORS>& ConversionStack,
                     string& result);

void main( void )
{
  CONVERSIONSTACK ConversionStack;

  string infix("4 * (16 + 2 * 8) + 22");
  string result("");
  int offset = 0;

  while(infix[offset] != '\0') {
    if(isdigit(infix[offset])) { // process values
      while(isdigit(infix[offset]))
        result += infix[offset++];
      result += " ";
  }
   else
     switch(infix[offset++]) { // process non-values
       case '(': ConversionStack.push(leftparenthesis);
                 break;
        case ')': while(ConversionStack.top() != leftparenthesis)
                  {
                        result += ConvertOpToString(ConversionStack.top());
                         ConversionStack.pop();
                  }

                       ConversionStack.pop();
                        break;
```

```
          case '+': processOperator(plusop, ConversionStack, result);
                    break;
        case '-': processOperator(minusop, ConversionStack, result);
                    break;
      case '*': processOperator(multiplyop, ConversionStack, result);
                    break;
      case '/': processOperator(divideop, ConversionStack, result);
                    break;
    }
  }

  while(!ConversionStack.empty()) { // empty the stack
    result += ConvertOpToString(ConversionStack.top());
    ConversionStack.pop();
  }
  cout << result;
}

string ConvertOpToString(OPERATORS CurrentOperator)
{
  switch(CurrentOperator) {
    case plusop     : return " + ";
    case minusop    : return " - ";
    case multiplyop : return " * ";
    case divideop   : return " / ";
  }
}

void processOperator(OPERATORS currentOperator, stack<OPERATORS>&
ConversionStack,
                string& result)
{
  while( (!ConversionStack.empty()) && (currentOperator <
ConversionStack.top()) ) {
    result += ConvertOpToString(ConversionStack.top());
    ConversionStack.pop();
  }
  ConversionStack.push(currentOperator);
}
```

The program begins by defining the stack element type OPERATORS:

```
typedef enum tagOPERATORS { leftparenthesis, plusop,
                            minusop, multiplyop,
                            divideop } OPERATORS;
```

Next, using Microsoft styling conventions, a typedef creates the *CON-VERSIONSTACK* type. Notice that the stack element type is *OPERATORS*.

```
typedef stack<OPERATORS> CONVERSIONSTACK;
```

The instantiation of *ConversionStack* takes the form (seen inside main()):

```
CONVERSIONSTACK ConversionStack;
```

For the sake of clarity, a sample Infix expression is wired into the program avoiding superfluous I/O statements to interactively accept and verify any Infix expression:

```
string infix("4 * (16 + 2 * 8) + 22");
```

The algorithm parses the *infix* string, immediately appending numeric constants to the *result* string:

```
while(infix[offset] != '\0') {
    if(isdigit(infix[offset])) { // process values
      while(isdigit(infix[offset]))
        result += infix[offset++];
      result += " ";
    }
```

Operators such as + and * cannot be output until both their arguments have been processed. Therefore, they must be saved on the *Conversion-Stack*. If an operator being pushed onto the stack has a lower precedence level than the current top of stack, then the top of stack is popped and appended to *result*:

```
while( (!ConversionStack.empty()) && (currentOperator <
ConversionStack.top()) ) {
    result += ConvertOpToString(ConversionStack.top());
    ConversionStack.pop();
  }
  ConversionStack.push(currentOperator);
```

A left parenthesis is immediately pushed on the *ConversionStack*, regardless of the precedence of the current top of stack:

```
case '(': ConversionStack.push(leftparenthesis);
```

The left parenthesis will be considered to have a precedence lower than any other symbol, and thus will never be popped off the stack. Instead, the right parenthesis will cause the stack to be popped and output until the corresponding left parenthesis is found. Notice the use of the template function top(), used to access the current stack top *OPERATORS*.

```
case ')': while(ConversionStack.top() != leftparenthesis)
          {
            result += ConvertOpToString(ConversionStack.top());
            ConversionStack.pop();
```

```
}
ConversionStack.pop();
```

The left parenthesis is popped, but not appended to *result*. Finally, when the end of the *infix* expression is reached, the *ConversionStack* is popped until empty, appending symbols to the *result* string. The code segment uses the template function empty() to know when all *OPERATORS* have been processed:

```
while(!ConversionStack.empty()) { // empty the stack
     result += ConvertOpToString(ConversionStack.top());
     ConversionStack.pop();
  }
```

It is necessary to convert the enumerated representation of operators to strings that can be appended to *result,* and explains the presence of *ConvertOpToString()*:

```
string ConvertOpToString(OPERATORS CurrentOperator)
{
   switch(CurrentOperator) {
     case plusop      : return " + ";
     case minusop     : return " - ";
     case multiplyop  : return " * ";
     case divideop    : return " / ";
   }
}
```

The output from the program looks like:

```
4  16  2  8    *    +    *  22    +
```

STL Queues and Double-ended Queues

The <queue> template, like the <stack> template, is implemented as an adaptor that wraps around an underlying container. As with the <stack> template, the <queue> adaptor does not actually provide any new functionality, but simply modifies the interface. Operations are provided with their conventional queue-like names, but are actually performed using operations on the underlying containers.

Containers in the standard library that implement the necessary operations for the <queue> adaptor include the <list> data structure, and the <deque> data structure that we will introduce later in the chapter. Unlike the <stack> template, the <queue> class in STL provides the ability to access both the front and back elements of the queue, while the conventional description of the queue data abstraction only permits access to the front.

The `<deque>` Template

The `<deque>` template provides one of the most interesting data structures in the STL. Of all of the STL code provided, the `<deque>` is the least conventional. The `<deque>` template represents a data type that is seldom considered to be one of the classic data abstractions, such as vectors, lists, sets, or trees.

Upon close examination, you will discover that the operations provided by `<deque>` are a combination of those provided by the classes `<vector>` and `<list>`. For example, like a vector, the deque is randomly accessible. This means that instances of the class deque can be used in many of the same situations as a vector. Similarly, like a list, elements may be inserted into the middle of a deque, although such insertions are not as efficient as in the list equivalent.

Officially, deque stands for double-ended queue, and the name defines the structure as well. The deque is a combination of a stack and queue, allowing elements to be inserted at either end. Whereas a vector only allows efficient insertion at one end, the deque can perform insertions in constant time at either the front or the back of the container. Like a vector, a deque is a very space-efficient structure, using far less memory for a given size collection than will a list, for example. However, note as with a vector, insertions into the middle of the structure are permitted, but are not time-efficient. An insertion into a deque may require the movement of every element in the collection!

Typically a deque is used as an underlying container for either a stack or a queue. The deque is the preferred container whenever the size of the collection remains relatively stable during the course of execution, although if the size varies widely, a list or vector is a better container choice. Ultimately, for time-critical applications, you will have to write the algorithm using the different forms and performing direct measurement of program size and run-time efficiency.

`<queue>` and `<deque>` Example Programs

The following sample applications illustrate various `<queue>` and `<deque>` methods, and emphasize areas of caution when using these templates.

THE FIFO.CPP APPLICATION

The following application illustrates the `<queue>` template's most frequently used methods, highlighting the actions of a logical queue's first-in-first-out (FIFO) algorithm. The `<queue>` is implemented as a `<list>` container. The `fifo.cpp` application instantiates both an integer and character queue for comparison purposes.

```cpp
// fifo.cpp
// Testing <queue>
// push(), pop(), empty() ,back(), front(), size()
// Chris H. Pappas and William H. Murray, 1999


#include <list> // access to front() template function
#include <queue>
#include <iostream>

using namespace std ;

// queue implemented as <list> container
typedef list<int> INT_LIST_TYPE;
typedef queue<int>  INT_QUEUE_TYPE;
typedef queue<char*> CHAR_QUEUE_TYPE;

#define SPACER cout << "\n\n"

void main( void )
{
  int queueSize;

  INT_QUEUE_TYPE intQ;
  CHAR_QUEUE_TYPE charQ;

  // Pushing elements onto the queue
  intQ.push(1);
  intQ.push(2);
  intQ.push(3);
  intQ.push(4);
  intQ.push(5);
  intQ.push(6);


  // Verify queue size
  queueSize = intQ.size();
  cout << "The intQ contains " << queueSize << " elements\n\n";

  // Print queue elements in order
  // Elements accessed using front()
  // Elements removed using pop()
  while( !intQ.empty() )
  {
    cout << intQ.front() << endl;
    intQ.pop();

  }

  // Insert items in the queue(uses deque)
```

```
charQ.push("First   in Q");
charQ.push("Second in Q");
charQ.push("Third  in Q");
charQ.push("Fourth in Q");
charQ.push("Fifth  in Q");

SPACER;

// Output the item inserted last using back()
cout << "The last item inserted into charQ: "
     << "\"" << charQ.back() << "\"" << endl;

// Output the size of queue
queueSize = charQ.size();
cout << "\nThe size of charQ is:" << queueSize << endl;

SPACER;

// Output items in queue using front()
// and use pop() to get to next item until
// queue is empty
while (!charQ.empty())
{
   cout << charQ.front() << endl;
   charQ.pop();

}
}
```

Both *intQ* and *charQ* use the push() template function to add items to the back of their respective queues. Notice that the size() template function reports the actual number of elements contained within each queue.

The empty() template function provides an easy, reliable way to traverse queue list elements and drives the **while** loop test conditions:

```
while( !intQ.empty() )
  {
     cout << intQ.front() << endl;
     intQ.pop();

  }
```

The <list> template class provides the underlying front() template function required by the <queue> adaptor class, providing access to the container's front element. Note, however, that accessing the front element does not remove the element and explains the call to pop(), which officially deletes the front element after output.

The output from the program looks like:

```
The intQ contains 6 elements

1
2
3
4
5
6


The last item inserted into charQ: "Fifth  in Q"

The size of charQ is:5


First  in Q
Second in Q
Third  in Q
Fourth in Q
Fifth  in Q
```

THE DOUBLEQ.CPP APPLICATION

For a slight change of pace, the doubleq.cpp application illustrates several of the overloaded deque operators, such as equality, less-than, and greater-than. The application also uses the assign() template function to copy the contents of *intDQ2* to *intDQ1*.

```cpp
// doubleq.cpp
// Testing <intDQ>
// Overloaded operators ==, >, <,
// push_front(), begin(), end(), and assign()
// Chris H. Pappas and William H. Murray, 1999

#include <deque>
#include <iostream>

using namespace std;

typedef deque<int>  INT_DEQUE_TYPE;
void printDeque (INT_DEQUE_TYPE  intDQ, char*);

void main( void )
{
  // intDQ1 initialized with 4 1s
  INT_DEQUE_TYPE  intDQ1(4,1);

  // a 2 pushed to the front of intDQ1
  intDQ1.push_front(2);
```

```
// intDQ2's initialized with 3 0s
INT_DEQUE_TYPE   intDQ2(3,0);

// print current container elements
  printDeque (intDQ1,"intDQ1");
  printDeque (intDQ2,"intDQ2");

// check equality of intDQ1 and intDQ2
if( intDQ1 == intDQ2 )
  cout <<"intDQ1 is equal to intDQ2"<<endl;
else if( intDQ1 > intDQ2 )
    cout <<"intDQ1 is greater than intDQ2"<<endl;
  else
    cout <<"intDQ1 is less than intDQ2" <<endl;

//assign the contents of intDQ2 to intDQ1
intDQ1.assign(intDQ2.begin(),intDQ2.end());
printDeque (intDQ1,"intDQ1");
printDeque (intDQ2,"intDQ2");

//compare intDQ1 and intDQ2 again
if( intDQ1 == intDQ2 )
  cout <<"intDQ1 is equal to intDQ2"<<endl;
else if( intDQ1 < intDQ2 )
    cout <<"intDQ1 is less than intDQ2"<<endl;
  else
    cout <<"intDQ1 is greater than intDQ2" <<endl;

}

void printDeque (INT_DEQUE_TYPE  intDQ, char *name)
{
  INT_DEQUE_TYPE::iterator pintDQ;

  cout << name <<" contains these elements: ";
  for(pintDQ = intDQ.begin(); pintDQ != intDQ.end();
      pintDQ++) {
    cout << *pintDQ <<" " ;
  }
  cout<<endl;
}
```

The first overloaded operator (==) compares two objects of template class <deque>. The function returns the following: intDQ1.size() == intDQ2.size(). For equality, the number of elements must be equal in both deque objects.

The second overloaded operator (>) compares two objects of template class <deque>. The function returns the following: lexicographical_compare `(intDQ1.begin(), intDQ1.end(), intDQ2.begin(), intDQ2.end())`. Because a lexicographic (as in a dictionary) compare is used, the number of elements does not matter while using the overloaded operator >. For this reason, `intDQ1` is greater than `intDQ2`, *not* because it has more elements, but because *2* is greater than *0*.

The output from the program looks like:

```
intDQ1 contains these elements: 2 1 1 1 1
intDQ2 contains these elements: 0 0 0
intDQ1 is greater than intDQ2
intDQ1 contains these elements: 0 0 0
intDQ2 contains these elements: 0 0 0
intDQ1 is equal to intDQ2
```

Summary

In this chapter, you learned all of the necessary fundamentals for using a `<vector>` container. You learned about: various dimension descriptors and template functions, how to traverse a vector container with iterators, the do's and don'ts of finding the beginning and ending address for a container via the template functions `begin()` and `end()`, how to insert and erase elements, and finally, that the `end()` template function does *not* return an iterator to the last element, but one beyond. The `<vector>` is a simple container because all the action takes place at only one end, the top.

Next, the chapter introduced you to the logical operation of a stack: last-in-first-out, or LIFO. You also discovered that the `<stack>` template does not directly implement its own data structures, but instead is considered one example of an adaptor class. Adaptors modify existing container functionality. The sample program demonstrated the most frequently used `<stack>` template functions, `empty()`, `push()`, `pop()`, and `top()`, to convert an arithmetic expression from Infix to Postfix form, most familiar to Hewlett Packard calculator users. In the next chapter, you will see how the `<queue>` and `<deque>` STL templates perform similar logical data manipulations as stacks, only at both ends of a container.

Finally, the chapter explored both the `<queue>` and `<deque>` templates; both structures maintain collections of values in a linear sequence. In a queue, values are inserted at one end and removed from the other, unlike the `<stack>`, which inserts and removes elements from one end. You learned that while queues can be built on top of list structures, the advantage of a vector or deque implementation is improved performance, while the advantage of a list implementation is greater flexibility because the number of elements need not be known in advance.

The deque, or double-ended queue, is a data structure that provides a combination of features from both the vector and list types. Like a vector, a deque is a randomly accessible and indexed data structure. Like a list, elements can be efficiently inserted at either the front or the end of the structure. This actually provides a deque that exhibits the actions of either a stack-like or a queue-like behavior.

Additional Containers

A `<list>` container is your best choice when the number of elements in a collection cannot be bounded, or varies widely during the course of execution. Like a vector, a list maintains values of uniform type. Unlike a vector, a list can hold any number of values. Lists are not indexed. Instead, elements must be examined one by one in sequence. For this reason, the amount of time required to access an element in a list depends upon the position the element holds in the list.

Using an iterator to denote a given location, insertion into or deletion from a list can be performed in constant time. As with a vector, to determine whether or not a specific value occurs in a list requires a sequential search. While a list can be ordered, it is not possible to perform a binary search on a list, and therefore the sequential search time is generally the best that can be achieved.

List reallocation occurs when a method must insert or erase elements within a container. In all such cases, only iterators or references that point at erased portions of the list become invalid.

Typedefs Used by the <list> Template

There are ten list-specific `typedefs` associated with the `<list>` template. They are reproduced here to help you understand their syntax and use.

allocator_type

The *allocator_type* is a synonym for the template parameter A and has the following syntax:

```
typedef A allocator_type;
```

size_type

The *size_type* is defined as an unsigned integer that can represent the length of any list type. The syntax looks like:

```
typedef A::size_type size_type;
```

difference_type

The *difference_type* is defined as a signed integer that can represent the difference between the addresses of any two elements in a list. The syntax looks like:

```
typedef A::difference_type difference_type;
```

reference

The *reference* type describes an object that can serve as a reference to an element of a list. The syntax looks like:

```
typedef A::reference reference;
```

const_reference

The *const_reference* describes an object that can serve as a constant reference to an element of a list. The syntax looks like:

```
typedef A::const_reference const_reference;
```

value_type

The *value_type* is a synonym for the template parameter T. The syntax looks like:

```
typedef A::value_type value_type;
```

(2) iterator

The *iterator* type describes an object that can serve as a bidirectional iterator for a list. It is described here as a synonym for the unspecified type T0. The syntax looks like:

```
typedef T0 iterator;
```

const_iterator

The *const_iterator* describes an object that can serve as a constant bidirectional iterator for a list. It is described here as a synonym for the unspecified type T1. The syntax looks like:

```
typedef T1 const_iterator;
```

reverse_iterator

The *reverse_iterator* defines an object that can serve as a reverse bidirectional iterator for a list. The syntax looks like:

```
typedef reverse_bidirectional_iterator<iterator,
    value_type, reference, A::pointer,
        difference_type> reverse_iterator;
```

const_reverse_iterator

The *const_reverse_iterator* describes an object that can serve as a constant reverse bidirectional iterator for a list. The syntax looks like:

```
typedef reverse_bidirectional_iterator<const_iterator,
    value_type, const_reference, A::const_pointer,
        difference_type> const_reverse_iterator;
```

<list> Example Programs

The following three example programs, initlist.cpp, pushlist.cpp, and revrlist.cpp, demonstrate the more frequently used components of list containers. The example programs demonstrate how to instantiate, initialize, insert, copy, delete, and traverse list containers.

The initlist.cpp Application

The first example demonstrates the use of four **char**-type lists. *ListA* and *ListB* are initialized when they are instantiated, while *ListC* and *ListD* are initialized at run-time with the insert() method:

```
// initlist.cpp
// Testing <list>
// insert(), begin(), end()
// Chris H. Pappas and William H. Murray, 1999

#include <list>
#include <iostream>

using namespace std ;

typedef list<char> CHAR_LIST_TYPE;

void main( void )
{
  char ListA[] = {'a','b','c'};
  char ListB[] = {'x','y','z','w'};
```

```
CHAR_LIST_TYPE ListC;
CHAR_LIST_TYPE ListD;
CHAR_LIST_TYPE::iterator ListIterator;

// After inserts ListC contains: m f q
ListC.insert (ListC.begin(), 'f');
ListC.insert (ListC.begin(), 'm');
ListC.insert (ListC.end(), 'q');

// Print m f q
for (ListIterator = ListC.begin(); ListIterator != ListC.end();
     ++ListIterator)
  cout << *ListIterator << " ";
cout << endl;

// Insert 4 ks
ListC.insert (ListC.end(), 4, 'k');

// Print m f q k k k k
for (ListIterator = ListC.begin(); ListIterator != ListC.end();
     ++ListIterator)
  cout << *ListIterator << " ";
cout << endl;

// Add a b c to ListC
ListC.insert (ListC.end(), ListA, ListA + 3);
// Print m f q k k k a b c
for (ListIterator = ListC.begin(); ListIterator != ListC.end();
     ++ListIterator)
  cout << *ListIterator << " ";
cout << endl;

// ListD is appended with first two elements of ListB: x y
ListD.insert (ListD.begin(), ListB, ListB+2);

// ListC gets an entire copy of ListD from begin() to end()
ListC.insert (ListC.end(), ListD.begin(), ListD.end());

// Print ListC's copied contents of ListD
for (ListIterator = ListC.begin(); ListIterator != ListC.end();
     ++ListIterator)
    cout << *ListIterator << " ";
  cout << endl;
}
```

The straightforward output from the program looks like:

```
m f q
m f q k k k k
m f q k k k k a b c
m f q k k k k a b c x y
```

The next application adds to your understanding of list manipulation by adding the methods push_front(), push_back(), assign(), and erase().

The pushlist.cpp Application

The following program highlights the stack capabilities of a list with push_front(), and the queue logic of push_back() or adding an element at the end of a list. *ListB* sees a lot of action with initiailizations and multiple element reassignments with the use of the assign() method. Finally, *ListB* is deleted entirely with a call to the erase() method.

```cpp
// pushlist.cpp
// Testing <list>
// push_front(), push_back(), assign(), begin(0, end(), erase()
// Chris H. Pappas and William H. Murray, 1999

#include <list>
#include <iostream>

using namespace std ;

typedef list<int> INT_LIST_TYPE;

void main( void )
{
  INT_LIST_TYPE ListA;
  INT_LIST_TYPE ListB;
  INT_LIST_TYPE::iterator ListIterator;

  // Initialize ListA with 4 values: 11 12 40 44
  ListA.push_front(12);
  ListA.push_front(11);
  ListA.push_back(40);
  ListA.push_back(44);

  cout << "ListA contains: ";
  for (ListIterator = ListA.begin(); ListIterator != ListA.end();
       ++ListIterator)
    cout << *ListIterator << " ";
  cout << endl;

  // Initialize ListB with 5
  ListB.push_front(5);

  // Print ListB
  cout << "ListB contains: ";
  for (ListIterator = ListB.begin(); ListIterator != ListB.end();
       ++ListIterator)
```

```
      cout << *ListIterator << " ";
  cout << endl;

  // Reassing ListB to ListA's contents
  ListB.assign(ListA.begin(), ListA.end());

  // Reprint ListB
  cout << "ListB now looks like ListA: ";
  for (ListIterator = ListB.begin(); ListIterator != ListB.end();
      ++ListIterator)
    cout << *ListIterator << " ";
  cout << endl;

  ListB.assign(5,2);

  // Reassign ListB to 5 2s
  cout << "ListB reassigned 5 2s: ";
  for (ListIterator = ListB.begin(); ListIterator != ListB.end();
      ++ListIterator)
    cout << *ListIterator << " ";
  cout << endl;


  // Erase the first element in ListB
  ListB.erase(ListB.begin());

  // Reprint ListB minus first 2
  cout << "ListB minus the first element: ";
  for (ListIterator = ListB.begin(); ListIterator != ListB.end();
      ++ListIterator)
    cout << *ListIterator << " ";
  cout << endl;

  // Erase all of ListB and verify with if...empty()
  ListB.erase(ListB.begin(), ListB.end());
  if( ListB.empty() )
    cout << "ListB has been erased!";
}
```

Pay particular attention to the order in which *ListA* is initialized in the following four lines of source code:

```
ListA.push_front(12);
ListA.push_front(11);
ListA.push_back(40);
ListA.push_back(44);
```

The second call to push_front() inserts the *11* in front of the first value placed into the container, or *12*. The calls to push_back(), however, add list elements in the order you would expect. The output from the program looks like:

```
ListA contains: 11 12 40 44
ListB contains: 5
ListB now looks like ListA: 11 12 40 44
ListB reassigned 5 2s: 2 2 2 2 2
ListB minus the first element: 2 2 2 2
ListB has been erased!
```

The revrlist.cpp Application

This next application reverses *ListA*'s contents, displays the list's size() and max_size(), then sort()s the list and finally splices the middle of *ListB* after the first element in *ListA*.

```cpp
// revrlist.cpp
// Testing <list>
// size(), max_size(), sort(), reverse(), splice(), begin(), end()
// Chris H. Pappas and William H. Murray, 1999

#include <list>
#include <iostream>

using namespace std ;

typedef list<int> INT_LIST_TYPE;

void main( void )
{
  INT_LIST_TYPE ListA;
  INT_LIST_TYPE ListB;
  INT_LIST_TYPE::iterator ListIterator;

  //Print size() and max_size() of ListA;
  cout << "ListA's size: " << ListA.size() << endl;
  cout << "ListA's max_size " << ListA.max_size() << endl;

  // Initialize ListA with 4 values: 10 11 12 13
  ListA.push_front(11);
  ListA.push_front(10);
  ListA.push_back(12);
  ListA.push_back(13);

  //Print size() and max_size() of ListA;
  cout << "ListA's size: " << ListA.size() << endl;
  cout << "ListA's max_size " << ListA.max_size() << endl;

  cout << "ListA contains: ";
```

```cpp
for (ListIterator = ListA.begin(); ListIterator != ListA.end();
     ++ListIterator)
  cout << *ListIterator << " ";
cout << endl;

// Reverse ListA
ListA.reverse();

// Reversed ListA
cout << "ListA reversed: ";
for   (ListIterator = ListA.begin(); ListIterator != ListA.end();
       ++ListIterator)
  cout << *ListIterator << " ";
cout << endl;

// Sort ListA
ListA.sort();

// ListA after a call to the method sort()
cout << "ListA sorted  : ";
for (ListIterator = ListA.begin(); ListIterator != ListA.end();
     ++ListIterator)
  cout << *ListIterator << " ";
cout << endl;

// Initialize Listb
ListB.insert(ListB.end(),1);
ListB.insert(ListB.end(),2);
ListB.insert(ListB.end(),3);
ListB.insert(ListB.end(),4);
ListB.insert(ListB.end(),5);

// ListB after being initialized
cout << "ListB contains: ";
for (ListIterator = ListB.begin(); ListIterator != ListB.end();
     ++ListIterator)
  cout << *ListIterator << " ";
cout << endl;

// Splicing ListB's 2 3 4, after ListA's 10
ListA.splice(++ListA.begin(),ListB, ++ListB.begin(), --ListB.end());

// ListA after splicing with subrange of ListB
cout << "ListA reversed: ";
for (ListIterator = ListA.begin(); ListIterator != ListA.end();
     ++ListIterator)
  cout << *ListIterator << " ";
cout << endl;

// ListB after the splice()
  cout << "ListB contains: ";
```

```
    for (ListIterator = ListB.begin(); ListIterator != ListB.end();
        ++ListIterator)
      cout << *ListIterator << " ";
    cout << endl;
}
```

Of the methods used in `revrlist.cpp`. the one needing additional explanation is `splice()`.

```
// Splicing ListB's 2 3 4, after ListA's 10
ListA.splice(++ListA.begin(),ListB, ++ListB.begin(), --ListB.end());
```

The `splice()` method has four arguments: the insertion point for the receiving list, the source list's location, where within the source list to begin transferring information, and where to end. These parameters are, in order: *++ListA.begin(), ListB, ++ListB.begin(), --ListB.end()*. Notice the use of the prefix increment ++ and decrement -- operators to shift these default starting and ending points.

You will notice from the program's output, seen below, that `splice()` doesn't just copy the source's subrange, but transfers the elements:

```
ListA's size: 0
ListA's max_size 1073741823
ListA's size: 4
ListA's max_size 1073741823
ListA contains: 10 11 12 13
ListA reversed: 13 12 11 10
ListA sorted  : 10 11 12 13
ListB contains: 1 2 3 4 5
ListA reversed: 10 2 3 4 11 12 13
ListB contains: 1 5
```

The Map Container

Many languages support the concept of a map, sometimes referred to as a table, dictionary, associative array, or vector, meaning an indexed collection of data. However, unlike a vector with integer indices, maps may be keyed on different data types. You can think of a map as a collection of associations of key and value pairs. Certainly, a phone book meets this definition with the phone number being the key and the associated value being the owner's name.

Containers Revisited

Since most people learn by way of repetition, the following **Cont** template is reproduced to remind you of those characteristics common to all containers:

```
namespace std {
template<class T, class A>
    class Cont;
//    TEMPLATE FUNCTIONS
template<class T, class A>
    bool operator==(
        const Cont<T, A>& lhs,
        const Cont<T, A>& rhs);
template<class T, class A>
    bool operator!=(
        const Cont<T, A>& lhs,
        const Cont<T, A>& rhs);
template<class T, class A>
    bool operator<(
        const Cont<T, A>& lhs,
        const Cont<T, A>& rhs);
template<class T, class A>
    bool "operator>(
        const Cont<T, A>& lhs,
        const Cont<T, A>& rhs);
template<class T, class A>
    bool operator<=(
        const Cont<T, A>& lhs,
        const Cont<T, A>& rhs);
template<class T, class A>
    bool ="operator>=(
        const Cont<T, A>& lhs,
        const Cont<T, A>& rhs);
template<class T, class A>
    void swap(
        const Cont<T, A>& lhs,
        const Cont<T, A>& rhs);
};
```

Remember that a container is an STL template class that manages a sequence of elements. These elements can be of any object type that supplies a default constructor, a destructor, and an assignment operator. Also, particular container template classes can have additional template parameters and additional methods. The STL template container classes are: deque, list, map, multimap, multiset, set, and vector. Even the standard C++ library template class **string** meets the requirements for a template container class.

<map> Example Program

The declaration of a map follows the pattern we have seen repeatedly throughout the use of other STL elements. A map is a template data structure, specialized by the type of the key elements and the type of the associated values. There is an optional third template argument that defines the function to be used in comparing key values. Like dynamic <vector> containers, a map initially contains no elements. Some example definitions look like:

```
map<double, string> a_string_map;
map<int, float> a_float_map;
map<int, int> an_int_map;
```

The <map> STL also defines several container-specific typd definitions. These are most commonly used in declaration statements. For example, an iterator for a map of integers to floats can be defined as:

```
map<int, float>::iterator it;
```

In addition to the iterator, the following other types are defined: *key_type*—the type associated with the keys used to index the map, and *value_type*—the type of the pair used to store entries in the map. The constructor for this type is used to create new container entries.

You insert entries into a map using the insert() method. Notice that the actual arguments must be a key-value pair. This pair is easily generated using the constructor for the value_type specification, as in:

```
a_float_map.insert(a_float_map::value_type(1, 1.1));
```

Of course values can be removed from a map by providing the key_value. The following example erases element 3:

```
an_int_map.erase(3);
```

Also, elements being removed can be referenced by means of an iterator, as, for example, the iterator yielded by a find() operation. The following two statements first locate the value 3, then delete the container entry:

```
an_int_map::iterator it = an_int_map.find(3);
an_int_map.erase(it);
```

Entire subranges of container elements are removed by making a call to erase(). The next example erases all values between 3 and 5:

```
an_int_map::iterator start = an_int_map.find(3);
an_int_map::iterator end = an_int_map.find(5);
an_int_map.erase(start, end);
```

Remember from previous chapters that the methods `begin()` and `end()` represent bidirectional map iterators. Dereferencing a map iterator yields a map element pair of key and value. You can use the types *first_type* and *second_type* (seen below) to reference these values individually. The *first_type* is a constant that cannot be modified. The *second_type* field, however, can be used to change the value being held in association with a given key, and will modify the value being maintained in the container. Elements will be generated in the container based on the ordering of the key fields. The iterators generated by calls to `rbegin()` and `rend()` allow you to access container elements in reverse.

pair
```
template<class T, class U>
    struct pair {
    typedef T first_type;
    typedef U second_type
    T first;
    U second;
    pair();
    pair(const T& x, const U& y);
    template<class V, class W>
        pair(const pair<V, W>& pr);
    };
```

To traverse or count map elements, you use the `find()`, `empty()`, and `size()` methods. The method `size()` returns the number of elements held by the container, while `empty()` returns a Boolean true if the container is empty. This is faster than testing the value returned by `size()` with zero. The method `find()` takes a key_type argument and returns an iterator denoting the associated key and value pair.

Advanced container element searches are possible with the methods `lower_bound()` and `upper_bound()`. The `lower_bound()` method yields the first entry that matches the argument key, while the `upper_bound()` method returns the first value past the last entry matching the argument. The method `equal_range()` returns a pair of iterators holding both the lower and upper bounds. The `count()` method returns the number of elements that match the key value supplied as the argument.

The `paircntnr.cpp` Application

If you have been following all of the examples throughout the previous chapters, you should genuinely feel a sense of learned accomplishment as you scan the following program's STL syntax and logic. What you should begin discovering at this point, is just how many of the earlier chapter's contents are beginning to congeal. For example, what once was an ethereal concept, iterators, is now a concrete, commonplace STL regular. You deserve some well-earned congratulations at this point for hanging in there!

First, take a look at paircntnr.cpp and prove to yourself just how much you have learned as you knowledgeably interpret each statement:

```cpp
// paircntnr.cpp
// Testing <map>
// insert(), begin(), end(), size(), erase(),
// upper_bound(), lower_bound(), find(),
// rbegin(), rend(), empty(), count(), equal_range()
// Chris H. Pappas and William H. Murray, 1999

#pragma warning(disable:4786)
// "Microsoft has confirmed this to be a bug in the Microsoft
// products listed at the beginning of this article. We are
// researching this bug and will post new information here in
// the Microsoft Knowledge Base as it becomes available."

#include <map>
#include <string>
#include <iostream>

using namespace std;

typedef map<string, string, less<string> > STR2STR;
typedef pair<STR2STR::iterator,STR2STR::iterator> STR2STRPAIR;

void main( void )
{
  STR2STR phoneBook;
  STR2STR::iterator it, upperBound, lowerBound;


  // Inserting five pairs
  phoneBook.insert(STR2STR::value_type("111-111-1111",
                                       "Adam Smith"));
  phoneBook.insert(STR2STR::value_type("555-555-5555",
                                       "Tina Smith"));
  phoneBook.insert(STR2STR::value_type("222-222-2222",
                                       "Fred Smith"));
  phoneBook.insert(STR2STR::value_type("444-444-4444",
                                       "John Smith"));
  phoneBook.insert(STR2STR::value_type("333-333-3333",
                                       "Jane Smith"));

  // Print phoneBook
  cout << "phoneBook now contains:\n";
  for(it = phoneBook.begin(); it != phoneBook.end(); it++)
    cout << it->first << " " << it->second << endl;
```

```
// Print phoneBook's size
cout << "\n\nphoneBook size = " << phoneBook.size();

// Print phoneBook in reverse
cout << "\n\nphoneBook in reverse order:\n";

STR2STR::reverse_iterator rit;
for(rit = phoneBook.rbegin(); rit != phoneBook.rend(); rit++)
  cout << rit->first << " " << rit->second << endl;

// Find key value "333-333-3333"
cout << "\n\nName for phone number 333-333-3333 = ";
it = phoneBook.find("333-333-3333");
cout << it->second << endl;

// Find subrange of key_values
cout << "\n\nPairs between 222-222-222 and 444-444-444:\n";
lowerBound = phoneBook.lower_bound("222-222-2222");
upperBound = phoneBook.upper_bound("444-444-4444");
for(it = lowerBound; it!= upperBound; it++)
  cout << it->first << it->second << endl;

// Declare iterator pair
STR2STRPAIR itPair;
itPair = phoneBook.equal_range("444-444-4444");

// Print one equal_range() value
cout << "\n\nequal_range() = ";
for(it = itPair.first; it != itPair.second; it++)
  cout << it->first << endl;

// Find key value "333-333-3333" again
it = phoneBook.find("333-333-3333");
it->second = "New Name";
cout << "\n\n333-333-3333 with new paired name: ";
cout << it->second << endl;


// Counting key values matching "555-555-5555"
cout << "\n\nNumber of 555-555-5555s = "
     << phoneBook.count("555-555-5555");

// Erasing key value pair "111-111-1111"
cout << "\n\nphoneBook minus 111-111-1111:\n";
phoneBook.erase("111-111-1111");
for(it = phoneBook.begin(); it != phoneBook.end(); it++)
  cout << it->first << " " << it->second << endl;

// Erasing entire phoneBook
phoneBook.erase(phoneBook.begin(),phoneBook.end());
```

```
   if(phoneBook.empty())
      cout << "\n\nThe phoneBook is empty!";
}
```

The discussion of `paircntnr.cpp` begins with the Microsoft-specific need to include the **#pragma** pre-processor directive to avoid four screens' worth of warning messages. Microsoft is working on this "bug" and therefore the statement may not be needed in the Microsoft Visual C++ studio you are using.

```
#pragma warning(disable:4786)
```

The program code continues with an STL style of declaring appropriate types needed by `paircntnr.cpp`:

```
typedef map<string, string, less<string> > STR2STR;
typedef pair<STR2STR::iterator,STR2STR::iterator> STR2STRPAIR;
```

Remember that `<map>`, by definition, creates a container of paired elements. The identifier *STR2STR* represents a map container keyed on strings and containing string elements. This is ideal for our *phoneBook*, with the key being the phone number in string format, and the `value_type` being a string representing the name associated with the phone number.

Later on in the program, a call is made to `equal_range()`. This method returns a pair of iterators and therefore explains the need for the *STR2STRPAIR* typedef, which creates a pairing of two *STR2STR::iterators*.

These statements are logically followed by the instantiation of *phoneBook* and the creation of three iterators: *it*, *upperBound*, and *lowerBound*:

```
STR2STR phoneBook;
STR2STR::iterator it, upperBound, lowerBound;
```

The actual *phoneBook* entries are added using the *insert()* method:

```
// Inserting five pairs
   phoneBook.insert(STR2STR::value_type("111-111-1111",
                                        "Adam Smith"));
   phoneBook.insert(STR2STR::value_type("555-555-5555",
                                        "Tina Smith"));
   phoneBook.insert(STR2STR::value_type("222-222-2222",
                                        "Fred Smith"));
   phoneBook.insert(STR2STR::value_type("444-444-4444",
                                        "John Smith"));
   phoneBook.insert(STR2STR::value_type("333-333-3333",
                                        "Jane Smith"));
```

Using a now-familiar iterator-controlled **for** loop, `paircntnr.cpp` outputs the current container's contents:

```
// Print phoneBook
  cout << "phoneBook now contains:\n";
  for(it = phoneBook.begin(); it != phoneBook.end(); it++)
    cout << it->first << " " << it->second << endl;
```

While the calls to begin() and end(), and **why** *it* is not tested with <, and instead is appropriately tested using != are all old news by now (you do not know any relationship to container addresses, so testing against a pointer <, >, <=, or >= makes no sense), the **cout** statement needs some clarification.

Since map elements are **pairs,** you access their individual components using their respective data member names *first* and *second*. In previous chapters, accessing container elements with an iterator, i.e., *it,* only required the use of the dereference operator, as in:

```
*it
```

However, now *it* points to more complex data types. You could actually write the syntax out long-hand, as in:

```
*it.first
*it.second
```

But this syntax presents an operator precedence-level nightmare since the period member operator, ., binds or has a higher precedence than the dereference operator, *. A knowledgeable and syntactically legal fix uses a set of parentheses to raise the priority of the dereference operator, as in:

```
(*it).first
(*it).second
```

A kludgey, greasy, squeaky way to solve the problem is to use the C and C++ special operator designed to eliminate this syntax nightmare, namely the arrow, or pointer operator, ->. This operator *requires* a pointer type to its left and a **class** or **struct** member name to its right. The **for** loop's **cout** statement uses this syntactically cleaner style:

```
cout << it->first << " " << it->second << endl;
```

The program then proceeds to demonstrate a method for determining the container's current number of entries with a call to the size() method:

```
// Print phoneBook's size
  cout << "\n\nphoneBook size = " << phoneBook.size();
```

Next, paircntnr.cpp demonstrates the syntax and logic necessary to access a map container in reverse:

```
// Print phoneBook in reverse
  cout << "\n\nphoneBook in reverse order:\n";
```

```
STR2STR::reverse_iterator rit;
for(rit = phoneBook.rbegin(); rit != phoneBook.rend(); rit++)
  cout << rit->first << " " << rit->second << endl;
```

First, a **reverse_iterator** is declared and immediately initialized to the address of the *last* container element with a call to rbegin(). Once again, the **for** loop test condition for continued iteration is **not** *it* <, but *it !* =. And **contrary** what you might expect, the third statement in the **for** loop does **not** decrement *rit,* but instead increments the **reverse_iterator** *rit*! Just when you think you can outguess STL, it humbles. . .

With pairentnr.cpp attempting to illustrate all of the common demands a program could put on a map container, the source code moves on to demonstrating how you would syntactically search a map container for a specific key using find():

```
// Find key value "333-333-3333"
  cout << "\n\nName for phone number 333-333-3333 = ";
  it = phoneBook.find("333-333-3333");
  cout << it->second << endl;
```

The **cout** statement in this case does not print the key, but instead only the associated value.

Remembering that map containers are sorted by the specified key makes it very easy to scan for subranges. This next code segment does exactly that by searching for all pairs with keys >= "222-222-2222" and <= "444-444-4444", using calls to lower_bound() and upper_bound():

```
// Find subrange of key_values
  cout << "\n\nPairs between 222-222-222 and 444-444-444:\n";
  lowerBound = phoneBook.lower_bound("222-222-2222");
  upperBound = phoneBook.upper_bound("444-444-4444");
  for(it = lowerBound; it!= upperBound; it++)
    cout << it->first << it->second << endl;
```

While map containers by definition have unique key values, multimap containers may contain duplicate keys. The following code segment uses equal_range() to locate, in the case of map containers, a single matching pair, but could be used by multimap containers to locate key subranges. Notice the use of the typedef *STR2STRPAIR* to declare the variable *itPair,* which is *equal_range()*'s return type for this application:

```
// Declare iterator pair
  STR2STRPAIR itPair;
  itPair = phoneBook.equal_range("444-444-4444");

// Print one equal_range() value
  cout << "\n\nequal_range() = ";
  for(it = itPair.first; it != itPair.second; it++)
    cout << it->first << endl;
```

itPair's two iterators are referenced using the data member names **first** and **second,** and proceeded by the variable's name *itPair* and the period member operator.

Of course an applicataion using map containers could want to change a key's paired value, so this next code segment uses a call to the method find() to first locate the key, and then using the returned iterator's address, points to the value member *second* and updates the name associated with the key phone number:

```
// Find key value "333-333-3333" again
  it = phoneBook.find("333-333-3333");
  it->second = "New Name";
  cout << "\n\n333-333-3333 with new paired name: ";
  cout << it->second << endl;
```

The count() method is used with both map and multimap containers and returns the number of container pairs that have a key (map) or keys (multimap) that match the search key:

```
// Counting key values matching "555-555-5555"
  cout << "\n\nNumber of 555-555-5555s = "
       << phoneBook.count("555-555-5555");
```

The paircntnr.cpp application next moves on to the syntax necessary to locate and then entirely delete an element pair with a call to erase() using only one actual argument, the key to delete:

```
// Erasing key value pair "111-111-1111"
  cout << "\n\nphoneBook minus 111-111-1111:\n";
  phoneBook.erase("111-111-1111");
  for(it = phoneBook.begin(); it != phoneBook.end(); it++)
    cout << it->first << " " << it->second << endl;
```

And finally, the step that many programmers forget—the professional and clean removal of the container from memory. Here again, a call is made to erase() only this time, the overloaded method is passed the two actual iterator arguments returned by begin() and end():

```
// Erasing entire phoneBook
  phoneBook.erase(phoneBook.begin(),phoneBook.end());
  if(phoneBook.empty())
    cout << "\n\nThe phoneBook is empty!";
```

The output from the program looks like:

```
phoneBook now contains:
111-111-1111 Adam Smith
222-222-2222 Fred Smith
333-333-3333 Jane Smith
```

```
444-444-4444 John Smith
555-555-5555 Tina Smith


phoneBook size = 5

phoneBook in reverse order:
555-555-5555 Tina Smith
444-444-4444 John Smith
333-333-3333 Jane Smith
222-222-2222 Fred Smith
111-111-1111 Adam Smith


Name for phone number 333-333-3333 = Jane Smith


Pairs between 222-222-222 and 444-444-444:
222-222-2222Fred Smith
333-333-3333Jane Smith
444-444-4444John Smith


equal_range() = 444-444-4444


333-333-3333 with new paired name: New Name


Number of 555-555-5555s = 1

phoneBook minus 111-111-1111:
222-222-2222 Fred Smith
333-333-3333 New Name
444-444-4444 John Smith
555-555-5555 Tina Smith


The phoneBook is empty!
```

Summary

In this chapter, we examined the STL `<list>` template. A list is an unordered collection of values. Unlike a vector, a list has no fixed size, but instead grows or shrinks as elements are added to or removed from the structure. In the basic list structure, elements can be only added to or removed from the front or back of the list by means of iterators; elements can also be added to or removed from the middle of a list as was the case with `splice()`.

This chapter also showed how a map is like a vector except that it has a user-defined key field and an associated data value(s), or pair . Unlike a vector, the index key can be any ordered type, and the paired data member can be *any* data type. You also learned that like vectors, methods such as `find()`, `begin()`, `end()`, and `size()` are used to give iterators legal starting, current, or ending pointer values to access container elements instead of the usual `array[subscript]` notation. And while array[subscript] notation is a legal syntax for map containers, it is a more antique, error-prone syntax, superseded by the more robust STL method approach. In the next chapter, you will learn all about the `<numeric>` template library and its template functions, which are useful for computing numeric values.

The STL <numeric> Template

The <numeric> STL encompasses four template functions: accumulate(), inner_product(), partial_sum(), and adjacent_difference(). While these four functions are part of the original STL release by HP, the ANSI C++/ISO Committee standardized the template functions in the <numeric> section of the C++ standard. In the interest of completeness, this chapter will go ahead and document these four template functions. The STL wasn't trying to be an all-inclusive library for every numeric operation. But, the STL numeric functions do give you a glimpse of the kind of interface you could conceivably design for a template-based library of your own.

Of special import is the last sample program described in this chapter. This will be your first example of an STL being incorporated into a complete Windows application. If you are already familiar with Windows programming, after having looked at the first four procedural <numeric> sample programs, you will notice that incorporating STL technology is a straightforward process!

<numeric> Example Programs

The following sample applications illustrate the four <numeric> template functions. This section also includes a super example that combines the <numeric> STL with a complete Windows application generating a Fourier series!

The addup.cpp Application

This first sample program uses the <numeric> accumulate() template function. accumulate() repeatedly applies the template function to each member of a container, storing the result in a temporary location. The initial value of the result is determined by an input parameter to the template function itself. The template function is either the operator+() or a binary template function specified by the programmer.

First, a look at the complete program:

```
// addup.cpp
// Testing <numeric>
// accumulate(), char_traits< >, multiplies< >,
// copy(), begin(), end()
// Chris H. Pappas and William H. Murray, 1999

// "Symbols too long" warning disable #pragma
#pragma warning (disable : 4786)

#include <string>
#include <vector>
#include <numeric>
#include <iostream>
#include <iterator>
#include <functional>

using namespace std;

#define MAX_VALUES 5

typedef vector < float > FLOATVECTOR;
typedef vector < string > STRINGVECTOR;
typedef ostream_iterator <float, char,
                    char_traits <char> > OstreamFLOATit;

void main( void )
{
  // Naming convention for FVdfvVectorInstance
  // Instantiate FLOATVECTOR— FV, dynamic float vector—dfv
  FLOATVECTOR FVdfvVectorInstance;

  // Ostream iterator that outputs value followed by a space and comma
  OstreamFLOATit OstreamIt(cout," ,");

  // Vector created with 1.0, 0.5, 0.33333, 0.25, 0.2
  for (int i=0; i < MAX_VALUES; i++)
    FVdfvVectorInstance.push_back(1.0f/(i+1));

  // Display FVdfvVectorInstance
  copy(FVdfvVectorInstance.begin(),FVdfvVectorInstance.end(),OstreamIt);
  cout << "\n\n";

  // Sum FVdfvVectorInstance
  cout << "Accumulate generates the sum of     "
       << "1.0, 0.5, 0.33, 0.25, 0.2:\n"
```

```
           << accumulate(FVdfvVectorInstance.begin(),
                         FVdfvVectorInstance.end(),0.0f)
           << "\n\n";

     // Multiply FVdfvVectorInstance elements
     cout << "Accumulate generates the product of "
          << "1.0, 0.5, 0.33, 0.25, 0.2:\n"
          << accumulate(FVdfvVectorInstance.begin(),
                        FVdfvVectorInstance.end(),1.0f,
                                    multiplies<float>())
          << "\n\n";

     // Naming convention for SV
     // Instantiate STRINGVECTOR—   SV, dynamic string vector—dsv.
     // with individual words
     STRINGVECTOR SVdsvVectorInstance;
     SVdsvVectorInstance.push_back("Build a"          );
     SVdsvVectorInstance.push_back("sentence "        );
     SVdsvVectorInstance.push_back("from string "     );
     SVdsvVectorInstance.push_back("vector elements!");

     // Using Accumulate() to concatenate SVdsvVectorInstance elements
     cout << "Accumulate used on string elements:\n"
          << accumulate(SVdsvVectorInstance.begin(),
                     SVdsvVectorInstance.end(),string(""))
          << endl;
}
```

When using `accumulate()`, the first formal argument is a copy of the current intermediate value of the result. The second formal argument is the next value from the container. The two are processed by the template function , and the result is stored in the intermediate result.

The sample programs use an **ostream_iterator** of **char_traits:**

```
typedef ostream_iterator <float, char,
                    char_traits <char> > OstreamFLOATit;
```

The following **struct char_traits** definition is included here for reference:

```
struct char_traits<E> {
    typedef E char_type;
    typedef T1 int_type;
    typedef T2 pos_type;
    typedef T3 off_type;
    typedef T4 state_type;
    static void assign(E& x, const E& y);
    static E *assign(E *x, size_t n, const E& y);
    static bool eq(const E& x, const E& y);
    static bool lt(const E& x, const E& y);
    static int compare(const E *x, const E *y, size_t n);
```

```
static size_t length(const E *x);
static E *copy(E *x, const E *y, size_t n);
static E *move(E *x, const E *y, size_t n);
static const E *find(const E *x, size_t n, const E& y);
static E to_char_type(const int_type& ch);
static int_type to_int_type(const E& c);
static bool eq_int_type(const int_type& ch1, const int_type& ch2);
static int_type eof();
static int_type not_eof(const int_type& ch);
};
```

The addup.cpp application also uses accumulate() in the form requiring a binary template function, so once again, the syntax for declaring a **binary_function** is included here for easy reference:

```
template<class T>
    struct multiplies : public binary_function<T, T, T> {
    T operator()(const T& x, const T& y) const;
    };
```

The **binary_function()** template defines its method as returning x * y.

By now, the **<vector>** typedefs, declarations, initializations, and element display coding should be "old-hat." So the discussion begins by examining the use of accumulate():

```
// Sum FVdfvVectorInstance
  cout << "Accumulate generates the sum of     "
       << "1.0, 0.5, 0.33, 0.25, 0.2:\n"
       << accumulate(FVdfvVectorInstance.begin(),
                 FVdfvVectorInstance.end(),0.0f)
       << "\n\n";
```

The first actual argument to accumulate() is the STL syntax required to reference the pointer, or address, to the first vector element, *FVdfvVectorInstance.begin()*. The second actual argument uses the same logical approach provided by the *.end()* method syntax. The final, or third actual argument, *0.0*, represents the initial value required by the accumulate algorithm. For example, if you were using accumulate to add up a vector of integers, you would need to provide an **int** value of 0. As the accumulate() method call resides within a **cout <<** statement, the method's return value is directly output.

The second call to accumulate():

```
// Multiply FVdfvVectorInstance elements
  cout << "Accumulate generates the product of "
       << "1.0, 0.5, 0.33, 0.25, 0.2:\n"
       << accumulate(FVdfvVectorInstance.begin(),
                 FVdfvVectorInstance.end(),1.0f,
                       multiplies<float>())
       << "\n\n";
```

uses the overloaded version of accumulate() requiring a **binary_function()**, in this case, multiplies< >(). Remember that the **binary_function()** must be an object that obeys function semantics. It should take two formal arguments: one of type T and one of the type pointed to by the input iterators. The template function should also return an object of type T, which is updated to supply the new cumulative value. The preceding **cout <<** statement uses the multiplies< >() template function to generate the product of *FVdfvVectorInstance*.

The third significant code section in addup.cpp revisits the accumulate() template function, only this time using a **binary_function()** returning a concatenation of vector string elements:

```
// Using Accumulate() to concatenate SVdsvVectorInstance elements
  cout << "Accumulate used on string elements:\n"
       << accumulate(SVdsvVectorInstance.begin(),
                SVdsvVectorInstance.end(),string(""))
       << endl;
```

The program output looks like:

```
1, 0.5, 0.333333, 0.25, 0.2
Accumulate generates the sum of     1.0, 0.5, 0.33, 0.25, 0.2:
2.8333

Accumulate generates the product of 1.0, 0.5, 0.33, 0.25, 0.2:
0.00833333

Accumulate used on string elements:
Build a sentence from string vector elements:

1, 0.5, 0.333333, 0.25, 0.2
```

The multiply.cpp Application

The multiply.cpp application uses the <numeric> inner_product() template function along with familiar <vector> syntax:

```
// multiply.cpp
// Testing <numeric>
// product(), begin(), end(), copy(),
// inner_product(), char_traits< >, multiplies< >
// Chris H. Pappas and William H. Murray, 1999

#include <vector>
#include <numeric>
#include <iostream>
#include <iterator>
#include <functional>
```

```
#define MAX_VALUES 4

using namespace std;

typedef vector < float > FLOATVECTOR;
typedef ostream_iterator < float, char,
                           char_traits<char> > OstreamFLOATit;

void main( void )
{
  OstreamFLOATit itOstream(cout," ");

  // Instantiate and initialize
  //            FVdfvVectorInstance1 to iValue
  // Instantiate and initialize
  //            FVdfvVectorInstance2 to iValue squared
  FLOATVECTOR FVdfvVectorInstance1, FVdfvVectorInstance2;
  for(int iValue=1; iValue <= MAX_VALUES; iValue++) {
    FVdfvVectorInstance1.push_back(iValue);
    FVdfvVectorInstance2.push_back(iValue*iValue);
  };

  // Display both FVdfvVectorInstance1 and FVdfvVectorInstance2
  cout << "FVdfvVectorInstance1 : ";
  copy(FVdfvVectorInstance1.begin(),
       FVdfvVectorInstance1.end(),itOstream);
  cout << endl;
  cout << "FVdfvVectorInstance2 : ";
  copy(FVdfvVectorInstance2.begin(),
       FVdfvVectorInstance2.end(),itOstream);
  cout << endl;

  // Use inner_product() to calculate the Sum of Products
  float fTheSumOfProducts = inner_product(FVdfvVectorInstance1.begin(),
                                          FVdfvVectorInstance1.end(),

FVdfvVectorInstance2.begin(),0);
  cout << "\n\ninner_product() -> Sum of Products: "
       << fTheSumOfProducts
       << endl;

  // Use inner_product() to calculate the Product of Sums
  float fTheProductOfSums = inner_product(FVdfvVectorInstance1.begin(),
                                          FVdfvVectorInstance1.end(),

FVdfvVectorInstance2.begin(),1,

multiplies<float>(),plus<float>());
  cout << "\n\ninner_product() -> Product of Sums: "
```

```
        << fTheProductOfSums
        << endl;
}
```

The interesting portion of this application begins with the first call to `inner_product()`:

```
// Use inner_product() to calculate the Sum of Products
  float fTheSumOfProducts = inner_product(FVdfvVectorInstance1.begin(),
                                 FVdfvVectorInstance1.end(),
                          FVdfvVectorInstance2.begin(),0);
  cout << "\n\ninner_product() -> Sum of Products: "
       << fTheSumOfProducts
       << endl;
```

The variable *fTheSumOfProducts* is assigned the return value generated by the call to `inner_product()`, which accumulates the result of the operation on two input sequences, *FVdfvVectorInstance1* and *FVdfvVectorInstance2*. Notice that unlike the required ending point for the first vector, *FVdfvVectorInstance1.end()*, there is no related endpoint for the second vector. This is because both vectors *must* be of the same size.

The second call to `inner_product()` generates *fTheProductOfSums* by supplying the two binary operation actual arguments, *multiplies< >()* and *plus< >()*:

```
// Use inner_product() to calculate the Product of Sums
  float fTheProductOfSums = inner_product(FVdfvVectorInstance1.begin(),
                                 FVdfvVectorInstance1.end(),
                                   FVdfvVectorInstance2.begin(),1,
                                  multiplies<float>(),plus<float>());
  cout << "\n\ninner_product() -> Product of Sums: "
       << fTheProductOfSums
       << endl;
```

This overloaded version of `inner_product()` applies the second specified binary operation, *plus< >()*, to the two elements from the input containers. It then uses the first specified binary operation, *multiplies< >()*, with the result to update the accumulated value.

The program output looks like:

```
FVdfvVectorInstance1 : 1 2 3 4
FVdfvVectorInstance2 : 1 4 9 16

inner_product() -> Sum of Products: 100

innter_product() -> Product of Sums: 2880
```

The `runtotl.cpp` Application

The third sample program, runtotl.cpp, uses the partial_sum() <numeric> template function:

```
// runtotl.cpp
// Testing <numeric>
// begin(), end(), char_traits< >,
// partial_sum(), copy(), multiplies < >
// Chris H. Pappas and William H. Murray, 1999

#include <iostream>
#include <numeric>
#include <functional>
#include <vector>
#include <iterator>

#define MAX_VALUES 5

using namespace std;


typedef vector < float > FLOATVECTOR;
typedef ostream_iterator < float, char,
                           char_traits<char> > OstreamFLOATit;

void main( void )
{
  OstreamFLOATit itOstream(cout," ");

  // Instantiate and initialize FVdfvVectorInstance
  FLOATVECTOR FVdfvVectorInstance;
  for (int i=1; i <= MAX_VALUES; i++)
    FVdfvVectorInstance.push_back(i);

  // Display FVdfvVectorInstance
  cout << "FvdfvVectorInstance contains: ";
  copy(FVdfvVectorInstance.begin(),
       FVdfvVectorInstance.end(),itOstream);
  cout << endl;

  // Declare and initialize FVdfvVectorResultInstance
  FLOATVECTOR FVdfvVectorResultInstance(FVdfvVectorInstance.size());

  // Use partial_sum on FVdfvVectorInstance elements
  partial_sum(FVdfvVectorInstance.begin(),
              FVdfvVectorInstance.end(),
                  FVdfvVectorResultInstance.begin());

  // Display FVdfvVectorResultInstance partial_sum()s
```

```
cout << "\n\nFVdfvVectorResultInstance sum      : ";
copy(FVdfvVectorResultInstance.begin(),
      FVdfvVectorResultInstance.end(),itOstream);
cout << endl;

// Use partial_sum to calculate partial product
partial_sum(FVdfvVectorInstance.begin(),
            FVdfvVectorInstance.end(),
                FVdfvVectorResultInstance.begin(),multiplies<float>());

// Display FVdfvVectorResultInstance partial product
cout << "\n\nFVdfvVectorResultInstance product : ";
partial_sum(FVdfvVectorResultInstance.begin(),
            FVdfvVectorResultInstance.end(),itOstream);
cout << endl;
}
```

The interesting portion of the application begins with the call to `partial_sum()` seen below:

```
// Use partial_sum on FVdfvVectorInstance elements
  partial_sum(FVdfvVectorInstance.begin(),
            FVdfvVectorInstance.end(),
                FVdfvVectorResultInstance.begin());
```

> Here the template function creates a sequence of elements that represents a running total of the container's elements. The second use of `partial_sum()`:

```
// Use partial_sum to calculate partial product
  partial_sum(FVdfvVectorInstance.begin(),
            FVdfvVectorInstance.end(),

FVdfvVectorResultInstance.begin(),multiplies<float>());
```

> Notice the overloaded form where the fourth actual argument is a binary operation, in this case, `multiplies< >()`, which in turn generates the partial product.
>
> The program output looks like:

```
FvdfvVectorInstance contains: 1 2 3 4 5


FVdfvVectorResultInstance sum     : 1 3 6 10 15


FVdfvVectorResultInstance product : 1 3 9 33 153
```

The `adjdiff.cpp` Application

The adjdiff.cpp application uses the `adjacent_difference` <numeric> template function to return an output sequence containing the difference between adjacent container elements, in this case, telephone trunk lines:

```
// adjdiff.cpp
// Testing <numeric>
// adjacent_difference(), begin(), end()
// copy()
// Chris H. Pappas and William H. Murray, 1999

#include <vector>
#include <numeric>
#include <iterator>
#include <iostream>
#include <functional>

#define MAX_VALUES 5

using namespace std;


typedef vector < int > INTVECTOR;
typedef ostream_iterator < int, char,
                           char_traits<char> > OstreamINTit;

void main( void )
{
  OstreamINTit itOstream(cout," ");

  // Declare and initialize IVdivVectorInstance
  // containing trunk line lenghts in kilometers
  // with routing origin New York
  INTVECTOR IVdivVectorInstance;
  IVdivVectorInstance.push_back( 2786); // San Francisco to Berlin
  IVdivVectorInstance.push_back(11554); // to Cairo
  IVdivVectorInstance.push_back(13802); // to Calcutta
  IVdivVectorInstance.push_back(40021); // to Cape Town
  IVdivVectorInstance.push_back(75722); // to Hong Kong

  // Display IVdivVectorInstance trunk line entries
  cout << "IVdivVectorInstance contains    : ";
  copy(IVdivVectorInstance.begin(),
       IVdivVectorInstance.end(),itOstream);
  cout << endl;

  // Declare and initialize IVdivVectorDifferenceInstance
  // with the calculated distance between each trunk line
  INTVECTOR IVdivVectorDifferenceInstance(MAX_VALUES);
```

```
INTVECTOR::iterator Difference_it =
                 IVdivVectorDifferenceInstance.begin();
adjacent_difference(IVdivVectorInstance.begin(),
                 IVdivVectorInstance.end(),Difference_it);

// Display IVdivVectorDifferenceInstance differences
cout << "\n\nIVdivVectorInstance differences : ";
copy(IVdivVectorDifferenceInstance.begin()+1,
     IVdivVectorDifferenceInstance.end(),itOstream);
cout << endl;
           }
```

The first call to `adjacent_difference()` looks like:

```
// Declare and initialize IVdivVectorDifferenceInstance
// with the calculated distance between each trunk line
INTVECTOR IVdivVectorDifferenceInstance(MAX_VALUES);
INTVECTOR::iterator Difference_it =
                 IVdivVectorDifferenceInstance.begin();
adjacent_difference(IVdivVectorInstance.begin(),
                 IVdivVectorInstance.end(),Difference_it);
```

Notice that the template function requires the definition of a bidirectional iterator in the following form: `vector::iterator it`. The generated results are then simply output with a call to `copy()`, using the ostream iterator *itOstream*:

```
copy(IVdivVectorDifferenceInstance.begin()+1,
     IVdivVectorDifferenceInstance.end(),itOstream);
```

The program output looks like:

```
IVdivVectorInstance contains     : 2786 11554 13802 40021 75722


IVdivVectorInstance differences : 8768 2248 26219 35701
```

Combining Windows Coding with the STL `<numeric>` Template

The previous examples can be easily expanded into a full-blown Windows plotting example involving Fourier series calculations. The French mathematician, Baron Jean Baptiste Joseph Fourier (1768–1830), found that any periodic waveform could be constructed by simply adding the correct combinations of sine wave harmonics together. Using his techniques, a wide variety of waveforms, from square to triangular, can be created. Electrical engineers are often interested in square wave reproduction, because square waves are made from a fundamental sine wave and its associated overtones. The quality of amplifiers and other communication devices depends on how well they can reproduce these signals. (For a more detailed treatment of the Fourier series, refer to college-level physics or electrical engineering textbooks.) Fourier's formal equation is usually expressed as:

```
y = A + A1(sin wt) + A2(sin 2wt) + A3(sin 3wt) +
    A4(sin 4wt)...
```

Some periodic waveforms include just the odd or even harmonics only. In others, all terms are included. Also, in some periodic waveforms, the signs alternate between + and − for adjacent terms. This example constructs a square wave by adding the odd harmonic terms in a Fourier series together. The more terms that are used in the series, the more the final result will approach a precise square wave. For a square wave, the general Fourier series equation becomes:

```
y = (sin wt) + (1/3)(sin 3wt) + (1/5)(sin 5wt) +
    (1/7)(sin 7wt)...
```

You can now see that the work done in the previous example is ideal for calculating a Fourier series of terms. Notice that only odd harmonics will contribute to the final result. Can you see from the equation that if only one harmonic is chosen, the result will be a sine wave? Notice, also, that each successive term uses a fractional multiplier—in other words, each successively higher harmonic affects the waveform less and less.

To fully appreciate what this application is about to accomplish, remember that each term in a Fourier series will be calculated separately by the program, for each angle. Individual values will be saved in an array by using the vector push_back() member function. The sum of the individual calculations, for a given angle is then found by using the accumulate() member function to sum each value in the array. Before going on to the next angle, the values are removed from the array by using the pop_back() member function.

If you ask the application to use 1000 harmonic terms, then 1000 separate sine values will be scaled, calculated, and saved to the array for each angle. When the array values are accumulated (summed together), the value will represent one point on the Fourier series plot. This procedure must be repeated for each point that is to be plotted on the window. Therefore, 1000 calculations times 400 points (along the horizontal) = 400,000 calculations.

To create this project, use the MFC Application Wizard to create a project named Fourier. Accept the defaults offered by the Application Wizard to create the base code. To this code, you will need to add a data entry dialog box and associated member variables.

Modify the FourierView.cpp code to reflect the changes shown in a bold font in the following listing. These modifications will provide the code necessary to include the Fourier series calculations.

```
// FourierView.cpp : implementation of the CFourierView class
//
```

```
#include "stdafx.h"
#include "Fourier.h"

#include "FourierDoc.h"
#include "FourierView.h"
#include "FourierDlg.h"
#include "FourierDlg2.h"
#include <iostream>
#include <numeric>
#include <functional>
#include <vector>
#include <iterator>
#include <string>
#include <math.h>

// turn off warning for symbols
// too long for debugger
#pragma warning (disable : 4786)

using namespace std;

typedef vector <float> FourierArray;

#ifdef _DEBUG
#define new DEBUG_NEW
#undef THIS_FILE
static char THIS_FILE[] = __FILE__;
#endif

/////////////////////////////////////////////////////////////////
// CFourierView

IMPLEMENT_DYNCREATE(CFourierView, CView)

BEGIN_MESSAGE_MAP(CFourierView, CView)
    //{{AFX_MSG_MAP(CFourierView)
    ON_WM_SIZE()
    ON_COMMAND(IDM_FOURIER, OnFourier)
    //}}AFX_MSG_MAP
END_MESSAGE_MAP()

/////////////////////////////////////////////////////////////////
// CFourierView construction/destruction

CFourierView::CFourierView()
{
}

CFourierView::~CFourierView()
{
```

```
    }

BOOL CFourierView::PreCreateWindow(CREATESTRUCT& cs)
  {
      return CView::PreCreateWindow(cs);
  }

/////////////////////////////////////////////////////////////////////
// CFourierView drawing

void CFourierView::OnDraw(CDC* pDC)
{
    CFourierDoc* pDoc = GetDocument();
    ASSERT_VALID(pDoc);

    int ltitle;
    double y, yp;
    double vertscale, horzscale;

    // vertical plotting scaling factor
    vertscale = 180.0;
    // convert degrees to radians and scale
    // horozontal for 360 degrees in 400 points
    horzscale = 3.1415927 * 360 / (180 * 400);

    // define a vector of floats
    FourierArray rgFA;

    // set mapping mode, viewport, and so on
    pDC->SetMapMode(MM_ISOTROPIC);
    pDC->SetWindowExt(500,500);
    pDC->SetViewportExt(m_cxClient,-m_cyClient);
    pDC->SetViewportOrg(m_cxClient/20,m_cyClient/2);

    // draw x & y coordinate axes
    pDC->MoveTo(0,240);
    pDC->LineTo(0,-240);
    pDC->MoveTo(0,0);
    pDC->LineTo(400,0);
    pDC->MoveTo(0,0);

    // i represents a given angle for the series
    for (int i = 0; i <= 400; i++) {
        // calculate Fourier terms for the angle
        // place each term in the array
        for (int j=1; j<=pDoc->myterms; j++) {
            y = (vertscale / ((2.0 * j)-1.0)) * \
                sin(((j *  2.0)-1.0) * horzscale * i);
            rgFA.push_back(y);
        }
```

```
            // accumulate the individual array terms
            // for the angle
            yp = accumulate(rgFA.begin(),rgFA.end(),0.0f);
            // draw the scaled point in the client area
            pDC->LineTo(i, (int)yp);
            yp-=yp;

            // clean out the array and prepare for
            // with next angle's values.
            for (j=1; j<=pDoc->myterms; j++) {
                rgFA.pop_back();
            }
        }

        // print waveform title
        ltitle=strlen(pDoc->mytext);
        pDC->TextOut(200-(ltitle*8/2),200,pDoc->mytext,ltitle);
}

/////////////////////////////////////////////////////////////////////
// CFourierView diagnostics

#ifdef _DEBUG
void CFourierView::AssertValid() const
{
    CView::AssertValid();
}

void CFourierView::Dump(CDumpContext& dc) const
{
    CView::Dump(dc);
}

CFourierDoc* CFourierView::GetDocument() // non-debug version is inline
{
    ASSERT(m_pDocument->IsKindOf(RUNTIME_CLASS(CFourierDoc)));
    return (CFourierDoc*)m_pDocument;
}
#endif //_DEBUG

/////////////////////////////////////////////////////////////////////
// CFourierView message handlers

void CFourierView::OnSize(UINT nType, int cx, int cy)
{
    CView::OnSize(nType, cx, cy);
    // TODO: Add your message handler code here

    // WHM: added for sizing and scaling window
    m_cxClient = cx;
    m_cyClient = cy;
```

```
}

void CFourierView::OnFourier()
{
    // TODO: Add your command handler code here

    // WHM: added to process dialog information
    FourierDlg dlg (this);
    int result = dlg.DoModal();

    if(result==IDOK) {
        CFourierDoc* pDoc = GetDocument();
        ASSERT_VALID(pDoc);

        pDoc->mytext=dlg.m_text;
        pDoc->myterms=dlg.m_terms;

        Invalidate();
    }
}
```

MFC Windows applications built with the Application Wizard are quite intimidating. You'll learn programming details for this type of application starting with the next chapter.

FOURIER SERIES CALCULATION

The actual Fourier calculations are made within two **for** loops and drawn with the LineTo() function:

```
// i represents a given angle for the series
    for (int i = 0; i <= 400; i++) {
        // calculate Fourier terms for the angle
        // place each term in the array
        for (int j=1; j<=pDoc->myterms; j++) {
            y = (vertscale / ((2.0 * j)-1.0)) * \
                sin(((j *  2.0)-1.0) * horzscale * i);
            rgFA.push_back(y);
        }
        // accumulate the individual array terms
        // for the angle
        yp = accumulate(rgFA.begin(),rgFA.end(),0.0f);
        // draw the scaled point in the client area
        pDC->LineTo(i, (int)yp);
        yp-=yp;

        // clean out the array and prepare for
        // with next angle's values.
        for (j=1; j<=pDoc->myterms; j++) {
```

```
            rgFA.pop_back();
        }
    }
```

The outer loop, using the i index, increments the horizontal plotting position across the window. This value represents the scaled angle for one set of Fourier series of terms. The inner loop, using the j index, calculates the appropriate number of Fourier values for the given angle. For example, if i is pointing to a value representing 45 degrees and the number of Fourier terms is 10, then 10 calculations will be made in the inner loop for each i value and pushed onto the array. Outside this loop, the individual array values are accumulated (added together) to form a single point that will be scaled and drawn to the window.

Figure 6.1 is the default waveform created by calculating four terms in the Fourier series for each point on the plot.

Figure 6.2 shows a plot created by opening the dialog box and requesting one harmonic.

Figure 6.3 shows a plot created by requesting forty harmonics.

If you increase the number of harmonics to 1000 or 5000, you'll end up with a pretty good square wave.

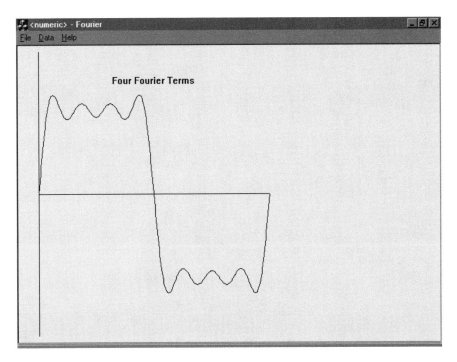

Figure 6.1   *The default Fourier series showing four harmonics.*

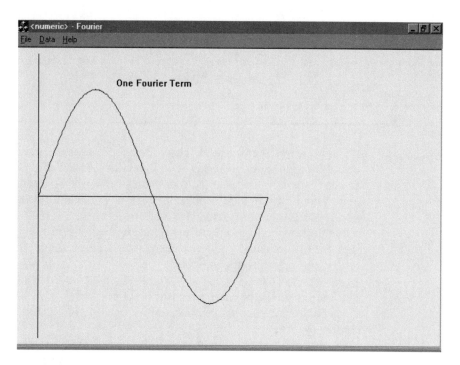

Figure 6.2   *A Fourier series created by requesting one harmonic.*

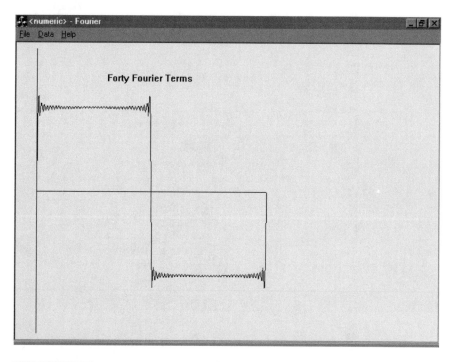

Figure 6.3   *A Fourier series created by requesting forty harmonics.*

174

Summary

In this chapter, you discovered just how easy it is to use the <numeric> template functions `accumulate()`, `inner_product()`, `partial_sum()`, and `adjacent_difference()`. In addition, you saw your first STL-ready Windows application using `accumulate()` to generate a Fourier series. The next chapter will describe the STL <set> and <memory> templates to complete your formal introduction to and use of the most significant addition to C++ by the ANSI C++/ISO Committee—namely STL!

The Microsoft Foundation Class (MFC) Library

In Chapter 1, you learned the reasons for developing parent classes and the techniques for deriving child classes from those parents. In this chapter, you will learn how Microsoft developed a family of classes that can be called upon when developing object-oriented Windows applications. This family of classes is called the Class MFC library.

The use of a class library is a radical departure from the use of functions in traditional procedure-oriented programming. Class libraries are the exclusive property of the developer. The MFC is owned and licensed by Microsoft Corporation. Microsoft introduced the Microsoft Foundation Class (MFC) library and warned developers that object-oriented programming with the MFC (of course) was the development path to take. At this writing, it seems apparent that the MFC has become the standard for class libraries. The common denominator, among all C/C++ compiler manufacturers is the MFC library. The strategies for developing a good library as well as simple program development will be discussed in Chapter 8. In this chapter, we will take a careful look at how the MFC library has evolved to version 6.0 in terms of class hierarchy.

Class Hierarchy

The MFC library is a collection of related classes. The relationship of one class to another depends upon where it falls in the class hierarchy for the MFC. For example, CTabCtrl and CSliderCtrl are two closely related classes. CSemaphore and CPropertySheet are not as closely related. However, in the larger scheme, they are all decendents of the CObject class. CObject is the base class for all derived MFC classes. CObject is discussed in more detail in Chapter 8 as it relates to the development of a simple programming example. In the following sections, we'll examine the class hierarchy of the MFC as it has evolved over the past several years. You'll gain a better understanding of how the various classes interact in the MFC, and perhaps understand how your applications can further derive child classes from this important library. There are a few classes that are not derived from CObject; they will also be examined.

CObject

CObject is the base class for almost all derived MFC classes. In the hierarchy scheme, groups of related classes are derived immediately from CObject, as shown in the following list:

```
CObject–
  Arrays
  CCmdTarget (architecture)
  Command Line
  Control
  Database
  Dialog Boxes
  Drawing Objects
  Exceptions
  File
  Graphics
  Lists
  Maps
  Menus
  Property Sheets
  Sockets
  Synchronization
```

The contents of each of these categories, along with a short description of their use, will be examined in the sections which follow.

Arrays

The CArray class allows arrays the use of arrays that shrink and grow as needed. They are most closely associated with normal C/C++ arrays. Memory is allocated to the upper bound. CArray is part of the template-based collection classes. As such, it provides a type-safe collection for containing objects of any type.

All remaining classes are not of the template-based collection type. These classes are used to efficiently manipulate and store the array data types mentioned.

```
CObject -
  Carray
  CByteArray
```

```
CDWordArray
CObArray
CPtrArray
CStringArray
CUIntArray
CWordArray
```

CCmdTarget (Architecture)

CCmdTarget is the base class for all classes of objects that receive and respond to messages. Messages are sent by menus, dialog boxes, controls, and
so on. These commands are sent from interface objects to target objects.

```
CObject -
  CCmdTarget
    CWinThread
    CWinApp
      COleControlModule
    CDocTemplate
      CSingleDocTemplate
      CMultiDocTemplate
    COleObjectFactory
      COleTemplateServer
    COleDataSource
    COleDropSource
    COleDropTarget
    COleMessageFilter
    CConnectionPoint
    Cdocument
      COleDocument
        COleLinkingDoc
          COleServerDoc
            CRichEditDoc
    CDocItem
      COleClientItem
        COleDocObjectItem
        CRichEditCntrlItem
    COleServerItem
      CDocObjectServerItem
    CDocObjectServer
  CWnd
```

For example, CDocTemplate serves as the base class for all document
templates. This class is not used directly. Instead, either CSingleDocTemplate or CMultiDocTemplate would be selected. CSingleDocTemplate
is a template for documents using the Single Document Interface (SDI).
CMultiDocTemplate is a template for documents using the Multiple Document Interface (MDI).

CWnd

This class is the base class for all window classes in the MFC library. The CWnd class lets you create a main window or child window for an application. A class is derived from CWnd, then member variables and functions are added. Other classes are derived from CWnd, including CDialog, CFrameWnd, CMDIChildWnd, CMDIFrameWnd, CView, and so on.

```
CObject -
  CCmdTarget
  Cwnd
      Control Bars
      Controls
      Dialog Boxes
      Frame
      Property Sheets
      Views
```

CONTROL BARS • Control bars are most closely associated with a frame window. They include buttons, dialog template, status panes and so on. They are easy to use because they are integrated with the frame window. CControlBar is the base class for CDialogBar, COleResizeBar, CStatusBar, and CToolBar.

```
CObject -
 CCmdTarget
  Cwnd
     CControlBar
        CDialogBar
        COleResizeBar
        CReBar
        CStatusBar
        CToolBar
```

CONTROLS • Control classes provide an interface between Windows controls such as buttons, combo boxes, list boxes, sliders, tabs, toolbars, and so on and your application. Classes ending with "Ctrl" are part of the common control being used extensively by programmers today.

```
CObject -
  CCmdTarget
    Cwnd
        CAnimateCtrl
        Cbutton
          CBitmapButton
        CComboBox
        Cedit
        CHeaderCtrl
        CHotKeyCtrl
        CIPPAddressCtrl
```

```
CListBox
  CCheckListBox
  CDragListBox
CListCtrl
CMonthCalCtrl
COleControl
CProgressCtrl
CRichEditCtrl
CScrollBar
CSliderCtrl
CSpinButtonCtrl
Cstatic
CStatusBarCtrl
CTabCtrl
CToolBarCtrl
CToolTipCtrl
CTreeCtrl
```

For example, common controls are used in dialog boxes, form views, record views, and so on. Common controls function as child windows that send notification messages to the parent window when events occur in the control. These messages can include WM_NOTIFY and WM_COMMAND Windows messages.

DIALOG BOXES • The CDialog class is the base class used for all dialog boxes. An object based on this class is made up of a dialog template and a class derived from CDialog.

```
CObject -
  CCmdTargeT
    CWnd
      CDialog
        CCommonDialog
          CColorDialog
          CFileDialog
          CFindReplaceDialog
          CFontDialog
          COleDialog
            COleBusyDialog
            COleChangeIconDialog
            COleChangeSourceDialog
            COleConvertDialog
            COleInsertDialoG
            COleLinksDialog
              ColeUpdateDialog
            COlePasteSpecialDialog
            COlePropertiesDialog
          CPageSetupDialog
          CPrintDialog
```

```
COlePropertyPage
CPropertyPage
  CPropertyPageEx
```

Member variables can be added to the derived dialog class for storing data received by controls contained in the dialog box.

FRAME • CFRameWnd is the base class for frame windows. It supports an SDI, overlapped, or pop-up frame window. In a user application, a class is derived from CFrameWnd, then member variables are added to store specific data for the particular application. Frame windows can be created by using Create(), LoadFrame(), or via a document template.

```
CObject -
  CCmdTarget
    Cwnd
      CFrameWnd
        CMDICChildWnd
        CMDIFrameWnd
        CMiniFrameWnd
        COleIPFrameWnd
        CSplitterWnd
```

PROPERTY SHEETS • The CPropertySheet class is used to create property sheet or tab dialog objects. Property sheets contain a CPropertySheet object and at least one CPropertyPage object. Property sheets are displayed in the framework as windows with tab indices. Property sheets can relieve the congestion found on single-sheet dialog boxes.

```
CObject -
  CCmdTarget
    Cwnd
      CPropertySheetEx
```

VIEWS • The CView class is the base class for all view classes. A view becomes part of a document and serves as an interface between the document and the user.

```
CObject -
  CCmdTarget
    Cwnd
      Cview
        CCtrlView
          CEditView
          CListView
          CRichEditView
          CTreeView
        CScrollView
          CFormView
```

```
CDaoRecordView
CHtmlView
COleDBRecordView
CRecordView
```

A view is simply the child of a frame window. New views are constructed by the framework and attached to a document as requested. Views receive commands from the frame window.

Control

An image list is a group of images of the same size. Image lists are used to manage large groups of icons and bitmapped images.

```
CObject -
  CDockState
  CImageList
```

Database

The CDatabase class allows an object to represent a connection to a data source. A data source might be provided by a database application such as Microsoft Access.

A CDaoDatabase class also allows an object to represent a connection to a data source. The basic difference between this class and CDatabase is that CDaoDatabase gains access to data via the Data Access Object (DAO). This object is based on the Microsoft Jet database engine. The CDatabase object, on the other hand, gains access through Open Database Connectivity (ODBC).

```
CObject -
  Cdatabase
  Crecordset
  CLongBinary
  CDaoDatabase
  CDaoQueryDef
  CDaoRecordset
  CDaoTableDef
  CDaoWorkspace
```

Drawing Objects

The CGdiObject class is the base class for Windows GDI objects. These objects include bitmaps, brushes, palettes, pens, and so on. User classes are based on classes derived from CGdiObject.

```
CObject -
  CGdiObject
    Cbitmap
```

```
Cbrush
Cfont
Cpalette
Cpen
CRgn
```

For example, the CBrush class encapsulates a Windows brush. A CBrush object can be used by any CDC member function.

Exceptions

In this group, CException serves as the base class for all exceptions in the MFC library. The derived exception classes include CArchiveException, CDaoException, CDBException, CFileException, CMemoryException, CNot-SupportedException, COleDispatchException, COleException, CResourceEx-ception, and CUserException.

```
CObject -
  Cexception
    CArchiveException
    CDaoException
    CDBException
    CFileException
    CInternetException
    CMemoryException
    CNotSupportedException
    COleException
    COleDispatchException
    CResourceException
    CUserException
```

Specific exceptions are captured using one of the previously mentioned classes. All exceptions can be captured with the CException class.

File

The CFile class serves as the base class for all MFC file classes using un-buffered disk input/output. Text files and memory files can also be supported via a derived child class.

```
CObject -
  CFile
    CMemFile
      CSharedFile
    COleStreamFile
     CMonikerFile
       CAsyncMonikerFile
         CDataPathProperty
           CCachedDataPathProperty
    CSocketFile
```

```
CStdioFile
   CInternetFile
   CGopherFile
   CHttpFile
CRecentFileList
```

For example, a `CStdioFile` class object can be used for a C run-time stream file. These files are buffered and can be used in text or binary mode.

Graphics

The `CDC` class provides device context objects for use in a device context. The device context can be the normal client area of a window or, for example, a printer.

Member functions are provided for all GDI graphics task, including coordinate system manipulation, clipping, device extents, and graphics figures.

```
CObject -
  CDC
    CCleintDC
    CMetaFileDC
    CPaintDC
    CWindowDC
```

`CPaintDC`, for example, encapsulates calls to **BeginPaint()** and **EndPaint()**. `CPaintDC` objects are used to respond to a WM_PAINT message. They are typically located in the `OnPaint` message handler member function.

Lists

The `CList` class acts as a double-linked list for ordered lists. Sequential searches are used to find list elements by value or index. Element insertion can be fast at the beginning or end of the list.

The `CStringList` class, for example, supports lists of `CString` objects. In this case, comparisons are done by value (characters instead of addresses).

```
CObject -
  Clist
  CPtrList
  CObList
  CStringList
```

Maps

The `CMap` class serves as a dictionary collection class. This class links specific keys to values, making retrieves or deletes very efficient.

Some classes serve very specific purposes. For example, the CMap-WordToPtr class is used to support maps of void pointers keyed by 16-bit words (pointers).

```
CObject -
  Cmap
  CMapWordToPtr
  CMapPtrToWord
  CMapPtrToPtr
  CMapWordToOb
  CMapStringToPtr
  CMapStringToOb
  CMapStringToString
```

Menus

The CMenu class encapsulates HMENU. CMenu provides the functionality for all menu implementation, including creating, updating, and destroying.

```
CObject -
  CMenu
```

Sockets

The CAsyncSocket class provides support for a Windows socket. Applications must handle blocking, order differences, and various string conversions. Sockets are used in Windows communications.

```
CObject -
  CAsyncSocket
    CSocket
```

Synchronization

The CSyncObject class allows the synchronization of objects. For example, CSemaphore is derived from CSyncObject. CSemaphore supports semaphores. Semaphores are used to limited the number of threads in a process. CSemaphore objects are used to hold the count of the number of threads accessing a resource.

```
CObject -
  CSyncObject
    CCriticalSection
    Cevent
    Cmutex
    CSemaphore
```

Classes Not Based On CObject

There are several small groups of classes not based on CObject. These groups are briefly discussed in the following sections.

Automation

These classes are typically used to encapsulate a particular type of OLE automation. For example, the COleCurrency class is used to create objects that encapsulate the CURRENCY data type of OLE automation. The CURRENCY data type is used for financial calculations or for any fixed-point calculation requiring accuracy.

```
COleCurrency
COleDateTime
COleDateTimeSpan
COleVariant
```

Object Model

These classes provide run-time object support. For example, CArchive is a class that permits a complex network of objects to be saved in a permanent binary form. This form exists even after the objects are deleted. The process of making data persistent is called *serialization*.

```
Carchive
DumpContext
CRuntimeClass
```

Structures

These classes provide structures for other MFC classes. For example, the framework uses the CCreateContext structure when implementing a frame window and views. The structure provides the required information for connecting the components of a document and the view of the document's data.

```
CCreateContext
CMemoryState
COleSafeArray
CPrintInfo
```

Support

This group of classes offers support for the indicated item. For example, the CDataExchange class provides support for the Dialog Data Exchange (DDX) and Dialog Data Validation (DDV) routines. The object provides the context information needed for DDX and DDV to take place.

```
CCmdUI
  COleCmdUI
CDaoFieldExchange
CDataExchange
CFieldExchange
COleDataObject
COleDataObject
COleDispatchDriver
CPropExchange
CRectTracker
CWaitCursor
```

Synchronization

The CSingleLock class allows objects to represent the access control mechanism used in controlling access to a resource in a multi-threaded program. Likewise, the CMultiLock class is used when multiple objects are needed.

```
CMultiLoc
CSingleLock
```

Typed Templates

These classes are often used as type-safe wrappers. For example, the CTypedPtrArray class supplies a wrapper for objects of class CPtrArray or CObArray. The type-checking facility of C++ helps eliminate mismatched pointer errors.

```
CTypedPtrArray
CTypedPtrList
CTypedPtrMap
```

Types

These classes are similar to required Windows structures. For example, the CRect class is similar to the RECT structure. CRect includes member functions required to manipulate CRect objects and Windows RECT structures.

```
Cpoin
Crect
Csize
Cstring
Ctime
CTimeSpan
```

Wrappers

These classes are used to encapsulate the functionality of a font or picture object and the appropriate interface. These classes are used when it is desirable to customize font or picture properties for an application.

```
CFontHolde
CPictureHolder
```

More On MFC Classes

This chapter was designed to be a very brief overview of the MFC class hierarchy. In Chapter 8, you'll learn more detail about CObject and the related classes necessary to build complete Windows applications with the MFC library.

An Object-Oriented Approach

In this chapter, we'll examine Microsoft's solution to making object-oriented programming easier. The Microsoft Visual C++ compiler provides a class library containing a new set of tools for the development of C++ and C++ Windows applications. While the Microsoft Foundation Class (MFC) library is available in 16- and 32-bit versions, only the 32-bit version will be discussed in this book. The 32-bit version is used exclusively for Windows 95/98/2000 and Windows NT applications. The 32-bit version offers an expanded library providing additional class support for control bars, property sheets, OLE, etc.

This chapter examines the advantages of using the MFC library for Windows code development. It discusses terms, definitions, and techniques that are common across all MFClass versions. The material you learn in this chapter is important for all MFC code developed in later chapters.

WHY SWITCH?

The MFC library provides easy-to-use objects for programmers. Windows, from its very inception, has followed many principles of object-oriented programming design, within the framework of a non-object-oriented language such as C. The use of the C++ language for developing 32-bit Windows applications is a natural because it can take full advantage of object-oriented programming features. The Microsoft development team designed a library that includes a comprehensive implementation of the Windows Application Program Interface (API). This library encapsulates the most important data structures and API function calls within a group of reusable classes.

Class libraries, in general, offer many advantages over the traditional function libraries used by procedure-oriented programmers. These advantages include:

- Encapsulation of code and data within the class.
- Final classes appear to be natural extensions of the language.
- Inheritance capabilities.
- Reduced code size as a result of well-designed class libraries.
- Reduction of function and variable name collisions.

By using the MFC library, the code required to establish a window has been reduced to approximately one-third the length of a conventional application. development, This allows you, the developer, to spend less time communicating with Windows and more time developing your application's code.

DESIGN TECHNIQUES

To make the library easy to use, the design team set design principles and guidelines that had to be followed. These principles and guidelines included the following:

- Capture the power of C++ without overwhelming the programmer.
- Power and efficiency must strike a balance in the design of class libraries.
- The class library must be portable from one platform to another, for example, Windows 95/98/2000 or Windows NT.
- The transition from the use of API function calls to the use of class libraries is to be as simple as possible.
- Traditional functions calls can be mixed with class libraries.

From the onset, the design team felt that a well-designed application had to start with a well-designed class library. The MFC classes are designed to be small in size and fast in execution speed. The current implementation of the MFC is easy to use with speeds approaching the older function libraries of C.

The MFC classes were developed so that new classes were named in a fashion similar to the function names known by experienced procedure-oriented Windows programmers. Microsoft achieved these results by carefully naming and designing class features. The "mixed-mode" concept was also implemented. With this approach, classes and traditional function calls can be intermixed in the same source code.

The original version of the MFC was designed to be portable. Windows NT was already on the market, and these programmers knew that Windows 95/98/2000 were on the horizon. This dynamic architecture allowed the classes to be easily scaled to the growing Windows environment. Thus, the MFC library is fully integrated across all platforms, Windows NT and Windows 95/98/2000.

KEY MFC FEATURES

Class libraries for Windows are available from other C++ compiler manufacturers, but Microsoft claims several real advantages for its MFC library:

- Data object type determination at run-time. This permits dynamic manipulation of a field when classes are instantiated.
- Diagnostics support that includes the ability to send information about objects to a file and to also validate member variables.
- Extensive exception-handling design that makes application code less subject to failure.
- Reduction of switch/case statements that are prone to error. Messages are mapped to member functions within a class. Direct message-to-method mapping is available for all messages.
- Same class-naming convention as the conventional function-based Windows API. Thus, the action of a class is immediately recognized by its name.
- Small code means fast implementation. With minimal object code overhead, MFC applications execute almost as quickly as conventional C Windows applications.
- Support for all Windows controls, dialog boxes, functions, GDI graphics, messages, menus, and dialog boxes.
- Support for the Component Object Model (COM).

Traditional procedure-oriented Windows programmers will appreciate two of these features: first, the familiar class-naming convention and the message-to-method mapping: second, the elimination of error-prone switch/case statements. As a developer, you will appreciate Microsoft's commitment to better diagnostics and the small code overhead imposed by the MFC library.

A PARENT CLASS, COBJECT

A class library, such as the MFC, develops a hierarchy of classes by deriving characteristics from a base or parent class. Microsoft uses a few classes as base or parent classes. Additional classes in the library are then derived from the parent classes. **CObject** is the one parent class used extensively in developing Windows applications. The MFC library header files, located in the MFC/INCLUDE subdirectory, provide a wealth of information on defined classes. **CObject** is defined in the `afx.h` header file. This code has been edited slightly for clarity.

```
Class Cobject
{
public:
// Object model (types, destruction, allocation)
    virtual CRuntimeClass* GetRuntimeClass() const;
```

```
    virtual ~CObject();   // virtual destructors are necessary
    // Diagnostic allocations
    void* PASCAL operator new(size_t nSize);
    void* PASCAL operator new(size_t, void* p);
    void PASCAL operator delete(void* p);
protected:
    Cobject();
private:
    CObject(const CObject& objectSrc);
    void operator=(const CObject& objectSrc);
// Attributes
public:
    BOOL IsSerializable() const;
    BOOL IsKindOf(const CRuntimeClass* pClass) const;
// Implementation
public:
    static const AFX_DATA CRuntimeClass classCObject;
};
```

If you examine the previous listing, notice which components make up the class definition. First, like most class definitions, **CObject** is divided into public, protected, and private parts. **CObject** also provides normal and dynamic typechecking and serialization. Dynamic type-checking allows the type of an object to be determined at run-time. The state of an object can be saved to a storage medium, such as a disk, through a concept called *persistence*. This object persistence permits class member functions to also be persistent, permitting retrieval of object data.

Child classes are derived from parent classes. **CGdiObject** and **CDC** are examples of classes derived from **CObject**. Here is a portion of the **CDC** definition found in the afxwin.h header file. Again, this partial listing has been edited for clarity.

```
    class CDC : public Cobject
{
    DECLARE_DYNCREATE(CDC)
public:
// Attributes
    HDC m_hDC;             // The output DC (must be first data member)
    HDCm_hAttribDC;        // The Attribute DC
    operator HDC() const;
    HDC GetSafeHdc() const; // Always returns the Output DC
    CWnd* GetWindow() const;

    static CDC* PASCAL FromHandle(HDC hDC);
    static void PASCAL DeleteTempMap();
    BOOL Attach(HDC hDC);   // Attach/Detach affects only the Output DC
    HDC Detach();

    virtual void SetAttribDC(HDC hDC);  // Set the Attribute DC
```

```
    virtual void SetOutputDC(HDC hDC);    // Set the Output DC
    virtual void ReleaseAttribDC();       // Release the Attribute DC
    virtual void ReleaseOutputDC();       // Release the Output DC

    BOOL IsPrinting() const;              // TRUE if printing

    CPen* GetCurrentPen() const;
    CBrush* GetCurrentBrush() const;
    CPalette* GetCurrentPalette() const;
    CFont* GetCurrentFont() const;
    CBitmap* GetCurrentBitmap() const;

    // for bidi and mirrored localization
    DWORD GetLayout() const;
    DWORD SetLayout(DWORD dwLayout);

// Constructors
    CDC();
    BOOL CreateDC(LPCTSTR lpszDriverName, LPCTSTR lpszDeviceName,
        LPCTSTR lpszOutput, const void* lpInitData);
    BOOL CreateIC(LPCTSTR lpszDriverName, LPCTSTR lpszDeviceName,
        LPCTSTR lpszOutput, const void* lpInitData);
    BOOL CreateCompatibleDC(CDC* pDC);

    BOOL DeleteDC();

// Device-Context Functions
    virtual int SaveDC();
    virtual BOOL RestoreDC(int nSavedDC);
    int GetDeviceCaps(int nIndex) const;
    UINT SetBoundsRect(LPCRECT lpRectBounds, UINT flags);
    UINT GetBoundsRect(LPRECT lpRectBounds, UINT flags);
    BOOL ResetDC(const DEVMODE* lpDevMode);

// Drawing-Tool Functions
    CPoint GetBrushOrg() const;
    CPoint SetBrushOrg(int x, int y);
    CPoint SetBrushOrg(POINT point);
    int EnumObjects(int nObjectType,
            int (CALLBACK* lpfn)(LPVOID, LPARAM), LPARAM lpData);

// Type-safe selection helpers
public:
    virtual CGdiObject* SelectStockObject(int nIndex);
    CPen* SelectObject(CPen* pPen);
    CBrush* SelectObject(CBrush* pBrush);
    virtual CFont* SelectObject(CFont* pFont);
    CBitmap* SelectObject(CBitmap* pBitmap);
    int SelectObject(CRgn* pRgn);           // special return for regions
    CGdiObject* SelectObject(CGdiObject* pObject);
            // Color and Color Palette Functions
```

```
        COLORREF GetNearestColor(COLORREF crColor) const;
        CPalette* SelectPalette(CPalette* pPalette, BOOL bForceBackground);
        UINT RealizePalette();
        void UpdateColors();

// Drawing-Attribute Functions
        COLORREF GetBkColor() const;
        int GetBkMode() const;
        int GetPolyFillMode() const;
        int GetROP2() const;
        int GetStretchBltMode() const;
        COLORREF GetTextColor() const;

        virtual COLORREF SetBkColor(COLORREF crColor);
        int SetBkMode(int nBkMode);
        int SetPolyFillMode(int nPolyFillMode);
        int SetROP2(int nDrawMode)
        int SetStretchBltMode(int nStretchMode);
        virtual COLORREF SetTextColor(COLORREF crColor);

        BOOL GetColorAdjustment(LPCOLORADJUSTMENT lpColorAdjust) const;
        BOOL SetColorAdjustment(const COLORADJUSTMENT* lpColorAdjust);

// Mapping Functions
        int GetMapMode() const;
        CPoint GetViewportOrg() const;
        virtual int SetMapMode(int nMapMode);
        // Viewport Origin
        virtual CPoint SetViewportOrg(int x, int y);
                CPoint SetViewportOrg(POINT point);
        virtual CPoint OffsetViewportOrg(int nWidth, int nHeight);

        // Viewport Extent
        CSize GetViewportExt() const;
        virtual CSize SetViewportExt(int cx, int cy);
                CSize SetViewportExt(SIZE size);
        virtual CSize ScaleViewportExt(int xNum, int xDenom,
                        int yNum, int yDenom);

        // Window Origin
        CPoint GetWindowOrg() const;
        CPoint SetWindowOrg(int x, int y);
        CPoint SetWindowOrg(POINT point);
        CPoint OffsetWindowOrg(int nWidth, int nHeight);

        // Window extent
        CSize GetWindowExt() const;
        virtual CSize SetWindowExt(int cx, int cy);
                CSize SetWindowExt(SIZE size);
```

```
        virtual CSize ScaleWindowExt(int xNum, int xDenom,
                      int yNum, int yDenom);

// Coordinate Functions
    void DPtoLP(LPPOINT lpPoints, int nCount = 1) const;
    void DPtoLP(LPRECT lpRect) const;
    void DPtoLP(LPSIZE lpSize) const;
    void LPtoDP(LPPOINT lpPoints, int nCount = 1) const;
    void LPtoDP(LPRECT lpRect) const;
    void LPtoDP(LPSIZE lpSize) const;

// Special Coordinate Functions
    void DPtoHIMETRIC(LPSIZE lpSize) const;
    void LPtoHIMETRIC(LPSIZE lpSize) const;
    void HIMETRICtoDP(LPSIZE lpSize) const;
    void HIMETRICtoLP(LPSIZE lpSize) const;

// Region Functions
    BOOL FillRgn(CRgn* pRgn, CBrush* pBrush);
    BOOL FrameRgn(CRgn* pRgn, CBrush* pBrush, int nWidth);
    BOOL InvertRgn(CRgn* pRgn);
    BOOL PaintRgn(CRgn* pRgn);

// Clipping Functions
    virtual int GetClipBox(LPRECT lpRect) const;
    virtual BOOL PtVisible(int x, int y) const;
            BOOL PtVisible(POINT point) const;
    virtual BOOL RectVisible(LPCRECT lpRect) const;
            int SelectClipRgn(CRgn* pRgn);
            int ExcludeClipRect(LPCRECT lpRect);
            int ExcludeUpdateRgn(CWnd* pWnd);
            int IntersectClipRect(LPCRECT lpRect);
            int OffsetClipRgn(int x, int y);
            int OffsetClipRgn(SIZE size);
    int SelectClipRgn(CRgn* pRgn, int nMode);

// Line-Output Functions
    CPoint GetCurrentPosition() const;
    CPoint MoveTo(int x, int y);
    CPoint MoveTo(POINT point);
    BOOL LineTo(int x, int y);
    BOOL LineTo(POINT point);
    BOOL Arc(LPCRECT lpRect, POINT ptStart, POINT ptEnd);
    BOOL Polyline(LPPOINT lpPoints, int nCount);

    BOOL ArcTo(LPCRECT lpRect, POINT ptStart, POINT ptEnd);
    int GetArcDirection() const;
    int SetArcDirection(int nArcDirection);

    BOOL PolylineTo(const POINT* lpPoints, int nCount);
```

```
        BOOL PolyPolyline(const POINT* lpPoints,
             const DWORD* lpPolyPoints, int nCount);

        BOOL PolyBezier(const POINT* lpPoints, int nCount);
        BOOL PolyBezierTo(const POINT* lpPoints, int nCount);

// Simple Drawing Functions
        void FillRect(LPCRECT lpRect, CBrush* pBrush);
        void FrameRect(LPCRECT lpRect, CBrush* pBrush);
        void InvertRect(LPCRECT lpRect);
        BOOL DrawIcon(int x, int y, HICON hIcon);
        BOOL DrawIcon(POINT point, HICON hIcon);

// Ellipse and Polygon Functions
        BOOL Chord(int x1, int y1, int x2, int y2, int x3, int y3,
             int x4, int y4);
        BOOL Chord(LPCRECT lpRect, POINT ptStart, POINT ptEnd);
        void DrawFocusRect(LPCRECT lpRect);
        BOOL Ellipse(int x1, int y1, int x2, int y2);
        BOOL Ellipse(LPCRECT lpRect);
        BOOL Pie(LPCRECT lpRect, POINT ptStart, POINT ptEnd);
        BOOL Polygon(LPPOINT lpPoints, int nCount);
        BOOL Rectangle(int x1, int y1, int x2, int y2);
        BOOL Rectangle(LPCRECT lpRect);
        BOOL RoundRect(LPCRECT lpRect, POINT point);

// Bitmap Functions
        BOOL PatBlt(int x, int y, int nWidth, int nHeight, DWORD dwRop);
        BOOL BitBlt(int x, int y, int nWidth, int nHeight, CDC* pSrcDC,
             int xSrc, int ySrc, DWORD dwRop);
        COLORREF GetPixel(int x, int y) const;
        COLORREF GetPixel(POINT point) const;
        COLORREF SetPixel(int x, int y, COLORREF crColor);
        COLORREF SetPixel(POINT point, COLORREF crColor);
        BOOL FloodFill(int x, int y, COLORREF crColor);
        BOOL SetPixelV(int x, int y, COLORREF crColor);
        BOOL SetPixelV(POINT point, COLORREF crColor);

// Text Functions
        virtual BOOL TextOut(int x, int y, LPCTSTR lpszString, int nCount);
        CSize GetTextExtent(LPCTSTR lpszString, int nCount) const;
        CSize GetTextExtent(const CString& str) const;
        CSize GetOutputTextExtent(LPCTSTR lpszString, int nCount) const;
        CSize GetOutputTextExtent(const CString& str) const;
        CSize GetTabbedTextExtent(LPCTSTR lpszString, int nCount,
             int nTabPositions, LPINT lpnTabStopPositions) const;
        CSize GetTabbedTextExtent(const CString& str,
             int nTabPositions, LPINT lpnTabStopPositions) const;
```

```
    CSize GetOutputTabbedTextExtent(LPCTSTR lpszString, int nCount,
        int nTabPositions, LPINT lpnTabStopPositions) const;
    CSize GetOutputTabbedTextExtent(const CString& str,
        int nTabPositions, LPINT lpnTabStopPositions) const;
    virtual BOOL GrayString(CBrush* pBrush,
        BOOL (CALLBACK* lpfnOutput)(HDC, LPARAM, int), LPARAM lpData,
            int nCount, int x, int y, int nWidth, int nHeight);
    UINT GetTextAlign() const;
    UINT SetTextAlign(UINT nFlags);
    int GetTextFace(int nCount, LPTSTR lpszFacename) const;
    int GetTextFace(CString& rString) const;
    BOOL GetTextMetrics(LPTEXTMETRIC lpMetrics) const;
    BOOL GetOutputTextMetrics(LPTEXTMETRIC lpMetrics) const;
    int SetTextJustification(int nBreakExtra, int nBreakCount);
    int GetTextCharacterExtra() const;
    int SetTextCharacterExtra(int nCharExtra);


// Scrolling Functions
    BOOL ScrollDC(int dx, int dy, LPCRECT lpRectScroll,
        LPCRECT lpRectClip,
        CRgn* pRgnUpdate, LPRECT lpRectUpdate);


// Font Functions
    BOOL GetCharWidth(UINT nFirstChar, UINT nLastChar,
    LPINT lpBuffer) const;
    BOOL GetOutputCharWidth(UINT nFirstChar, UINT nLastChar,
    LPINT lpBuffer) const;
    DWORD SetMapperFlags(DWORD dwFlag);
    CSize GetAspectRatioFilter() const;


    BOOL GetCharABCWidths(UINT nFirstChar, UINT nLastChar,
    LPABC lpabc) const;
    DWORD GetFontData(DWORD dwTable, DWORD dwOffset,
    LPVOID lpData, DWORD cbData) const;
    int GetKerningPairs(int nPairs,
    LPKERNINGPAIR lpkrnpair) const;
    UINT GetOutlineTextMetrics(UINT cbData,
    LPOUTLINETEXTMETRIC lpotm) const;
    DWORD GetGlyphOutline(UINT nChar, UINT nFormat,
    LPGLYPHMETRICS lpgm,
        DWORD cbBuffer, LPVOID lpBuffer,
    const MAT2* lpmat2) const;


    BOOL GetCharABCWidths(UINT nFirstChar, UINT nLastChar,
        LPABCFLOAT lpABCF) const;
    BOOL GetCharWidth(UINT nFirstChar, UINT nLastChar,
        float* lpFloatBuffer) const;
```

CDC and its member functions allow the drawing of all the basic graphics primitives for Windows. These graphics primitives include lines, circles, arcs, polylines, rectangles, rounded rectangles, and so on.

While Microsoft has provided detailed information about the MFC library, it is not really necessary to completely understand the class definitions to use them efficiently.

For example, in traditional C Windows applications, the **Delete-Object**() function can be called with the following syntax:

```
DeleteObject(hPen);   /*hPen is the pen handle*/
```

In C++, when using the MFC library, the same results will be achieved by accessing the member function with the following syntax:

```
newpen.DeleteObject(); //newpen is current pen
```

While this is a simple example, you should see that switching between C Windows function calls and class library objects can be intuitive. Microsoft has used this same approach in developing all Windows classes. This makes the transition from traditional function calls used in procedure-oriented applications to MFC library objects very easy.

PARENT CLASS HIERARCHY

Table 8.1 lists important 32-bit MFC library classes. All classes in this table are derived from **CObject**.

Table 8.1	MFC Parent Class Hierarchy

```
Cobject
    CException
        CMemoryException
        CFileException
        CArchiveException
        CNotSupportedException
        CUserException
        COleException
            COleDispatchException
        CDBException
    CFile
        CStdioFile
        CMemFile
        COleStreamFile
    CDC
        CClientDC
        CWindowDC
```

| Table 8.1 | *MFC Parent Class Hierarchy (Continued)* |

```
            CPaintDC
            CMetaFileDC
    CGdiObject
            CPen
            CBrush
            CFont
            CBitmap
            CPalette
            CRgn
    CMenu
    CArray
    CByteArray
    CWordArray
    CDWordArray
    CPtrArray
    CObArray
    CStringArray
    CUIntArray
    CList
    CPtrList
    CObList
    CStringList
    CMap
    CMapWordToPtr
    CMapPtrToWord
    CMapPtrToPtr
    CMapWordToOb
    CMapStringToPtr
    CMapStringToOb
    CMapStringToString
    CDatabase
    CRecordSet
    CLongBinary
```
CCmdTarget
```
        CWinThread
                CWinApp
        CDocTemplate
                CSingleDocTemplate
                CMultiDocTemplate
        COleObjectFactory
                COleTemplateServer
        COleDataSource
        COleDropSource
        COleDropTarget
        COleMessageFilter
        CDocument
```

(continued)

Table 8.1	*MFC Parent Class Hierarchy (Continued)*

```
                        COleDocument
                                COleLinkingDoc
                                        COleServerDoc
                CDocItem
                        COleClientItem
                        COleServerItem
CWnd
        CFrameWnd
                CMDIChildWnd
                CMDIFrameWnd
                CMiniFrameWnd
                COleIPFrameWnd
        CControlBar
                CToolBar
                CStatusBar
                CDialogBar
                COleResizeBar
        CSplitterWnd
        CPropertySheet
        CDialog
                COleDialog
                        COleInsertDialog
                        COleChangeIconDialog
                        COlePasteSpecialDialog
                        COleConvertDialog
                        COleBusyDialog
                        COleLinksDialog
                                COleUpdateDialog
        CFileDialog
        CColorDialog
        CFontDialog
        CPrintDialog
        CFindReplaceDialog
        CPropertyPage
        CView
                CScrollView
                        CFormView
                                CRecordView
        CEditView
        CStatic
        CButton
                CBitmapButton
        CListBox
        CComboBox
        CScrollBar
        CEdit
```

Table 8.2 is a list of the 32-bit run-time object model support.

Table 8.2	*Run-Time Object Model Support*

CArchive
CCmdUI
CCreateContext
CDataExchange
CDumpContext
CFieldExchange
CFileStatus
CMemoryState
COleDataObject
COleDispatchDriver
CPoint
CPrintInfo
CRect
CRectTracker
CRuntimeClass
CSize
CString
CTime
CTimeSpan
CTypedPtrArray
CTypedPtrList
CTypedPtrMap

Tables 8.1 and 8.2 will help you maintain an understanding of where classes fit into the overall hierarchy as you continue your study of the MFC in future chapters. Mark this spot!

AN MFC APPLICATION, WINVERMFC.CPP

The purpose of WinVerMFC.cpp is to:

- Draw simple GDI graphics in the client area.
- Establish a window on the screen.
- Make a calculation to determine whether the operating system is Windows NT or Windows 95.

THE WinVerMFC.h HEADER FILE • The WinVerMFC.h header file is used to indicate class definitions that are unique to the application. The definitions for two classes are contained in this file. First, **CMainWnd** is derived from Microsoft's **CWinApp**. Next, **CWinVerMFCApp** is derived from Microsoft's **CFrameWnd**.

Here is the WinVerMFC.h header file listing:

```
class CMainWnd : public CFrameWnd
{
```

```
public:
  CMainWnd();
  afx_msg void OnPaint();
  DECLARE_MESSAGE_MAP();
};

class CWinVerMFCApp : public CWinApp
{
public:
   BOOL InitInstance();
};
```

Note   Putting these class definitions in a separate header file is a matter of style—a style of programming encouraged by Microsoft.

The class **CWinVerMFC** overrides the member function, **InitInstance()** of **CWinApp**. You will find that overriding member functions occurs frequently. By overriding **InitInstance()**, you can customize the initialization and execution of the application. In **CWinApp**, it is also possible to override **InitApplication()**, **ExitInstance()**, and **OnIdle()**, but for most applications, this will not be necessary.

Here is an edited portion of the **CWinApp** class description, as found in the afxwin.h header file:

```
class CWinApp : public Cobject
{
  DECLARE_DYNAMIC(CWinApp)
public:
  CWinApp(const char* pszAppName=NULL);
  void SetCurrentHandles();

  const char* m_pszAppName;
  HANDLE m_hInstance;
  HANDLE m_hPrevInstance;
  LPSTR m_lpCmdLine;
  int m_nCmdShow;

  CWnd* m_pMainWnd;

  HCURSOR LoadCursor(LPSTR lpCursorName);
  HCURSOR LoadCursor(WORD nIDCursor);
  HCURSOR LoadStandardCursor(LPSTR lpCursorName);
  HCURSOR LoadOEMCursor(WORD nIDCursor);

  HICON LoadIcon(LPSTR lpIconName);
  HICON LoadIcon(WORD nIDIcon);
  HICON LoadStandardIcon(LPSTR lpIconName);
  HICON LoadOEMIcon(WORD nIDIcon);
```

```
      BOOL PumpMessage();

      virtual BOOL InitApplication();
      virtual BOOL InitInstance();

       virtual int Run();

      virtual BOOL PreTranslateMessage(MSG* pMsg);
      virtual BOOL OnIdle(LONG lCount);
      virtual int ExitInstance();

protected:
      MSG m_msgCur;
};
```

The **CWinApp** class is responsible for establishing and implementing the Windows message loop. This action alone eliminates many lines of repetitive code.

As you continue examining the WinVerMFC.h header file, notice that **CMainWnd** contains a function declaration, **OnPaint()**, and a message map. For member functions such as **OnPaint()**, the **afx_msg** keyword is used instead of **virtual**. **OnPaint()** is a member function of the **CFrameWnd** class that the **CMainWnd** class overrides. This allows the client area of the window to be altered. The **OnPaint()** function is automatically called when a WM_PAINT message is sent to a **CMainWnd** object.

DECLARE_MESSAGE_MAP is used in virtually all object-oriented MFC Windows applications. This permits class overrides when handling certain messages. (See the body of the source code.) The MFC makes use of message maps, instead of virtual functions, because they are more space-efficient.

THE WinVerMFC.CPP APPLICATION FILE • The C++ source code file is straightforward. Examine the complete WinVerMFC.cpp file, which follows, and notice the length of the code listing.

```
//
//  WinVerMFC.cpp
//  A 32-bit application for Windows 95 or Windows NT.
//  This application illustrates the newer
//  object-oriented approach for designing
//  Windows 95 and/or Windows NT applications.
//  The program determines if your operating system is
//  Windows 95 or Windows NT.
//  Copyright (c) 1999 William H. Murray and Chris H. Pappas
//

#include <afxwin.h>
#include "WinVerMFC.h"

CWinVerMFCApp theApp;
```

```
CMainWnd::CMainWnd()
{
  Create(NULL,"Windows 95 or Windows NT?",
         WS_OVERLAPPEDWINDOW,rectDefault,NULL,NULL);
}

void CMainWnd::OnPaint()
{
  CPaintDC dc(this);

  DWORD dwVersion;
  char szVersion[25];
  int I;

  dwVersion=GetVersion();

  dc.Ellipse(10,10,210,210);
  dc.Ellipse(220,10,540,210);

  for (i=60;i>10;i-=10)
    dc.Rectangle(320-i,380-i,320+i,380+i);

  if (dwVersion < 0x80000000) {
    wsprintf(szVersion,
             "This is Windows NT, Version %u.%u",
             (LOBYTE(LOWORD(dwVersion))),
             (HIBYTE(LOWORD(dwVersion))));
    dc.TextOut(210,240,szVersion,strlen(szVersion));
  } else
    wsprintf(szVersion,
             "This is Windows 95, Version %u.%u",
             (LOBYTE(LOWORD(dwVersion))),
             (HIBYTE(LOWORD(dwVersion))));
    dc.TextOut(210,240,szVersion,strlen(szVersion));
    }
}
BEGIN_MESSAGE_MAP(CMainWnd,CFrameWnd)
  ON_WM_PAINT()
END_MESSAGE_MAP()

BOOL CWinVerMFCApp::InitInstance()
{
  m_pMainWnd=new CMainWnd();
  m_pMainWnd->ShowWindow(m_nCmdShow);
  m_pMainWnd->UpdateWindow();

  return TRUE;
}
```

In the next sections, we'll examine the details concerning the various parts of this source code file.

The afxwin.h *Header File*   The first header file to be included in the source code listing is afxwin.h. The afxwin.h header file provides the entrance to the world of MFC programming. This header file is equivalent to the windows.h header file used by procedure-oriented applications. Like its windows.h counterpart, this header file calls all subsequent header files, including windows.h, as they are needed. Using one header file also aids in creating precompiled header files. Precompiled header files save time when repeated compilation is being done during application development.

Note   You'll see extremely large precompiled header files, files with .pch extensions, after you build an application. They are only useful where subsequent rebuilds will take place.

We recommend that you print a copy of afxwin.h for future reference as you develop applications using the MFC library.

Note   32-bit version of afxwin.h is approximately 100 pages in length.

The CFrameWnd *Class*   The application window, established by the CMain-Wnd class, is defined from the base class, CFrameWnd. Here, the CMainWnd constructor defines the window style:

```
CMainWnd::CMainWnd()
{
   Create(NULL,"Windows 95 or Windows NT?",
          WS_OVERLAPPEDWINDOW,rectDefault,NULL,NULL);
}
```

The constructor for the class, **CMainWnd()**, calls the **Create()** member function to establish initial window parameters. In this application, the window's style and caption are provided as parameters. It is also possible to specify a menu name and an accelerator table with the **Create()** member function.

Here is a small, edited portion of **CFrameWnd**, which is also found in the afxwin.h header file:

```
class CFrameWnd : public Cwnd
{
   DECLARE_DYNAMIC(CFrameWnd)

protected:
   HANDLE m_hAccelTable;

public:
   static const CRect rectDefault;
```

```
CFrameWnd();

BOOL LoadAccelTable(const char FAR* lpAccelTableName);
BOOL Create(const char FAR* lpClassName,
            const char FAR* lpWindowName,
            DWORD dwStyle = WS_OVERLAPPEDWINDOW,
            const RECT& rect = rectDefault,
            const CWnd* pParentWnd = NULL,
            const char FAR* lpMenuName = NULL);
public:
  virtual ~CFrameWnd();
  virtual CFrameWnd* GetParentFrame();
  virtual CFrameWnd* GetChildFrame();

protected:
  virtual BOOL PreTranslateMessage(MSG* pMsg);
};
```

Notice that the first parameter in the **Create()** member function allows a class name to be specified in compliance with the traditional Windows API **RegisterClass()** function. Normally, this will be set to NULL in the applications you develop and a class name will not be required.

Using Member Functions   Recall that the derived CWinVerMFCApp class object overrode the InitInstance() member function. Here is how this application implements InitInstance():

```
BOOL CWinVerMFCApp::InitInstance()
{
  m_pMainWnd=new CMainWnd();
  m_pMainWnd->ShowWindow(m_nCmdShow);
  m_pMainWnd->UpdateWindow();

  return TRUE;
}
```

The **new** operator invokes the constructor **CMainWnd**, discussed in the previous section. The *m_pMainWnd* member variable (*m_* indicates a member variable) holds the location for the application's main window. The member function **ShowWindow()**, is required to display the window on the screen. The parameter *m_nCmdShow* is initialized by the application's constructor. The **UpdateWindow()** member function displays and paints the window being sent to the screen.

The Constructor   The application's constructor is invoked at startup with this piece of code:

```
CWinVerApp theApp;
```

The application code for this example is very simple and straightforward. The application merely establishes a window; it does not permit you to draw anything in the window.

The `OnPaint()` *Message Handler*   The function part of this application results from the inclusion of the `OnPaint()` message handler function. Examine the following portion of source code:

```
void CMainWnd::OnPaint()
{
  CPaintDC dc(this);

  DWORD dwVersion;
  char szVersion[25];
  int I;

  dwVersion=GetVersion();

  dc.Ellipse(10,10,210,210);
  dc.Ellipse(220,10,540,210);

  for (i=60;i>10;i-=10)
    dc.Rectangle(320-i,380-i,320+i,380+i);

if (dwVersion < 0x80000000) {
    wsprintf(szVersion,
            "This is Windows NT, Version %u.%u",
            (LOBYTE(LOWORD(dwVersion))),
            (HIBYTE(LOWORD(dwVersion))));
    dc.TextOut(210,240,szVersion,strlen(szVersion));
  } else {
    wsprintf(szVersion,
            "This is Windows 95, Version %u.%u",
            (LOBYTE(LOWORD(dwVersion))),
            (HIBYTE(LOWORD(dwVersion))));
    dc.TextOut(210,240,szVersion,strlen(szVersion));
  }
}
```

A device context is created for handling `WM_PAINT` messages. Windows GDI functions are encapsulated in the device context in this section. When the **OnPaint()** function ends, the destructor for **CPaintDC** is called automatically.

This application uses a fairly short message map, as the following code indicates:

```
BEGIN_MESSAGE_MAP(CMainWnd,CFrameWnd)
  ON_WM_PAINT()
END_MESSAGE_MAP()
```

Two classes are specified by BEGIN_MESSAGE_MAP: **CMainWnd** and **CFrameWnd**. **CMainWnd** is the target class, and **CFrameWnd** is a class based on **CWnd**. The **ON_WM_PAINT()** function handles all WM_PAINT messages and directs them to the **OnPaint()** member function just discussed. In later chapters, you'll see many additional functions added to the message map.

Remember that one of the biggest advantages of using message maps is the elimination of error-prone switch/case statements. Switch/case statements are a hallmark of procedure-oriented Windows applications.

BUILDING THE WinVerMFC APPLICATION • Enter the source code, WinVerMFC.cpp and the header file code, WinVerMFC.h for this application. Next, create a project workspace named WinVerMFC. When you create the project workspace, make sure that you mark it as an MFC application. This can be done from the compiler's Build menu by selecting the Settings... menu item. When the selection is made, the Project Settings dialog box will appear, as shown in Figure 8.1. From the list box, select the option Use MFC in a Static Library. Otherwise, you will get a series of strange errors when building the executable.

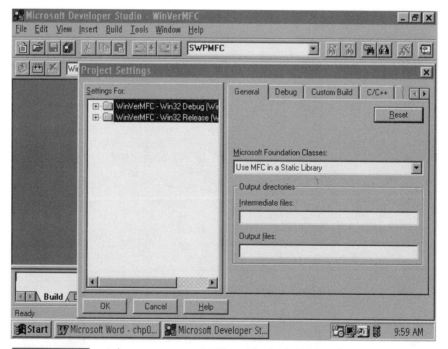

Figure 8.1   *Selecting a static MFC library for the build operation.*

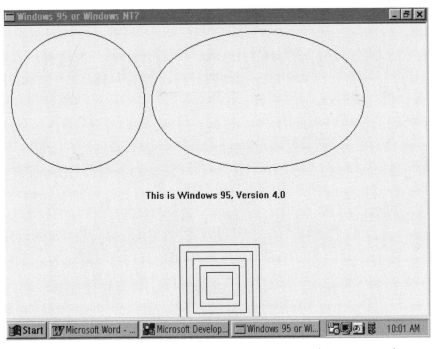

Figure 8.2 *The window created by* `WinVerMFC.cpp` *when running under Windows 95.*

Once you have entered the source and header code and created a project workspace with the proper compiler options set, it is time to build the application. From the compiler's `Build` menu, select the `Rebuild All` menu item. If no errors occur, run the application. Depending on your version of Windows, you should see a screen similar to Figure 8.2.

This 32-bit application can also be run under Windows NT.

FILE SIZES

Remember that the Microsoft Visual C++ compiler is an optimizing compiler. If you check the file sizes in this chapter, you'll find that the object-oriented `WinVerMFC.cpp` version has a debug file size of 932 KB and a release version size of 99 KB.

So, while the source code file lengths are much shorter for equivalent MFC applications, there is a penalty in executable file sizes to be paid when using the MFC library. The questions you must answer are: Does it matter? Is it worth it?

In the following chapters, we'll try to give you sound reasons for adopting the MFC library and the object-oriented approach.

Using the MFC AppWizard

This chapter will introduce you to the use of Microsoft's wizards for Microsoft Foundation Class (MFC) application development. The Microsoft AppWizard is an automatic MFC code generator that generates specific features for an application, all controlled by the programmer. But why is a code generator necessary? To answer that question, this chapter will examine a short history of MFC Windows program development, before the use of code generators, and then make a strong case for their use. The two programming examples in this chapter will illustrate parallel code development with and without the use of the AppWizard.

The first programming example will develop a single source code application whose project workspace is named NoWiz. The second programming example will develop a similar application with the use of the AppWizard. Its project workspace is named YesWiz.

When working with the AppWizard, you might be surprised that the code generator generates several source code files for each application. Do not become alarmed; the source code in YesWiz is essentially the same code used in the NoWiz application. The Microsoft AppWizard breaks application code into functioning units. For example, if an application is named YesWiz, you might find these five files: StdAfx.cpp, YesWiz.cpp, MainFrm.cpp, YesWizDoc.cpp, and YesWizView.cpp. The YesWiz.cpp is the main source code file for the application. The MainFrm.cpp file is used to describe the document interface for the application. The YesWizDoc.cpp file is used to describe the document data. The YesWizView.cpp file is used for viewing objects. The separate source code files are combined, using the linker, into a single executable application. In this example, the executable file would be named YesWiz.exe.

Code Generators

In Chapter 8, you learned how to develop a simple object-oriented Windows application. Since almost every Windows application establishes a basic window in the same manner, this code could be used again and again. When code remains essentially unchanged, it can copied or "boilerplated" from one application to another. Then, any unique code to the current application could be added to make a complete application. If coding is so easy, why is a code generator needed? You'll find that while the question is simple, the answer is multifaceted.

Remembering When...

In 1985, Microsoft released the first version of Windows. Almost as quickly, authors such as Petzold, Murray, and Pappas published procedure-oriented C programming books for Windows. These were the good old days! Programming books concentrated on getting programmers started in the new Windows environment. Programmers needed to know what cursors, icons, scroll bars, menus, dialog boxes, and bitmaps were and how to use them. The developed applications were short and to the point—teaching a few new concepts in each chapter. Early Windows programming books seldom contained program code that exceeded five or six book pages in length. In the good old days, there was no need for code generators.

In the early days, if a programmer saw that a new application would be similar to a previous application, the programmer simply cut and pasted the code from the first application to the next. When code was used in this "boilerplate" fashion, it was being used as a static template, with basically no changes from one application to another. The use of static templates worked well for those early, short, procedure-oriented applications.

A programmer's life, however, was not to remain so easy. Since 1985, users and programmers have learned the language of Windows. Even if you, the programmer, have never implemented the code for a menu or dialog box, you certainly know what they are and how they function within the Windows environment. As Windows hardware and compilers evolved, users and programmers alike wanted more. Life and programming was moving toward the fast lane.

Picking Up the Pace of Life

When hardware and software evolved, Windows evolved with it. From a sleepy 16-bit DOS overlay, we now work in a truly powerful 32-bit multitasking environment under Windows 98 or Windows 2000 (NT). Multitasking capabilities in Windows increased the demand for the ability to connect multiple applications. OLE was introduced as Microsoft's solution for object linking and embedding. The seamless connection was made, but not without a price.

During its evolutionary trip, Windows continued to add new capabilities. Functions for multimedia sound and video, task bars, tool tips, security, OLE, and COM more than tripled the original number of Windows function calls. No evolutionary step made as many changes as the inclusion of OLE, however. Almost overnight, the slope of the Windows learning curve tripled. If you wanted to be a Windows programmer and wanted to write applications across the breadth of capabilities for this environment, then you were faced with a huge task: understanding hundreds of new function calls and how to implement them.

There were a few daring pioneers that actually tackled this task and wrote procedure-oriented OLE applications. But hundreds of hours of work were involved with these projects.

Microsoft quickly saw the problem and went to work on a solution. That solution is the AppWizard and associated ClassWizard, contained in the Visual C++ compiler. The AppWizard is a dynamic code generator that creates MFC object-oriented code templates with a set of customizable features. These features include editing, file and printing capabilities, OLE container and server support, database and so on.

The AppWizard instantly puts you on the MFC Windows interstate highway, doing 70 mph, in the fast lane. No room for procedure-oriented coding here! Buckle up—its the law!

Developing the NoWiz Project

You will learn shortly that Microsoft's AppWizard typically generates five separate object-oriented source code files and five separate header files. The linker then combines these files to produce the executable application.

In the NoWiz project, you will see an application written with a single source code file and single header file. After all, this is the style that most C++ programming books use when developing simple applications. We'll then show you how the Microsoft AppWizard divides a single source code application into five separate source code files. Having seen how this is done, future AppWizard files should be less of a mystery to you.

Remember, the purpose of this section is not to build a specific application or explain application code. This section will illustrate how a single source code file can be broken into five source code components, similar to the technique used by the Microsoft AppWizard to generate project code.

The NoWiz.rc Resource File

The AppWizard generates resource files that describe a variety of Windows resources. These resources can include menus, dialog boxes, keyboard accelerators, and string tables. We have to give you this file, without a lot of description, because it is generated by the Resource Compiler for even the simplest applications. This file will be named NoWiz.rc:

```
//Microsoft Developer Studio generated resource script.
//
#include "resource.h"

#define APSTUDIO_READONLY_SYMBOLS
/////////////////////////////////////////////////////////////////
//
// Generated from the TEXTINCLUDE 2 resource.
//
#include "afxres.h"


/////////////////////////////////////////////////////////////////
#undef APSTUDIO_READONLY_SYMBOLS


/////////////////////////////////////////////////////////////////
// English (U.S.) resources

#if !defined(AFX_RESOURCE_DLL) || defined(AFX_TARG_ENU)
#ifdef _WIN32
LANGUAGE LANG_ENGLISH, SUBLANG_ENGLISH_US
#pragma code_page(1252)
#endif //_WIN32

#ifdef APSTUDIO_INVOKED
/////////////////////////////////////////////////////////////////
//
// TEXTINCLUDE
//

1 TEXTINCLUDE DISCARDABLE
BEGIN
   "resource.h\0"
END

2 TEXTINCLUDE DISCARDABLE
BEGIN
   "#include ""afxres.h""\r\n"
   "\0"
END

3 TEXTINCLUDE DISCARDABLE
BEGIN
```

```
    "#define _AFX_NO_SPLITTER_RESOURCES\r\n"
    "#define _AFX_NO_OLE_RESOURCES\r\n"
    "#define _AFX_NO_TRACKER_RESOURCES\r\n"
    "#define _AFX_NO_PROPERTY_RESOURCES\r\n"
    "\r\n"
    "#if !defined(AFX_RESOURCE_DLL) || defined(AFX_TARG_ENU)\r\n"
    "#ifdef _WIN32\r\n"
    "LANGUAGE 9, 1\r\n"
    "#pragma code_page(1252)\r\n"
    "#endif //_WIN32\r\n"
    "#include ""res\\NoWiz.rc2""  // non-Microsoft resources\r\n"
    "#include ""afxres.rc""        // Standard components\r\n"
    "#endif\r\n"
    "\0"
END


#endif  // APSTUDIO_INVOKED


/////////////////////////////////////////////////////////////
//
// Icon
//

// Icon with lowest ID value—first to ensure application icon
// remains consistent on all systems.
IDR_MAINFRAME  ICON  DISCARDABLE  "res\\NoWiz.ico"
IDR_NOWIZTYPE  ICON  DISCARDABLE  "res\\NoWizDoc.ico"

/////////////////////////////////////////////////////////////
//
// Menu
//

IDR_MAINFRAME MENU PRELOAD DISCARDABLE
BEGIN
  POPUP "&File"
  BEGIN
  MENUITEM "E&xit",       ID_APP_EXIT
  END
  POPUP "&Help"
  BEGIN
  MENUITEM "&About NoWiz...",    ID_APP_ABOUT
  END
END


/////////////////////////////////////////////////////////////
//
// Dialog
```

```
//

IDD_ABOUTBOX DIALOG DISCARDABLE  0, 0, 235, 55
STYLE DS_MODALFRAME | WS_POPUP | WS_CAPTION | WS_SYSMENU
CAPTION "About NoWiz"
FONT 8, "MS Sans Serif"
BEGIN
   ICON    IDR_MAINFRAME,IDC_STATIC,11,17,20,20
   LTEXT   "NoWiz Version 1.0",IDC_STATIC,40,10,119,8,SS_NOPREFIX
   LTEXT   "Copyright (C) 1999",IDC_STATIC,40,25,119,8
   DEFPUSHBUTTON   "OK",IDOK,178,7,50,14,WS_GROUP
END


#ifndef _MAC
/////////////////////////////////////////////////////////////
//
// Version
//

VS_VERSION_INFO VERSIONINFO
 FILEVERSION 1,0,0,1
 PRODUCTVERSION 1,0,0,1
 FILEFLAGSMASK 0x3fL
#ifdef _DEBUG
 FILEFLAGS 0x1L
#else
 FILEFLAGS 0x0L
#endif
 FILEOS 0x4L
 FILETYPE 0x1L
 FILESUBTYPE 0x0L
BEGIN
  BLOCK "StringFileInfo"
  BEGIN
  BLOCK "040904b0"
  BEGIN
   VALUE "Comments", "\0"
   VALUE "CompanyName", "\0"
   VALUE "FileDescription", "NoWiz MFC Application\0"
   VALUE "FileVersion", "1, 0, 0, 1\0"
   VALUE "InternalName", "NoWiz\0"
   VALUE "LegalCopyright", "Copyright (C) 1999\0"
   VALUE "LegalTrademarks", "\0"
   VALUE "OriginalFilename", "NoWiz.EXE\0"
   VALUE "PrivateBuild", "\0"
   VALUE "ProductName", "NoWiz Application\0"
   VALUE "ProductVersion", "1, 0, 0, 1\0"
   VALUE "SpecialBuild", "\0"
  END
```

```
   END
   BLOCK "VarFileInfo"
   BEGIN
   VALUE "Translation", 0x409, 1200
   END
END


#endif  // !_MAC


//////////////////////////////////////////////////////////////
//
// DESIGNINFO
//

#ifdef APSTUDIO_INVOKED
GUIDELINES DESIGNINFO DISCARDABLE
BEGIN
  IDD_ABOUTBOX, DIALOG
  BEGIN
  LEFTMARGIN, 7
  RIGHTMARGIN, 228
  TOPMARGIN, 7
  BOTTOMMARGIN, 48
  END
END
#endif  // APSTUDIO_INVOKED


//////////////////////////////////////////////////////////////
//
// String Table
//

STRINGTABLE PRELOAD DISCARDABLE
BEGIN
  IDR_MAINFRAME   "NoWiz\nNo Wizards Here\nNoWiz\n\n\
                   nNoWiz.Document\nNoWiz Document"
END

STRINGTABLE PRELOAD DISCARDABLE
BEGIN
  AFX_IDS_APP_TITLE  "NoWiz"
  AFX_IDS_IDLEMESSAGE  "Ready"
END

STRINGTABLE DISCARDABLE
BEGIN
  ID_APP_ABOUT    "Display prog info, version & copyright\nAbout"
  ID_APP_EXIT     "Quit the application; save documents\nExit"
```

```
END

STRINGTABLE DISCARDABLE
BEGIN
  AFX_IDS_SCSIZE   "Change the window size"
  AFX_IDS_SCMOVE   "Change the window position"
  AFX_IDS_SCMINIMIZE   "Reduce the window to an icon"
  AFX_IDS_SCMAXIMIZE   "Enlarge the window to full size"
  AFX_IDS_SCNEXTWINDOW   "Switch to the next document window"
  AFX_IDS_SCPREVWINDOW   "Switch to the previous document window"
  AFX_IDS_SCCLOSE    "Close window and save the documents"
END

STRINGTABLE DISCARDABLE
BEGIN
  AFX_IDS_SCRESTORE   "Restore the window to normal size"
  AFX_IDS_SCTASKLIST   "Activate Task List"
END

#endif  // English (U.S.) resources
/////////////////////////////////////////////////////////////


#ifndef APSTUDIO_INVOKED
/////////////////////////////////////////////////////////////
//
// Generated from the TEXTINCLUDE 3 resource.
//
#define _AFX_NO_SPLITTER_RESOURCES
#define _AFX_NO_OLE_RESOURCES
#define _AFX_NO_TRACKER_RESOURCES
#define _AFX_NO_PROPERTY_RESOURCES

#if !defined(AFX_RESOURCE_DLL) || defined(AFX_TARG_ENU)
#ifdef _WIN32
LANGUAGE 9, 1
#pragma code_page(1252)
#endif //_WIN32
#include "res\NoWiz.rc2"   // non-Microsoft edited resources
#include "afxres.rc"       // Standard components
#endif

/////////////////////////////////////////////////////////////
#endif  // not APSTUDIO_INVOKED
```

This is a complicated resource script file. As you glance through the listing, you might be able to pick out the description of the application's menus, dialog boxes, string tables, and accelerators. There will be more on these features in Chapters 10 through 12.

The `NoWiz.h` Header File

The `NoWiz.h` header file contains the class descriptions, similar to the header file used in the previous chapter.

```
// NoWiz.h : main header file for the NOWIZ application
//

#if _MSC_VER > 1000
#pragma once
#endif // _MSC_VER > 1000

#define VC_EXTRALEAN        //Exclude rarely-used stuff
#include "resource.h"
#include <afxwin.h>         // MFC core and standard components
#include <afxext.h>         // MFC extensions

class CMainFrame : public CFrameWnd
{

protected: // create from serialization only
     CMainFrame();
     DECLARE_DYNCREATE(CMainFrame)

// Attributes
public:

// Operations
public:

// Overrides
     // ClassWizard generated virtual function overrides
     //{{AFX_VIRTUAL(CMainFrame)
     virtual BOOL PreCreateWindow(CREATESTRUCT& cs);
     //}}AFX_VIRTUAL

// Implementation
public:
     virtual ~CMainFrame();
#ifdef _DEBUG
     virtual void AssertValid() const;
     virtual void Dump(CDumpContext& dc) const;
#endif

// Generated message map functions
protected:
     //{{AFX_MSG(CMainFrame)
     //}}AFX_MSG
     DECLARE_MESSAGE_MAP()
};
```

```
class CNoWizApp : public CWinApp
{
public:
    CNoWizApp();

// Overrides
    // ClassWizard generated virtual function overrides
    //{{AFX_VIRTUAL(CNoWizApp)

    public:
    virtual BOOL InitInstance();
    //}}AFX_VIRTUAL

// Implementation
    //{{AFX_MSG(CNoWizApp)
    afx_msg void OnAppAbout();
    //}}AFX_MSG
    DECLARE_MESSAGE_MAP()
};

class CNoWizDoc : public Cdocument
{
protected: // create from serialization only
    CNoWizDoc();
    DECLARE_DYNCREATE(CNoWizDoc)

// Attributes
public:

// Operations
public:

// Overrides
    // ClassWizard generated virtual function overrides
    //{{AFX_VIRTUAL(CNoWizDoc)
    public:
    virtual BOOL OnNewDocument();
    virtual void Serialize(CArchive& ar);
    //}}AFX_VIRTUAL

// Implementation
public:

    virtual ~CNoWizDoc();
#ifdef _DEBUG
    virtual void AssertValid() const;
    virtual void Dump(CDumpContext& dc) const;
#endif

protected:
```

```cpp
// Generated message map functions
protected:
    //{{AFX_MSG(CNoWizDoc)
    //}}AFX_MSG
    DECLARE_MESSAGE_MAP()
};

class CNoWizView : public Cview
{
protected: // create from serialization only
    CNoWizView();
    DECLARE_DYNCREATE(CNoWizView)

// Attributes
public:
    CNoWizDoc* GetDocument();
// Operations
public:

// Overrides

    // ClassWizard generated virtual function overrides
    //{{AFX_VIRTUAL(CNoWizView)
    public:
    virtual void OnDraw(CDC* pDC);   //overridden to draw view
    virtual BOOL PreCreateWindow(CREATESTRUCT& cs);
    protected:
    //}}AFX_VIRTUAL

// Implementation
public:
    virtual ~CNoWizView();
#ifdef _DEBUG
    virtual void AssertValid() const;
    virtual void Dump(CDumpContext& dc) const;
#endif

protected:

// Generated message map functions
protected:
    //{{AFX_MSG(CNoWizView)
    //}}AFX_MSG
    DECLARE_MESSAGE_MAP()
};

#ifndef _DEBUG  // debug version in NoWizView.cpp
inline CNoWizDoc* CNoWizView::GetDocument()
   { return (CNoWizDoc*)m_pDocument; }
#endif
```

Remember, the NoWiz.h header file wasn't included in this chapter for you to type in and then build the application. Rather, the file is used to illustrate how Microsoft's AppWizard generates similar code in five separate source code and five separate header files.

The NoWiz.cpp Source Code File

The source code file is similar to the applications you saw in the previous chapter, but perhaps a bit more complicated. The application uses a number of separate classes, such as CNoWizApp, CNoWizDoc, and CNoWizView, that will lend themselves to separate source code files when projects are generated by the AppWizard.

This application will identify whether it is executing under Windows 98 or Windows NT (2000) and give the proper version number.

```
//
// NoWiz.cpp : Source code file.
// Defines the class behaviors for the application.
// by William H. Murray and Chris H. Pappas, Copyright 1999
//

#include "NoWiz.h"

#ifdef _DEBUG
#define new DEBUG_NEW
#undef THIS_FILE
static char THIS_FILE[] = __FILE__;
#endif

IMPLEMENT_DYNCREATE(CMainFrame, CFrameWnd)

BEGIN_MESSAGE_MAP(CMainFrame, CFrameWnd)
    //{{AFX_MSG_MAP(CMainFrame)
    //}}AFX_MSG_MAP
END_MESSAGE_MAP()

CMainFrame::CMainFrame()
{
}

CMainFrame::~CMainFrame()
{
}

BOOL CMainFrame::PreCreateWindow(CREATESTRUCT& cs)
{
    if( !CFrameWnd::PreCreateWindow(cs) )
    return FALSE;
    return TRUE;
```

```
}

#ifdef _DEBUG
void CMainFrame::AssertValid() const
{

    CFrameWnd::AssertValid();
}

void CMainFrame::Dump(CDumpContext& dc) const
{
    CFrameWnd::Dump(dc);
}

#endif //_DEBUG

BEGIN_MESSAGE_MAP(CNoWizApp, CWinApp)
    //{{AFX_MSG_MAP(CNoWizApp)
    ON_COMMAND(ID_APP_ABOUT, OnAppAbout)
    //}}AFX_MSG_MAP
    // Standard file based document commands
END_MESSAGE_MAP()

CNoWizApp::CNoWizApp()
{
}

CNoWizApp theApp;

BOOL CNoWizApp::InitInstance()
{
    // Change registry key where settings are stored.
    SetRegistryKey(_T("Local AppWizard-Generated Applications"));

    LoadStdProfileSettings();  //Load std INI file options
    // Register document templates

    CSingleDocTemplate* pDocTemplate;
    pDocTemplate = new CSingleDocTemplate(
        IDR_MAINFRAME,
        RUNTIME_CLASS(CNoWizDoc),
        RUNTIME_CLASS(CMainFrame), // main SDI frame window
        RUNTIME_CLASS(CNoWizView));
    AddDocTemplate(pDocTemplate);

    // Parse command line for standard shell commands
    CCommandLineInfo cmdInfo;
    ParseCommandLine(cmdInfo);
    // Dispatch commands specified on the command lin
```

```
      if (!ProcessShellCommand(cmdInfo))
            return FALSE;
      m_pMainWnd->ShowWindow(SW_SHOW);
      m_pMainWnd->UpdateWindow();

      return TRUE;
}

class CAboutDlg : public Cdialog
{
public:
      CAboutDlg();

// Dialog Data
      //{{AFX_DATA(CAboutDlg)
      enum { IDD = IDD_ABOUTBOX };
      //}}AFX_DATA

      // ClassWizard generated virtual function overrides
      //{{AFX_VIRTUAL(CAboutDlg)
      protected:
      virtual void DoDataExchange(CDataExchange* pDX);     // DDX/DDV support
      //}}AFX_VIRTUAL

// Implementation
protected:
      //{{AFX_MSG(CAboutDlg)
            // No message handlers
      //}}AFX_MSG
      DECLARE_MESSAGE_MAP()
};

CAboutDlg::CAboutDlg() : CDialog(CAboutDlg::IDD)
{
      //{{AFX_DATA_INIT(CAboutDlg)
      //}}AFX_DATA_INIT
}

void CAboutDlg::DoDataExchange(CDataExchange* pDX)
{
      CDialog::DoDataExchange(pDX);
      //{{AFX_DATA_MAP(CAboutDlg)
      //}}AFX_DATA_MAP
}

BEGIN_MESSAGE_MAP(CAboutDlg, Cdialog)
      //{{AFX_MSG_MAP(CAboutDlg)
            // No message handlers
      //}}AFX_MSG_MAP
```

```
END_MESSAGE_MAP()

// App command to run the dialog
void CNoWizApp::OnAppAbout()
{
     CAboutDlg aboutDlg;

     aboutDlg.DoModal();
}

IMPLEMENT_DYNCREATE(CNoWizDoc, Cdocument)

BEGIN_MESSAGE_MAP(CNoWizDoc, Cdocument)
     //{{AFX_MSG_MAP(CNoWizDoc)
     //}}AFX_MSG_MAP
END_MESSAGE_MAP()

CNoWizDoc::CNoWizDoc()
{
}

CNoWizDoc::~CNoWizDoc()
{
}

BOOL CNoWizDoc::OnNewDocument()
{
     if (!CDocument::OnNewDocument())
          return FALSE;
     return TRUE;
}

void CNoWizDoc::Serialize(CArchive& ar)
{
     if (ar.IsStoring())

{
     }
     else
     {
     }
}

#ifdef _DEBUG
void CNoWizDoc::AssertValid() const
{
     CDocument::AssertValid();
}

void CNoWizDoc::Dump(CDumpContext& dc) const
```

```
{
     CDocument::Dump(dc);
}
#endif //_DEBUG

IMPLEMENT_DYNCREATE(CNoWizView, Cview)

BEGIN_MESSAGE_MAP(CNoWizView, Cview)
     //{{AFX_MSG_MAP(CNoWizView)
     //}}AFX_MSG_MAP
END_MESSAGE_MAP()

CNoWizView::CNoWizView()
{
}

CNoWizView::~CNoWizView()
{
}

BOOL CNoWizView::PreCreateWindow(CREATESTRUCT& cs)
{
     return CView::PreCreateWindow(cs);
}

void CNoWizView::OnDraw(CDC* pDC)
{
     CNoWizDoc* pDoc = GetDocument();
     ASSERT_VALID(pDoc);
     DWORD dwVersion;
     char szVersion[25];
     int I;

     dwVersion=GetVersion();

     pDC->Ellipse(10,10,210,210);
     pDC->Ellipse(220,10,540,210);

     for (i=60;i>10;i-=10)
      pDC->Rectangle(320-i,380-i,320+i,380+i);

     if (dwVersion < 0x80000000) {
       wsprintf(szVersion,
               "This is Windows NT (2000), Version %u.%u",
               (LOBYTE(LOWORD(dwVersion))),
               (HIBYTE(LOWORD(dwVersion)))));
       pDC->TextOut(210,240,szVersion,strlen(szVersion));
     } else {
       wsprintf(szVersion,
               "This is Windows 98, Version %u.%u",
```

```
            (LOBYTE(LOWORD(dwVersion)))),
            (HIBYTE(LOWORD(dwVersion)))));
     pDC->TextOut(210,240,szVersion,strlen(szVersion));
    }

}

#ifdef _DEBUG
void CNoWizView::AssertValid() const
{
     CView::AssertValid();
}

void CNoWizView::Dump(CDumpContext& dc) const
{
     CView::Dump(dc);
}

CNoWizDoc* CNoWizView::GetDocument() // non-debug version is inline
{
     ASSERT(m_pDocument->IsKindOf(RUNTIME_CLASS(CNoWizDoc)));
     return (CNoWizDoc*)m_pDocument;
}
#endif //_DEBUG
```

Our NoWiz project is identical in operation and *almost* identical in actual code to the AppWizard's generated project named YesWiz. The YesWiz application will be examined and explained in the remainder of this chapter.

Developing the YesWiz Project

In the previous section, we developed a single source code and single header file project named NoWiz. This project was crafted so that it could be easily divided into five source code files and five header files. This is exactly the way the AppWizard will generate the YesWiz project.

Confession: *Actually, we reverse-engineered the NoWiz project from information we gained from the YesWiz project discussed in this section.*

In the next section, we'll generate the YesWiz project by using the AppWizard. You're going to see portions of code that are very similar to the NoWiz.cpp source code file.

Now that you know how it's done, get ready to *write* a project without ever actually writing one single line of code! What is even better is that when you are ready to develop OLE projects, you'll have access to over 20,000 lines of OLE code. Just remember, by using the AppWizard, it's code that you'll never have to write.

Working with the AppWizard

In this section, we'll take you step-by-step through the application creation process using the AppWizard. You will learn all of the steps necessary to create a simple application named `YesWiz`. In the first section, we'll discuss the six common steps that will take you through the development of code with the AppWizard. For this application, you will find that it won't even be necessary to use the ClassWizard, as all important classes will be provided by the AppWizard.

Start your Visual C++ compiler and follow along as we create the `YesWiz` project using this simple step-by-step approach.

THE APPWIZARD'S EASY STEPS

To create a new project and workspace, select the `File` menu and then the `New` menu item from the menu list given by the Visual C++ compiler (Figure 9.1). When this selection is made, a dialog box will appear that allows you to select a new project workspace, as shown in Figure 9.2.

The `New Project` dialog box will allow you to select the project type, name the project, set the project's platform, and pick a location where the

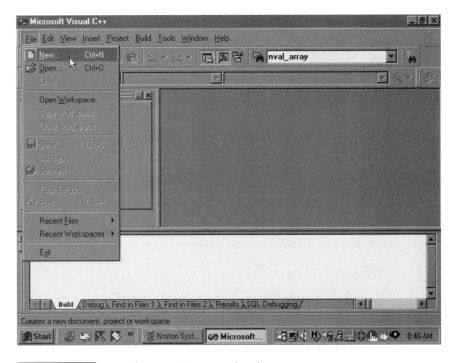

Figure 9.1   *Use the `File` Menu to select the `New` menu item.*

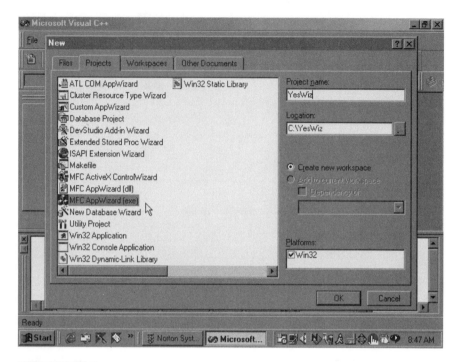

Figure 9.2 *Use the* New Project *dialog box to set project options.*

project is to be built. Figure 9.2 shows the YesWiz project and other perti-nent information. Notice that the MFC AppWizard (exe) option was chosen as the project's type.

The first step in generating a project with the AppWizard involves making a decision on how the project will handle single, multiple, or dialog-based doc-uments. For this example, a Single document interface is selected, as shown in Figure 9.3. Use the Next button to continue to the next step.

The second step is used only when database support is to be included. In this case, None is selected, as shown in Figure 9.4. Use the Next button to continue.

The third step allows the developer to specify the type of OLE docu-ment and OLE support. In this example, None is selected, as shown in Figure 9.5. Use the Next button to continue.

The fourth step allows the programmer the opportunity to add special features to the project. For example, a toolbox or status bar could be added at this point. In the example, however, no special features are added, as shown in Figure 9.6. Use the Next button to continue.

Additional features can be selected in the fifth step. For example, we'll request that no comments be generated for the source file and that a static

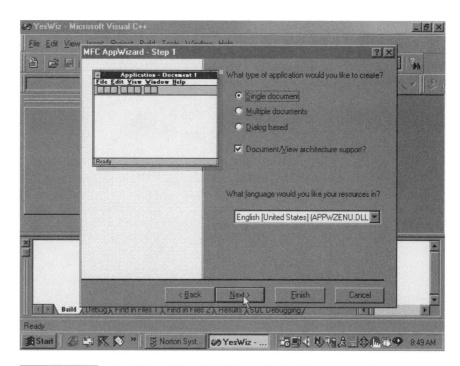

Figure 9.3　　AppWizard Step #1: Select a Single document interface.

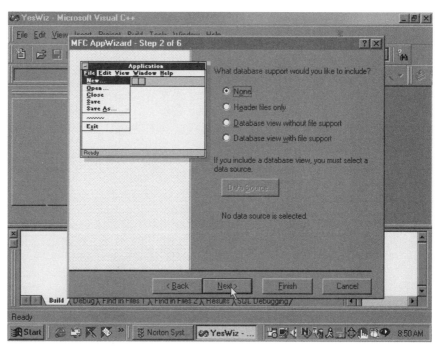

Figure 9.4　　AppWizard Step #2: Selecting no database support.

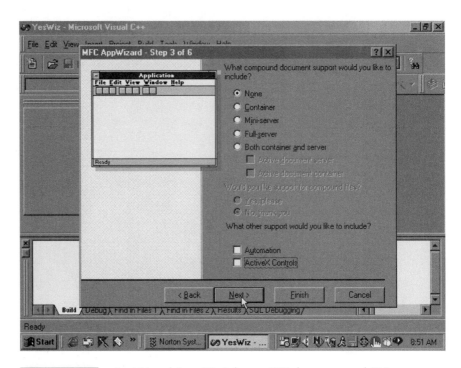

Figure 9.5   *AppWizard Step #3: Selecting OLE documents and OLE support.*

MFC library be used. Figure 9.7 illustrates these selections. Use the Next button to continue.

The sixth step lists the new classes that the AppWizard will automatically generate. These are shown in Figure 9.8. Use the Finish button to complete the wizard.

The four classes that will be created for this application include: CYesWizApp, CMainFrame, CYesWizDoc and CYesWizView.

If you select CYesWizView in the list box, the Base Class list box will expand to allow your class, CYesWizView, to be derived from the CEditView, CFormView, CScrollView, or CView base classes.

The CView class, derived from the CWnd class, is used to create the base for user-defined view classes. Views serve as a buffer between the document and the user and are actually children of frame windows. Views produce an image of the document (screen, printer, etc.) and use input (keyboard, mouse, etc.) as operations on the document.

Two other classes, just mentioned, are derived from the CView base class. They are CFormView and CEditView. CFormView describes a scrollable view. This view is based upon a dialog template resource and includes dialog box controls. CEditView describes a simple text editor.

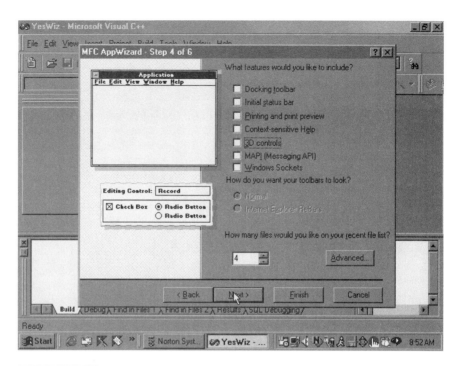

Figure 9.6 AppWizard Step #4: Selecting application features.

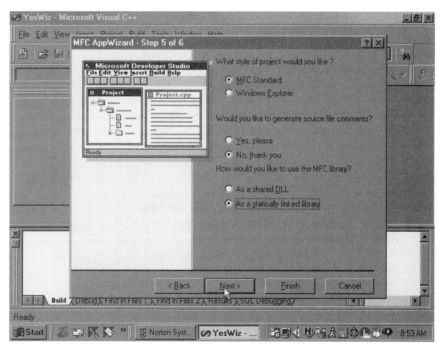

Figure 9.7 AppWizard Step #5: Selecting additional features for the project.

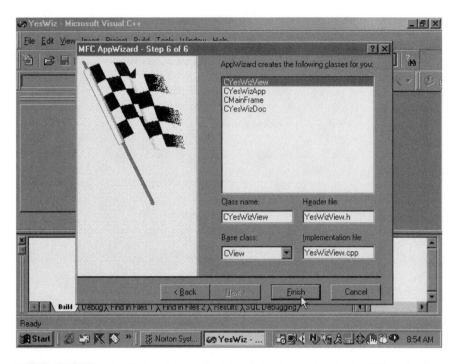

AppWizard Step #6: A list of the classes that the AppWizard will generate.

The `YesWiz` application, however, will use `CView` as the base class. As a matter of fact, all of the default classes shown in the `Classes` dialog box are acceptable. Just click the Finish button to generate the base project code. Figure 9.9 shows a list of source and header files generated by the AppWizard.

Note that there is a matching header file in the list for each source code file. We'll investigate the contents of these files shortly.

BUILDING THE APPLICATION

The AppWizard code is now complete enough to actually create and place a window on the screen.

Select the `Rebuild All` menu item from the compiler's `Build` menu, as shown in Figure 9.10.

During the build operation, details of the compile and link operations are displayed on the screen. Notice, in particular, that five source code files will be compiled then linked: `StdAfx.cpp`, `YesWiz.cpp`, `MainFrm.cpp`, `YesWizDoc.cpp`, and `YesWizView.cpp`. These files represent only a small portion of the total number of files involved with this project. When the build process is complete, examine the sub-directory where these files are stored.

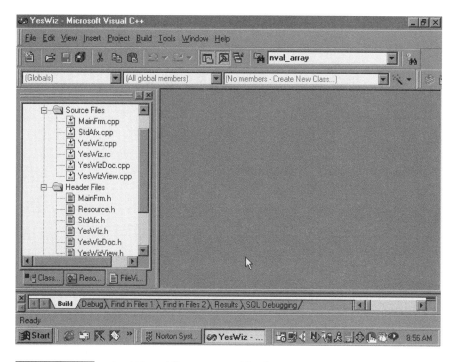

Figure 9.9   *AppWizard files generated for the YesWiz project.*

You will find over 35 files stored in the sub-directory. Obviously, there is a price to be paid for this automation.

One of the files present, in the previously mentioned sub-directory, is the executable file for the project. For this example, the executable file should be named YesWiz.exe, and it will probably be found in the project's Debug sub-directory. Run the application from within the Visual C++ compiler. You should see a screen similar to Figure 9.11.

In the next section, we'll investigate how the AppWizard's code actually works and show you how to add a little code to the application to make it useful.

Understanding the AppWizard's Code

The AppWizard generated five important C++ files for the YesWiz project: StdAfx.cpp, YesWiz.cpp, MainFrm.cpp, YesWizDoc.cpp, and YesWiz-View.cpp. Each of these C++ files has an associated header file: StdAfx.h, YesWiz.h, MainFrm.h, YesWizDoc.h, and YesWizView.h. The header files contain the declarations of the specific classes in each C++ file. The purpose of each important C++ file will be examined in the following sections.

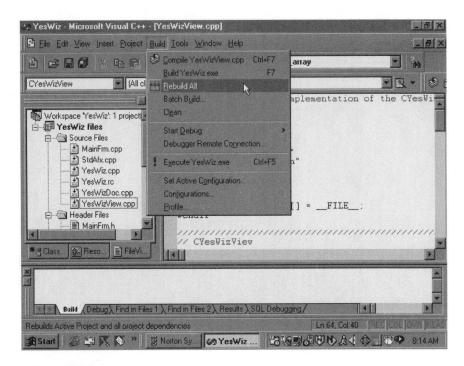

Figure 9.10   *Build the project by selecting the* `Rebuild All` *menu item from the compiler's Build menu.*

THE `STDAFX.CPP` FILE

The `StdAfx.cpp` file is used to include standard information. In this example, it allows access to the `stdafx.h` header file.

```
// stdafx.cpp : source file that includes just the standard includes
// YesWiz.pch will be the pre-compiled header
// stdafx.obj will contain the pre-compiled type information

#include "stdafx.h"
```

Remember that the AppWizard is creating files in a style that can handle much larger projects than our initial `YesWiz` project.

THE `YESWIZ.CPP` FILE

The `YesWiz.cpp` file serves as the main file for the application. It contains the `CYesWizApp` class that is derived from Microsoft's `CWinApp` class.

```
// YesWiz.cpp : Defines the class behaviors for application.
//
```

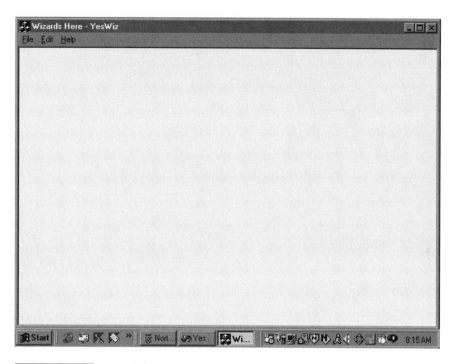

Figure 9.11   *The default window for the YesWiz application.*

```
#include "stdafx.h"
#include "YesWiz.h"

#include "MainFrm.h"
#include "YesWizDoc.h"
#include "YesWizView.h"

#ifdef _DEBUG
#define new DEBUG_NEW
#undef THIS_FILE
static char THIS_FILE[] = __FILE__;
#endif

/////////////////////////////////////////////////////////////
// CYesWizApp

BEGIN_MESSAGE_MAP(CYesWizApp, CWinApp)
    //{{AFX_MSG_MAP(CYesWizApp)
    ON_COMMAND(ID_APP_ABOUT, OnAppAbout)
    //}}AFX_MSG_MAP
```

```
    // Standard file based document commands
    ON_COMMAND(ID_FILE_NEW, CWinApp::OnFileNew)
    ON_COMMAND(ID_FILE_OPEN, CWinApp::OnFileOpen)
END_MESSAGE_MAP()

/////////////////////////////////////////////////////////
// CYesWizApp construction

CYesWizApp::CYesWizApp()
{
}

/////////////////////////////////////////////////////////
// The one and only CYesWizApp object

CYesWizApp theApp;

/////////////////////////////////////////////////////////
// CYesWizApp initialization

BOOL CYesWizApp::InitInstance()
{
    // Standard initialization

    //Change the registry key where settings are stored.
    SetRegistryKey(_T("Local AppWizard-Generated Applications"));

    LoadStdProfileSettings();  // Load standard INI file options

    // Register document templates

    CSingleDocTemplate* pDocTemplate;
    pDocTemplate = new CSingleDocTemplate(
        IDR_MAINFRAME,
        RUNTIME_CLASS(CYesWizDoc),
        RUNTIME_CLASS(CMainFrame),          // main SDI frame window
        RUNTIME_CLASS(CYesWizView));
    AddDocTemplate(pDocTemplate);

    // Parse command line for standard shell commands
    CCommandLineInfo cmdInfo;
    ParseCommandLine(cmdInfo);

    // Dispatch commands specified on the command line
    if (!ProcessShellCommand(cmdInfo))
        return FALSE;
    m_pMainWnd->ShowWindow(SW_SHOW);
    m_pMainWnd->UpdateWindow();
```

```
      return TRUE;
}


//////////////////////////////////////////////////////////////
// CAboutDlg dialog used for App About

class CAboutDlg : public Cdialog
{
public:
   CAboutDlg();

// Dialog Data
   //{{AFX_DATA(CAboutDlg)
   enum { IDD = IDD_ABOUTBOX };
   //}}AFX_DATA

   // ClassWizard generated virtual function overrides
   //{{AFX_VIRTUAL(CAboutDlg)
   protected:
   virtual void DoDataExchange(CDataExchange* pDX);
   //}}AFX_VIRTUAL

// Implementation
protected:
   //{{AFX_MSG(CAboutDlg)
         // No message handlers
   //}}AFX_MSG
   DECLARE_MESSAGE_MAP()
};

CAboutDlg::CAboutDlg() : CDialog(CAboutDlg::IDD)
{
   //{{AFX_DATA_INIT(CAboutDlg)
   //}}AFX_DATA_INIT
}

void CAboutDlg::DoDataExchange(CDataExchange* pDX)
{
   CDialog::DoDataExchange(pDX);
   //{{AFX_DATA_MAP(CAboutDlg)
   //}}AFX_DATA_MAP
}

BEGIN_MESSAGE_MAP(CAboutDlg, Cdialog)
    //{{AFX_MSG_MAP(CAboutDlg)
         // No message handlers
         //}}AFX_MSG_MAP
END_MESSAGE_MAP()
```

```
// App command to run the dialog
void CYesWizApp::OnAppAbout()
{
    CAboutDlg aboutDlg;
    aboutDlg.DoModal();
}
```

```
///////////////////////////////////////////////////////////////
// CYesWizApp message handlers
```

Our class, CYesWizApp, is derived from Microsoft's CWinApp class. The CWinApp class holds the code that initializes, runs, and terminates the application. CWinApp itself is derived from several other classes:

```
Cobject→
        CCmdtarget→
                CWinThread→
                        CWinApp
```

The message map near the top of the previous listing belongs to the CYesWizApp class. This message map specifically links the ID_APP_ABOUT messages with their member function, OnAppAbout(). When you examine the listing, you will also notice that a constructor, initial instance (InitInstance()), and member function (OnAppAbout()) are implemented. In this portion of code, you will also see the use of a template for single documents. CSingleDocTemplate is responsible for constructing the object.

CSingleDocTemplate is derived from several other classes:

```
CObject→
        CCmdtarget→
                CDocTemplate→
                        CSingleDocTemplate
```

The About dialog box is derived from the CDialog class. CDialog serves as the base class for all dialog boxes. CDialog is derived from several other classes:

```
CObject→
        CCmdtarget→
                CWnd→
                        CDialog
```

The lower portion of code in the previous listing contains a description for a message map, constructor, and member function, CDialog:: DoDataExchange().

This listing contains several placeholders for user entries. Examine the listing once again and find the occurrence of statements such as // No message handlers.

THE MAINFRM.CPP FILE

This file contains the frame class, CMainFrame. This class is derived from Microsoft's CFrameWnd class, and serves as the base class used to control all Single Document Interface (SDI) frame features.

```cpp
// MainFrm.cpp : implementation of the CMainFrame class
//
#include "stdafx.h"
#include "YesWiz.h"

#include "MainFrm.h"

#ifdef _DEBUG
#define new DEBUG_NEW
#undef THIS_FILE
static char THIS_FILE[] = __FILE__;
#endif

/////////////////////////////////////////////////////////////
// CMainFrame

IMPLEMENT_DYNCREATE(CMainFrame, CFrameWnd)

BEGIN_MESSAGE_MAP(CMainFrame, CFrameWnd)
    //{{AFX_MSG_MAP(CMainFrame)
    //}}AFX_MSG_MAP
END_MESSAGE_MAP()

/////////////////////////////////////////////////////////////
// CMainFrame construction/destruction

CMainFrame::CMainFrame()


}

CMainFrame::~CMainFrame()
{
}

BOOL CMainFrame::PreCreateWindow(CREATESTRUCT& cs)
{
   if( !CFrameWnd::PreCreateWindow(cs) )
        return FALSE;
   return TRUE;
}

/////////////////////////////////////////////////////////////
// CMainFrame diagnostics
```

```
#ifdef _DEBUG
void CMainFrame::AssertValid() const
{
    CFrameWnd::AssertValid();
}

void CMainFrame::Dump(CDumpContext& dc) const
{
    CFrameWnd::Dump(dc);
}

#endif //_DEBUG

/////////////////////////////////////////////////////////////////
// CMainFrame message handlers
```

CFrameWnd is derived from several other classes:

```
CObject→
        CCmdtarget→
                    CWnd→
                            CFrameWnd
```

Examine this listing and notice that the message map, constructor, and destructor initially contain no code. Member functions such as Assert-Valid() and Dump() use definitions contained in the parent class. CMainFrame initially contains no message handlers.

THE YESWIZDOC.CPP FILE

The YesWizDoc.cpp file contains the CYesWizDoc class. This class will contain code unique to your application when the application is designed to hold document data. It is also used for file loading and saving. CYesWizDoc is derived from Microsoft's CDocument class. The CDocument class serves as the base class for all application-specific documents.

```
// YesWizDoc.cpp : implementation of the CYesWizDoc class
//

#include "stdafx.h"
#include "YesWiz.h"

#include "YesWizDoc.h"

#ifdef _DEBUG
#define new DEBUG_NEW
#undef THIS_FILE
static char THIS_FILE[] = __FILE__;
#endif

/////////////////////////////////////////////////////////////////
```

```
// CYesWizDoc

IMPLEMENT_DYNCREATE(CYesWizDoc, Cdocument)

BEGIN_MESSAGE_MAP(CYesWizDoc, Cdocument)
    //{{AFX_MSG_MAP(CYesWizDoc)
    //}}AFX_MSG_MAP
END_MESSAGE_MAP()

/////////////////////////////////////////////////////////
// CYesWizDoc construction/destruction

CYesWizDoc::CYesWizDoc()
{
}

CYesWizDoc::~CYesWizDoc()
{
}

BOOL CYesWizDoc::OnNewDocument()
{
    if (!CDocument::OnNewDocument())
         return FALSE;
    return TRUE;
}




/////////////////////////////////////////////////////////
// CYesWizDoc serialization

void CYesWizDoc::Serialize(CArchive& ar)
{
    if (ar.IsStoring())
    {
    }
    else
    {
    }
}

/////////////////////////////////////////////////////////
// CYesWizDoc diagnostics

#ifdef _DEBUG
void CYesWizDoc::AssertValid() const
{
    CDocument::AssertValid();
}
```

```
void CYesWizDoc::Dump(CDumpContext& dc) const
{
    CDocument::Dump(dc);
}
#endif //_DEBUG

/////////////////////////////////////////////////////////////////
// CYesWizDoc commands
```

CDocument is derived from several other classes:

```
CObject→
            CCmdtarget→
                        CDocument
```

As you examine this listing, you will notice once again that the message map, constructor, and destructor contain no code. Several member functions can be used to provide vital document support. For example, OnNewDocument() uses the definition provided by the parent class to create a new document. Serialize() supports persistent objects. This member function is used to aid in file I/O. The member functions AssertValid() and Dump() use definitions contained in the parent class.

THE YESWIZVIEW.CPP FILE

The YesWizView.cpp file provides the view of the document. In this implementation, our CYesWizView class is derived from Microsoft's CView class. CView is derived from several other classes:

```
CObject→
            CCmdtarget→
                        CWnd→
                                CView
```

CView serves as the base, or parent, class for all specific views of the document's data. In other words, CYesWizView objects are used to view CYesWizDoc objects.

```
// YesWizView.cpp : implementation of the CYesWizView class
//

#include "stdafx.h"
#include "YesWiz.h"

#include "YesWizDoc.h"
#include "YesWizView.h"

#ifdef _DEBUG
#define new DEBUG_NEW
#undef THIS_FILE
```

```
static char THIS_FILE[] = __FILE__;
#endif

/////////////////////////////////////////////////////////////////
// CYesWizView

IMPLEMENT_DYNCREATE(CYesWizView, Cview)

BEGIN_MESSAGE_MAP(CYesWizView, Cview)
    //{{AFX_MSG_MAP(CYesWizView)
    //}}AFX_MSG_MAP
END_MESSAGE_MAP()

/////////////////////////////////////////////////////////////////
// CYesWizView construction/destruction

CYesWizView::CYesWizView()
{
}

CYesWizView::~CYesWizView()
{
}

BOOL CYesWizView::PreCreateWindow(CREATESTRUCT& cs)
{
    return CView::PreCreateWindow(cs);
}

/////////////////////////////////////////////////////////////////
// CYesWizView drawing

void CYesWizView::OnDraw(CDC* pDC)
{
    CYesWizDoc* pDoc = GetDocument();
    ASSERT_VALID(pDoc);
}

/////////////////////////////////////////////////////////////////
// CYesWizView diagnostics

#ifdef _DEBUG
void CYesWizView::AssertValid() const
{
    CView::AssertValid();
}
void CYesWizView::Dump(CDumpContext& dc) const
{
    CView::Dump(dc);
}
```

```
CYesWizDoc* CYesWizView::GetDocument() //non-debug ver is inline
{
    ASSERT(m_pDocument->IsKindOf(RUNTIME_CLASS(CYesWizDoc)));
    return (CYesWizDoc*)m_pDocument;
}
#endif //_DEBUG

/////////////////////////////////////////////////////////////////
// CYesWizView message handlers
```

The OnDraw() member function uses the pointer *pDoc* to point to the document. The member functions AssertValid() and Dump() use definitions contained in the parent class.

Normally, the CYesWizView message handler area is empty unless the ClassWizard has been used to add specific message-handling abilities. Simple GDI graphics functions can be inserted in the OnDraw() member function.

DRAWING IN THE CLIENT AREA

The initial file generation using the AppWizard produced an SDI application. The view class was derived from the parent class, CView. The following code, shown in bold font, can now be added to the YesWizView.cpp file, under the OnDraw() member function.

```
void CYesWizView::OnDraw(CDC* pDC)
{
    CYesWizDoc* pDoc = GetDocument();
    ASSERT_VALID(pDoc);

    DWORD dwVersion;
    char szVersion[25];
    int I;

    dwVersion=GetVersion();
    pDC->Ellipse(10,10,210,210);
    pDC->Ellipse(220,10,540,210);
    for (i=60;i>10;i-=10)
      pDC->Rectangle(320-i,380-i,320+i,380+i);

    if (dwVersion < 0x80000000) {
      wsprintf(szVersion,
              "This is Windows NT (2000), Version %u.%u",
              (LOBYTE(LOWORD(dwVersion))),
              (HIBYTE(LOWORD(dwVersion)))));
      pDC->TextOut(210,240,szVersion,strlen(szVersion));
    } else {
      wsprintf(szVersion,
              "This is Windows 98, Version %u.%u",
              (LOBYTE(LOWORD(dwVersion))),
              (HIBYTE(LOWORD(dwVersion)))));
```

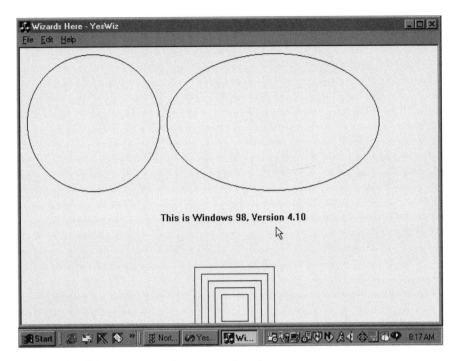

Figure 9.12   *A completed AppWizard application.*

```
    pDC->TextOut(210,240,szVersion,strlen(szVersion));
    }
}
```

Build this application. When executed under Windows 98, a screen similar to Figure 9.12 should appear on your computer.

If you test the various menus provided by the AppWizard, you will note that most are not functional. Why? They are not functional because no additional code was added to handle menu responses. You'll learn more about menus in Chapter 11.

What's the Difference?

Have you taken the time to compare the code in the NoWiz and YesWiz projects? You'll find that the code is very similar, save for the fact that NoWiz contains only one source code file and YesWiz is broken into five source code files.

If you feel that the AppWizard has over-reacted when generating project files, keep two points in mind. First, this project, in itself, is a very simple application. Second, most commercially designed applications have very large source code files that certainly benefit from this type of division.

In Chapters 10 through 12, we'll continue working with relatively small AppWizard projects until you have learned all of the Windows programming fundamentals, such as the use of icons, cursors, bitmaps, fonts, sounds, menus, keyboard accelerators, dialog boxes, and various graphics primitives. By Chapter 13, you will be well-prepared to venture into larger and larger projects involving the STL and MFC.

Windows Resources

In the previous chapter, the AppWizard was used to generate dynamic template code. By adding a minimum of code to this base template, you learned how to create an application that reports the current operating system.

The remainder of this book will be devoted to working with the code developed by the AppWizard and enhanced with the ClassWizard. In later chapters, you'll see the inclusion of the STL with MFC Windows applications.

In this chapter, you will learn how to add important resources to the base code created by the AppWizard. These resources include bitmaps, icons, cursors, fonts, and sound resources. In Chapters 11 and 12 you will learn how to add other types of resources including menus, keyboard accelerators, and dialog boxes. The addition of resources allows you to build professional-quality MFC applications.

Resources involving bitmaps are usually divided into three groups; bitmaps, cursors, and icons. However, bitmaps, cursors, and icons are all basically the same thing; graphics images created or drawn in a graphics editor and saved in a binary format. The advantage of bitmap resources is that they can be snapped to the screen in the shortest possible time. In the following sections, you will learn how to create each of these resources and add them to a simple application. In a later section, you will learn how to use the sound recorder to create your own custom wave (sound) files.

The Microsoft Visual Studio's Bitmap Editors

The Microsoft Visual Studio contains a variety of fully integrated resource editors that can be used within the Visual C++ environment. Bitmaps, cursors, and icons are saved as binary files with unique file extensions. Bitmaps use the .bmp file extension, cursors the .cur file extension, and icons the .ico file extension. These separate resources are included in projects, with other resources, with the inclusion of a resource script file using the .rc file extension. The Microsoft Resource Compiler then compiles the resource script file into a file with an .res file extension and combines this file with the project's code using the linker.

Today it is an easy process to design, create, maintain, and implement all types of resources as a result of integrating these resource editors into the Visual Studio.

The path to creating unique bitmap resources is almost always the same. To add a resource to a project that is already being developed, follow these steps:

- Choose the Insert menu from within the Visual C++ compiler.
- Select the Resource...menu item (see Figure 10.1).
- Choose the resource you wish to add from the list given in the Insert Resource dialog box (see Figure 10.2).

Notice, in Figure 10.2, that the resource list includes accelerators, bitmaps, cursors, dialog boxes, icons, menus, string tables, and other Win-

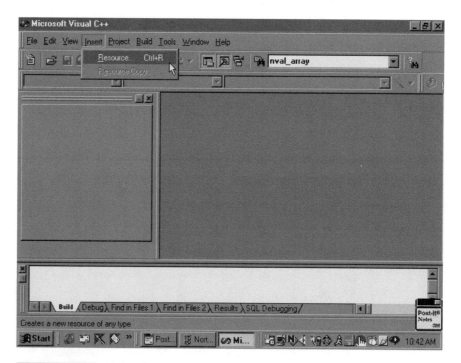

Figure 10.1 *Select the* Resource . . . *menu item in the* Insert *menu to add a new resource to a project.*

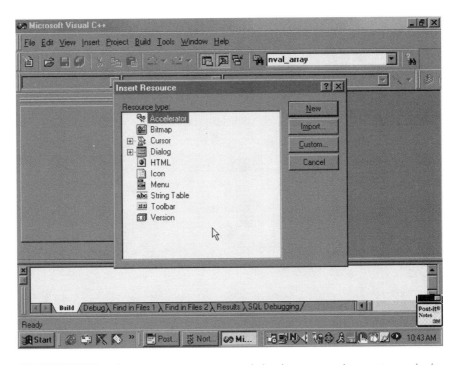

Figure 10.2 *The* Insert Resource *dialog box permits the creation and editing of a variety of Windows resources.*

dows resources. When a particular resource is selected from this list, the correct Visual Studio editor will be opened. Each editor has different design criterion for the resource being developed.

In the following sections, we'll examine the steps necessary to create three different bitmap resources; icons, cursors, and bitmaps.

Icons

Icons are used as small graphical reminders that applications are running or activated in Windows. However, you'll also find icons being used in menus and in the title bars of applications. When they are used in this manner, they convey, in a limited way, information about the application. In earlier versions of Windows, the standard icon measured 32x32 pixels. Starting with Windows 95, applications now use an icon that is 16x16 pixels..

If you follow the steps in the previous section and select an icon from the Insert Resource dialog box, you will enter a bitmap editor for iconic bitmaps. Figure 10.3 shows the initial screen for designing and editing icons.

By default, the drawing size of the iconic bitmap surface is set to 32x32 pixels. Windows will convert 32x32 bitmaps to 16x16 bitmaps when necessary.

Figure 10.3   *Icons are designed and edited in a Visual Studio bitmap editor.*

Notice, in Figure 10.3, a toolbox of drawing tools just to the right of the main drawing area. Likewise, a default palette of 16 colors is provided just under the toolbox. The small iconic symbol toward the left of the drawing area is how the icon will actually appear on the screen.

Figure 10.4 shows a completed icon designed for the PicturePerfect image company. Remember the icon should convey something about the application or product.

By default, the Visual Studio editor selects an ID value for the resource. The ID for this icon is IDI_ICON1. Can you find this ID value in the title bar?

If you are designing Windows 98 or Windows NT (2000) projects, you have two choices when it comes to icon sizes. You can choose to use the default 32x32 icon size, which is now officially called a normal icon, and let Windows automatically shrink it to 16x16 pixels. However, since these results are not always what you might have desired, you might choose instead to create a 16x16 icon in the Visual Studio's editor. The 16x16 icon is now officially called a small icon.

To design a 16x16 icon, open the Visual Studio's iconic editor in the normal manner. Select the size icon, shown in Figure 10.5, to open the New Icon Image dialog box.

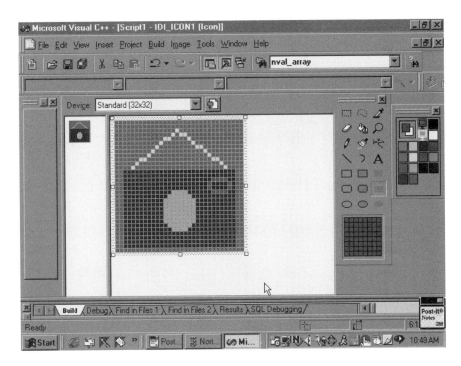

Figure 10.4   *A completed 32x32 iconic resource.*

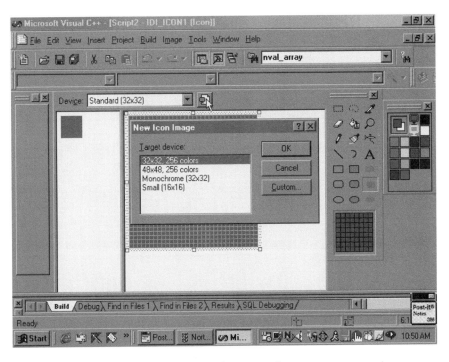

Figure 10.5   *To create a 16x16-pixel icon, use the size icon to open the* New
Icon Image *dialog box.*

251

From the New Icon Image dialog box, select the Custom... button to open the Custom Image dialog box, shown in Figure 10.6.

If you examine Figure 10.7, you will notice that the entire drawing area has been reduced. It's a little hard to create meaningful icons in a 16x16-pixel drawing area, but Figure 10.7 shows a new icon designed for the Sunshine Vacation Company.

That is really all there is to designing icons. If you take time in designing meaningful and colorful icons, your projects will be greatly enhanced.

If you decide that you don't want to use the default ID value assigned to a resource by the editor, the ID value can be changed in the Icon Properties dialog box for the resource, as shown in Figure 10.8.

The Icon Properties dialog box can be brought to the screen by double-clicking on the iconic image by selecting the Edit menu and choosing the Properties...menu item. The example application, developed later in this chapter, will show you how easy it is to include iconic resources in a project.

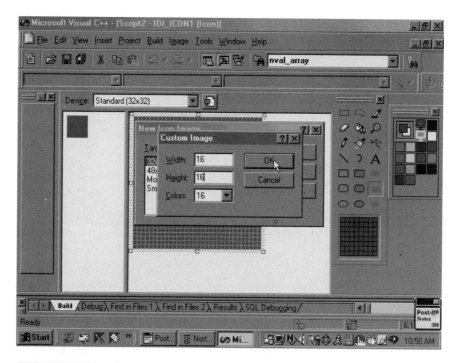

Figure 10.6   *The Customer Image dialog box allows you to set the size of the icon in pixels and the number of colors desired.*

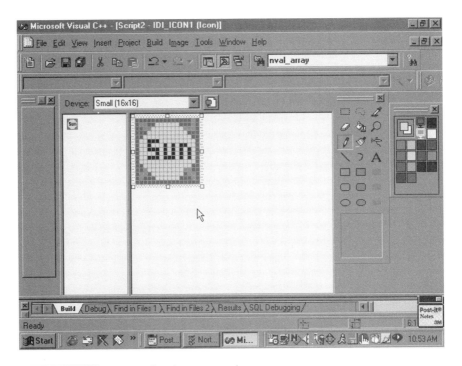

Figure 10.7   *A completed 16x16-pixel icon.*

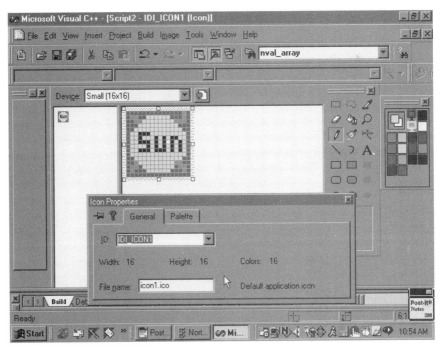

Figure 10.8   *ID values and filenames can be changed for a resource.*

Cursors

Cursors are also small bitmap images that are used as pointers, prompts, and reminders. Windows provides a group of stock cursors that can be selected for use. It is also possible to design custom cursors with the use of the Visual Studio. The stock cursors, also called standard cursors, are defined in the winuser.h header file. Here is a portion of the file showing the standard cursors:

```
/*
 * Standard Cursor Ids
 */
#define IDC_ARROW           MAKEINTRESOURCE(32512)
#define IDC_IBEAM           MAKEINTRESOURCE(32513)
#define IDC_WAIT            MAKEINTRESOURCE(32514)
#define IDC_CROSS           MAKEINTRESOURCE(32515)
#define IDC_UPARROW         MAKEINTRESOURCE(32516)

/* OBSOLETE: use IDC_SIZEALL */
#define IDC_SIZE            MAKEINTRESOURCE(32640)

/* OBSOLETE: use IDC_ARROW */
#define IDC_ICON            MAKEINTRESOURCE(32641)

#define IDC_SIZENWSE        MAKEINTRESOURCE(32642)
#define IDC_SIZENESW        MAKEINTRESOURCE(32643)
#define IDC_SIZEWE          MAKEINTRESOURCE(32644)
#define IDC_SIZENS          MAKEINTRESOURCE(32645)
#define IDC_SIZEALL         MAKEINTRESOURCE(32646)

/* not in win3.1 */
#define IDC_NO              MAKEINTRESOURCE(32648)
#if(WINVER >= 0x0500)
#define IDC_HAND            MAKEINTRESOURCE(32649)
#endif /* WINVER >= 0x0500 */

/* not in win3.1 */
#define IDC_APPSTARTING     MAKEINTRESOURCE(32650)
#if(WINVER >= 0x0400)
#define IDC_HELP            MAKEINTRESOURCE(32651)
#endif /* WINVER >= 0x0400 */
```

To create a new cursor resource, use the Insert menu and select the Resource...menu item as you did for iconic resources. The Insert Resource dialog box allows you to open a Visual Studio editor for cursor bitmaps. Figure 10.9 shows the initial screen for designing and editing cursor resources.

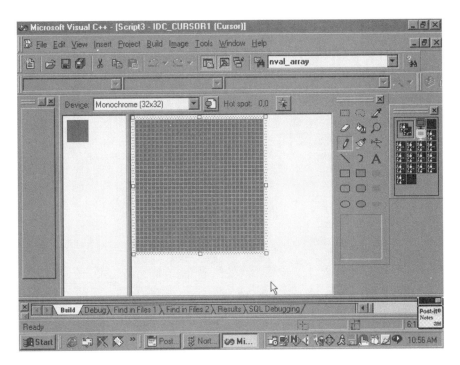

Figure 10.9   *Cursors are designed and edited in a Visual Studio bitmap editor.*

By default, the color and size of the bitmap is set to monochrome color and 32x32 pixels, respectively. The defaults can be changed, just as we did for icons, by selecting the size icon in the editor.

When you examine Figure 10.9, notice a toolbox of drawing tools just to the right of the main drawing area. Likewise, a palette of colors or monochrome patterns is provided just under the toolbox. The small cursor symbol to the left of the design area is how the cursor will actually appear on the screen.

Figure 10.10 shows a completed, colorful cursor designed for the BentArrow Trading Company. Remember, the cursor should be useful as well as unique.

By default, the editor selects an ID value for the resource. The ID for this cursor is IDC_CURSOR1. This value can be changed by using the Cursor Properties dialog box.

By this point, you probably know that good cursor design takes time. Keep in mind that your product's cursor is ever-present as a consumer uses your application.

In the example application that is discussed later in this chapter, you will find that cursor resources are very easy to add to a project.

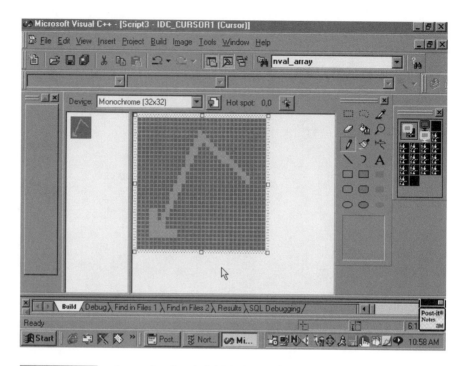

Figure 10.10 *A completed, colorful 32x32 pixel cursor.*

Bitmaps

Bitmaps are resource images that can vary in size from iconic-sized images up to whole screens. Bitmaps can be designed and created in a manner similar to icons and cursors, or they can be created in an entirely different way. For example, the Paint application supplied with Windows allows images to be saved in a bitmap format. Scanners can also be used to scan documents and photographs, or digital cameras can directly save photographs as bitmapped images. In other words, there are numerous sources in addition to the Visual Studio bitmap editor that will allow you to include unique bitmaps in your projects.

If you choose to use the Visual Studio bitmap editor to create a bitmap, just select the bitmap option from the New Resource dialog box as you have done for icons and cursors. Figure 10.11 shows the initial editing window for a new bitmap. It looks similar to the icon and cursor windows, except the drawing area is, by default, larger.

The width and height of the bitmap drawing area can be stretched with the mouse. Figure 10.12 shows a large bitmap being created with the editor. Multiple colors, shapes, and text can be added with this editor.

Notice that the ID value assigned to this resource is IDB_BITMAP1. That default ID name can be changed by using the Bitmap Properties dialog box.

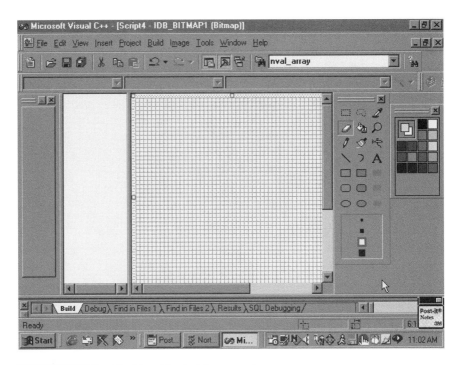

Figure 10.11   The Visual Studio's bitmap editor.

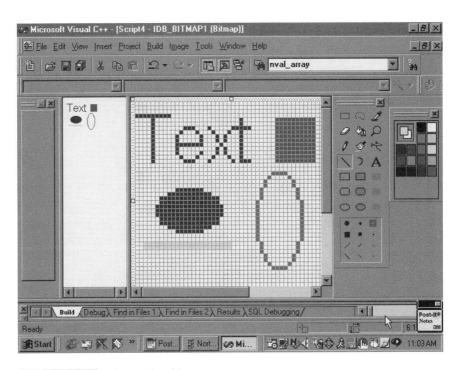

Figure 10.12   A completed bitmap image.

257

New users often have the attitude that there is no limit when it comes to bitmap image sizes. After all, a full screen photograph of Uncle John and Aunt Mildred is what you've always wanted. However, caution is in order. For large bitmaps with many colors, the memory for storing the image becomes enormous.

In our example application developed later in this chapter, a cropped bitmap image supplied by a digital camera will be used to illustrate Windows' ability to incorporate external bitmapped images.

Microsoft's Sound Recorder

A sound recorder is supplied with all versions of Windows. This recorder is most likely the easiest tool you will ever use for creating resources. Most likely, you will find the sound recorded in the `Accessories` group under the `Entertainment` menu item.

Sound resources are saved as wave files with .wav file extensions. To create a sound file, start the sound recorder and select the `File | New` option. Next, click on the record button when you are ready to start. The record button is the right-most button shown in Figure 10.13.

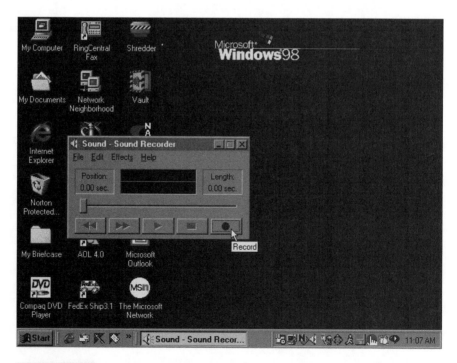

Figure 10.13   *Use the record button to record a wave file sound resource.*

A microphone or other audio device must be connected to your multimedia sound board. Recording is stopped by using the stop button. The stop button is the button with the rectangular image. If the file is what you want, save the file by selecting the `File | Save` option.

You can use the `Edit` or `Effects` menu to respectively shorten or add special effects, like echo, to your recording.

We'll show you how to incorporate sound resources into the project developed later in this chapter.

Fonts

Fonts are probably one of the resources you will change most frequently in your applications. However, unlike icons, cursors, and bitmaps, they are almost never completely designed from scratch. The reason is, of course, the extreme amount of time and patience required to complete a whole family of characters and digits. Unique fonts are available from Microsoft and from other sources such as Corel Draw.

What is a font? A font is a complete set of characters of the same typeface and size, including letters, punctuation marks, and other symbols. Font sizes are measured in points. For example, a 12-point TrueType Courier New font is different from a 10-point TrueType Courier New bold font. A point is the smallest unit of measure used in typography. There are 72 points in an inch.

The following font constants show the various font families. These definitions can be found in the `wingdi.h` header file.

```
/* Font Families */
#define FF_DONTCARE         (0<<4)
#define FF_ROMAN            (1<<4)
#define FF_SWISS            (2<<4)
#define FF_MODERN           (3<<4)
#define FF_SCRIPT           (4<<4)
#define FF_DECORATIVE       (5<<4)
```

Fonts are also supplied with a number of defining constants. To illustrate a portion of these constants, examine the font weight constants in the following partial listing. All of the various font constants can be found in the `wingdi.h` header file.

```
/* Font Weights */
#define FW_DONTCARE         0
#define FW_THIN             100
#define FW_EXTRALIGHT       200
#define FW_LIGHT            300
#define FW_NORMAL           400
```

```
#define FW_MEDIUM           500
#define FW_SEMIBOLD         600
#define FW_BOLD             700
#define FW_EXTRABOLD        800
#define FW_HEAVY            900

#define FW_ULTRALIGHT       FW_EXTRALIGHT
#define FW_REGULAR          FW_NORMAL
#define FW_DEMIBOLD         FW_SEMIBOLD
#define FW_ULTRABOLD        FW_EXTRABOLD
#define FW_BLACK            FW_HEAVY

#define PANOSE_COUNT                10
#define PAN_FAMILYTYPE_INDEX         0
#define PAN_SERIFSTYLE_INDEX         1
#define PAN_WEIGHT_INDEX             2
#define PAN_PROPORTION_INDEX         3
#define PAN_CONTRAST_INDEX           4
#define PAN_STROKEVARIATION_INDEX    5
#define PAN_ARMSTYLE_INDEX           6
#define PAN_LETTERFORM_INDEX         7
#define PAN_MIDLINE_INDEX            8
#define PAN_XHEIGHT_INDEX            9

#define PAN_CULTURE_LATIN            0
```

These constants are used as parameter values for the various font function calls and structures. You'll see these values used throughout the remainder of this book.

The TEXTMETRIC Structure

The TEXTMETRIC structure, used in versions prior to Windows 98 and Windows NT (2000), has been redefined to include new structure types. TEXT-METRIC is now associated with either TEXTMETRICA or TEXTMETRICW. TEXTMETRICW is used in Unicode applications. The NEWTEXTMETRIC structure is associated with NEWTEXTMETRICA or NEWTEXTMETRICW. NEWTEXTMETRICW is used in Unicode applications. You can find all of these structures in wingdi.h. Here is the NEWTEXTMETRICA structure:

```
struct tagNEWTEXTMETRICA
{
  LONG   tmHeight;
  LONG   tmAscent;
  LONG   tmDescent;
  LONG   tmInternalLeading;
  LONG   tmExternalLeading;
  LONG   tmAveCharWidth;
  LONG   tmMaxCharWidth;
```

```
    LONG  tmWeight;
    LONG  tmOverhang;
    LONG  tmDigitizedAspectX;
    LONG  tmDigitizedAspectY;
    BYTE  tmFirstChar;
    BYTE  tmLastChar;
    BYTE  tmDefaultChar;
    BYTE  tmBreakChar;
    BYTE  tmItalic;
    BYTE  tmUnderlined;
    BYTE  tmStruckOut;
    BYTE  tmPitchAndFamily;
    BYTE  tmCharSet;
    DWORD ntmFlags;
    UINT  ntmSizeEM;
    UINT  ntmCellHeight;
    UINT  ntmAvgWidth;
} NEWTEXTMETRICA;
```

The last four structure members are used only by TrueType fonts. If you examine TEXTMETRICA and NEWTEXTMETRICA, you will find that they are very similar.

The LOGFONTA Structure

In addition to the TEXTMETRIC structures just discussed, the LOGFONTA data structure is also frequently used in applications. The use of this structure makes creating logical fonts an easy process. The following is the LOG-FONTA data structure:

```
struct tagLOGFONTA
{
    LONG      lfHeight;
    LONG      lfWidth;
    LONG      lfEscapement;
    LONG      lfOrientation;
    LONG      lfWeight;
    BYTE      lfItalic;
    BYTE      lfUnderline;
    BYTE      lfStrikeOut;
    BYTE      lfCharSet;
    BYTE      lfOutPrecision;
    BYTE      lfClipPrecision;
    BYTE      lfQuality;
    BYTE      lfPitchAndFamily;
    BYTE      lfFaceName[LF_FACESIZE];
} LOGFONTA;
```

The data members of this structure allow various font characteristics to be manipulated. For example, it is possible to specify the boldness of a character or its height and width.

TrueType Fonts

TrueType font technology was introduced in Windows 3.1. TrueType fonts are easy to scale. When a TrueType font of a particular size is created, information is embedded within the font's specification. This information is used to draw the lines and curves of the font. Once the character is drawn, it is converted to a bitmap. The embedded information then aids in scaling the font.

You will find that there are two important font functions; CreatFont() and CreateFontIndirect(). These functions will be discussed in the next two sections of this chapter.

CreateFont()

The CreateFont() function is defined in the wingdi.h header file. The syntax for this function is:

```
CreateFont(Height, Width, Escapement,
           Orientation, Weight, Italic,
           Underline, StrikeOut,
           CharSet, OutputPrecision,
           ClipPrecision, Quality,
           PitchAndFamily, Facename);
```

This font has fourteen parameters. Each time a call is made to Create-Font(), specifications must be provided for each of the fourteen parameters. These parameters are discussed in Table 10.1.

Table 10.1   *CreateFont () Parameters*

Parameter	Use
(int) Height	Desired font height in logical units.
(int) Width	Average font width in logical units.
(int) Escapement	Angle (tenths of a degree) for each line written in the font.
(int) Orientation	Angle (tenths of a degree) for each character's baseline.
(int) Weight	Weight of font (0 to 1000); 400 is normal, 700 is bold.
(byte) Italic	Italic font.
(byte) Underline	Underline font.

Table 10.1	CreateFont () Parameters (Continued)
Parameter	**Use**
(byte) StrikeOut	Strike through font.
(byte) CharSet	Character set (ANSI_CHARSET, DEFAULT_CHARSET, OEM_CHARSET, SYMBOL_CHARSET.
(byte) OutputPrecision	How closely output must match the requested specifications (OUT_CHARACTER _PRECIS, OUT_DEFAULT_PRECIS, OUT_DE-VICE_PRECIS, OUT_RASTER_PRECIS, OUT_STRING_PRECIS, OUT_STROKE_PRECIS, OUT_TT_PRECIS).
(byte) ClipPrecision	How to clip characters outside of clipping range (CLIP_CHARAC-TER_PRECIS, CLIP_DEFAULT_PRECIS, CLIP_ENCAPSULATE, CLIP_LH_ANGLES, CLIP_STROKE_PRECIS, CLIP_MASK, CLIP_TT_AL-WAYS).
(byte) Quality	How carefully logical attributes are mapped to the physical font (DE-FAULT_QUALITY, DRAFT_QUALITY, PROOF_QUALITY.
(byte) PitchAndFamily	Pitch and family of font (DEFAULT_PITCH, FIXED_PITCH, PROOF_QUALITY, FF_DECORATIVE, FF_DONTCARE, FF_MODERN, FF_ROMAN, FF_SCRIPT, FF_SWISS).
(lpstr) Facename	A string pointing to the name of the desired font's typeface.

The CreateFont() function selects a logical font from the GDI's pool of physical fonts. Once the logical font is created, it can be used by any device including printers.

CreateFontIndirect()

The CreateFontIndirect() function frees the programmer from parameter specifications. This function is used to create or modify logical fonts. The modifications are specified in a LOGFONTA data structure. The programmer only needs to specify the characteristics that are to change. The syntax for this function is:

```
HFONT CreateFontIndirect(lpLogFont)
```

Here, the parameter lpLogFont points to a LOGFONTA data structure.

Manipulating fonts is an easy task when using either the Create-Font() or CreateFontIndirect() functions. The sample application developed in the next section will show you how to add a number of resources to a project, including font resources.

Adding Resources To A Windows Project

In this section, you'll learn how to develop a project named PlusRes with the AppWizard. You'll then learn how to modify the application's base code to include a custom icon, cursor, bitmap, font, and wave (sound) resource.

You'll find that adding these resources is a snap since the AppWizard has done all of the code writing (well, almost all) for us.

Our first task will be to generate a base template for this application. Use the same steps that were explained in the previous chapter, or refer to the next section for an outline of the steps necessary for creating a new MFC project named PlusRes.

Base Code

Use the following steps to complete the base code for the PlusRes project:

- Open the Microsoft C++ compiler.
- Choose the File menu and select the New menu item.
- Select Project Workspace from the New dialog box.
- From the New Project Workspace dialog box:
  - Name the workspace PlusRes.
  - Set the location of the workspace (for example, C:\PlusRes).
  - Select MFC AppWizard (exe) from the list box.
- Step 1—Select a Single document application type.
- Step 2—Select no database support.
- Step 3—Select None for OLE compound document support.
- Step 4—Select no additional features.
- Step 5—Do not select comments. Use a statically linked library.
- Step 6—View your settings and Finish the AppWizard process.

When the final step has been completed, the AppWizard will generate all of the base files needed for the PlusRes project.

Modifications with the ClassWizard

After the AppWizard has generated the base code for the project, we are going to add two member functions to the project.

From the Visual C++ compiler's menu, use the View menu to select the ClassWizard...menu item. This will open the MFC ClassWizard dialog box, as shown in Figure 10.14.

Make sure the Project specification in this dialog box is set to Plus-Res and that the Class Name is set to CPlusResView.

The first member function that we'll add is a member function that will respond to WM_SIZE messages. To do this, scroll down the Messages list box until you encounter WM_SIZE. Using the left mouse button, double click

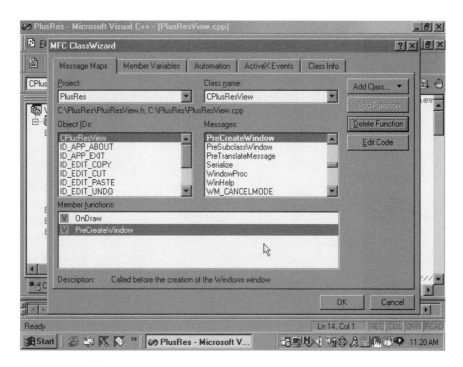

Figure 10.14   *The* `MFC ClassWizard` *dialog box will allow us to add two member functions to the project.*

on `WM_SIZE` to add the member function to the class. The `MFC ClassWizard` dialog box should now take on the appearance of Figure 10.15.

The new member function will appear in the `Member` function list. Code can be added to this member function by selecting the `Edit Code` button. We'll show you the additional code shortly. First, we need to add another member function.

Repeat the procedure for adding a new member function, but this time select `Create` from the `Messages` list box. Double clicking the left mouse button on `Create` will add the member function to the `Member` function list, as shown in Figure 10.16.

We'll show you the code for each of these member functions in the next section.

The AppWizard Files

The AppWizard generates numerous source code files, including `PlusRes.cpp`, `PlusResDoc.cpp`, `MainFrame.cpp`, `StdAfx.cpp`, and `PlusResView.cpp`. Also generated are the associated header files and a resource script file. Of all the base code files, only `PlusResView.cpp` needs to be altered to include

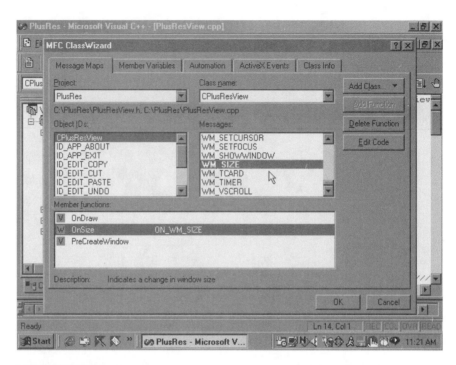

Figure 10.15   The MFC ClassWizard *dialog box after a member function to handle* WM_SIZE *messages has been added.*

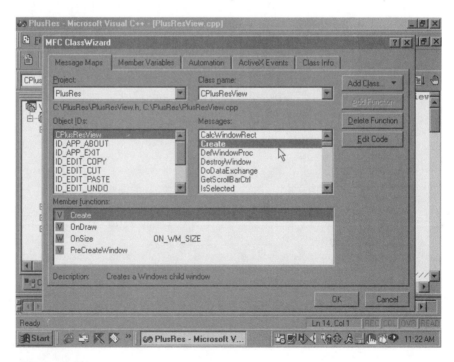

Figure 10.16   The MFC ClassWizard *dialog box after the* Create *member function has been added.*

our icon, cursor, bitmap, sound, and font resources. Here is the complete listing for the `PlusResView.cpp` file. The bolded lines are lines that we added
to the base code generated by the AppWizard.

```cpp
// PlusResView.cpp : implementation of the CPlusResView class
//

#include "stdafx.h"
#include "PlusRes.h"

#include "PlusResDoc.h"
#include "PlusResView.h"

#include <mmsystem.h>
static char szWave[]= "res\\MyWav.wav";

#ifdef _DEBUG
#define new DEBUG_NEW
#undef THIS_FILE
static char THIS_FILE[] = __FILE__;
#endif

/////////////////////////////////////////////////////////////////
// CPlusResView

IMPLEMENT_DYNCREATE(CPlusResView, Cview)

BEGIN_MESSAGE_MAP(CPlusResView, Cview)
  //{{AFX_MSG_MAP(CPlusResView)
  ON_WM_SIZE()
  //}}AFX_MSG_MAP
END_MESSAGE_MAP()

/////////////////////////////////////////////////////////////////
// CPlusResView construction/destruction

CPlusResView::CPlusResView()
{
}

CPlusResView::~CPlusResView()
{
}

BOOL CPlusResView::PreCreateWindow(CREATESTRUCT& cs)
{
  return CView::PreCreateWindow(cs);
}

/////////////////////////////////////////////////////////////////
```

```
// CPlusResView drawing

void CPlusResView::OnDraw(CDC* pDC)
{
  CPlusResDoc* pDoc = GetDocument();
  ASSERT_VALID(pDoc);

  BITMAP bm;

  CBitmap m_bitmap;
  CFont newfont;
  CFont* oldfont;

  m_bitmap.LoadBitmap(IDB_BITMAP1);
  m_bitmap.GetObject(sizeof(bm),&bm);

  CDC dcMem;
  if (!dcMem.CreateCompatibleDC(pDC))
    return;
  CBitmap* pBitmapOld = dcMem.SelectObject(&m_bitmap);
  if (pBitmapOld == NULL)
    return;

  pDC->BitBlt(0,0,bm.bmWidth,bm.bmHeight,&dcMem,0,0,SRCCOPY);
  pDC->StretchBlt(bm.bmWidth,bm.bmHeight,2*bm.bmWidth,
                  2*bm.bmHeight,&dcMem,0,0,bm.bmWidth,
                  bm.bmHeight,SRCCOPY);

  dcMem.SelectObject(pBitmapOld);

  newfont.CreateFont(20,20,0,0,FW_BOLD,
                     FALSE,FALSE,FALSE,0,
                     OUT_DEFAULT_PRECIS,
                     CLIP_DEFAULT_PRECIS,
                     DEFAULT_QUALITY,
                     34,"Arial");
  oldfont=pDC->SelectObject(&newfont);
  pDC->TextOut(170,90,"Fly to new heights",18);
}

////////////////////////////////////////////////////////////
// CPlusResView diagnostics

#ifdef _DEBUG
void CPlusResView::AssertValid() const
{
  CView::AssertValid();
}

void CPlusResView::Dump(CDumpContext& dc) const
```

```
{
  CView::Dump(dc);
}

CPlusResDoc* CPlusResView::GetDocument() //non-debug ver inline
{
  ASSERT(m_pDocument->IsKindOf(RUNTIME_CLASS(CPlusResDoc)));
  return (CPlusResDoc*)m_pDocument;
}
#endif //_DEBUG

/////////////////////////////////////////////////////////////////
// CPlusResView message handlers

void CPlusResView::OnSize(UINT nType, int cx, int cy)
{
  CView::OnSize(nType, cx, cy);

  // TODO: Add your message handler code here

  // Play a wave file when window is resized
  sndPlaySound(szWave,SND_ASYNC);
}

BOOL CPlusResView::Create(LPCTSTR lpszClassName,
                          LPCTSTR lpszWindowName,
                          DWORD dwStyle, const RECT& rect,
                          CWnd* pParentWnd, UINT nID,
                          CCreateContext* pContext)
{
  // TODO: Add specialized code here and/or call base class

  lpszClassName = AfxRegisterWndClass(CS_HREDRAW|CS_VREDRAW,
                    LoadCursor(AfxGetInstanceHandle(),
                    MAKEINTRESOURCE(IDC_CURSOR1)),
                    (HBRUSH) CreateSolidBrush(RGB(0,255,255)),
                    NULL);

  return CWnd::Create(lpszClassName, lpszWindowName, dwStyle,
                      rect, pParentWnd, nID, pContext);
}
```

In the following sections, we will examine the specific code that was added for each resource.

ADDING AN ICON

An icon resource was created using the icon resource editor provided by the Visual Studio and discussed earlier in the chapter. Figure 10.17 shows this application's icon during design.

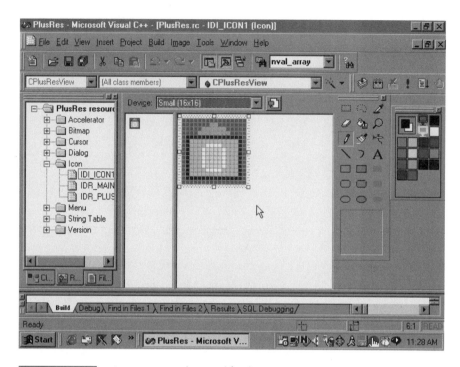

Figure 10.17   *A new icon is designed for the* PlusRes *project.*

Since the AppWizard's base code already supplies a default icon, no additional code is needed to incorporate a custom icon. When you leave the resource editor, save the icon resource file as icon1.ico in the PlusRes\Res subdirectory.

Now, edit the following line in the PlusRes.rc resource script file so that it points to the new icon:

```
IDR_MAINFAME ICON DISCARDABLE "res\icon1.ico"
```

Hint

Open the PlusRes.rc file by using the compiler's File menu, selecting the PlusRes.rc file, and specifying that the file be opened as a text file.

When the application is built, the new icon will be used instead of the icon provided by the AppWizard.

ADDING SOUND

To include a sound resource, the mmsystem.h header file must be included at the start of the PlusResView.cpp file. The sound resource is identified in a character string, *szWave[]*, as MyWav.wav. Find these lines in the program source code just given:

```
#include <mmsystem.h>
static char szWave[]= "MyWav.wav";
```

Sound resources can be played with just a call to the sndPlaySound() function. To use this function, simply specify the wave source and SND_ASYNC or SND_SYNC. If SND_ASYNC is specified, the program will continue as the sound resource is played. If SND_SYNC is specified, the application will halt until the sound is completed.

We added the following code to the WM_SIZE member function so that a sound would play anytime the window was resized. Can you find these lines of code in the program listing shown earlier?

```
// Play a wave file when window is resized
  sndPlaySound(szWave,SND_ASYNC);
```

Now there is just one tiny catch at this point. When you are ready to build the application, the winmm.lib must be specified for the linker, as shown in Figure 10.18.

Now a sound resource, added to this project, will sound each time the screen is resized.

ADDING A BITMAP

The bitmap resource for this project could be retrieved from a digital camera or scanned from a photograph. This image, seagull43.bmp, is added as a resource to the project and given the ID value IDB_BITMAP1. This is an image of a seagull soaring in the air. In the PlusRes.rc resource script file, you'll want to make sure the following line of code appears:

```
IDB_BITMAP1 BITMAP "seagull42.bmp"
```

Then be sure to include the bitmap resource file in the PlusRes subdirectory.

The code for actually loading the bitmap is just a little more complicated. Here is that portion of code:

```
BITMAP bm;

  CBitmap m_bitmap;
```

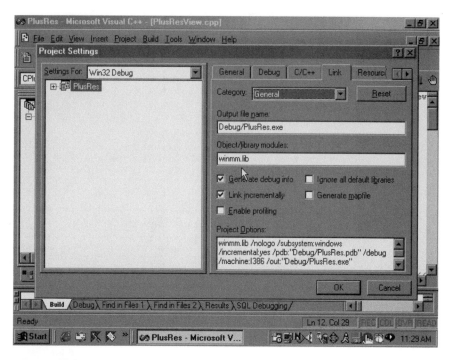

Figure 10.18   *Specify* `winmm.lib` *for the linker if multimedia resources are included with the project.*

```
m_bitmap.LoadBitmap(IDB_BITMAP1);
m_bitmap.GetObject(sizeof(bm),&bm);

CDC dcMem;
if (!dcMem.CreateCompatibleDC(pDC))
  return;
CBitmap* pBitmapOld = dcMem.SelectObject(&m_bitmap);
if (pBitmapOld == NULL)
  return;

pDC->BitBlt(0,0,bm.bmWidth,bm.bmHeight,&dcMem,0,0,SRCCOPY);
pDC->StretchBlt(bm.bmWidth,bm.bmHeight,2*bm.bmWidth,
            2*bm.bmHeight,&dcMem,0,0,bm.bmWidth,
            bm.bmHeight,SRCCOPY);

dcMem.SelectObject(pBitmapOld);
```

The `LoadBitmap()` function loads the bitmap resource identified by `IDB_BITMAP1`. When the bitmap is loaded it is attached to the `CBitmap` object. The first parameter specifies the number of bytes to copy into the buffer.

The second parameter is a pointer to a buffer that receives the bitmap information.

The CreateCompatibleDC() function creates a *memory device context* that is compatible with the device given by *pDC*. A memory device context is a block of memory that represents the display surface. Images can be created here and quickly transferred to the device.

The SelectObject() function selects an object into the device context. The BitBlt() and StretchBlt() functions are used to transfer the bitmap image to the screen.

The *pDC* parameter points to the device context where the image will be drawn. The first two parameters in this function specify the start of the bitmap image, while the third and fourth parameters give the width and height of the bitmap image. The *dcMem* parameter is the location where the bitmapped image is stored. The seventh and eighth parameters specify the upper-left coordinates of the source bitmap. The final parameter indicates the raster operation to be performed—in this case, SCRCOPY, which copies the source bitmap to the destination bitmap. You can find additional information on available raster operations with the Microsoft Visual Studio's Help facility.

The StretchBlt() function is similar to the BitBlt() function, but its parameters allow you to stretch a bitmap image to a larger size.

ADDING A FONT

A new font is created using the CreateFont() function, discussed earlier in this chapter.

```
newfont.CreateFont(20,20,0,0,FW_BOLD,
                   FALSE,FALSE,FALSE,0,
                   OUT_DEFAULT_PRECIS,
                   CLIP_DEFAULT_PRECIS,
                   DEFAULT_QUALITY,
                   34,"Arial");
oldfont=pDC->SelectObject(&newfont);
pDC->TextOut(170,90,"Fly to new heights",18);
```

The specifications call for an Arial TrueType font, 20 points by 20 points. The font will be bolded. All other parameters are system defaults.

A text string is drawn to the window with a call to the TextOut() function.

THE Create() member FUNCTION

Recall that the ClassWizard was used to add a Create() member function to the PlusResView.cpp file. The code shown in bold is the code we wrote for this member function.

```
BOOL CPlusResView::Create(LPCTSTR lpszClassName,
                          LPCTSTR lpszWindowName,
                          DWORD dwStyle, const RECT& rect,
                          CWnd* pParentWnd, UINT nID,
                          CCreateContext* pContext)
{
    // TODO: Add specialized code here and/or call base class

    lpszClassName = AfxRegisterWndClass(CS_HREDRAW|CS_VREDRAW,
               LoadCursor(AfxGetInstanceHandle(),
               MAKEINTRESOURCE(IDC_CURSOR1)),
               (HBRUSH) CreateSolidBrush(RGB(0,255,255)),
               NULL);

    return CWnd::Create(lpszClassName, lpszWindowName, dwStyle,
                        rect, pParentWnd, nID, pContext);
}
```

This member function can be used to create a class with a unique cursor, icon, and background color. Here is the syntax for using Afx-RegisterWndClass():

```
LPCTSTR AFXAPI AfxRegisterWndClass(UINT nClassStyle,
                          HCURSOR hCursor = 0,
                          HBRUSH hbrBackground = 0,
                          HICON hIcon = 0 );
```

The *nClassStyle* parameter gives the class style for the window. The *hCursor* parameter gives the handle to the cursor resource. This cursor is used whenever a window of this class is created. The *hbrBackground* gives the handle to the brush that is used to paint the window. The final parameter, *hIcon,* is used to identify the icon resource that will be used when a window is created from this class. The function returns a null-terminated string with the class name.

To add a unique cursor to the project, the PlusRes.rc resource script file should contain the following line of code:

```
IDC_CURSOR1 CURSOR DISCARDABLE "res\cursor1.cur"
```

Figure 10.19 shows the unique cursor designed for the PlusRes project. The CreateSolidBrush() function is used to create a new background brush. Can you tell from the RGB specifications what the background color will be? Recall that the new icon is not specified here, since the App-Wizard provides a default implementation for this resource.

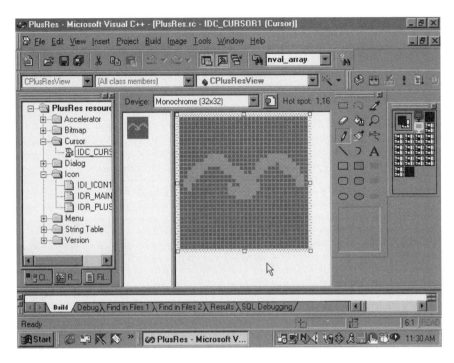

Figure 10.19   *The cursor resource designed for the* `PlusRes` *project.*

CLEANING UP

Before building the application, you'll probably want to clean up a few details. First, the AppWizard provides menus and menu items for `File`, `Edit` and `Help`. Our project will use the `Help` menu to provide access to the `About` dialog box. It will use the `File` menu to provide access to the `Exit` option. The `Edit` menu isn't used, nor are many menu items in the `File` menu. These unused menus and menu items can be removed by opening the menu resource editor provided by the Visual Studio. Simply click on the menu or menu item and use the Delete key.

By default, the title bar of this project will contain the name `untitled` since no documents are being opened. This default can be replaced simply by opening the `String Table` resource, as shown in Figure 10.20.

Doubleclick on the `IDR_MAINFRAME` string to bring up the `String Properties` dialog box. Insert the text `Picture Perfect` in the location shown in Figure 10.21.

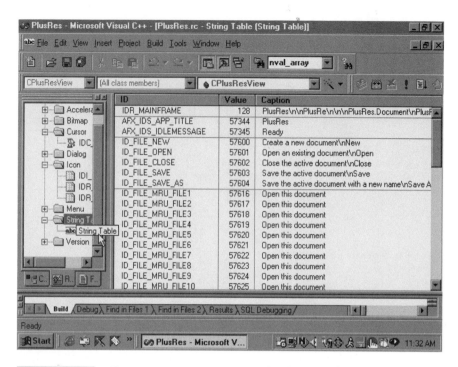

Figure 10.20   The String Table *is opened in the resource editor.*

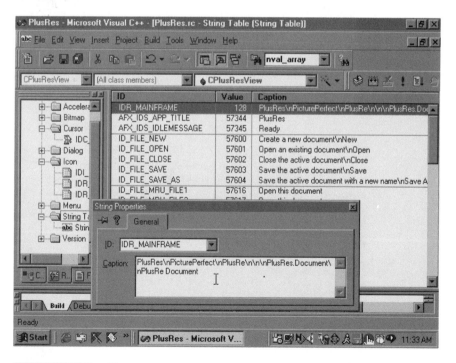

Figure 10.21   *Changing* untitled *to* Picture Perfect *in the project's title bar.*

276

| **Figure 10.22** | *The* `PlusRes` *application showing several unique resources added to the project.* |

That's all of the modifications we need to make. Now it is time to build the project!

Building and Testing the PlusRes Application

Build the `PlusRes` executable file by using the `Build` menu and selecting the `Rebuild All` menu item. When a successful compilation results, execute the application from the `Build` menu by selecting the `Execute PlusRes.exe` menu item.

Your screen should be similar to Figure 10.22.

Figure 10.22 shows the unique icon in the upperleft corner of the screen, a bitmap drawn in the client area, and a unique cursor. You'll probably agree that resources can make an application come alive.

Menu and Keyboard Accelerator Resources

In the previous chapter, you learned how to add bitmap resources such as icons, cursors, bitmaps, and fonts to a project. You also learned that adding multimedia sound resources were just as easy to add as bitmap resources. Bitmap resources are easy to add and really enhance the appearance of any project.

Menus and keyboard accelerators are two additional Windows resources that greatly enhance the performance of a project. Menus serve as a gateway for consistent operation from one application to another. By using the menu resource editor provided with the Microsoft Visual Studio, you will create consistent menu designs. Many developers consider menus the most important of all Windows resources.

Simple menus permit a user to point and click on menu items that have been predefined by the programmer. Menu items often allow users to select items such as screen colors, object colors, sizing options, directory listings, and so on. Menu items can also serve as the interface to dialog boxes. Dialog boxes, discussed in Chapter 12, are important resources because they permit the user to communicate interactively with the application. Dialog boxes are used for all types of data entry, including character strings and numeric information. The proper way to access a dialog box is through a menu item. This makes menus even more important!

Menus are used in most of the projects in the remaining chapters of this book, so this chapter will concentrate on presenting one complete menu project. You will learn how to generate a base project with the AppWizard and then how to add a custom menu resource. The example application for this chapter will allow the user to select the color of objects drawn in the client area by selecting a menu item or using a keyboard accelerator.

Menu and Keyboard Accelerators

Before tackling the project for this chapter, it is important to understand menu and keyboard accelerator terms and definitions. You will find that both menus and keyboard accelerators are both easy to create and include in any project.

Menu Fundamentals

Menus typically contain a list of items or names that represent options that the user can select. Menu item selections are made with the mouse or a combination of keyboard keys. Menu items, the list of options that appear when the menu is opened, usually include simple predefined choices. These choices are used to select options or open dialog boxes and bitmaps. When a user selects a menu item, Windows automatically sends a message to the application stating which menu item was selected.

Windows draws and manages menus automatically. This feature allows menus to have a consistent appearance from one application to another. Menus are designed and created with the use of the menu resource editor provided with the Microsoft Visual Studio. Most frequently, new menus are added to the existing menu bar that was created for the project by the App-Wizard. Recall that the AppWizard creates a menu bar when it generates the base code for a project. This menu resource information is saved in a resource script file. Resource script files have `.rc` file extensions. The resource script file is compiled using the resource compiler. The resource compiler is an integral part of the Microsoft Visual Studio. Compiled resource files are combined with the project code by the linker. This combined code is then used to create the final executable file for the project.

Keyboard Accelerator Fundamentals

Keyboard accelerators are used by Windows to provide an alternative method of selecting menu items. As such, they can be used as a "hot-key" method of making menu selections. For example, a menu may allow the user to select between twelve colors that are in turn used to set the brush color for filling closed objects such as ellipses and rectangles. With a menu of this type, the normal approach for selecting a color choice would be to open the menu and select the menu item with the mouse. Keyboard accelerators can be used to speed up this selection process. For example, the function keys (F1 to F12) can be designated as accelerator keys and allow the user to quickly select a color without having to select the menu or menu item at all! A simple click of the F1 through F12 keys would make the color choice automatically, without the need to even open the menu!

When a menu uses keyboard accelerators as an optional selection method, it is usual practice to list them to the right of the menu item.

Basic Project Code

For the project described in this chapter, you will need to generate the basic project code using the AppWizard. Proceed to do this, as you have in Chapters 9 and 10, by naming the project. This project will be named `ColorMenu`. Now, use the following steps to complete the initial project using the AppWizard from within the Microsoft Visual Studio.

- Choose the `File` menu and select the `New` menu item.
- Select `Project Workspace` from the `New` dialog box.
- From the `New Project Workspace` dialog box:
  - Name the workspace `ColorMenu`.
  - Set the location of the workspace (for example, `C:\ColorMenu`)
  - Select `MFC AppWizard (.exe)` from the list box.
- Step 1—Select a `Single` document application type.
- Step 2—Select no database support.
- Step 3—Select `None` for OLE compound document support.
- Step 4—Select no additional project features.
- Step 5—Do not select comments. Select a statically linked library.
- Step 6—View your settings and `Finish` the AppWizard process.
- If the information in the `New Project Information` dialog box is correct, select `OK`.

These are the steps you followed in Chapters 9 and 10. When the final step has been completed, the AppWizard generates all of the basic files needed for the `ColorMenu` project.

If you examine the generated files you should find the following source code files: `MainFrm.cpp`, `ColorMenu.cpp`, `ColorMenuDoc.cpp`, `Color-MenuView.cpp`, and `StdAfx.cpp`. You will also find the associated header files for the above source code files as well as a `resource.h` header file and a `ColorMenu.rc` resource script file.

Creative Designs

In this project, `ColorMenu,` one menu will be used that will permit the user to select a new drawing color. This menu will contain twelve predefined color choices that can be selected directly from the menu or by keyboard accelerators.

A Unique Menu

From the Microsoft Visual Studio, use the `Resource` tab to open the Resource pane. This pane is just to the left of the area where code appears while using the Visual Studio. Double-click on `Resource Files` and select `Menu` from the list of items that appears. Since a menu has already been created by the AppWizard, the ID for this menu should be present. Use `IDR_MAINFRAME` to open the menu, as shown in Figure 11.1.

This project will not use the `Edit` menu or many `File` menu items, so the first step will be to remove the `Edit` menu and `File` menu items not used by the project. Move the mouse over the `Edit` menu, as shown in Figure 11.2, and click on this menu.

Now use the Delete key (`Del` or `Delete`) to cut this menu from the menu bar.

The `File` menu has several menu items that will not be used in this project. Menu items can be removed just like menus. Click the mouse on the `File` menu to open the menu, as shown in Figure 11.3.

Select a menu item by positioning and clicking the mouse. Use the Delete key (`Del` or `Delete`) to remove the menu item from the menu.

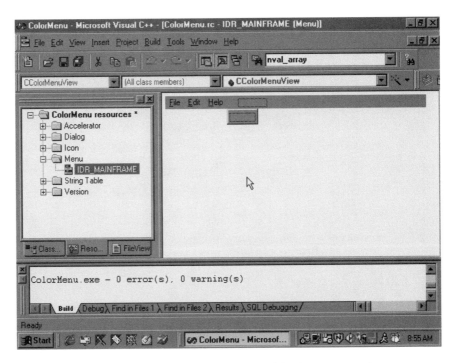

Figure 11.1   *The default menu resource created by the AppWizard.*

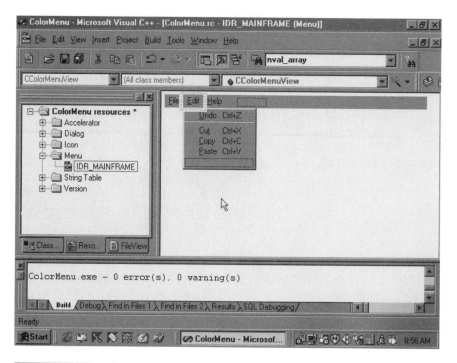

Figure 11.2   *The unused* Edit *menu will be removed from this project.*

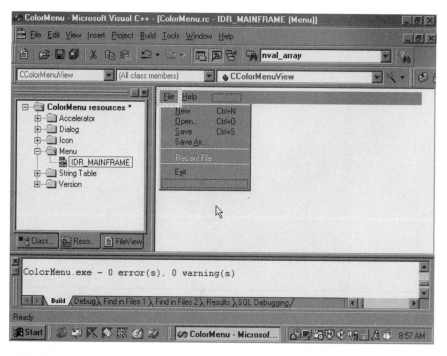

Figure 11.3   *Several menu items will be removed from the* File *menu.*

282

For the `File` menu, remove all menu items except the `Exit` menu item, as shown in Figure 11.4.

To add a new menu to the menu bar, select the outlined rectangular shape on the menu bar, position it where you would like the new menu to appear, and type in the menu name. Figure 11.5 shows a new menu named `Colors`.

When you type in the new menu name, the `Menu Item Properties` dialog box is opened automatically. The ampersand character (&) placed just before a letter will produce an underlined character in the resulting menu. There is no ID value associated with the menu name.

Now, individual menu items can be added to the menu. Figure 11.6 shows the first of twelve menu items.

Each time you select the outlined rectangular shape beneath the menu name, the `Menu Item Properties` dialog box will allow you to enter the menu item caption, ID, and any special features. Notice, in Figure 11.6, that keyboard accelerators will be used with this project. The accelerator key notation is added to the menu caption with `\tF1`. The `\t` represents a Tab key for the menu, and F1 will be the accelerator key corresponding to this selection. The menu item is initially checked, because this will be the default

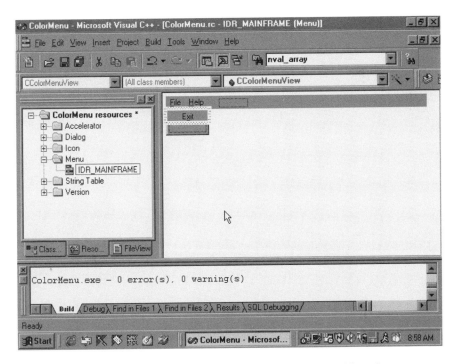

| **Figure 11.4** | *All menu items except* `Exit` *have been removed from the* `File` *menu.* |

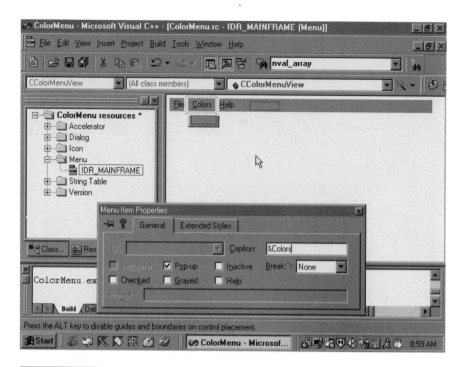

Figure 11.5   *A new menu is added to the menu bar.*

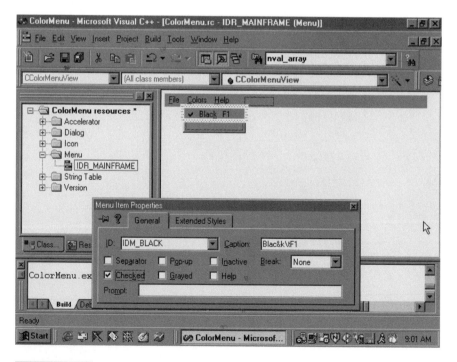

Figure 11.6   *Menu items are added to a new menu by selecting the outlined rectangular shape immediately under the menu name.*

284

color. Note: No other menu items should have the check option set at this point. Menu items traditionally use an ID value starting with `IDM` (for menu). Thus, our first menu color choice has an ID value of `IDM_BLACK`.

Add the remaining eleven menu items so that the `Colors` menu takes on the appearance of Figure 11.7.

The menu design phase is now complete. Now it is time to add the accelerator keys. Remember, the F1..F12 designations shown in the previous menu are only prompts, they are not the implementations of the keyboard accelerators.

Unique Keyboard Accelerators

Keyboard accelerators are also easy to add to a project. Return to the `Resource` pane, select `Resource Files`, and then open the `Accelerator` resource. Since the default project already defines keyboard accelerators, simply use `IDR_MAINFRAME` to edit the default list.

Figure 11.8 shows the default keyboard accelerator list produced by the AppWizard when it generated the base code for this project.

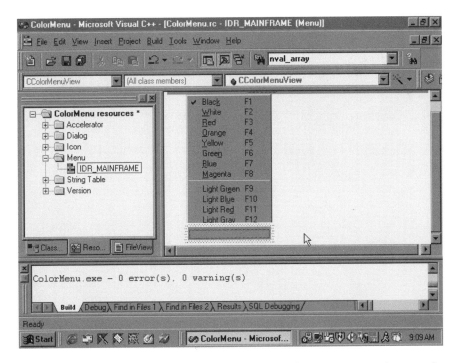

Figure 11.7   *The* `Colors` *menu now contains twelve menu items and prompts for the accelerator keys.*

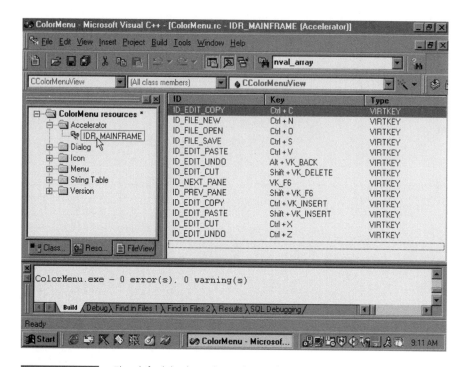

Since most `File` menu items and the `Edit` menu have already been removed, many of these keyboard accelerators are meaningless. Remove them by selecting the item and deleting it with the Delete key (`Del` or `Delete`).

New keyboard accelerators can now be added to the empty list. Figure 11.9 shows the start of a new keyboard accelerator list.

To add a new accelerator key to the list, click on the outlined rectangular shape to bring up the `Accel Properties` dialog box. Select the key from the list of key options or use the `Next Key Typed` button. If you select the VK_F2 key option from the list, the F2 function key will now become an accelerator key. Now, an ID value must be associated with the key. For this case, the F2 key will represent the second menu color choice, so it is assigned the menu ID value of `IDM_WHITE`. The `IDM_WHITE ID` value can be selected from the list of available ID values. All other accelerator keys are added in a similar manner.

Figure 11.10 shows the completed accelerator key list.

Why isn't the `IDM_WHITE` accelerator key the second key listed? The accelerator key list is maintained in alphabetical order by the `Key` value.

The keyboard accelerator design phase of the project is now completed.

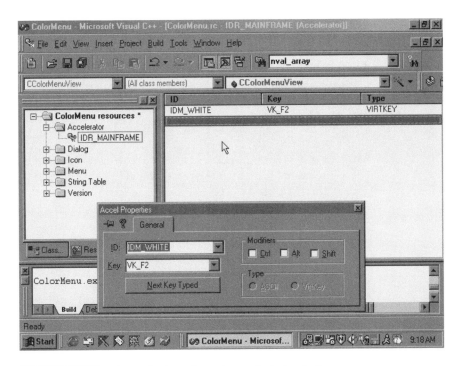

Figure 11.9   *A new keyboard accelerator list being built.*

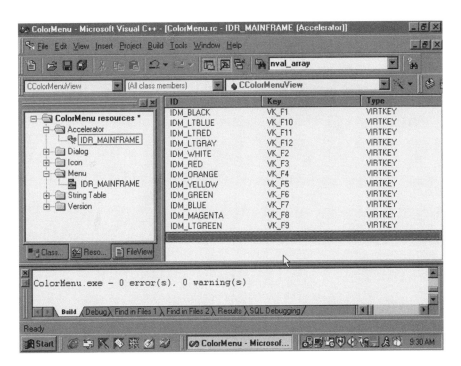

Figure 11.10   *The complete accelerator key list for the* `ColorMenu` *project.*

The ColorMenu Project Files

The AppWizard generated numerous files for this project. In the previous section, you were editing the ColorMenu.rc resource script file when you included a new menu, menu items, and keyboard accelerators. It is now time to alter various source code files to interact with these new resources.

The list of source code files includes MainFrm.cpp, ColorMenu.cpp, ColorMenuDoc.cpp, ColorMenuView.cpp, and StdAfx.cpp. The associated header files for the above source code files are also provided. To add the new menu and keyboard accelerators to this project and make them functional will require changes to the ColorMenu.h header file, and the Color-Menu.cpp and ColorMenuView.cpp source code files. These changes will be described in the following sections.

A Look at the ColorMenu.h and ColorMenu.cpp Files

The project files starting with just the name of the project, such as Color-Menu, can be used to hold variables that will be accessed with various source code files. The following listing is the complete ColorMenu.h header file, showing the addition of a *ColorValue[]* variable of type COLORREF.

```
// ColorMenu.h : main header file for the COLORMENU application
//

#if !defined(AFX_COLORMENU_H__4A619BA4_2D2F_11D3_9D69_0080AE000001__INCLUDED_)
#define AFX_COLORMENU_H__4A619BA4_2D2F_11D3_9D69_0080AE000001__INCLUDED_

#if _MSC_VER > 1000
#pragma once
#endif // _MSC_VER > 1000

#ifndef __AFXWIN_H__
    #error include 'stdafx.h' before including this file for PCH
#endif

#include "resource.h"        // main symbols

extern COLORREF NEAR ColorValue[];

/////////////////////////////////////////////////////////////////////////////
// CColorMenuApp:
// See ColorMenu.cpp for the implementation of this class
//

class CColorMenuApp : public CWinApp
{
```

```
public:
    CColorMenuApp();

// Overrides
    // ClassWizard generated virtual function overrides
    //{{AFX_VIRTUAL(CColorMenuApp)
    public:
    virtual BOOL InitInstance();
    //}}AFX_VIRTUAL

// Implementation
    //{{AFX_MSG(CColorMenuApp)
    afx_msg void OnAppAbout();
    //}}AFX_MSG
    DECLARE_MESSAGE_MAP()
};


/////////////////////////////////////////////////////////////////////

//{{AFX_INSERT_LOCATION}}
// Microsoft Visual C++ will insert additional declarations immediately before
the previous line.

#endif //
!defined(AFX_COLORMENU_H__4A619BA4_2D2F_11D3_9D69_0080AE000001__INCLUDED_)
```

The *ColorValue[]* array will easily transfer information between the menu items and the code implementing the color changes. These items are often in separate files, too.

The definition of the *ColorValue[]* array is coded in the Color-Menu.cpp source code file.

```
// ColorMenu.cpp : Defines class behaviors for application.
//

#include "stdafx.h"
#include "ColorMenu.h"

#include "MainFrm.h"
#include "ColorMenuDoc.h"
#include "ColorMenuView.h"

#ifdef _DEBUG
#define new DEBUG_NEW
#undef THIS_FILE
static char THIS_FILE[] = __FILE__;
#endif

COLORREF NEAR ColorValue[]={RGB(0,0,0),        //Black
```

```
                              RGB(255,255,255),  //White
                              RGB(255,0,0),      //Red
                              RGB(255,96,0),     //Orange
                              RGB(255,255,0),    //Yellow
                              RGB(0,255,0),      //Green
                              RGB(0,0,255),      //Blue
                              RGB(255,0,255),    //Magenta
                              RGB(128,255,0),    //Lite Green
                              RGB(0,255,255),    //Lite Blue
                              RGB(255,0,159),    //Lite Red
                              RGB(180,180,180)};//Lite Gray

/////////////////////////////////////////////////////////////
// CColorMenuApp

BEGIN_MESSAGE_MAP(CColorMenuApp, CWinApp)
    //{{AFX_MSG_MAP(CColorMenuApp)
    ON_COMMAND(ID_APP_ABOUT, OnAppAbout)
    //}}AFX_MSG_MAP
    // Standard file based document commands
    ON_COMMAND(ID_FILE_NEW, CWinApp::OnFileNew)
    ON_COMMAND(ID_FILE_OPEN, CWinApp::OnFileOpen)
END_MESSAGE_MAP()

/////////////////////////////////////////////////////////////
// CColorMenuApp construction

CColorMenuApp::CColorMenuApp()
{
}

/////////////////////////////////////////////////////////////
// The one and only CColorMenuApp object

CColorMenuApp theApp;

/////////////////////////////////////////////////////////////
// CColorMenuApp initialization

BOOL CColorMenuApp::InitInstance()
{
    // Standard initialization

    // Change the registry key under where settings are stored.
    SetRegistryKey(_T("Local AppWizard-Generated Applications"));

    LoadStdProfileSettings();  // Load standard INI file options

    // Register document templates
```

```
    CSingleDocTemplate* pDocTemplate;
    pDocTemplate = new CSingleDocTemplate(
        IDR_MAINFRAME,
        RUNTIME_CLASS(CColorMenuDoc),
        RUNTIME_CLASS(CMainFrame),          // main SDI frame window
        RUNTIME_CLASS(CColorMenuView));

    AddDocTemplate(pDocTemplate);

    // Parse command line for standard shell commands
    CCommandLineInfo cmdInfo;
    ParseCommandLine(cmdInfo);

    // Dispatch commands specified on the command line
    if (!ProcessShellCommand(cmdInfo))
        return FALSE;
    m_pMainWnd->ShowWindow(SW_SHOW);
    m_pMainWnd->UpdateWindow();

    return TRUE;

}

/////////////////////////////////////////////////////////////
// CAboutDlg dialog used for App About
class CAboutDlg : public Cdialog
{

public:
    CAboutDlg();

// Dialog Data
    //{{AFX_DATA(CAboutDlg)
    enum { IDD = IDD_ABOUTBOX };
    //}}AFX_DATA

    // ClassWizard generated virtual function overrides
    //{{AFX_VIRTUAL(CAboutDlg)
    protected:
    virtual void DoDataExchange(CDataExchange* pDX); // DDX/DDV
    //}}AFX_VIRTUAL

// Implementation
protected:
    //{{AFX_MSG(CAboutDlg)
        // No message handlers
    //}}AFX_MSG
    DECLARE_MESSAGE_MAP()
};
```

```
CAboutDlg::CAboutDlg() : CDialog(CAboutDlg::IDD)
{
    //{{AFX_DATA_INIT(CAboutDlg)
    //}}AFX_DATA_INIT
}

void CAboutDlg::DoDataExchange(CDataExchange* pDX)
{
    CDialog::DoDataExchange(pDX);
    //{{AFX_DATA_MAP(CAboutDlg)
    //}}AFX_DATA_MAP
}

BEGIN_MESSAGE_MAP(CAboutDlg, Cdialog)
    //{{AFX_MSG_MAP(CAboutDlg)
        // No message handlers
    //}}AFX_MSG_MAP
END_MESSAGE_MAP()

// App command to run the dialog
void CColorMenuApp::OnAppAbout()

{
    CAboutDlg aboutDlg;
    aboutDlg.DoModal();
}

/////////////////////////////////////////////////////////////
// CColorMenuApp message handlers
```

The *ColorValue[]* array holds twelve RGB color definitions. RGB values specify the amount of red, green, and blue (RGB) each color value will use. The values for each color range between 0 and 255. Thus, pure red is (255, 0, 0), while pure blue is (0, 0, 255). All other colors are specified with combinations of values, as shown in the previous listing. This array is available to all ColorMenu files.

Changing to the `ColorMenuView.cpp` File

The ClassWizard will be used to add member functions to the Color-MenuView.cpp file. Open the ClassWizard from the View menu of the Microsoft Visual Studio. The Project name is ColorMenu and the Class name that we wish to work with is CColorMenuView, as shown in Figure 11.11.

There are twelve menu colors. Usually you will add a separate member function for each menu choice, but this application is designed a little differ-

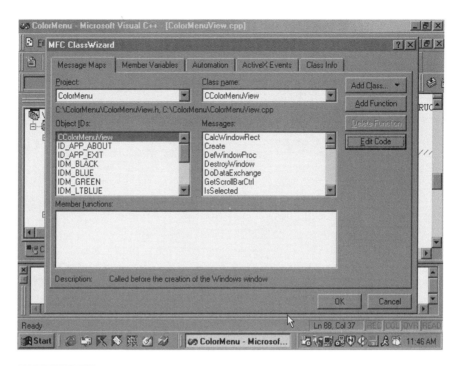

Figure 11.11   The ClassWizard is used to add member functions to the `CColor-MenuView` class.

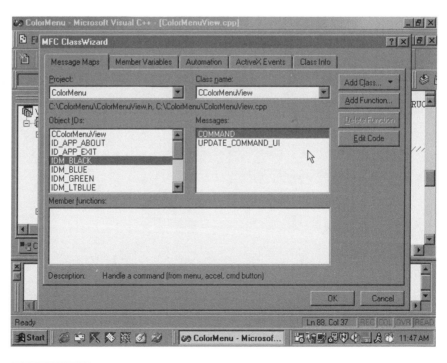

Figure 11.12   Menu items are usually processed via system commands.

ently. From the ClassWizard dialog box, choose IDM_BLACK from the Object ID, list as shown in Figure 11.12.

Select the COMMAND message from the Message list box. Click the Add Function...button to add a function for processing this information. The Add Member Function dialog box will appear with a default name for the member function. Do not use the default name. Change the name to OnColor, as shown in Figure 11.13.

By selecting a common member function name, each color will be evaluated within the same member function. Otherwise, this application would have had twelve member functions, each corresponding to a different color.

Now, another member function must be added to update information after a menu selection changes. In this application, the update information will be used to correctly check the menu item with a check symbol. Again, from the ClassWizard dialog box, choose IDM_BLACK from the Object ID, list as shown in Figure 11.14.

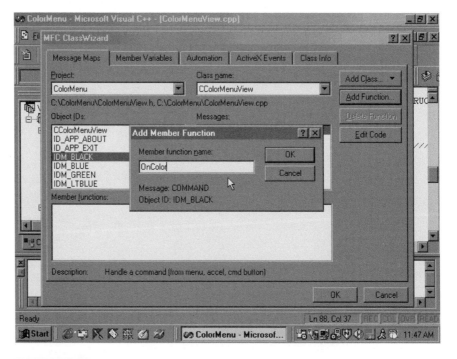

Figure 11.13 *As member functions are added for each color, they will all use On-Color as their member function name.*

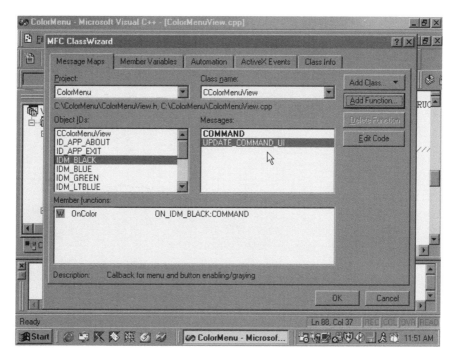

Figure 11.14   *Updated information resulting from menu changes are usually processed via the* UPDATE_COMMAND_UI *message.*

Select UPDATE_COMMAND_UI from the Message list box. Click the Add Function...button to add a function for processing this information. The Add Member Function dialog box will appear with a default name for the member function. Do not use the default name. Change the name to OnUpdateColor, as shown in Figure 11.15.

By selecting a common member function name, each time a menu item is selected, its update information will be evaluated by the same member function.

Figure 11.16 shows a partial list of all of the added member functions.

Remember, as you examine the list of member functions, notice that all menu colors use the OnColor member function. Likewise, all update messages are processed by the OnUpdateColor member function.

Once these changes are made, the ClassWizard will update the Color-MenuView.cpp file. Here is a complete listing of this file. Code that we've added is shown in a bold font. All other code has been generated by the App-pWizard and ClassWizard.

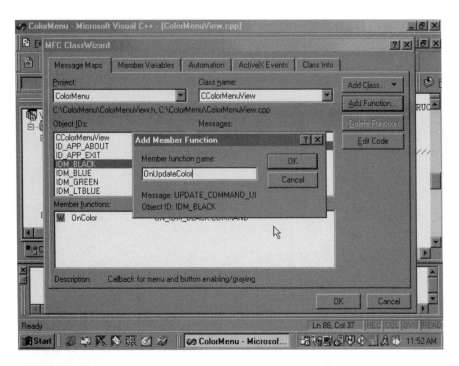

Figure 11.15   As member functions are added for each color, they will all use `OnUpdateColor` as the member function name.

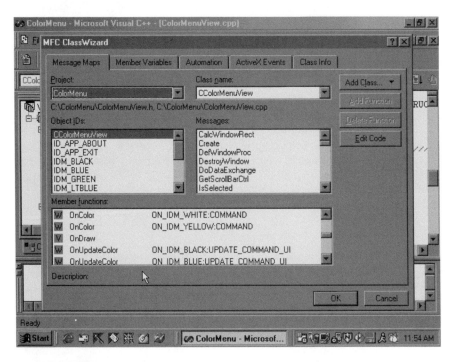

Figure 11.16   A partial view of the completed list of member functions.

```
// ColorMenuView.cpp : implementation of CColorMenuView class
//

#include "stdafx.h"
#include "ColorMenu.h"

#include "ColorMenuDoc.h"
#include "ColorMenuView.h"

#ifdef _DEBUG
#define new DEBUG_NEW
#undef THIS_FILE
static char THIS_FILE[] = __FILE__;
#endif

UINT m_nColor;
UINT m_clrBrush;

/////////////////////////////////////////////////////////////////
// CColorMenuView

IMPLEMENT_DYNCREATE(CColorMenuView, Cview)

BEGIN_MESSAGE_MAP(CColorMenuView, Cview)
    //{{AFX_MSG_MAP(CColorMenuView)
    ON_COMMAND(IDM_BLACK, OnColor)
    ON_UPDATE_COMMAND_UI(IDM_BLACK, OnUpdateColor)
    ON_COMMAND(IDM_WHITE, OnColor)
    ON_UPDATE_COMMAND_UI(IDM_WHITE, OnUpdateColor)
    ON_COMMAND(IDM_RED, OnColor)
    ON_UPDATE_COMMAND_UI(IDM_RED, OnUpdateColor)
    ON_COMMAND(IDM_ORANGE, OnColor)
    ON_UPDATE_COMMAND_UI(IDM_ORANGE, OnUpdateColor)
    ON_COMMAND(IDM_YELLOW, OnColor)
    ON_UPDATE_COMMAND_UI(IDM_YELLOW, OnUpdateColor)
    ON_COMMAND(IDM_GREEN, OnColor)
    ON_UPDATE_COMMAND_UI(IDM_GREEN, OnUpdateColor)
    ON_COMMAND(IDM_BLUE, OnColor)
    ON_UPDATE_COMMAND_UI(IDM_BLUE, OnUpdateColor)
    ON_COMMAND(IDM_MAGENTA, OnColor)
    ON_UPDATE_COMMAND_UI(IDM_MAGENTA, OnUpdateColor)
    ON_COMMAND(IDM_LTGREEN, OnColor)
    ON_UPDATE_COMMAND_UI(IDM_LTGREEN, OnUpdateColor)
    ON_COMMAND(IDM_LTBLUE, OnColor)
    ON_UPDATE_COMMAND_UI(IDM_LTBLUE, OnUpdateColor)
    ON_COMMAND(IDM_LTRED, OnColor)
    ON_UPDATE_COMMAND_UI(IDM_LTRED, OnUpdateColor)
    ON_COMMAND(IDM_LTGRAY, OnColor)
    ON_UPDATE_COMMAND_UI(IDM_LTGRAY, OnUpdateColor)
```

```
     //}}AFX_MSG_MAP
END_MESSAGE_MAP()

/////////////////////////////////////////////////////////
// CColorMenuView construction/destruction

CColorMenuView::CColorMenuView()
{
    m_nColor = IDM_BLACK;
    m_clrBrush = RGB(0,0,0);
}

CColorMenuView::~CColorMenuView()
{
}

BOOL CColorMenuView::PreCreateWindow(CREATESTRUCT& cs)
{
    return CView::PreCreateWindow(cs);
}

/////////////////////////////////////////////////////////
// CColorMenuView drawing

void CColorMenuView::OnDraw(CDC* pDC)
{
    CColorMenuDoc* pDoc = GetDocument();
    ASSERT_VALID(pDoc);

    CBrush newbrush;
    CBrush* oldbrush;
    newbrush.CreateSolidBrush(m_clrBrush);
    oldbrush=pDC->SelectObject(&newbrush);

    pDC->Ellipse(10,10,60,60);
    pDC->Rectangle(80,40,300,100);
    pDC->Ellipse(20,200,50,400);
    pDC->Rectangle(150,170,400,420);
}

/////////////////////////////////////////////////////////
// CColorMenuView diagnostics

#ifdef _DEBUG
void CColorMenuView::AssertValid() const
{
    CView::AssertValid();
}

void CColorMenuView::Dump(CDumpContext& dc) const
{
```

```
    CView::Dump(dc);
}

CColorMenuDoc* CColorMenuView::GetDocument() // non-debug inline
{
    ASSERT(m_pDocument->IsKindOf(RUNTIME_CLASS(CColorMenuDoc)));
    return (CColorMenuDoc*)m_pDocument;
}
#endif //_DEBUG

/////////////////////////////////////////////////////////////////
// CColorMenuView message handlers

void CColorMenuView::OnColor()
{
    // TODO: Add your command handler code here
    m_nColor = LOWORD(GetCurrentMessage()->wParam);
    m_clrBrush = ColorValue[m_nColor—IDM_BLACK];
    InvalidateRect(NULL, TRUE);
}

void CColorMenuView::OnUpdateColor(CCmdUI* pCmdUI)
{
    // TODO: Add your command update UI handler code here
    pCmdUI->SetCheck(pCmdUI -> m_nID == m_nColor);
}
```

The first block of code shown in a bold font is used to identify the member variables *m_nColor* and *m_clrBrush*. These unsigned integers will be used to identify menu items and to set brush colors.

Examine the listing and notice the inclusion of the ON_COMMAND and ON_UPDATE_COMMAND_UI lines for each menu color in the file's message map. This block of code was inserted by the ClassWizard.

The class constructor is used to initialize the default brush ID and brush color, before any menu selections are made. In this project, the color black is chosen as the default color.

```
    m_nColor = IDM_BLACK;
    m_clrBrush = RGB(0,0,0);
```

Several graphical shapes drawn with the Ellipse() and Rectangle() functions are placed in the client area of the window and filled with the current brush color. These functions are handled within the OnDraw() member function.

```
    CBrush newbrush;
    CBrush* oldbrush;

    newbrush.CreateSolidBrush(m_clrBrush);
```

```
oldbrush=pDC->SelectObject(&newbrush);

pDC->Ellipse(10,10,60,60);
pDC->Rectangle(80,40,300,100);
pDC->Ellipse(20,200,50,400);
pDC->Rectangle(150,170,400,420);
```

The CBrush class is used for creating a new brush object. A new solid brush is then created by calling the CreateSolidBrush() function and passing it a brush color via the *m_clrBrush* member variable. Since an ellipse and rectangle are closed shapes, they are automatically filled with the current brush color.

A separate member function, OnColor(), allows the brush color to be changed to match the menu selection.

```
m_nColor = LOWORD(GetCurrentMessage()->wParam);
m_clrBrush = ColorValue[m_nColor—IDM_BLACK];
InvalidateRect(NULL,TRUE);
```

The *wParam* value contains the menu color selection when a color is selected from the menu or by a keyboard accelerator. This value is sent as a message when the menu selection is made. The GetCurrentMessage() function intercepts the complete message. The color value resides in the LOWORD of the message.

The *m_nColor* member variable contains an integer value reflecting the menu item selected. This value is actually the ID number assigned to the color selection by the AppWizard. You can view these ID values in the re-source.h header file.

Imagine that IDM_BLACK is assigned an ID value of 32771 and IDM_GREEN a value of 32776. The difference between these two numbers is 5. 5 is then used as the index value into the *ColorValue[]* array. Remember that the array index starts at 0, so IDM_green is defined in the sixth position with an index value of 5.

Once the color value is selected, it is available to all project files. However, the graphics colors on the screen won't change until you force a repaint of the client area. This is done with a call to the InvalidateRect() function. No handle is used, so a NULL value is specified. A TRUE value for the second parameter forces the whole client area to be repainted.

The final step is to check the selected color in the menu. If you've been programming in Windows for a while, you might be tempted to use the CheckMenuItem() function. However, the use of this function has been replaced with the SetCheck() member function:

```
pCmdUI->SetCheck(pCmdUI->m_nID==m_nColor);
```

The framework passes the handler a pointer to a CCmdUI object when routing the update command to the handler. In this case, the object is a menu item that must be checked. A pointer is used by the update handler for call-

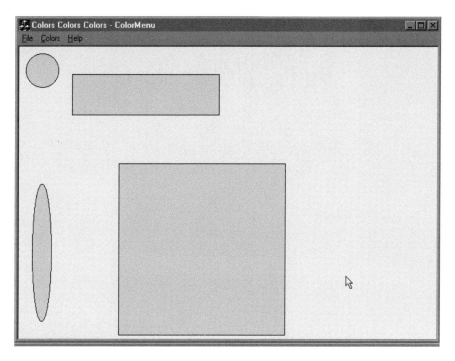

Figure 11.17   *Colored graphics shapes drawn in the client area.*

ing member functions of the CCmdUI structure. Once completed, the correct menu item will be checked.

Running the ColorMenu Application

Build the executable file for this project by selecting the Rebuild All menu item from the Microsoft Visual Studio's Build menu.

Execute the ColorMenu.exe file by selecting the Execute menu item, also found in the Build menu.

Your results should be similar to those shown in Figure 11.17.

More Menus?

Menus are relatively easy resources to incorporate in a project. You'll see additional menu applications as you work through the remaining chapters in this book. Remember, menus are the gateway to dialog boxes, and Chapter 12 is devoted exclusively to dialog boxes!

Dialog Box Resources

The concepts taught in Chapter 11 regarding menus and keyboard accelerators allow applications to have a small degree of user interaction. In this
chapter, you will learn about the most significant means of user interaction—
the dialog box. Menus serve as a path to dialog boxes. Menu items folowed
by an ellipsis (...) indicate that when the menu item is selected, it will in
turn bring up a dialog box. Dialog boxes are constructed of many components and often make the greatest use of Windows controls. Controls include
push buttons, radio buttons, list boxes, edit boxes, static text boxes, and so
on. The use of standard controls in a dialog box gives your application the
interactive capabilities of commercially produced applications.

This chapter will teach you the fundamentals of creating and using dialog
boxes. You will create dialog boxes with standard controls and learn how to
pass data from the dialog box resource to the application. You will also find additional examples of dialog boxes in the remaining chapters of this book.

Dialog Boxes as Resources

Dialog boxes are child windows that pop up when a dialog box menu item is
selected. Dialog box complexity can range from simple About boxes to complicated data entry forms involving the use of numerous controls. When a user
selects a dialog box control, such as a push button, check box, or edit box, Windows supplies the means necessary to process the message information.

Dialog boxes are created as a resource from within the Microsoft Visual
Studio. When dialog box specifications are saved, they are saved to a resource script file. Resource script files, with .rc file extensions, hold resource
information for string tables, menus, and so on.

The Dialog Box Design Environment

To create a new dialog box resource, use the `Insert` menu and select the `Resource`...menu item as you have done for icons, cursors, menus, and so on. When the selection is made, the `Insert Resource` dialog box lists possible resources that can be created, as shown in Figure 12.1.

When the `Dialog` resource is selected, the dialog box resource editor will appear. The editor provides a default dialog box, a toolbox of controls, and a toolbar of dialog box alignment items, as shown in Figure 12.2.

Examine Figure 12.2 and the fourteen buttons in the toolbar, located at the bottom of the design window. Table 12.1 describes the function of each of these buttons.

Table 12.1   *Dialog Box Resource Editor Toolbar Button Functions*

Button	Function
Test	Allows the programmer to test the dialog box.
Align Left	Allows a group of selected controls to be aligned to the left.
Align Right	Allows a group of selected controls to be aligned to the right.
Align Top	Allows a group of selected controls to be aligned to the top.
Align Bottom	Allows a group of selected controls to be aligned to the bottom.
Center Vertical	Allows a group of selected controls to be centered vertically.
Center Horizontal	Allows a group of selected controls to be centered horizontally.
Space Across	Allows a group of selected controls to be evenly spaced horizontally.
Space Down	Allows a group of selected controls to be evenly spaced vertically.
Make Same Width	Makes a group of selected controls the same width.
Make Same Height	Makes a group of selected controls the same height.
Toggle Grid	Turns the design grid on and off.
Toggle Guide	Turns the design guide on and off.

The dialog box `Controls` toolbox is shown at the right of the default dialog box in Figure 12.2. The `Controls` toolbox contains a grid of cells that contains small icons. The small icons represent the controls. Controls can be transferred from the toolbox to the dialog box under construction by placing the pointer on the control, clicking the left mouse button, and dragging the control to the dialog box.

Brief explanations of the most frequently used toolbox controls are given in the following sections. Refer to Figure 12.2 for the location of individual controls in the toolbox. Additional information for any toolbox control

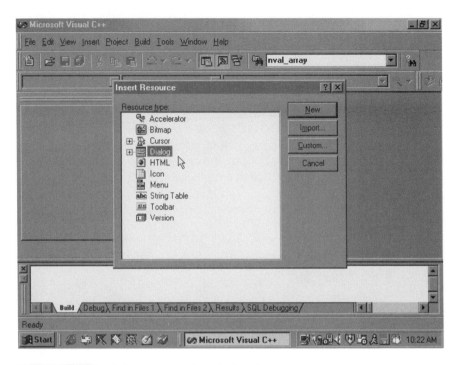

Figure 12.1   *Select* `Dialog` *from the list of available resources.*

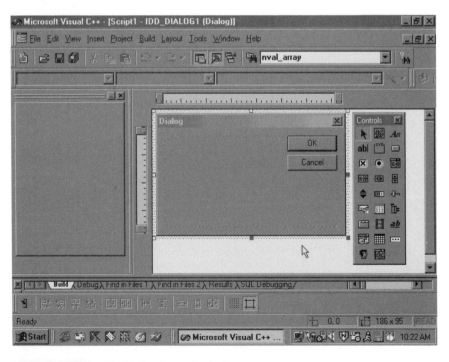

Figure 12.2   *The dialog box editor's design environment.*

304

can be found by using the on-line help facilities provided with your Visual C++ compiler.

The Button (Push Button) Control

The icon for the button control is in the third column, second row. The button control is a small, rounded rectangle that can also be sized. The button control contains a label. Buttons are used for making an immediate choice, such as accepting or canceling the dialog box selections made by the user. The dialog boxes in this chapter usually contain one or two buttons: OK and/or Cancel.

The Check Box Control

The icon for the check box control is in the first column, third row. The check box control draws a small square box (a check box) with a label to its right. Check boxes are marked, or checked, by clicking the left mouse button while positioned over the check box. Check boxes can also be selected by using the keyboard. Check boxes usually appear in groups and allow the user to check one or more features at the same time.

The Combo Box Control

The icon for the combo box control is in the third column, third row. The combo box control is made up of two elements. It is a combination of a single-line edit field (a static text control) and a list box. The combo box gives the user the ability to enter text into the edit box or to scroll through the list box looking for an appropriate selection. Windows provides several styles of combo boxes.

The Custom Control

The icon for the custom control is in the first column, ninth row. The custom control option allows the creation of customized controls. Many such controls can be created and saved in a catalog recognized by the resource editor. Custom controls are made up of dynamic link libraries (DLLs) that also contain the window procedure for the control. The catalog is contained in the win.ini file.

The Date Time Picker Control

The icon for the date time picker control is in the first column, eighth row. The date time picker control is a control that can provide the current date or time to the user. This is useful when an application prompts the user for such information, as in the case of a product registration questionnaire.

The Edit Box Control

The icon for the edit box control is in the first column, second row. The edit box control draws a small interactive rectangle on the screen. The user can enter string information within the rectangle from the keyboard. The edit box control can be sized to accept short or long strings. The string information can be processed directly (as character or numeric integer data) and indirectly (as real number data). The edit box is the most important control for data entry. Several applications in this chapter use edit box controls.

The Group Box Control

The icon for the group box control is in the second column, second row. The group box control draws a rectangular outline within a dialog box. The outline encloses a group of controls that are to be used together. These controls often share a common feature. For example, a group box might contain check boxes and radio buttons for setting foreground and background colors and so on. The group box has a user-defined label at its upper-left edge.

The List Control

The icon for the list control is in the second column, sixth row. The list control allows the user to make a selection from a list of presented options.

The List Box Control

The icon for the list box control is in the first column, fourth row. The list box control draws a rectangular outline with a vertical scroll bar. List boxes are useful when scrolling is needed for long lists.

The Month Calendar Control

The icon for the month calendar control is in the second column, eighth row. This month calendar control draws the current month's calendar to the screen when selected. The control provides a variety of properties that allow dates to be selected, changed, and so on. This control is very easy to implement and provides outstanding visual effects.

The Progress Control

The icon for the progress control is in the second column, fifth row. The progress control is used to show the progress of an operation such as a file transfer.

The Radio Button Control

The icon for the radio button control is in the second column, third row. The radio button control draws a small circle (a radio button) with a label at its right. Radio button controls, like check box controls, typically appear in groups. However, unlike check box controls, only one radio button control at a time can be selected in any given group. Radio button controls can be selected with the mouse or keyboard.

The Scroll Bar Controls

The icon for the vertical and horizontal scroll bar controls are in the second and third columns, fourth row. The horizontal and vertical scroll bar controls draw the horizontal or vertical scroll bars for a dialog box. These are usually used in conjunction with another window or control that contains text or graphics information. Scroll bar controls can be placed anywhere within a dialog box and are not restricted to the bottom or right edges of the dialog box.

The Slider Control

The icon for the slider control is in the third column, fifth row. The slider control behaves like a sliding volume control on a stereo. It can be moved from left-to-right or designed to move from top-to-bottom.

The Spin Control

The icon for the spin control is in the first column, fifth row. The spin control provides two arrows (up and down). By clicking on either arrow, the user can move up or down in a selection. Spin controls behave like the up and down arrows in a scroll bar control.

The Static Text Control

The icon for the static text control is in the third column, first row. The static text control allows the insertion of labels and strings within the dialog box. These can be used, for example, to place labels before edit box controls.

The Tab Control

The icon for the tab control is in the first column, seventh row. The tab control is frequently used to divide a large dialog box into related folders. The individual folders are then selected via the tab control.

Basic Project Code

There are two projects described in this chapter. To create each project, you will have to follow the basic steps, shown below, for the AppWizard. Let's start with the first example and create a project named DataInput.

Use the following steps to create the basic project files using the AppWizard:

- Enter the Microsoft Visual Studio (Visual C++ compiler).
- Choose the File menu and select the New menu item.
- Select Project Workspace from the New dialog box.
- From the New Project Workspace dialog box:
  - Name the workspace DataInput.
  - Set the location of the workspace (for example, C:\DataInput).
  - Select MFC AppWizard (exe) from the list box.
- Step 1—Select a Single document application type.
- Step 2—Select no database support.
- Step 3—Select None for OLE compound document support.
- Step 4—Select no additional features.
- Step 5—Do not select comments. Select a statically linked library.
- Step 6—View your settings and Finish the AppWizard process.
- If the information in the New Project Information dialog box is correct, select OK.

When the final step has been completed, the AppWizard generates all of the basic files needed for the DataInput project.

You can create the basic files for the second project in this chapter by simple repeating the process one more time. This time, create a project named Colors. We'll use that basic code later in this chapter.

Creating A New About Dialog Box For The Project

When you used the AppWizard to generate the DataInput project, described in the previous section, a default About dialog box was generated. To view and modify this About dialog box, open the DataInput.rc file while in the Microsoft Visual Studio. You'll be able to select the About dialog box from the list of resources, as shown in Figure 12.3.

When you have selected the About dialog box for editing, the Microsoft Visual Studio will take you to the dialog box resource editor and place the About box in the window. Figure 12.4 shows the default About dialog box designed by the AppWizard for this project.

Any control now present in the dialog box can be eliminated or modified. Select any control by positioning the mouse over the control and click-

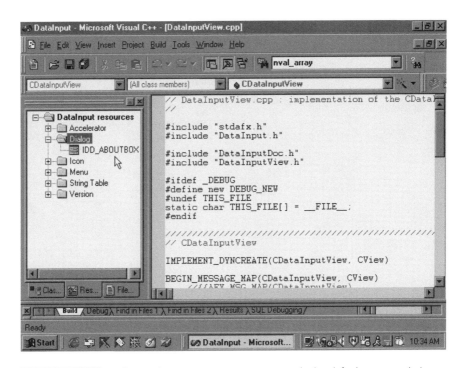

Figure 12.3 — *Choose the* `IDD_ABOUTBOX` `ID` *to edit the default* `About` *dialog box.*

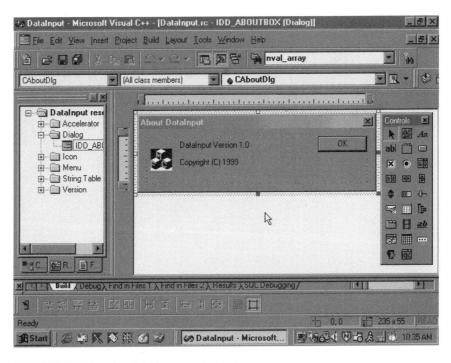

Figure 12.4 — *The default* `About` *dialog box.*

309

ing the left mouse button. Once the control is selected, it can be eliminated by pressing the Del or Delete key. Controls can be modified by clicking the right mouse button and selecting the control's Properties dialog box from the list of items. From the Properties dialog box, the text in the two static text controls can be modified, as shown in Figure 12.5.

As you view Figure 12.5, also notice that the icon has been deleted, the push button has been moved and resized, the dialog box dimensions have been changed, the default font has been changed to an Arial TrueType font, and the static text has been centered horizontally.

About boxes are mostly used to convey information to the user concerning the application, the developers involved, and any copyright information. Since About dialog boxes are automatically added by the AppWizard, just a little editing customizes the About box for your project. What could be easier?

Creating A Data Entry Dialog Box For The Project

A new dialog box that will allow data to be entered from the keyboard will be added to the DataInput project. To reach the dialog box, a special menu and menu item will be created.

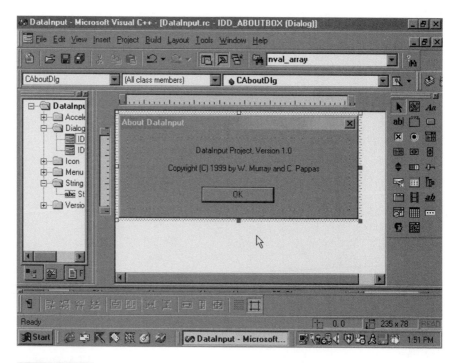

Figure 12.5   *Modifications to the default* About *dialog box.*

A New Menu

Recall that the AppWizard creates a default menu bar, so creating a new menu will be a matter of opening and editing the current menu resource. Chapter 11 discussed the steps necessary for altering menu resources.

IDR_MAINFRAME is the ID given to the menu resource. Figure 12.6 shows the modified menu bar with a new menu named Data. Data contains a menu item named Data Entry..., which will allow access to a new dialog box.

The Data Entry...menu item must be assigned an ID value. For this project, use ID_DATA_DATAINPUT.

Note

As with the menus developed in Chapter 11, unused menus and menu items are eliminated from the default menu bar.

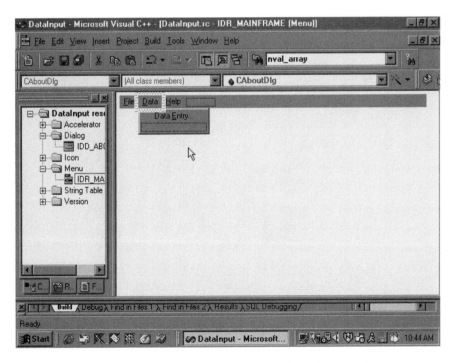

| Figure 12.6 | *A new menu and menu item are added to the menu bar.* |

A New Dialog Box

It is now time to create an entirely new dialog box to house various data entry controls. To add an additional dialog resource, use the `Insert` menu and choose the `Resource...` menu item. The `Insert Resource` dialog box allows you to select the resource type. In this case, a `Dialog` resource is selected.

Use the default dialog box provided by the dialog box resource editor, then modify and add controls so that it appears similar to Figure 12.7.

The original default dialog box was resized and the `OK` and `Cancel` push buttons were moved to new locations. Next, a group box was added and titled `Shape Selection`. Two radio buttons were added to this group. One radio button is named `Rectangle` and the other `Ellipse`. Four static text controls were then added. Their titles include `Title`, `Size`, `x =`, and `y =`. Three edit box controls were added to allow user input. These were the white rectangles shown earlier in Figure 12.7.

To communicate with the dialog box and the dialog box controls, each is given a unique ID value when created. We'll use the defaults assigned by the editor for this project. The dialog box itself is assigned ID of `IDD_DIA-LOG1`. The `Ellipse` radio button is assigned `IDC_RADIO2`, and the `Rectangle` radio button `IDC_RADIO1`. The edit box to the right of the title text

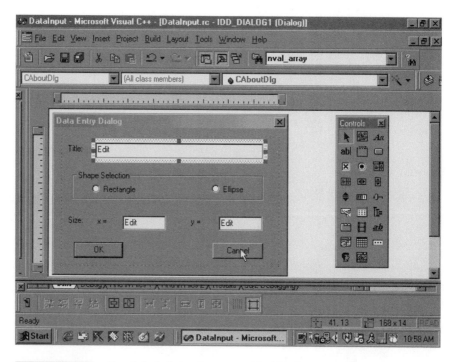

Figure 12.7   *The default dialog box is modified for the* `DataInput` *project.*

is assigned `IDC_EDIT1`, the next `IDC_EDIT2`, and the last `IDC_EDIT3`. These are the only controls that will be directly involved with data transfer.

Once the dialog box design has been completed, it will be necessary to create a new class to process information from the various controls.

Using the ClassWizard

Use the `View` menu and select the `ClassWizard` menu item. The `Class-Wizard` option will bring up the `Adding a Class` dialog box, which allows you to create a new class, as shown in Figure 12.8. You can also use the Add Class push button provided with the ClassWizard dialog box.

The `New Class` dialog box is displayed, as shown in Figure 12.9, when a new class is requested.

In this application, the new class name will be `CDataInput1`. The controls included in the dialog box will require additional member functions. Figure 12.10 shows the `CDataInput` class with the `DoDataExchange()` member function already added.

The three edit controls and two radio buttons will pass information from the dialog box to the application. These controls will require member variables to assist in this transfer of information. Select the `Member Vari-`

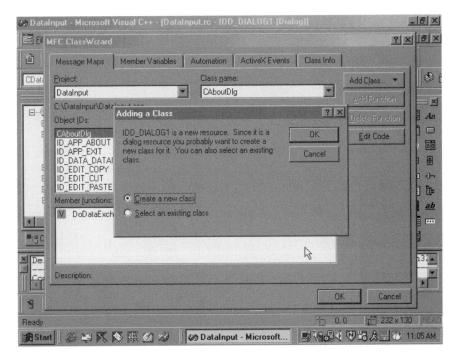

Figure 12.8   *Use the* `Adding A Class` *dialog box to add a new class to this project.*

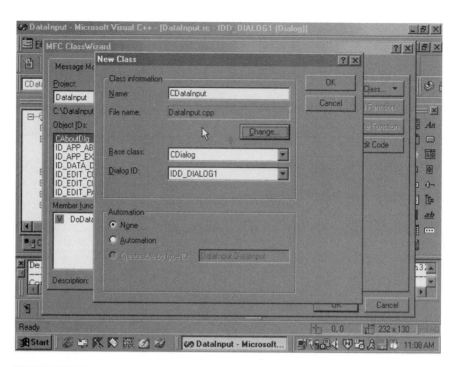

Figure 12.9 The New Class *dialog box permits a new dialog box class to be derived from a* CDialog *base class.*

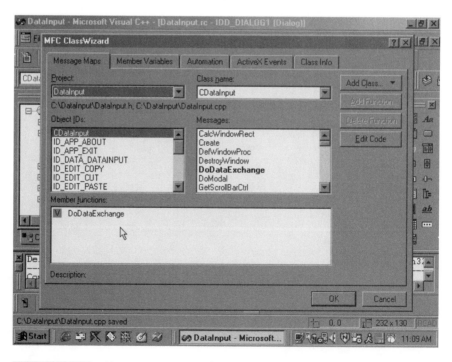

Figure 12.10 The CDataInput *class already contains a* DoDataExchange() *member function.*

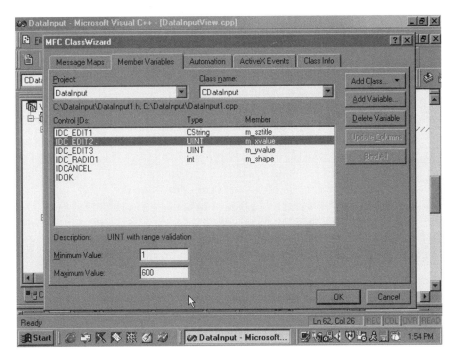

Figure 12.11   *Member variables are used with each edit box control.*

ables folder to reveal a list of control IDs used in data transfer. Select the `IDC_EDIT1`, `IDC_EDIT2`, and `IDC_EDIT3` controls, one at a time, and add member variables by using the `Add Variable...` button. A small dialog box will permit you to name the member variable, its type, and the data it will transfer. Figure 12.11 shows member variables for all three edit controls. `IDC_EDIT2` is currently selected in this figure. Note that you can also view a preset range of acceptable values (1 to 600).

To access the dialog box from the menu when the `Data Entry...` menu item is selected, a member function must also be added to the `CDataInputView` class described in the `DataInputView.cpp` file. Figure 12.12 shows the object ID, the message and member, function, `OnDataDatainput()`, that will be added by the ClassWizard.

Remember that `ID_DATA_DATAINPUT` is the ID value assigned to the `Data Entry...` menu item.

When the message handler was added to the `DataInputView.cpp` file, the following small amount of code had to be added to the message handler to process dialog box information:

```
CDataInput dlg;
```
.

```
        .
        .
// CDataInputView message handlers
void CDataInputView::OnDataDataInput()
{
  dlg.DoModal();
  InvalidateRect(NULL,TRUE);
  UpdateWindow();
}
```

The portion of code printed in bold is the actual code added to this member function's description. This allows the application to draw the dialog box when the menu item selection is made.

In the next section, you'll learn about the code that must be included to make this control operational.

Editing the `DataInput.cpp` File

The `DataInput1.cpp` file contains a large amount of new code. This is a result of the member function added to the data entry dialog box in the previous section. The following listing is the complete `DataInput1.cpp` file:

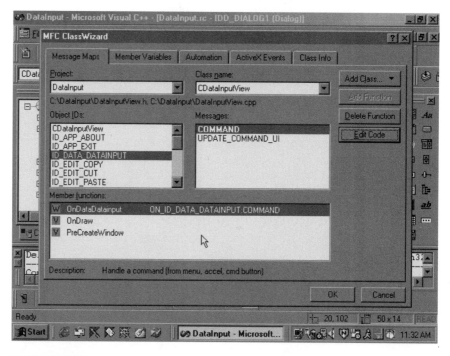

Figure 12.12   *Adding a member function in* `CDataInput`.

```cpp
// DataInput1.cpp : implementation file
//

#include "stdafx.h"
#include "DataInput.h"
#include "DataInput1.h"

#ifdef _DEBUG
#define new DEBUG_NEW
#undef THIS_FILE
static char THIS_FILE[] = __FILE__;
#endif

/////////////////////////////////////////////////////////////////
// CDataInput dialog


CDataInput::CDataInput(CWnd* pParent /*=NULL*/)
    : CDialog(CDataInput::IDD, pParent)
{
    //{{AFX_DATA_INIT(CDataInput)
    m_shape = 1;
    m_sztitle = _T("Title");
    m_xvalue = 50;
    m_yvalue = 80;
    //}}AFX_DATA_INIT
}


void CDataInput::DoDataExchange(CDataExchange* pDX)
{
    CDialog::DoDataExchange(pDX);
    //{{AFX_DATA_MAP(CDataInput)
    DDX_Radio(pDX, IDC_RADIO1, m_shape);
    DDX_Text(pDX, IDC_EDIT1, m_sztitle);
    DDV_MaxChars(pDX, m_sztitle, 40);
    DDX_Text(pDX, IDC_EDIT2, m_xvalue);
    DDV_MinMaxUInt(pDX, m_xvalue, 1, 600);
    DDX_Text(pDX, IDC_EDIT3, m_yvalue);
    DDV_MinMaxUInt(pDX, m_yvalue, 1, 400);
    //}}AFX_DATA_MAP
}

BEGIN_MESSAGE_MAP(CDataInput, Cdialog)
    //{{AFX_MSG_MAP(CDataInput)
        // NOTE: the ClassWizard adds message map macros here
    //}}AFX_MSG_MAP
END_MESSAGE_MAP()

/////////////////////////////////////////////////////////////////
// CDataInput message handlers
```

As you examine the previous listing, note the four member variables shown in bold. The member variables are declared in the `DataInput1.h` header file and start with the characters `"m_"`. Examine the listing further and note that we edited the initial values for these member variables in the class constructor.

DATA EXCHANGE

The `DoDataExchange()` member function uses `DDX_` and `DDV_` macros. `DDX_` macros are used for data exchange and `DDV_` macros are used for data validation. These macros help to interface your application's variables with the various dialog box controls. `DDX_` is used to represent the exchange function name. `DDX_` names include `DDX_Check`, `DDX_Control`, `DDX_Radio`, `DDX_Text`, and so on. `DDV_` macros are used to validate data. They make sure data is of the proper type and in the proper range. Message boxes are used to warn users of potential violations. `DDV_` names include `DDV_Max-Chars`, `DDV_MinMaxInt`, `MinMaxUInt`, and so on.

Examine the `DoDataExchange()` member function in the `DataInput1.cpp` file. You should note several lines with `DDX_` and `DDV_`. For example, find the following lines that describe how the window's title information will be exchanged.

```
      .
      .
      .
  DDX_Text(pDX, IDC_EDIT1, m_sztitle);
  DDV_MaxChars(pDX, m_sztitle, 40);
      .
      .
      .
```

In the previous portion of code, the `DDX_Text` function uses the pointer to the `CDataExchange` object. The ID value of the control is the second parameter and the data member involved with the data exchange is the third parameter. `DDV_MaxChars` checks the data member against the maximum number of characters. There are eleven `DDX_` functions. The `DDX_Text` function is overloaded, as you can see in Table 12.2.

Table 12.2	*Important DDX_Data Exchange Functions*
DDX_Function	***Member Variable Type***
DDX_CBIndex	int
DDX_CBString	CString
DDX_CBStringExact	CString
DDX_Check	int

Table 12-2	*Important DDX_Data Exchange Functions (Continued)*
DDX_Function	**Member Variable Type**
DDX_Control	CWnd
DDX_HexText	long
DDX_LBIndex	int
DDX_LBString	Cstring
DDX_LBStringExact	Cstring
DDX_Radio	int
DDX_Scroll	int
DDX_Text	BYTE
	ColeCurrency
	ColeDateTime
	CString
	double
	DWORD
	float
	int
	long
	short
	UINT

The direction of data exchange is controlled by the m_bSaveAndVali-date flag. When this flag is TRUE, data transfer moves from the controls to the class member variables. When it is FALSE, data moves from the class member variables to the controls. When data exchange occurs outside the specified range, DDV_ functions will post the appropriate error messages to the system.

The DDX_Radio function handles the transfer of integer (int) data between a radio control group in a dialog box and an integer data member of the dialog box. The first radio button in a group will be assigned a value of 0, the second a value of 1, and so on. When DDX_Radio is called, the value is set to the current state of the radio control group. It is important to make sure the first radio button in a group has its group property checked when creating the dialog box. Subsequent radio buttons in the group must occur, in order, at the next corresponding tab stops for the group.

The DDX_Text function handles the transfer of integer (int), UINT, long, DWORD, CString, float, or double data between an edit control in a dialog box and a CString data member of the dialog box.

Editing the `DataInputView.cpp` File

During the operation of the application, information will be passed from the dialog box controls to the functions in the `DataInputView.cpp` file. Here is a complete listing of the `DataInputView.cpp` file, with our code additions in bold.

```
// DataInputView.cpp : implementation of CDataInputView class
//

#include "stdafx.h"
#include "DataInput.h"
#include "DataInput1.h"

#include "DataInputDoc.h"
#include "DataInputView.h"

CDataInput dlg;

#ifdef _DEBUG
#define new DEBUG_NEW

#undef THIS_FILe
static char THIS_FILE[] = __FILE__;
#endif

/////////////////////////////////////////////////////////////
// CDataInputView

IMPLEMENT_DYNCREATE(CDataInputView, Cview)

BEGIN_MESSAGE_MAP(CDataInputView, Cview)
    //{{AFX_MSG_MAP(CDataInputView)
    ON_COMMAND(ID_DATA_DATAINPUT, OnDataDatainput)
    //}}AFX_MSG_MAP
END_MESSAGE_MAP()

/////////////////////////////////////////////////////////////
// CDataInputView construction/destruction

CDataInputView::CDataInputView()
{
}

CDataInputView::~CDataInputView()
{
}

BOOL CDataInputView::PreCreateWindow(CREATESTRUCT& cs)
{
    return CView::PreCreateWindow(cs);
```

```
}

//////////////////////////////////////////////////////////////
// CDataInputView drawing

void CDataInputView::OnDraw(CDC* pDC)
{
    CDataInputDoc* pDoc = GetDocument();
    ASSERT_VALID(pDoc);

    CBrush newbrush;
    CBrush* oldbrush;

    newbrush.CreateSolidBrush(RGB(255,0,0));
    oldbrush=pDC->SelectObject(&newbrush);

    if(dlg.m_shape == 0)
      pDC->Rectangle(20,40,dlg.m_xvalue,dlg.m_yvalue);
    if (dlg.m_shape == 1)
      pDC->Ellipse(20,40,dlg.m_xvalue,dlg.m_yvalue);

    pDC->TextOut(20,10,dlg.m_sztitle,strlen(dlg.m_sztitle));

    pDC->SelectObject(&newbrush);
    newbrush.DeleteObject();
}

//////////////////////////////////////////////////////////////
// CDataInputView diagnostics

#ifdef _DEBUG
void CDataInputView::AssertValid() const
{
    CView::AssertValid();
}

void CDataInputView::Dump(CDumpContext& dc) const
{
    CView::Dump(dc);
}

CDataInputDoc* CDataInputView::GetDocument() //non-debug inline
{
    ASSERT(m_pDocument->IsKindOf(RUNTIME_CLASS(CDataInputDoc)));
    return (CDataInputDoc*)m_pDocument;
}
#endif //_DEBUG

//////////////////////////////////////////////////////////////
// CDataInputView message handlers

void CDataInputView::OnDataDatainput()
```

```
{
    // TODO: Add your command handler code here
    dlg.DoModal();
    InvalidateRect(NULL,TRUE);
    UpdateWindow();
}
```

Recall that this application uses two radio buttons and three edit boxes. The information returned by the radio buttons is treated as a flag in determining whether a rectangle or ellipse is drawn in the client area. The title for the figure is returned by the first edit box in a string accessed by dlg.m_sztitle. The size of the figure is determined by the values returned by the remaining two edit boxes. These values are returned in dlg.m_xvalue and dlg.m_yvalue.

An example of the execution of this application, after a complete build, is shown in Figure 12.13.

Dialog boxes require a large amount of time to plan, develop and implement. They should be intuitive in their use and user-friendly.

Certain Windows operations, such as file, font, and color selections, are common among many applications. Because of this fact, Microsoft has designed a group of common dialog boxes for these tasks. The use of common dialog boxes will save hours of development time and make your applica-

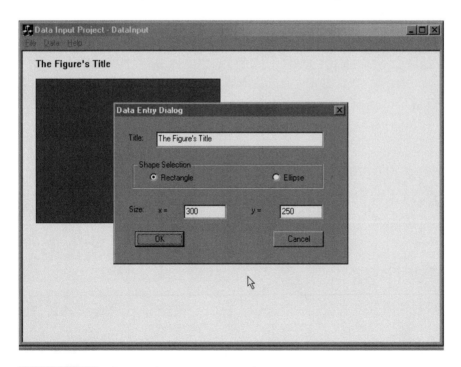

Figure 12.13   *Running the* DataInput *application.*

tions consistent with others on the market. The common dialog approach will be discussed in the next section.

Common Dialog Boxes

Microsoft has designed common dialog boxes to provide consistent dialog box styles for operations such as color, file, font, and print selection. Every common dialog uses its own special class. The common color dialog box uses the CColorDialog class. CFileDialog, CFontDialog, and CPrint-Dialog correspond to the remaining classes.

The use of each common dialog box is similar, but each common dialog box uses its own group of parameters, flags, filters, and so on.

The AppWizard generates applications that can access the file and print common dialog boxes. In this section, we'll illustrate how to use the common color dialog box.

If you have been working along with the code development for this chapter, you have already created a project named Colors with the AppWizard. This code will now be modified to allow access to the common color dialog box. If you have not completed this step, just use the AppWizard to create a project named Colors with the options we have been using throughout the book.

The AppWizard creates a basic application that will be modified to accommodate a new menu, menu item, and permit access to the common color dialog box. Before modifying the actual program code, we'll modify the menus on the menu bar so that they take on the appearance of Figure 12.14.

Use IDC_MYCOLOR for the ID value associated with the Pick a color ... menu item.

Next, use the ClassWizard to create a new class named CCustomColor, which is based on the CColorDialog base class. Use the Add Class... button, as shown in Figure 12.15, to add this class.

Note   All Microsoft common dialog boxes have a base class associated with them in the MFC library.

Use the ClassWizard to access the CColorsView class found in the ColorsView.cpp file. To make this application operational, we'll have to add an additional member function to this class. The new member function will respond to a command message. Choose IDC_MYCOLOR in the Object IDs list box. Select COMMAND from the Messages list box. Then, add the function by selecting the Add Function button, as shown in Figure 12.16.

When this project is built, a CustomColor.cpp file will be added to support the CCustomColor class. Remember, this class is based on the CColorDialog base class. Here is a complete listing for this file:

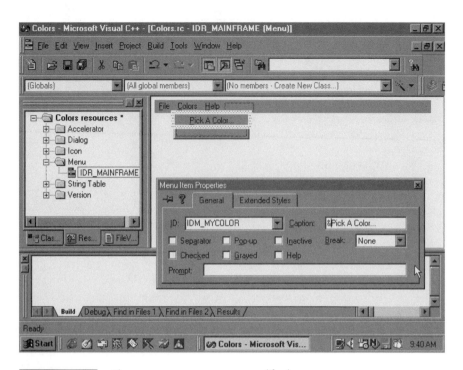

Figure 12.14 The `Colors` project uses a modified menu.

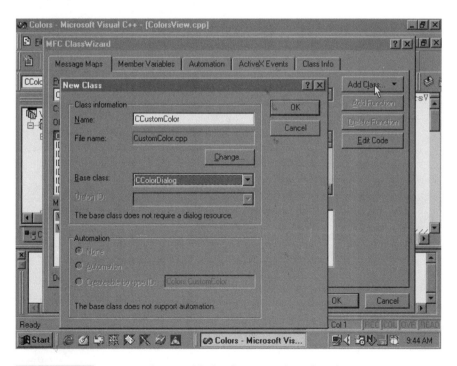

Figure 12.15 A new class is added to the project based on the `CColorDialog` base class.

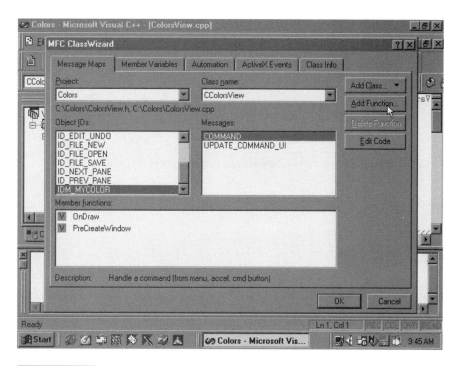

Figure 12.16   Adding the `OnMyColor()` member function to the project.

```
// CustomColor.cpp : implementation file
//

#include "stdafx.h"
#include "Colors.h"
#include "CustomColor.h"

#ifdef _DEBUG
#define new DEBUG_NEW
#undef THIS_FILE
static char THIS_FILE[] = __FILE__;
#endif

/////////////////////////////////////////////////////////////////
// CCustomColor

IMPLEMENT_DYNAMIC(CCustomColor, CColorDialog)

CCustomColor::CCustomColor(COLORREF clrInit, DWORD dwFlags,
                           CWnd* pParentWnd) :
    CColorDialog(clrInit, dwFlags, pParentWnd)
{
}
```

```
BEGIN_MESSAGE_MAP(CCustomColor, CColorDialog)
    //{{AFX_MSG_MAP(CCustomColor)
    // NOTE—ClassWizard adds and removes mapping macros.
    //}}AFX_MSG_MAP
END_MESSAGE_MAP()
```

This listing is fairly short since no specific message handlers were added. To complete this project, modifications were also made to the ColorsView.cpp file. The code we added is shown in bold in the following listing:

```
// ColorsView.cpp : implementation of the CColorsView class
//

#include "stdafx.h"
#include "Colors.h"

#include "ColorsDoc.h"
#include "ColorsView.h"

#include "CustomColor.h"
CColorDialog dlg;

#ifdef _DEBUG
#define new DEBUG_NEW
#undef THIS_FILE
static char THIS_FILE[] = __FILE__;
#endif

/////////////////////////////////////////////////////////////
// CColorsView

IMPLEMENT_DYNCREATE(CColorsView, Cview)

BEGIN_MESSAGE_MAP(CColorsView, Cview)
    //{{AFX_MSG_MAP(CColorsView)
    ON_COMMAND(IDM_MYCOLOR, OnMyColor)
    //}}AFX_MSG_MAP
END_MESSAGE_MAP()

/////////////////////////////////////////////////////////////
// CColorsView construction/destruction

CColorsView::CColorsView()
{
}

CColorsView::~CColorsView()
{
}

BOOL CColorsView::PreCreateWindow(CREATESTRUCT& cs)
```

```
{
    return CView::PreCreateWindow(cs);
}

///////////////////////////////////////////////////////////////////
// CColorsView drawing

void CColorsView::OnDraw(CDC* pDC)
{
    CColorsDoc* pDoc = GetDocument();
    ASSERT_VALID(pDoc);

    COLORREF mycolor;
    CBrush newbrush;
    CBrush* oldbrush;

    // open the full dialog box
    dlg.m_cc.Flags |= CC_FULLOPEN;

    // get the selected color from the dialog box
    mycolor = dlg.GetColor();

    // create a new brush color
    newbrush.CreateSolidBrush(mycolor);
    oldbrush=pDC->SelectObject(&newbrush);

    // create a new text color
    pDC->SetTextColor(mycolor);

    // draw text and shapes
    pDC->TextOut(200,10,"The common color dialog box is used",
                 35);
    pDC->TextOut(240,360,"to select a new brush color.",28);
    pDC->Ellipse(100,100,300,300);
    pDC->Rectangle(400,100,600,300);

    pDC->SelectObject(&newbrush);
    newbrush.DeleteObject();
}

///////////////////////////////////////////////////////////////////
// CColorsView diagnostics

#ifdef _DEBUG
void CColorsView::AssertValid() const
{
    CView::AssertValid();
}

void CColorsView::Dump(CDumpContext& dc) const
{
```

```
    CView::Dump(dc);
}

CColorsDoc* CColorsView::GetDocument() //non-debug ver inline
{
    ASSERT(m_pDocument->IsKindOf(RUNTIME_CLASS(CColorsDoc)));
    return (CColorsDoc*)m_pDocument;
}
#endif //_DEBUG

/////////////////////////////////////////////////////////////
// CColorsView message handlers

void CColorsView::OnMyColor()
{
    // TODO: Add your command handler code here
    dlg.DoModal();
    InvalidateRect(NULL,TRUE);
    UpdateWindow();
}
```

The common colors dialog box returns the color selected in the dialog box to a variable of type COLORREF. In this application, that variable is named mycolor. The RGB color value is easy to obtain through a call to the GetColor() function.

The common color dialog box can be modified by using the m_cc member function. This member function uses a CHOOSECOLOR structure, which takes on the following appearance:

```
struct {
    DWORD         lStructSize;
    HWND          hwndOwner;
    HWND          hInstance;
    COLORREF      rgbResult;
    COLORREF*     lpCustColors;
    DWORD         Flags;
    LPARAM        lCustData;
    LPCCHOOKPROC  lpfnHook;
    LPCTSTR       lpTemplateName;
} CHOOSECOLOR;
```

In this structure, lStructSize, gives the length (bytes) of the structure. The hwndOwner value indicates which window generated the dialog box. The hInstance value is a handle to a data block holding the dialog box template. The rgbResult value gives the color selected when the dialog box was created. Black is the initial color if this value is NULL. The lpCustColors pointer points to an array of 16 DWORDS. Each array value maps to a custom color cell in the dialog box. The user can define custom colors within each cell. The Flags value gives the dialog box initialization flags. These flags may be ORed

together, and they include CC_ENABLEHOOK, CC_ENABLETEMPLATE, CC_EN-
ABLETEMPLATEHANDLE, CC_FULLOPEN, CC_PREVENTFULLOPEN, CC_RG-
BINIT, and CC_SHOWHELP. Additional information for each of these flags can
be found through the Microsoft Developer Studio's Help screen. The lCust-
Data value is used to pass data to the hook function identified by the lpfn-
Hook member. The hook member is used to process messages for the dialog
box. The lpstrTemplateName pointer points to a null-terminated string that
indicates a substitute dialog box template.

   If you examine the listing for the ColorsView.cpp file, you will notice
that the application changed one flag value in this structure:

```
// Open the full dialog box
  dlg.m_cc.Flags |= CC_FULLOPEN;
```

   Here, the CC_FULLOPEN flag fully opens the common dialog box. If
you examine Figure 12.17, you will see a common color dialog box in this
state.

   The default option is to show just the left half of the dialog box. The
full view immediately allows the user to create custom colors from the dialog
box options. The color selected by the user is then used to set a brush color

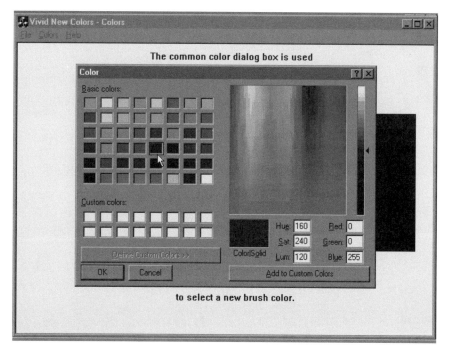

Figure 12.17   *A fully opened common color dialog box.*

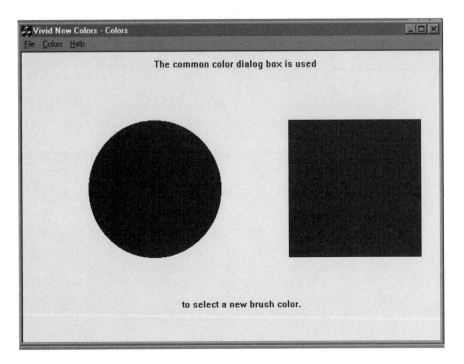

Figure 12.18   *Brush and text colors can be set with the color returned by the dialog box.*

and text color for this application. Two simple shapes and a text message are drawn to the screen in the new color. Figure 12.18 shows a vivid blue color for the graphics figures and text (trust us).

Experiment with the common color dialog box project by selecting other colors, changing flags, and so on.

More Dialog Boxes?

You'll gain even more experience with dialog boxes in the remaining chapters of this book. However, real experience is best gained by creating your own projects and working through the problems that may develop.

Using STL with Graphics Primitives

In the first section of this book, we concentrated on the details of using the STL. In the second section, the MFC (Microsoft Foundation Class) was explored with an emphasis on developing object-oriented Windows applications. In this section, starting with this chapter, we'll explore examples that combine the power of the STL and ease of the MFC when developing Windows applications. In the MFC section of this book, we used one or two graphics drawing primitives to draw a few GDIs to the client area of the window. In this chapter, you will explore the use of a wide variety of drawing primitives. Windows provides a number of functions for drawing basic graphical GDIs, such as arcs, lines, circles, and pie wedges. More complicated GDIs must be constructed with the use of these basic functions, hence the name *graphics primitives*.

You'll also learn how to perform fundamental operations within the graphics environment, such as changing text colors, drawing modes, and pens and brushes.

Graphics Device Interface

Windows uses a code module that handles graphics instructions. This module is called the Graphics Device Interface, or GDI. All graphics functions, including the drawing primitives mentioned in the last section, are contained in the GDI. In addition to providing support for all graphics functions, the GDI also supports the translation of these commands to output device drivers such as monitors, plotters, printers, and so on. Since the GDI operates as a device-independent interface, all graphics applications will draw correctly on any properly installed monitor, plotter, or printer.

The following sections will explain much of the basic terminology associated with the GDI environment.

Windows Environments

Windows 2000 (NT) and Windows 98 keep track of all installed software and hardware. The GDI uses the list of installed drivers to determine how to interface with the various hardware items making up the computer system. For example, information being sent to a printer must be handled differently than information being sent to a monitor. Further differences must be taken into account, even among printers, because printers have different resolutions, color capabilities, and so on. Windows handles all of this interfacing in an invisible manner, thus offering a high degree of portability.

The `GetDeviceCaps()` Function

The `GetDeviceCaps()` function can be used to obtain information concerning the hardware in a particular system. The `GetDeviceCaps()` function returns information on numerous hardware device attributes, including aspect ratios, color planes, resolution, and so on. The syntax for this function is simple:

```
dc.GetDeviceCaps(nIndex);
```

The value *nIndex* is an integer index value used to return information on a particular item. Table 13.1 gives a description of these attributes.

Table 13.1	*Device Capabilities*	
Index	**Meaning**	**Detail**
DRIVERVERSION	Version number.	
TECHNOLOGY	DT_CHARSTREAM	
	DT_DISPFILE	
	DT_METAFILE	
	DT_PLOTTER	
	DT_RASCAMERA	
	DT_RASDISPLA	
	DT_RASPRINTER	
HORZSIZE	Width of display in millimeters.	
VERTSIZE	Height of display in millimeters.	
HORZRES	Width of the display (pixels).	
VERTRES	Height of the display (raster lines).	

Table 13.1	Device Capabilities (Continued)	
Index	**Meaning**	**Detail**
LOGPIXELSX	Number of pixels in logical inch for display width.	
LOGPIXELSY	Number of pixels in logical inch for display height.	
BITSPIXEL	Number of adjacent color bits/pixels.	
PLANES	Number of color planes.	
NUMBRUSHES	Number of device-specific brushes.	
NUMPENS	Number of device-specific pens.	
NUMMARKERS	Number of device-specific markers.	
NUMFONTS	Number of device-specific fonts.	
NUMCOLORS	Number of entries in the device color table.	
ASPECTX	Relative width of device pixel.	
ASPECTY	Relative height of device pixel.	
ASPECTXY	Diagonal width of device pixel.	
PDEVICESIZE	Size of the PDEVICE internal structure (bytes).	
CLIPCAPS	Clipping capabilities supported:	
	CP_NONE	
	CP_RECTANGLE	
	CP_REGION	
SIZEPALETTE	Number of entries in the system palette.	
NUMRESERVED	Number of reserved entries in the system palette.	
COLORRES	Color resolution of the device (bits/pixels).	
RASTERCAPS	Raster capabilities supported:	
	RC_BANDING	Banding.
	RC_BIGFONT	Fonts larger than 64K.
	RC_BITBLT	Transfers bitmaps.
	RC_BITMAP64	Bitmaps larger than 64K.
	RC_DEVBITS	Device bitmaps.

(continued)

Table 13.1	Device Capabilities (Continued)	
Index	**Meaning**	**Detail**
RC_DI_BITMAP	SetDIBits and GetDIBits support.	
	RC_DIBTODEV	SetDIBitsToDevice support.
	RC_FLOODFILL	Flood fills supported.
	RC_GDI20_OUTPUT	Windows (ver 2.0) features.
	RC_GDI20_STATE	Puts a state block in device context.
	RC_NONE	Raster operations not support.
	RC_OP_DX_OUTPUT	Supports dev opaque and DX array.
	RC_PALETTE	Specifies a palette-based device.
	RC_SAVEBITMAP	Saves bitmaps locally.
	RC_SCALING	Scaling support.
	RC_STRETCHBLT	StretchBlt support.
	RC_STRETCHDIB	StretchDIBits support.
CURVECAPS	Curve capabilities the device supports:	
	CC_CHORD	Chords support.
	CC_CIRCLES	Circles support.
	CC_ELLIPSES	Ellipses support.
	CC_INTERIORS	Interiors support.
	CC_NONE	Curves support.
	CC_PIE	Pie wedges support.
	CC_ROUNDRECT	Rectangles with rounded corners support.
	CC_STYLED	Styled borders support.
	CC_WIDE	Wide borders support.
	CC_WIDESTYLED	Wide-styled borders support.
LINECAPS	Line capabilities the device supports:	
	LC_INTERIORS	Interiors support.
	LC_MARKER	Markers support.
	LC_NONE	No lines support.
	LC_POLYLINE	Polylines support.
	LC_POLYMARKER	Polymarkers support.
	LC_STYLED	Styled lines support.

Table 13.1   *Device Capabilities (Continued)*

Index	Meaning	Detail
	LC_WIDE	Wide lines support.
	LC_WIDESTYLED	Wide-styled lines support.
POLYGONALCAPS	Polygonal capabilities the device supports:	
	PC_INTERIORS	Interiors support.
	PC_NONE	No polygons support.
	PC_POLYGON	Alternate fill polygons support.
	PC_RECTANGLE	Rectangles support.
	PC_SCANLINE	Scan lines support.
	PC_STYLED	Styled borders support.
	PC_WIDE	Wide borders support.
	PC_WIDESTYLED	Wide-styled borders support.
	PC_WINDPOLYGON	Winding number fill polygons support.
TEXTCAPS	Text capabilities the device supports:	
	TC_CP_STROKE	Device can clip fonts to a pixel.
	TC_CR_90	90-degree character rotation.
	TC_CR_ANY	Any degree character rotation.
	TC_EA_DOUBLE	Double-weight characters.
	TC_IA_ABLE	Italics.
	TC_OP_CHARACTER	Device can place fonts at any pixel.
	TC_OP_STROKE	Device can omit any stroke of a font.
	TC_RA_ABLE	Raster fonts.
	TC_RESERVED	Reserved (must be zero).
	TC_SA_CONTIN	Multiples for exact scaling.
	TC_SA_DOUBLE	Doubled character scaling.
	TC_SA_INTEGER	Integer multiples for scaling.
	TC_SF_X_YINDEP	Independent scaling x and y direction.
	C_SO_ABLE	Strikeouts.
	TC_UA_ABLE	Underlining.
	TC_VA_ABLE	Vector fonts.
LOGPIXELSX	Pixels/inches in X direction.	
LOGPIXELSY	Pixels/inches in Y direction.	

You will also notice in Table 13.1 that some devices, such as plotters, can have a built-in capability to draw circles, ellipses, pie wedges, and so on. When these abilities are present, Windows does not have to use specific GDI routines. When the hardware device does not have these capabilities, Windows supplies the equivalent software routine through the GDI.

Mapping Modes

By default, the GDI uses the upper left part of the window as the origin. In this mode, the X axis increases positively as you move to the right and the Y axis increases positively as you move down, as shown in Figure 13.1.

This is the Windows default mapping mode. It is named the MM_TEXT mapping mode or pixel coordinate mode. Seven additional mapping modes are available. These mapping modes allow drawing in English, metric, or user-defined units. These mapping modes will be described in the next section. The default MM_TEXT mapping mode uses 0 to 639 pixels horizontally and 0 to 479 pixels vertically when drawing on a VGA screen. If the application is then run on a system with an SVGA monitor, the GDI will adjust the window accordingly.

MAPPING MODE PARAMETERS

GDI graphics functions are dependent on the mapping mode currently in use. Only the default mapping mode MM_TEXT measures point values in pixels. Table 13.2 lists the eight mapping modes.

Table 13.2	Windows' Eight Mapping Modes
Mode	**Description**
MM_ANISOTROPIC	Arbitrary units with arbitrarily scaled axes.
MM_HIENGLISH	Logical unit mapped to 0.001 inch. Positive x is to the right, positive y is up.
MM_HIMETRIC	Logical unit mapped to 0.01 millimeter. Positive x is to the right, positive y is up.
MM_ISOTROPIC	Arbitrary units with equally scaled axes.
MM_LOMETRIC	Logical unit mapped to 0.1 millimeter. Positive x is to the right, positive y is up.
MM_LOENGLISH	Logical unit mapped to 0.01 inch. Positive x is to the right, positive y is up.
MM_TEXT	Logical unit mapped to device pixel. Positive x is to the right, positive y is down.
MM_TWIPS	Logical unit mapped to 1/20 of printer's point. Positive x is to the right, positive y is up.

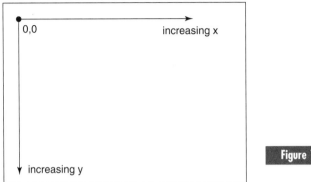

0,0   increasing x

increasing y

Figure 13.1 *The default Windows coordinate system with the origin in the upper left corner of the window.*

You'll see how mapping modes are changed in various examples throughout the remainder of this book.

CHANGING MAPPING MODES

A change to the default mapping mode can be made with a call to the `SetMapMode()` function:

```
dc.SetMapMode(fnMapMode);
```

The *fnMapMode* parameter is an integer value specifying one of the eight types shown in Table 13.2. The function returns an integer value. Regardless of which mapping mode is used, it is the responsibility of Windows to map the logical drawing coordinates to the physical device coordinates.

Drawing Primitives

Windows provides a large number of drawing functions for creating lines, arcs, rectangles, and so on. These graphics primitives are the building blocks of all other graphics drawing functions. Graphics primitives are the components of all Windows graphics applications.

There are numerous categories of drawing primitives. Most of these categories are composed of a single function. The most often used categories include functions for drawing arcs, chords, circles, ellipses, lines, pie wedges, polygons, polylines, rectangles, rectangles with rounded corners, and single pixels, plus techniques for setting cursor positions.

All drawing primitives draw with the current pen style and color and, where applicable, fill the shape with the current brush style and color. Details about pen and brush selections are included later in this chapter.

Arc() **and** ArcTo()

The Arc() function is used to draw an elliptical arc with the current pen. The arc is centered in a bounding rectangle described by the points x1,y1 and x2,y2, as shown in Figure 13.2.

The arc's length is described as lying between points x3,y3 and x4,y4. The arc is drawn in a counterclockwise direction. The Arc() function does not update the coordinates of the current point. All parameters are specified as integers. This function returns a type BOOL.

The function can be called by supplying parameters in the following manner:

```
pDC->Arc(x1,y1,x2,y2,x3,y3,x4,y4);
```

The ArcTo() function is similar to the Arc() function, except that it updates the current point.

Chord()

The Chord() function is similar to the Arc() function. The resulting figure is closed by a line between the two arc points x3,y3 and x4,y4. The chord is drawn using the current pen. Figure 13.3 shows these points.

Since the chord is a closed figure, it is filled with the current brush color. All parameters are integer values. This function returns a type BOOL.

The function uses the following syntax:

```
pDC->Chord(x1,y1,x2,y2,x3,y3,x4,y4);
```

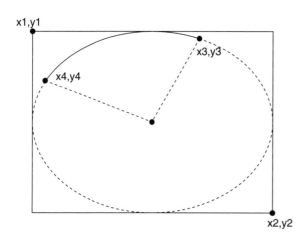

Figure 13.2   *The arc is centered in a bounding rectangle.*

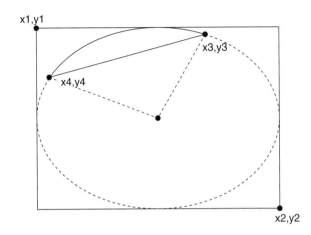

x1,y1

x3,y3

x4,y4

x2,y2

| **Figure 13.3** | *The chord is enclosed in a bounding rectangle.* |

`Ellipse()` (and Circle)

The `Ellipse()` function is used to draw an ellipse or a circle with the current pen. The center of the ellipse is a bounding rectangle described by the points x1,y1 and x2,y2, as shown in Figure 13.4.

Since the ellipse is a closed figure, it is filled with the current brush color. All parameters are integer values. This function returns a type BOOL.

The function uses the following syntax:

```
pDC->Ellipse(x1,y1,x2,y2);
```

Circles can be drawn with the `Ellipse()` function by making the bounding rectangle's points symmetric (a square).

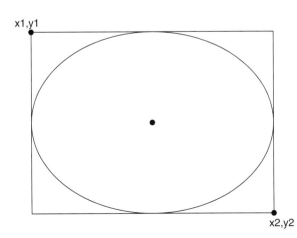

x1,y1

x2,y2

| **Figure 13.4** | *The ellipse is contained in the bounding rectangle.* |

LineTo()

The LineTo() function draws a line from the current point up to, but not including, the specified point with the current pen. The current point is set with the MoveTo() function. The current point will be x,y when the function is finished. All parameters are of type int. This function returns a type BOOL.
     The function uses the following syntax:

```
pDC->LineTo(x,y);
```

MoveTo() **and** MoveToEx()

The MoveTo() and MoveToEx() functions move the current point to the specified point. MoveToEx() returns the original point to a data structure. The x and y values are integers. This function returns a type BOOL. The x and y coordinates of the original point are returned in an *lpPoint* structure.
     This function uses the following syntax:

```
pDC->MoveTo(x,y);
pDC->MoveToEx(x,y,lpPt);
```

If the original point's values are not required, a NULL value can be inserted in the third parameter of the MoveToEx() function.

Pie()

The Pie() function is used to draw pie-shaped wedges with the current pen. The center of the elliptical pie arc is centered in the bounding rectangle described by the points x1,y1 and x2,y2, as shown in Figure 13.5.

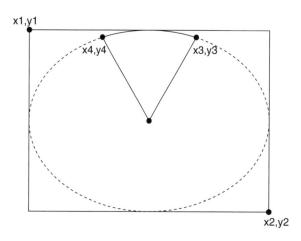

| Figure 13.5 | The pie slice is centered in the bounding rectangle. |

The starting and ending points of the arc are drawn counterclockwise from points x3,y3 to x4,y4. The pie wedge is filled with the current brush color since it is a closed figure. All parameters are integer values. This function returns a type BOOL.

This function uses the following syntax:

```
pDC->Pie(x1,y1,x2,y2,x3,y3,x4,y4);
```

Polygon()

The `Polygon()` function draws a polygon. Polygons are specified by points that are connected by lines. The polygon is a closed shape and is drawn with the current pen and filled with the current brush color. Figure 13.6 shows an example of a polygon.

The data points for the polygon are held in an array of type POINT. The number of points in the array is an integer. This function returns a type BOOL.

This function uses the following syntax:

```
pDC->Polygon(pointarray,nCount);
```

Polyline() and PolylineTo()

The `Polyline()` function draws a group of connected line segments given in a type POINT array with the current pen. This function does not return the starting point. However, the `PolylineTo()` is a Win32 function that behaves like `Polyline()` and also returns the starting point. The number of data points in the array is an integer. This function returns a type BOOL.

This function uses the following syntax:

```
pDC->Polyline(pointarray,nCount);
```

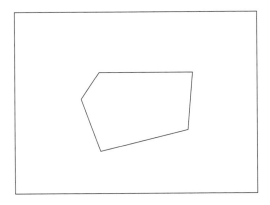

Figure 13.6   *A closed polygon shape.*

Rectangle()

The `Rectangle()` function draws a rectangle described by x1,y1 and x2,y2. The rectangle is drawn with the current pen and filled with the current brush color since it is a closed shape. All parameters are integer values. This function returns a type BOOL.

This function uses the following syntax:

```
pDC->Rectangle(x1,y1,x2,y2);
```

RoundRect()

The `RoundRect()` function draws a round-cornered rectangle described by x1,y1 and x2,y2 with the current pen. The values x3 and y3 give the width and height of the ellipse used to round the corners. The rounded rectangle is filled with the current brush color since it is a closed figure. All parameters are integer values. This function returns a type BOOL.

This function uses the following syntax:

```
pDC->RoundRect(x1,y1,x2,y2,x3,y3);
```

SetPixel() and GetPixel()

The `SetPixel()` function is used to light a pixel at position x,y. The function uses the RGB color closest to the color requested. The x and y parameters are integer values, and *crColor* is of type COLORREF. This function returns a type COLORREF.

This function uses the following syntax:

```
pDC->SetPixel(x,y,crColor);
```

The `GetPixel()` function retrieves the RGB color value at the point given by x,y and returns it as a type COLORREF.

This function uses the following syntax:

```
pointcolor = pDC->GetPixel(x,y);
```

Windows Graphics Tools

Windows provides a number of default drawing options. Stock tools such as brush and pen styles and colors can be used, or special tools can be designed. Most GDI stock items are described in the `wingdi.h` header file. For example, the stock brushes and pens described in Table 13.3 are found in the `wingdi.h` header file.

Table 13.3	*Stock Brushes and Pens*

Stock Brush and Pen Identifiers

WHITE_BRUSH

LTGRAY_BRUSH

GRAY_BRUSH

DKGRAY_BRUSH

BLACK_BRUSH

HOLLOW_BRUSH (or NULL_BRUSH)

WHITE_PEN

BLACK_PEN

NULL_PEN

A number of examples in this chapter and those that follow will illustrate the use of stock brushes and pens.

Pens

Pens draw the outlines for all graphics functions. Pens have three attributes: color, style, and width. The default pen is a black pen (BLACK_PEN) drawing a solid line (PS_SOLID) one device pixel wide. Additional stock pen colors include white (WHITE_PEN) and a pen that draws in invisible ink (NULL_PEN).

The stock pen line styles are shown in Table 13.4:

Table 13.4	*Stock Pen Line Styles*

Pen Style	**Description**
PS_SOLID	A solid line.
PS_DASH	A dashed line.
PS_DOT	A dotted line.
PS_DASHDOT	A dash-dot line.
PS_DASHDOTDOT	A dash-dot-dot line.
PS_NULL	An invisible line.
PS_INSIDEFRAME	A solid rule inside a frame.

Line widths are given in logical units as integer numbers. A width of 15 in the default drawing mode will draw a line 15 pixels wide. However, all pens greater than one logical unit default to either a null or a solid line drawing style.

Pens are created using the CPen class. Stock pens can be obtained with the GetStockObject() function. To change the pen just selected to the current pen, use the SelectObject() function. For example:

```
CPen   newpen;
       .
       .
       .
newpen = pDC->SelectObject(GetStockObject(WHITE_PEN));
```

A custom pen can be created and selected with the CreatePen() function, in conjunction with the SelectObject() function. The CreatePen() function creates a logical pen with the syntax:

```
newpen.CreatePen(nPenStyle,nWidth,rgbColor);
```

The parameter *nPenStyle* is an integer and can be specified by any of the PS_ values, for example, PS_SOLID. The value *nWidth* is an integer and is given in logical units. The *rgbColor* value is of type COLORREF and is given in terms of an RGB color value. For example:

```
CPen   newpen;
CPen*  oldpen;
       .
       .
       .
newpen.CreatePen(PS_SOLID,8,RGB(255,0,0));
oldpen = pDC->SelectObject(CreatePen(&newpen));
```

In this case, a pen is created and selected for drawing solid lines, eight pixels wide, in a red color. Once a pen is selected, only that pen can be used to draw within the device context. To use another pen, the first pen must be de-selected. This is done by calling the DeleteObject() function.

```
newpen.DeleteObject();
```

Only user-created pens should be deleted. Stock pens should not be deleted.

Brushes

Brushes are used to fill the closed figures created with the appropriate graphics functions. Brushes have several attributes, including color, brush style, and hatch style. The default brush is a white brush (WHITE_BRUSH) that fills the object with a solid pattern (BS_SOLID). A solid brush refers to the fill pattern used by the brush. Other stock brush color choices include BLACK_BRUSH, BKGRAY_BRUSH, GRAY_BRUSH, HOLLOW_BRUSH, or NULL_BRUSH, and LTGRAY_BRUSH.

The stock fill patterns used by brushes include those shown in Table 13.5:

Table 13.5	Stock Brush Fill Patterns
Brush Style	**Description**
BS_SOLID	The fill is the color of the brush.
BS_HOLLOW	The color of the brush is ignored.
BS_HATCHED	The hatching is the color of the brush.
BS_PATTERN	The color of the brush is ignored.
BS_INDEXED	The color is selected from a color table.
BS_DIBPATTERN	The color is defined by a device-independent bitmap.

Cross-hatching can be selected from the group of hatch patterns shown in Table 13.6:

Table 13.6	Stock Brush Hatch Patterns
Brush Hatch Patterns	**Description**
HS_HORIZONTAL	Horizontal hatch.
HS_VERTICAL	Vertical hatch.
HS_FDIAGONAL	Forward diagonal hatch.
HS_BDIAGONAL	Backward diagonal hatch.
HS_CROSS	+-pattern cross hatch.
HS_DIAGCROSS	x-pattern cross hatch.

Additional hatch patterns are described in the wingdi.h header file. Brushes are created via the CBrush class. Stock brushes can be obtained with the GetStockObject() function. The SelectObject() function changes the brush just selected to the current brush.

To create and select a custom brush, use one of the following functions: CreateSolidBrush(), CreateHatchBrush(), CreatePattern-Brush(), or CreateDIBPatternBrush(). Once the brush is created, it is selected with the SelectObject() function. Here is an example:

```
CBrush   newbrush;
CBrush*  oldbrush;
      .
      .
      .
newbrush.CreateSolidBrush(RGB(0,255,0));
oldbrush = pDC->SelectObject(&newbrush);
```

In this example, a solid green brush is created and selected.

Once a brush is selected, only that brush can be used to fill objects within the current device context. To use a brush of another color or pattern, the previous brush must be de-selected. This is done by calling the `Delete-Object()` function. For example:

```
newbrush.DeleteObject();
```

Only user-defined brushes should be deleted. Stock brushes should not be deleted.

Text Colors

The foreground and background colors of text drawn to the graphics screen are easy to change. The foreground color of text can be changed with a call to the `SetTextColor()` function. For example:

```
dc.SetTextColor(RGB(0,0,255));
```

This RGB value sets the text color to blue.

The background color of the text block is based on the background mode and color. The background mode is either opaque or transparent. An opaque mode background color fills the space between the letters with the new color. The default is white unless the background color has been changed. In transparent mode, the background color is ignored. The space between characters is not filled. The background mode is set with a call to the `SetBkMode()` function.

```
dc.SetBkMode(TRANSPARENT);
```

The background text color is set with a call to the `SetBkColor()` function.

```
dc.SetBkColor(RGB(0,255,0));
```

In this case, the background text color is set to green.

Drawing Mode Selection

Pens and brushes are combined with objects based on the selected drawing mode. The `SetROP2()` function is used to select the drawing mode. The syntax of the function is:

```
pDC->SetROP2(nDrawMode);
```

The `SetROP2()` function returns an integer. The *nDrawMode* parameter is also an integer. The value for *nDrawMode* can be any of the values shown in Table 13.7.

Table 13.7	*Drawing Mode Values*

Selected Value	**Description**
R2_BLACK	Pixel is black.
R2_COPYPEN	Pixel is pen color.
R2_MASKNOTPEN	Pixel is a combination of display and inverse of pen.
R2_MASKPEN	Pixel color is common to pen and display.
R2_MASKPENNOT	Pixel is a combination of pen color and inverse of screen.
R2_MERGENOTPEN	Pixel is display color and inverse pen color.
R2_MERGEPEN	Pixel is pen color and display color merged.
R2_MERGEPENNOT	Pixel is pen color and inverse display color merged.
R2_NOP	Pixel is unchanged.
R2_NOT	Pixel is inverse of display color.
R2_NOTCOPYPEN	Pixel is inverse of pen color.
R2_NOTMASKPEN	Pixel is inverse of R2_MASKPEN.
R2_NOTMERGEPEN	Pixel is inverse of R2_MERGEOPEN color.
R2_NOTXORPEN	Pixel is inverse of R2_XORPEN.
R2_WHITE	Pixel is white.
R2_XORPEN	Pixel is combination of colors in pen and display, but not colors in both.

Windows uses a default value of `R2_COPYPEN`. If the default drawing mode is satisfactory, the `SetROP2()` function will not need to be called.

A Simple Application Using The STL and GDI Tools

The project developed for this chapter will put many of the graphics functions just discussed into action. This straightforward application is designed to teach you how the various graphics primitives and drawing options can be used and how to weave simple STL code into a Windows project. The project is named GDI. You can use the AppWizard to create the initial template code for the project, as we have done in the past four chapters.

The Basic Project Code

To build the project for this chapter, you will first need to generate the project's template code with the AppWizard. The project name is GDI. Use the following steps to complete the project files.

- Enter the Microsoft Visual Studio (Visual C++ compiler).
- Choose the File menu and select the New menu item.
- Select Project Workspace from the New dialog box.
- From the New Project Workspace dialog box:
  - Name the workspace GDI.
  - Set the location of the workspace (for example, C:\GDI).
  - Select MFC AppWizard (exe) from the list box.
- Step 1—Select a Single document application type.
- Step 2—Select no database support.
- Step 3—Select None for OLE compound document support.
- Step 4—Select no additional features.
- Step 5—Do not select comments. Select a statically linked library.
- Step 6—View your settings and Finish the AppWizard process.
- If the information in the New Project Information dialog box is correct, select OK.

When the final step has been completed, as just described, the AppWizard generates all of the template code needed for the project.

Adding Unique Project Code

When the AppWizard generated the template code for the GDI project, it created numerous source code, header, and resource files. For example, the following source code files can be found in the GDI subdirectory: Main-Frm.cpp, GDI.cpp, GDIDoc.cpp, GDIView.cpp and StdAfx.cpp. For this simple example, only the GDIView.cpp file will have to be altered to support the graphics function calls.

Before adding various GDI drawing functions, edit the application's menu so that only a File menu with an Exit menu item and a Help menu with an About menu item are available, as shown in Figure 13.7.

Open the GDIView.cpp file for editing. You will need to enter the code shown in bold in the next listing.

```
// GDIView.cpp : implementation of the CGDIView class
//
```

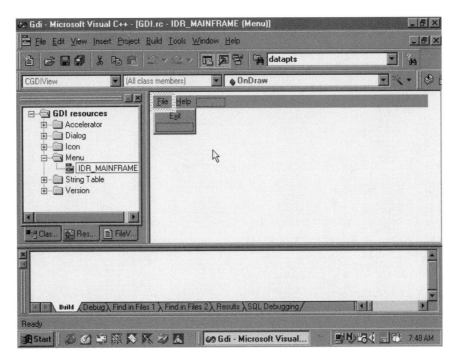

Figure 13.7   *A modified AppWizard menu with just* File *and* Exit *capabilities.*

```
#include "stdafx.h"
#include "GDI.h"

#include "GDIDoc.h"
#include "GDIView.h"

#include <list>

using namespace std;
typedef list <int> INTPTS;

#ifdef _DEBUG
#define new DEBUG_NEW
#undef THIS_FILE
static char THIS_FILE[] = __FILE__;
#endit

/////////////////////////////////////////////////////////////
// CGDIView

IMPLEMENT_DYNCREATE(CGDIView, Cview)
```

```
BEGIN_MESSAGE_MAP(CGDIView, Cview)
    //{{AFX_MSG_MAP(CGDIView)
    //}}AFX_MSG_MAP
END_MESSAGE_MAP()

////////////////////////////////////////////////////////////
// CGDIView construction/destruction

CGDIView::CGDIView()
{
}

CGDIView::~CGDIView()
{
}

BOOL CGDIView::PreCreateWindow(CREATESTRUCT& cs)
{
    return CView::PreCreateWindow(cs);
}

////////////////////////////////////////////////////////////
// CGDIView drawing

void CGDIView::OnDraw(CDC* pDC)
{
    CGDIDoc* pDoc = GetDocument();
    ASSERT_VALID(pDoc);

    POINT polylpts[4],polygpts[5];

    INTPTS datapts1, datapts2;
    INTPTS::iterator p1, p2;

    CBrush newbrush;
    CBrush* oldbrush;
    CPen newpen;
    CPen* oldpen;

    // draw several styled lines
    // using an STL list
    newpen.CreatePen(PS_DASHDOT,1,RGB(255,0,255));
    oldpen=pDC->SelectObject(&newpen);
    datapts1.insert (datapts1.end(), 40);
    datapts1.insert (datapts1.end(), 90);
    for (int y = 10; y<= 50; y+=5) {
        p1=datapts1.begin();
        pDC->MoveTo(*p1,y);
        ++p1;
        pDC->LineTo(*p1,y);
```

```
}
pDC->TextOut(100,20,"<- styled lines",15);
// de-select pen
pDC->SelectObject(&newpen);
newpen.DeleteObject();

// return to default pen values
newpen.CreatePen(PS_SOLID,1,RGB(0,0,0));
oldpen=pDC->SelectObject(&newpen);
// de-select pen
pDC->SelectObject(&newpen);
newpen.DeleteObject();

// use an STL list for drawing
// several pixels on screen
datapts2.insert (datapts2.begin(), 380);
datapts2.insert (datapts2.begin(), 385);
datapts2.insert (datapts2.begin(), 390);
datapts2.insert (datapts2.begin(), 395);
datapts2.insert (datapts2.begin(), 400);
datapts2.insert (datapts2.begin(), 405);
datapts2.insert (datapts2.begin(), 410);
datapts2.insert (datapts2.begin(), 415);
datapts2.insert (datapts2.begin(), 420);
datapts2.insert (datapts2.begin(), 425);
datapts2.insert (datapts2.begin(), 430);
datapts2.insert (datapts2.begin(), 435);
for (p2=datapts2.begin(); p2!=datapts2.end(); ++p2)
    pDC->SetPixel(*p2,55,0L);
pDC->TextOut(460,45,"<- pixels",9);

// draw an arc
pDC->Arc(25,125,175,225,175,225,100,125);
pDC->TextOut(70,160,"small arc ->",12);

// drawing several lines with Polyline
polylpts[0].x=10;
polylpts[0].y=30;
polylpts[1].x=10;
polylpts[1].y=100;
polylpts[2].x=50;
polylpts[2].y=100;
polylpts[3].x=10;
polylpts[3].y=30;
pDC->Polyline(polylpts,4);
pDC->TextOut(10,110,"polyline",8);

// draw a chord, fill with red
newbrush.CreateSolidBrush(RGB(255,0,0));
oldbrush=pDC->SelectObject(&newbrush);
```

```
pDC->Chord(130,125,275,225,275,225,200,130);
pDC->TextOut(280,150,"<- chord",8);
// de-select brush
pDC->SelectObject(&newbrush);
newbrush.DeleteObject();

// draw an ellipse, fill with blue
newbrush.CreateSolidBrush(RGB(0,0,255));
oldbrush=pDC->SelectObject(&newbrush);
pDC->Ellipse(270,300,200,270);
pDC->TextOut(220,250,"ellipse",7);
// de-select brush
pDC->SelectObject(&newbrush);
newbrush.DeleteObject();

// draw a circle with ellipse function
// fill with green
// set text color to blue
// fill green color between letters.
newbrush.CreateSolidBrush(RGB(0,255,0));
oldbrush=pDC->SelectObject(&newbrush);
pDC->Ellipse(375,75,525,225);
pDC->SetTextColor(RGB(0,0,255));
pDC->SetBkMode(TRANSPARENT);
pDC->SetBkColor(RGB(0,255,0));
pDC->TextOut(435,130,"circle",6);
// return to default values
pDC->SetTextColor(RGB(0,0,0));
pDC->SetBkMode(OPAQUE);
pDC->SetBkColor(RGB(255,255,255));
// de-select brush
pDC->SelectObject(&newbrush);
newbrush.DeleteObject();

// draw a pie wedge, fill with yellow
newbrush.CreateSolidBrush(RGB(255,255,0));
oldbrush=pDC->SelectObject(&newbrush);
pDC->Pie(200,0,300,100,200,50,250,100);
pDC->TextOut(260,70,"<- pie wedge",12);
// de-select brush
pDC->SelectObject(&newbrush);
newbrush.DeleteObject();

// draw a rectangle, fill with lite blue
newbrush.CreateSolidBrush(RGB(0,255,255));
oldbrush=pDC->SelectObject(&newbrush);
pDC->Rectangle(20,300,150,380);
pDC->TextOut(50,325,"rectangle",9);
// de-select brush
pDC->SelectObject(&newbrush);
newbrush.DeleteObject();
```

```
    // draw rounded rectangle, fill with gray
    // change pen width to 3 and color to red
    newpen.CreatePen(PS_SOLID,3,RGB(255,0,0));
    oldpen=pDC->SelectObject(&newpen);
    newbrush.CreateSolidBrush(RGB(127,127,127));
    oldbrush=pDC->SelectObject(&newbrush);
    pDC->RoundRect(350,250,400,380,20,20);
    pDC->TextOut (410,270,"<- rounded rectangle",20);
    // de-select brush
    pDC->SelectObject(&newbrush);
    newbrush.DeleteObject();
    // de-select pen
    pDC->SelectObject(&newpen);
    newpen.DeleteObject();

    // draw with Polygon, fill with a mixed color
    // change pen width to 5 and color to blue
    polygpts[0].x=40;
    polygpts[0].y=200;
    polygpts[1].x=100;
    polygpts[1].y=270;
    polygpts[2].x=80;
    polygpts[2].y=290;
    polygpts[3].x=20;
    polygpts[3].y=220;
    polygpts[4].x=40;
    polygpts[4].y=200;
    newpen.CreatePen(PS_SOLID,5,RGB(0,0,255));
    oldpen=pDC->SelectObject(&newpen);
    newbrush.CreateSolidBrush(RGB(127,155,55));
    oldbrush=pDC->SelectObject(&newbrush);
    pDC->Polygon(polygpts,5);
    pDC->TextOut(90,230,"<- polygon",10);
    // de-select brush
    pDC->SelectObject(&newbrush);
    newbrush.DeleteObject();
    // de-select pen
    pDC->SelectObject(&newpen);
    newpen.DeleteObject();
}

/////////////////////////////////////////////////////////////////
// CGDIView diagnostics

#ifdef _DEBUG
void CGDIView::AssertValid() const
{
    CView::AssertValid();
}

void CGDIView::Dump(CDumpContext& dc) const
```

```
{
    CView::Dump(dc);
}

CGDIDoc* CGDIView::GetDocument() // non-debug version inline
{
    ASSERT(m_pDocument->IsKindOf(RUNTIME_CLASS(CGDIDoc)));
    return (CGDIDoc*)m_pDocument;
}
#endif //_DEBUG

///////////////////////////////////////////////////////////////
// CGDIView message handlers
```

This application will make a handy reference when you want to remember how to code a particular graphics function. Examine the listing carefully, study the figure shown in Figure 13.8, and see if you can determine how each function operates.

Build the application from the Microsoft Visual Studio's Build menu, and then select the Rebuild All menu item.

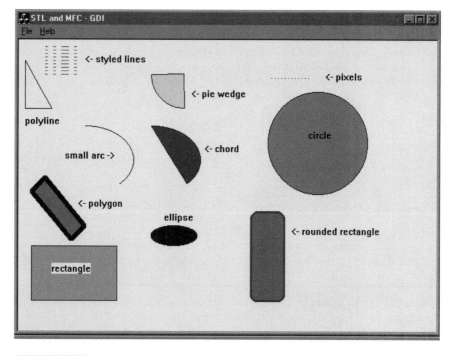

Figure 13.8   *The simple graphics of the GDI project.*

Examining the Project Code

The unique project code added to the basic code generated by the AppWizard is straightforward. You'll find that most GDI graphics functions are called in accordance with the function descriptions discussed earlier in this chapter. There are, however, two unique situations that involve the use of the STL.

The STL portion of `GDIView.cpp` begins with the following statement:

```
#include <list>
```

While the **#include** statement is not new to programmers, what it includes is a radical departure from typical header files. In Chapter 5, you learned that the STL `<list>` template defines a generic linked-list. The `<list>` template provides all of the necessary functionality for initializing, creating, inserting, deleting, searching, and counting list elements.

A `<list>` container is your best choice when the number of elements in a collection cannot be bounded, or varies widely during the course of execution. Like a vector, a list maintains values of uniform type. However, unlike vectors, lists are not indexed. Instead, elements must be examined one by one in sequence. For this reason, the amount of time required to access an element in a list depends upon the position the element holds in the list.

The following **using namespace std;** statement imports all STL-compatible definitions necessary for any application employing STL technology:

```
using namespace std;
typedef list <int> INTPTS;
```

Recall, from a discussion in Chapter 2, that the ANSI C++ Committee recommends a **typedef** definition for STL-style compatibility. Here, the **typedef** creates a new type called *INTPTS*, which associated with an STL list containing integer elements. This **typedef** is used in the *GDIView::OnDraw()* method.

The following statement instantiates two actual list objects: one called *datapts1*, and a second called *datapts2*.

```
INTPTS datapts1, datapts2;
```

The following code statement immediately follows the object instantiation:

```
INTPTS::iterator p1, p2;
```

This statement uses the *INTPTS* type to define two list iterators, *p1* and *p2*. Once again, from Chapter 5, you learned that to traverse a container, a list element type-specific pointer is needed to hold list element addresses.

However, in STL terminology, you do not call this variable a pointer, although that's structurally what it is; instead, you call it an iterator.

From an efficiency viewpoint, using an iterator to denote a given location, for insertion into or deletion from a list, can be performed in constant time. As with a vector, to determine whether or not a specific value occurs in a list requires a sequential search. While a list can be ordered, it is not possible to perform a binary search on a list, and therefore the sequential search time is generally the best that can be achieved.

Examine the following code statements:

```
datapts1.insert(datapts1.end(),40);
datapts1.insert(datapts1.end(),90);
```

These statements are used to define the starting and ending horizontal points on a styled line. These statements use two STL methods to *insert()* the points at the *end()* of the list container. This same code logic can be used to treat a list like a queue, where each new item added is placed at the end of the list.

The most crucial point to remember when using STL container technology is that even though an iterator is an element-specific-type pointer, you should *not* keep track of its address. Instead, STL technology employs data-independent, generic methods, like *end()*, to safely locate specific elements (in this case, the location of the next available list location). This approach, once you understand its design, is intended to *always* separate you from *how* a container is internally implemented, and allow you to simply concentrate on the behaviors necessary to get the container to do what you want.

The code that actually draws a styled line initializes the iterator *p1* to the first element in the list container (*40*) by using the *begin()* method:

```
p1=datapts1.begin();
```

Notice that it is this iterator's contents that are dereferenced (**p1*) in the call to the MoveTo() function:

```
pDC->MoveTo(*p1,y);
```

Once the current point is set to (**p1,y*), the following statement is used:

```
++p1;
```

This statement uses the prefix increment operator on the *p1* iterator to move its address to the next list container element (*90*). If you are an experienced linked list programmer, you'll appreciate this streamlined syntax. Notice that you do not have to point to a node structure's *next_nodes_address* member to retrieve the location of the next list element, as in:

```
p1 = p1->next_nodes_address;
```

Once again, you see code demonstrations of how the STL cloaks the underlying container's internal construction!

Finally, the `LineTo()` function is used to draw a line from the previously defined point to the final point. Since the `MoveTo()` and `LineTo()` functions are in a loop, several styled lines are drawn to the screen at various vertical positions.

While this is a fairly simple example, you can imagine the power of using a list when you realize that a list could contain the points for drawing many different line segments. These segments could define a complex graphics shape, such as a house, car and so on.

The next portion of code using STL technology is responsible for placing a number of colored pixels in the client area. Examine this portion of code:

```
        .
        .
        .
// use an STL list for drawing
// several pixels on screen
datapts2.insert (datapts2.begin(), 380);
datapts2.insert (datapts2.begin(), 385);
datapts2.insert (datapts2.begin(), 390);
datapts2.insert (datapts2.begin(), 395);
datapts2.insert (datapts2.begin(), 400);
datapts2.insert (datapts2.begin(), 405);
datapts2.insert (datapts2.begin(), 410);
datapts2.insert (datapts2.begin(), 415);
datapts2.insert (datapts2.begin(), 420);
datapts2.insert (datapts2.begin(), 425);
datapts2.insert (datapts2.begin(), 430);
datapts2.insert (datapts2.begin(), 435);
for (p2=datapts2.begin(); p2!=datapts2.end(); ++p2)
    pDC->SetPixel(*p2,55,0L);
pDC->TextOut(460,45,"<- pixels",9);
```

The concepts used in this portion of code are very similar to the logic used for the draw styled line algorithm described earlier. This code segment begins with:

```
datapts2.insert(datapts2.begin(), 380);
datapts2.insert(datapts2.begin(), 385);
```

Here, the *insert()* method is used to add a list container element. However, unlike the draw styled line code segment, this portion of the algorithm uses the *begin()* adapter method previously discussed in Chapter 4. By not using the *end()* method, the *begin()* approach instructs the list container to behave more like a stack (LIFO—Last In First Out). The segment that drew a styled line segment used the container like a queue (FIFO—First In

First Out). In this portion of code, the *last* horizontal pixel location used from the container is the 380 value.

A simple **for** loop controls the drawing of the individual pixels, which you should be able to see in Figure 13.8, shown earlier.

More GDI Primitives?

Did you know there are even more graphics primitives than those we've shown you in this chapter? Windows 2000 (NT), for example, supports a whole host of graphics functions that deal with world transformations. These functions allows the coordinate system to be rotated and scaled. By using these functions, it is possible to draw an ellipse on something other than the horizontal or vertical axis.

If you are interested in these additional concepts, start first by printing the header files we suggested earlier in this chapter. Next, use the help engine supplied with the Microsoft Visual Studio. Finally, don't neglect Microsoft's sample programs.

Vectors and Complex Numbers

In the previous chapter, you learned how to use various GDI drawing primitives and included the power of the STL `<list>` template. This chapter will continue the development of the STL and MFC Windows applications by making use of the `<numeric>` and `<vector>` templates in one application, and using the `<complex>` template in another.

The GDI drawing primitives used in this chapter are simple and straightforward, but you might want to review the details of their use in Chapters 11 through 13. We'll also revisit the Fourier application from Chapter 6, and add some interesting details.

A Fourier Applicaton

In the previous chapter, you learned how to use the `<list>` container in an MFC application. Recall that the `<list>` template provides all of the necessary functionality for initializing, creating, inserting, deleting, searching, and counting list elements. The `<list>` container is the best choice when the number of elements in a collection cannot be bounded, or varies widely during the course of execution. A list maintains values of uniform type; however the list is not indexed. A `<vector>` container can function in a manner very similar to a list, and the elements in a `<vector>` container can be indexed. This means vector elements do not have to be examined one by one in sequence. This can be an advantage since the amount of time required to access an element in a vector does not depend upon the position the element holds in the vector. You'll see how a `<vector>` container is implemented in the application later in this section.

To make this application more robust, we're going to combine the `<vector>` container with some simple GDI drawing primitives and calculate and plot a Fourier series.

The French mathematician Baron Jean Baptiste Joseph Fourier (1768-1830) found that any periodic waveform can be constructed by simply adding the correct combinations of sine wave harmonics together. Using his techniques, a wide variety of waveforms, from square to triangular, can be created. Electrical engineers are often interested in square wave reproduction, because square waves are made from a fundamental sine wave and its associated overtones. The quality of amplifiers and other communication devices depends on how well they can reproduce these signals. (More information can be found on Fourier series in college-level physics or electrical engineering textbooks.) Fourier's formal equation is usually expressed as:

```
y = A + A1(sin wt) + A2(sin 2wt) + A3(sin 3wt) +
    A4(sin 4wt) + A5(sin 5wt)...
```

Some periodic waveforms can be expressed using just the odd or even harmonics. In others, all harmonic terms are included. Also, in some periodic waveforms, the signs alternate between + and—for adjacent terms. For the Fourier series developed in this application, a square wave is constructed by adding the odd harmonic terms in a Fourier series together. The more terms that are used in the series, the more the final result will approach a precise square wave. To create a square wave, the general Fourier series equation becomes:

```
y = (sin wt) + (1/3)(sin 3wt) + (1/5)(sin 5wt) +
    (1/7)(sin 7wt)...
```

Note that only odd harmonics will contribute to the final result. Can you see from the equation that if only one harmonic is chosen, the result will be a sine wave? Notice also that each successive term uses a fractional multiplier—in other words, each successively higher harmonic affects the shape of the waveform less and less.

To fully appreciate what this application is about to accomplish, remember that each term in a Fourier series will be calculated separately by the program for each point plotted to the screen. Individual values will be saved in an array by using the vector `push_back()` member function. The sum of the individual calculations, for each given angle, is then found by using the `accumulate()` member function to sum each value in the array. Before going on to the next angle, the values are removed from the array by using the `pop_back()` member function.

If you ask the application to use 2000 harmonic terms, then 2000 separate sine values will be scaled, calculated, and saved to the array for each angle. When the array values are accumulated (summed together), the value will represent one point on the Fourier series plot. This procedure must be repeated for each point that is to be plotted on the window. Therefore, 2000 calculations times 400 points (along the horizontal) = 800,000 calculations.

The Basic Application Code

To build the project for this chapter, you will first need to generate the project's template code with the AppWizard. The project name is `Fourier`. Use the following steps to complete the project files;

- Enter the Microsoft Visual Studio (Visual C++ compiler).
- Choose the `File` menu and select the `New` menu item.
- Select `Project Workspace` from the `New` dialog box.
- From the `New Project Workspace` dialog box:
  - Name the workspace `Fourier`.
  - Set the location of the workspace (for example, `C:\Fourier`).
  - Select `MFC AppWizard (exe)` from the list box.
- Step 1—Select a `Single` document application type.
- Step 2—Select no database support.
- Step 3—Select `None` for OLE compound document support.
- Step 4—Select no additional features.
- Step 5—Do not select comments. Select a statically linked library.
- Step 6—View your settings and `Finish` the AppWizard process.
- If the information in the `New Project Information` dialog box is correct, select `OK`.

When the final step has been completed, as just described, the AppWizard generates all of the template code needed for the project.

Fourier Code Modifications

Modify the `FourierView.cpp` code to reflect the changes shown in bold in the following listing. These modifications will provide the code necessary to include the Fourier series calculations.

```
// FourierView.cpp : implementation of the CFourierView class
//

#include "stdafx.h"
#include "Fourier.h"

#include "FourierDoc.h"
#include "FourierView.h"
#include "FourierDlg.h"
#include "FourierDlg2.h"

#include <numeric>
#include <vector>
#include <math.h>
```

```
using namespace std;

typedef vector <float> FourierArray;

#ifdef _DEBUG
#define new DEBUG_NEW
#undef THIS_FILE
static char THIS_FILE[] = __FILE__;
#endif

/////////////////////////////////////////////////////////////
// CfourierView

IMPLEMENT_DYNCREATE(CFourierView, CView)

BEGIN_MESSAGE_MAP(CFourierView, CView)
    //{{AFX_MSG_MAP(CFourierView)
    ON_WM_SIZE()
    ON_COMMAND(IDM_FOURIER, OnFourier)
    //}}AFX_MSG_MAP
END_MESSAGE_MAP()

/////////////////////////////////////////////////////////////
// CFourierView construction/destruction

CFourierView::CFourierView()
{
}

CFourierView::~CFourierView()
{
}

BOOL CFourierView::PreCreateWindow(CREATESTRUCT& cs)
{
    return CView::PreCreateWindow(cs);
}

/////////////////////////////////////////////////////////////
// CFourierView drawing

void CFourierView::OnDraw(CDC* pDC)
{
    CFourierDoc* pDoc = GetDocument();
    ASSERT_VALID(pDoc);

    int ltitle;
    double y, yp;
    double vertscale, horzscale;

    // vertical plotting scaling factor
```

```
vertscale = 180.0;
// convert degrees to radians and scale
// horozontal for 360 degrees in 400 points
horzscale = 3.1415927 * 360 / (180 * 400);

// define a vector of floats
FourierArray rgFA;

// set mapping mode, viewport, and so on
pDC->SetMapMode(MM_ISOTROPIC);
pDC->SetWindowExt(500,500);
pDC->SetViewportExt(m_cxClient,-m_cyClient);
pDC->SetViewportOrg(m_cxClient/20,m_cyClient/2);

// draw x & y coordinate axes
pDC->MoveTo(0,240);
pDC->LineTo(0,-240);
pDC->MoveTo(0,0);
pDC->LineTo(400,0);
pDC->MoveTo(0,0);

// i represents a given angle for the series
for (int i = 0; i <= 400; i++) {
    // calculate Fourier terms for the angle
    // place each term in the array
    for (int j=1; j<=pDoc->myterms; j++) {
        y = (vertscale / ((2.0 * j)—1.0)) * \
            sin(((j * 2.0)—1.0) * horzscale * i);
        rgFA.push_back(y);
    }
    // accumulate the individual array terms
    // for the angle
    yp = accumulate(rgFA.begin(),rgFA.end(),0.0f);
    // draw the scaled point in the client area
    pDC->LineTo(i, (int)yp);
    yp-=yp;

    // clean out the array and prepare for
    // with next angle's values.
    for (j=1; j<=pDoc->myterms; j++) {
        rgFA.pop_back();
    }
}

// print waveform title
ltitle=strlen(pDoc->mytext);
pDC->TextOut(200-(ltitle*8/2),200,pDoc->mytext,ltitle);
}
```

//

```
// CFourierView diagnostics

#ifdef _DEBUG
void CFourierView::AssertValid() const
{
    CView::AssertValid();
}

void CFourierView::Dump(CDumpContext& dc) const
{
    CView::Dump(dc);
}

CFourierDoc* CFourierView::GetDocument() // non-debug is inline
{
    ASSERT(m_pDocument->IsKindOf(RUNTIME_CLASS(CFourierDoc)));
    return (CFourierDoc*)m_pDocument;
}
#endif //_DEBUG

/////////////////////////////////////////////////////////////
// CFourierView message handlers

void CFourierView::OnSize(UINT nType, int cx, int cy)
{
    CView::OnSize(nType, cx, cy);
    // TODO: Add your message handler code here

    // WHM: added for sizing and scaling window
    m_cxClient = cx;
    m_cyClient = cy;
}

void CFourierView::OnFourier()
{
    // TODO: Add your command handler code here

    // WHM: added to process dialog information
    FourierDlg dlg (this);
    int result = dlg.DoModal();

    if(result==IDOK) {
        CFourierDoc* pDoc = GetDocument();
        ASSERT_VALID(pDoc);

        pDoc->mytext=dlg.m_text;
        pDoc->myterms=dlg.m_terms;

        Invalidate();
    }
}
```

In addition to this modified code, you will need to alter the project's menu to match the menu resource shown in Figure 14.1.

A data entry dialog box will be necessary for this project, also. Figure 14.2 shows the data entry dialog box for the project.

This dialog box will allow the user to enter a title and the number of harmonics that will be included in the calculation.

Chapter 11 provides more detail on how to include dialog box resources in a project.

A Closer Look at the Code

At the start of the previous listing, note the following line of code:

```
typedef vector <float> FourierArray;
```

The angle brackets around the keyword **float** (<float>) instruct the compiler to fill in all vector-templatized date type definitions with the standard type **float**. This typedef is used in the instantiation of the actual vector:

```
FourierArray rgFA;
```

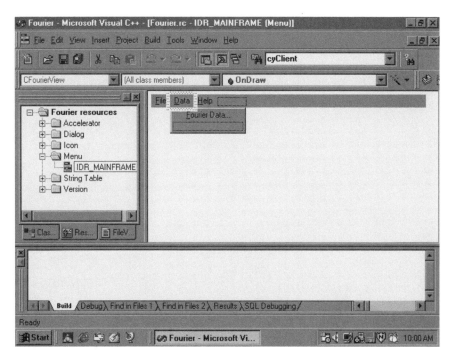

| Figure 14.1 | The default menu is modified for the Fourier project.

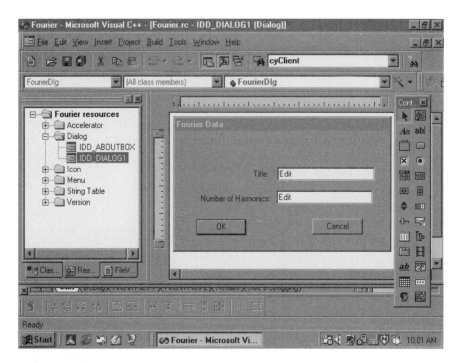

Figure 14.2   *A data entry dialog box is added to the project.*

The actual Fourier calculations are made within two **for** loops. The figure is drawn with the `LineTo()` function.

```
// i represents a given angle for the series
for (int i = 0; i <= 400; i++) {
    // calculate Fourier terms for the angle
    // place each term in the array
    for (int j=1; j<=pDoc->myterms; j++) {
        y = (vertscale / ((2.0 * j)-1.0)) * \
            sin(((j *  2.0)-1.0) * horzscale * i);
        rgFA.push_back(y);
    }
    // accumulate the individual array terms
    // for the angle
    yp = accumulate(rgFA.begin(),rgFA.end(),0.0f);
    // draw the scaled point in the client area
    pDC->LineTo(i, (int)yp);
    yp-=yp;

    // clean out the array and prepare for
    // with next angle's values.
    for (j=1; j<=pDoc->myterms; j++) {
```

```
        rgFA.pop_back();
    }
}
```

The outer **for** loop, using the i index, increments the horizontal plotting position across the window. This value represents the scaled angle for one set of Fourier series terms.

The inner **for** loop, using the j index, calculates the appropriate number of Fourier values for the given angle. For example, if i is pointing to a value representing 45 degrees and the number of Fourier terms is 10, then 10 calculations will be made in the inner loop for each i value and pushed onto the array. This is achieved with the STL dynamic array or vector approach to inserting elements with:

```
rgFA.push_back(y);
```

Thus, each Fourier term for a given angle is accumulated in this array. The individual values can be added together to form one data point by using the accumulate() method. This method is not part of the vector template, but is defined in the STL numeric template. The use of the numeric template was discussed in Chapter 6.

The accumulate() method is implemented in the following manner:

```
y = accumulate(rgFA.begin(),rgFA.end(), 0.0f);
```

The numeric accumulate() method initializes an accumulator, *yp*, with an initial value, *rgFA.begin()*, and then modifies it with $yp = yp + $ *double_prt* for every vector entry in the range, in order, until *rgFA.end()*. Normally, the accumulate() method is used to sum the numeric elements of a vector. The accumulate() method requires a container-specific iterator to locate the summation range. These iterator (or pointer values) are supplied by the begin() and end() methods.

Finally, the vector is cleared out using a similar **for** loop control statement:

```
for (j=1; j<=pDoc->myterms; j++) {
    rgFA.pop_back();
}
```

The pop_back() vector method removes the last element from the list. Another approach would be to call the vector method clear(), which in turn calls the erase() and end() methods to automatically delete the vector's contents from beginning to end().

Figure 14.3 is the default waveform created by calculating six terms in the Fourier series for each point on the plot.

Figure 14.4 shows a plot created by opening the dialog box and requesting ten harmonics.

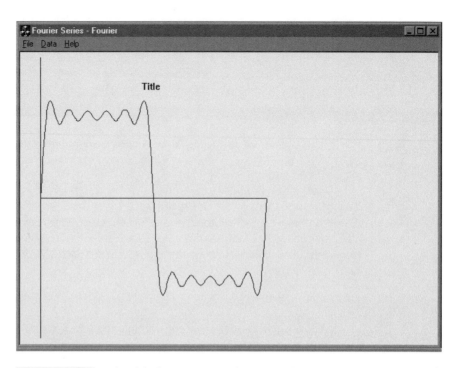

Figure 14-3   The default Fourier series showing six harmonics.

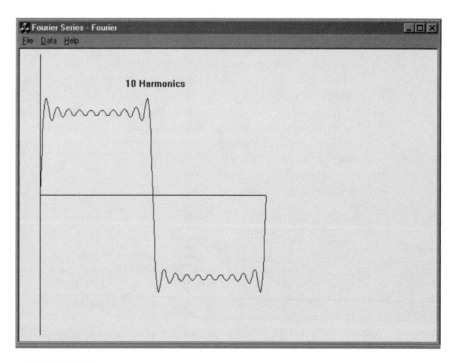

Figure 14.4   A Fourier series created by requesting ten harmonics.

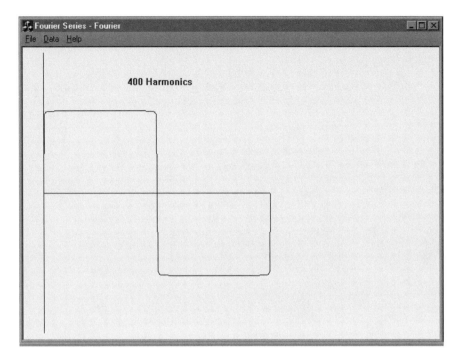

Figure 14.5   *A Fourier series created by requesting four hundred harmonics.*

Figure 14-5 shows a plot created by requesting four hundred harmonics.

As the number of harmonics increases, according to Fourier, the result-ing waveform will approach a perfect square wave.

A Vector Application

In the application discussed in this section, individual complex numbers will be plotted to the screen along with their sum. These complex numbers take advantage of the <complex> template.

A brief review of what complex numbers are is in order. If you have ever been involved with mathematical, engineering, or physics calculations, you have surely run into complex numbers. Complex numbers result from vectors (no relationship to STL vectors) or, better yet, phasors that have a magnitude and direction and can be described on an x-y coordinate system. The positive and negative x-axis represents the real component of a phasor, while the y-axis represents the imaginary component of a phasor. In engi-neering statics, phasors are often used to represent a force moving in a certain direction. In electrical engineering, phasors are often used to represent voltages and currents and their associated phase angles.

There are three basic ways to represent complex numbers or phasors: polar form, rectangular form, and exponential form. For example, imagine the representation of a phasor with a magnitude of 20 at an angle of 30 degrees measured counterclockwise from the positive x-axis.

Polar Form:

In polar form, this phasor could be represented as:

20 /_ 30 deg

Rectangular Form:

In rectangular form, the real component is found using:

20 * cos 30 = 20 * 0.86603 = 17.3205

The imaginary component is

20 * sin 30 = 20 * 0.5 = 10

This phasor could be presented as:

17.3205 + j10

Exponential Form:

In exponential form, the phasor is represented as:

$20 * e^{j30}$

Because phasors contain both real and imaginary components, they are called complex numbers.

It has always been difficult to perform mathematical operations on complex numbers using a computer since most mathematical operators are not overloaded. For example, it is not possible to add (+), subtract (-), multiply (x), or divide (/) complex numbers without operators overloaded for such purposes or without having a template to handle all of that work for you.

Phasors (complex numbers) that are represented in rectangular form are easy to add and subtract. For example:

(20 + j40) − (30 + j20) = − 10 +j20

(20 + j40) + (30 + j20) = 50 + j60

Multiplication and division of phasors (complex numbers) in rectangular form are not as easy, but they are not impossible. However, the easiest way to multiply and divide phasors is by working with them in polar form. For example:

(44.72 /_ 63.44 deg) * (36.05 /_ 33.7 deg) = (44.72 * 36.05) /_ (63.44 + 33.7) deg

= 1612.156 /_ 97.14 deg

(20 /_ 50 deg) / (15 /_ 30 deg) = (20 / 15) /_ (50 deg—30 deg)

= 1.333 /_ 20 deg

As a result of these various forms, conversion from one form to another is typical in most arithmetic operations involving phasors. The calculations can be tedious when using a calculator or computer program that cannot handle complex numbers.

If you would like more information on the use of complex numbers, we recommend any good technical mathematics book, any electrical engineering book dealing with ac circuits, or any college physics book.

In the following section, we'll investigate the capabilities of the <complex> template. Then you'll learn how the <complex> template can be used to build an MFC Windows application that will draw individual phasors and their sum to the screen.

The <complex> Template Syntax

The standard C++ header <complex> is used to define the template class complex and a large number of supporting template functions. The following listing gives the syntax for the <complex> template:

```
namespace std {
#define __STD_COMPLEX
//    TEMPLATE CLASSES
template<class T>
    class complex;
class "complex<float>;
class "complex<double>;
class "complex<long double>;
//    TEMPLATE FUNCTIONS
template<class T>
    complex<T> operator+(const complex<T>& lhs, const complex<T>& rhs);
template<class T>
    complex<T> operator+(const complex<T>& lhs, const T& rhs);
template<class T>
    complex<T> operator+(const T& lhs, const complex<T>& rhs);template<class T>
    complex<T> operator-(const complex<T>& lhs, const complex<T>& rhs);
template<class T>
    complex<T> operator-(const complex<T>& lhs, const T& rhs);
template<class T>
    complex<T> operator-(const T& lhs, const complex<T>& rhs);
template<class T>
    complex<T> operator*(const complex<T>& lhs, const complex<T>& rhs);
template<class T>
    complex<T> operator*(const complex<T>& lhs, const T& rhs);
template<class T>
    complex<T> operator*(const T& lhs, const complex<T>& rhs);
template<class T>
    complex<T> operator/(const complex<T>& lhs, const complex<T>& rhs);
template<class T>
    complex<T> operator/(const complex<T>& lhs, const T& rhs);
```

```
template<class T>
    complex<T> operator/(const T& lhs, const complex<T>& rhs);
template<class T>
    complex<T> operator+(const complex<T>& lhs);
template<class T>
    complex<T> operator-(const complex<T>& lhs);
template<class T>
    bool operator==(const complex<T>& lhs, const complex<T>& rhs);
template<class T>
    bool operator==(const complex<T>& lhs, const T& rhs);
template<class T>
    bool operator==(const T& lhs, const complex<T>& rhs);
template<class T>
    bool operator!=(const complex<T>& lhs, const complex<T>& rhs);
template<class T>
    bool operator!=(const complex<T>& lhs, const T& rhs);
template<class T>
bool operator!=(const T& lhs, const complex<T>& rhs);
template<class E, class Ti, class T>
    basic_istream<E, Ti>& "operator>>(basic_istream<E, Ti>& is,
        complex<T>& x);
template<class E, class T, class U>
    basic_ostream<E, T>& operator<<(basic_ostream<E, T>& os,
        const complex<U>& x);
template<class T>
    T real(const complex<T>& x);
template<class T>
    T imag(const complex<T>& x);
template<class T>
    T abs(const complex<T>& x);
template<class T>
    T arg(const complex<T>& x);
template<class T>
    T norm(const complex<T>& x);
template<class T>
    complex<T> conjg(const complex<T>& x);
template<class T>
    complex<T> polar(const T& rho, const T& theta = 0);
template<class T>
    complex<T> cos(const complex<T>& x);
template<class T>
    complex<T> cosh(const complex<T>& x);
template<class T>
    complex<T> exp(const complex<T>& x);
template<class T>
    complex<T> log(const complex<T>& x);
template<class T>
    complex<T> log10(const complex<T>& x);
template<class T>
    complex<T> pow(const complex<T>& x, int y);
template<class T>
    complex<T> pow(const complex<T>& x, const T& y);
```

```
template<class T>
    complex<T> pow(const complex<T>& x, const complex<T>& y);
template<class T>
    complex<T> pow(const T& x, const complex<T>& y);
template<class T>
    complex<T> sin(const complex<T>& x);
template<class T>
    complex<T> sinh(const complex<T>& x);
template<class T>
    complex<T> sqrt(const complex<T>& x);
    };
```

Note   At the time of this writing, the complex conjugate of a complex number is found by using conj(), not conjg(), as appears in Microsoft's references.

For this template class, functions that return multiple values will return an imaginary part in the half-open interval given by (-pi, pi].

Table 14.1 lists and describes the template functions for <complex>.

Table 14.1   *Template Functions for <complex>*

Template Functions

complex<T> operator+(const complex<T>& lhs, const complex<T>& rhs);

complex<T> operator+(const complex<T>& lhs, const T& rhs);

complex<T> operator+(const T& lhs, const complex<T>& rhs);

complex<T> operator-(const complex<T>& lhs, const complex<T>& rhs);

complex<T> operator-(const complex<T>& lhs, const T& rhs);

complex<T> operator-(const T& lhs, const complex<T>& rhs);

complex<T> operator*(const complex<T>& lhs, const complex<T>& rhs);

complex<T> operator*(const complex<T>& lhs, const T& rhs);

complex<T> operator*(const T& lhs, const complex<T>& rhs);

complex<T> operator/(const complex<T>& lhs, const complex<T>& rhs);

complex<T> operator/(const complex<T>& lhs, const T& rhs);

complex<T> operator/(const T& lhs, const complex<T>& rhs);

complex<T> operator+(const complex<T>& lhs);

complex<T> operator-(const complex<T>& lhs);

Bool operator==(const complex<T>& lhs, const complex<T>& rhs);

Bool operator==(const complex<T>& lhs, const T& rhs);

(continued)

Table 14.1	*Template Functions for* `<complex>` *(Continued)*

Template Functions

```
Bool operator==(const T& lhs, const complex<T>& rhs);
Bool operator!=(const complex<T>& lhs, const complex<T>& rhs);
Bool operator!=(const complex<T>& lhs, const T& rhs);
Bool operator!=(const T& lhs, const complex<T>& rhs);
basic_istream<E, Ti>& "operator>>(basic_istream<E, Ti>& is,complex<T>& x);
basic_ostream<E, T>& operator<<(basic_ostream<E, T>& os,const complex<U>& x);
```

The methods in this template class are listed and described in Table 14.2. All of the normal operations needed for manipulating complex numbers are provided with this template.

Table 14.2	*Various* *<complex>* *Template Methods*

Template Method	**Description**
`template<class T>` `  T abs(const complex<T>& x);`	Returns the magnitude of x.
`template<class T>` `  T arg(const complex<T>& x);`	Returns the phase angle of x.

`template<class T>`
`  complex<T> conjg(const`
`  complex<T>& x);`
	Returns the conjugate of x.
	Note: Use `conj()`, at this time, to find the complex conjugate.

`template<class T>` `  complex<T> cos(const complex<T>& x);`	Returns the cosine of x.

`template<class T>`
`  complex<T> cosh(const`
`  complex<T>& x);`
	Returns the hyperbolic cosine of x.

`template<class T>` `  complex<T> exp(const complex<T>& x);`	Returns the exponential of x.
`template<class T>` `  T imag(const complex<T>& x);`	Returns the imaginary part of x.
`template<class T>` `  complex<T> log(const complex<T>& x);`	Returns the logarithm of x. The branch cuts occur along the negative real axis.

`template<class T>`
`  complex<T> log10(const`
`  complex<T>& x);`
	Returns the base 10 logarithm of x. The branch cuts occur along the negative real axis.

Table 14.2	Various `<complex>` Template Methods (Continued)

Template Method	**Description**
`template<class T>` `  T norm(const complex<T>& x);`	Returns the squared magnitude of x.

`template<class T>`
`  complex<T> polar(const T& rho,`
`  const T& theta = 0);`
	Returns a complex value. The magnitude is rho and the phase angle is theta.

`template<class T>`
`  complex<T> pow(const complex<T>& x,`
`  int y);`
	Each function converts both operands to the given return type, then returns the converted x to the power y. The branch cut for x occurs along the negative real axis.

`template<class T>`
`  complex<T> pow(const complex<T>& x,`
`  const T& y);`	

`template<class T>`
`  complex<T> pow(const complex<T>& x,`
`  const complex<T>& y);`	

`template<class T>`
`  complex<T> pow(const T& x, const`
`  complex<T>& y);`	

`template<class T>` `  T real(const complex<T>& x);`	Returns the real part of x.
`template<class T>` `  complex<T> sin(const complex<T>& x);`	Returns the imaginary sine of x.

`template<class T>`
`  complex<T> sinh(const`
`  complex<T>& x);`
	Returns the hyperbolic sine of x.

`template<class T>`
`  complex<T> sqrt(const`
`  complex<T>& x);`
	Returns the square root of x. The phase angle occurs in the half-open interval (-pi/2, pi/2]. The branch cuts occur along the negative real axis.

The `<complex>` template class describes an object. This object stores two objects of type T. One object represents the real part of a complex number and the other object the imaginary part of the complex number.

Objects of class T have a public constructor, destructor, copy constructor, and assignment operator. Class T objects can be assigned integer or floating-point values, or they can **cast** to the desired values. Arithmetic operators are defined for the appropriate floating-point types.

In the next three sections, you'll see how the template class handles three floating-point types: float, double, and long double. For this version of Visual C++, a value of any other type T is **cast** to a double for actual calculations. The return type, a double, is assigned back to the object of type T.

CLASS COMPLEX <FLOAT>

The class complex <float> describes an object that stores two objects of type float. One object represents the real part of a complex number and the second object the imaginary part of the complex number.

```
class complex<float> {
public:
  complex(float re = 0, float im = 0);
  explicit complex(const complex<double>& x);
  explicit complex(const complex<long double>& x);
  // remainder identical to template class complex
};
```

Note that the only difference is in the defined constructors. The first constructor initializes the real part to re and the imaginary part to im. Two final constructors initialize the real part to x.real() and the imaginary part to x.imag().

CLASS COMPLEX <DOUBLE>

The class complex <double> describes an object that stores two objects of type double. One object represents the real part of a complex number and the second object the imaginary part of the complex number.

```
class complex<double> {

public:
  complex(double re = 0, double im = 0);
  complex(const complex<float>& x);
  explicit complex(const complex<long double>& x);
  // remainder identical to template class complex
};
```

Again, the only difference is in the defined constructors. The first constructor initializes the real part to re and the imaginary part to im. Two final constructors initialize the real part to x.real() and the imaginary part to x.imag().

CLASS COMPLEX <LONG DOUBLE>

The class complex <long double> describes an object that stores two objects of type long double. One object represents the real part of a complex number and the second object the imaginary part of the complex number.

```
class complex<long double> {
public:
  complex(long double re = 0, long double im = 0);
  complex(const complex<float>& x);
  complex(const complex<double>& x);
  // remainder identical to the template class complex
};
```

Again, the only difference is in the defined constructors. The first constructor initializes the real part to *re* and the imaginary part to *im*. Two final constructors initialize the real part to x.real() and the imaginary part to x.imag().

The Basic Application Code

To build the project for this chapter, you will first need to generate the project's template code with the AppWizard. The project name is Vectors. Use the following steps to complete the project files.

- Enter the Microsoft Visual Studio (Visual C++ compiler).
- Choose the File menu and select the New menu item.
- Select Project Workspace from the New dialog box.
- From the New Project Workspace dialog box:
  - Name the workspace Vectors.
  - Set the location of the workspace (for example, C:\Vectors).
  - Select MFC AppWizard (exe) from the list box.
- Step 1—Select a Single document application type.
- Step 2—Select no database support.
- Step 3—Select None for OLE compound document support.
- Step 4—Select no additional features.
- Step 5—Do not select comments. Select a statically linked library.
- Step 6—View your settings and Finish the AppWizard process.
- If the information in the New Project Information dialog box is correct, select OK.

When the final step has been completed, as just described, the AppWizard generates all of the template code needed for the project.

Modifications to the Basic Code

When the AppWizard has generated the source code and header files for the application, select the VectorsView.cpp source code file and modify it by adding the code shown in bold in the following listing:

```
// VectorsView.cpp : implementation of the CVectorsView class
//

#include "stdafx.h"
#include "Vectors.h"
```

```
#include "VectorsDoc.h"
#include "VectorsView.h"

#include <complex>

using namespace std;

#ifdef _DEBUG
#define new DEBUG_NEW
#undef THIS_FILE
static char THIS_FILE[] = __FILE__;
#endif

/////////////////////////////////////////////////////////////////
// CVectorsView

IMPLEMENT_DYNCREATE(CVectorsView, CView)

BEGIN_MESSAGE_MAP(CVectorsView, CView)
    //{{AFX_MSG_MAP(CVectorsView)
    ON_WM_SIZE()
    //}}AFX_MSG_MAP
END_MESSAGE_MAP()

/////////////////////////////////////////////////////////////////
// CVectorsView construction/destruction

CVectorsView::CVectorsView()
{
}

CVectorsView::~CVectorsView()
{
}

BOOL CVectorsView::PreCreateWindow(CREATESTRUCT& cs)
{
    return CView::PreCreateWindow(cs);
}

/////////////////////////////////////////////////////////////////
// CVectorsView drawing

void CVectorsView::OnDraw(CDC* pDC)
{
    CVectorsDoc* pDoc = GetDocument();
    ASSERT_VALID(pDoc);

    CPen bluepen, greenpen, magentapen, redpen;
    CPen* oldpen;
```

```
complex<double> x1, x2, x3, temp;

// phasor one
x2.real(-90.0);                     //-90.0—j60.0
x2.imag(-60.0);

// phasor two
x1 = polar(60.0, -0.523598);    //60.0 /_ -30 deg

// phasor three
x3.real(-80.0);                     //-80.0 + j120.0
x3.imag(120.0);

// set mapping modes and viewport
pDC->SetMapMode(MM_ISOTROPIC);
pDC->SetWindowExt(250,250);
pDC->SetViewportExt(m_cxClient,-m_cyClient);
pDC->SetViewportOrg(m_cxClient/2,m_cyClient/2);

// draw coordinate axes
pDC->MoveTo(-120,0);
pDC->LineTo(120,0);
pDC->MoveTo(0,-100);
pDC->LineTo(0,100);

// draw first phasor with blue pen
bluepen.CreatePen(PS_DASHDOT,0,RGB(0,0,255));
oldpen = pDC->SelectObject(&bluepen);
pDC->MoveTo(0,0);
pDC->LineTo(real(x1),imag(x1));
DeleteObject(oldpen);

temp = x1 + x2;   // add first two phasors

// draw second phasor with green pen
greenpen.CreatePen(PS_DASHDOT,0,RGB(0,255,0));
oldpen = pDC->SelectObject(&greenpen);
pDC->LineTo(real(temp),imag(temp));
DeleteObject(oldpen);

temp += x3;      // add in last phasor

// draw third phasor with magenta pen
magentapen.CreatePen(PS_DASHDOT,0,RGB(255,0,255));
oldpen = pDC->SelectObject(&magentapen);
pDC->LineTo(real(temp),imag(temp));
DeleteObject(oldpen);

// draw sum of phasors with wide red pen
redpen.CreatePen(PS_SOLID,3,RGB(255,0,0));
oldpen = pDC->SelectObject(&redpen);
```

```
    pDC->LineTo(0,0);
    DeleteObject(oldpen);
}


/////////////////////////////////////////////////////////////////////
// CVectorsView diagnostics

#ifdef _DEBUG
void CVectorsView::AssertValid() const
{
    CView::AssertValid();
}

void CVectorsView::Dump(CDumpContext& dc) const
{
    CView::Dump(dc);
}

CVectorsDoc* CVectorsView::GetDocument() // non-debug is inline
{
    ASSERT(m_pDocument->IsKindOf(RUNTIME_CLASS(CVectorsDoc)));
    return (CVectorsDoc*)m_pDocument;
}
#endif //_DEBUG


/////////////////////////////////////////////////////////////////////
// CVectorsView message handlers

void CVectorsView::OnSize(UINT nType, int cx, int cy)
{
    CView::OnSize(nType, cx, cy);

    // TODO: Add your message handler code here

    m_cxClient = cx;
    m_cyClient = cy;
}
```

To complete this application a few more steps are necessary. First, open the ClassWizard from the Visual C++ compiler's View menu. With all windows set to the values shown in Figure 14.6, you can add a WM_SIZE message handler.

The ClassWizard will add an OnSize() method to the Vectors-View.cpp source code file, as shown in Figure 14.7.

The code is modified to return information to two member variables, *m_cxClient* and *m_cyClient*, with regard to the size of the window:

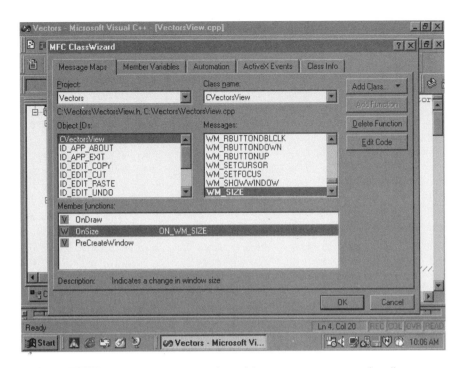

Figure 14.6 Use the ClassWizard to add a WM_SIZE message handler.

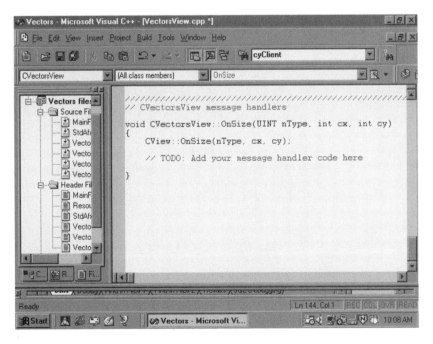

Figure 14.7 An OnSize() method is added to complex3View.cpp by the ClassWizard.

```
void CComplex3View::OnSize(UINT nType, int cx, int cy)
{
    CView::OnSize(nType, cx, cy);

    // TODO: Add your message handler code here

    m_cxClient = cx;
    m_cyClient = cy;
}
```

To make these variables visible, declare the member variables in the `VectorsView.h` header file. This is shown in Figure 14.8.

The following listing shows the actual code, in bold, that must be entered in this header file.

```
class CVectorsView : public CView
{
private:    // member variables for resized window
int m_cxClient;
```

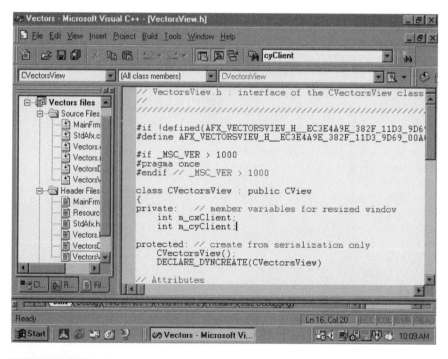

| Figure 14.8 | *The member variables are declared in the* `VectorsView.h` *header file.* |

```
int m_cyClient;

protected: // create from serialization only
    CVectorsView();
    DECLARE_DYNCREATE(CVectorsView)

// Attributes
public:
CVectorsDoc* GetDocument();
    .
    .
    .
```

The only thing left is to compile and execute this application. Figure 14.9 shows the output sent to the window.

The three phasors are shown with dash-dot line segments, and the result of adding the phasors together is shown with a solid, wide, red line.

The addition of the phasors (complex numbers) is now possible since the "+" operator is overloaded.

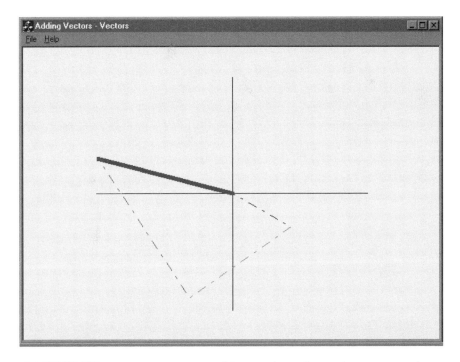

Figure 14.9   *The graphical results of the complex arithmetic drawn in a window.*

We're sure you'll agree that adding graphing capabilities to complex number arithmetic opens new possibilities to engineering and mathematical calculations.

This Chapter

The <vector>, <numeric> and <complex> template header files provide powerful new abilities to the programmer, mathematician, and engineer alike. The <complex> template provides a new tool for viewing the results of complex number calculations.

Robust Windows Applications with the STL

In the previous two chapters of this book, you learned how to use the STL and MFC libraries together. In this chapter, you will learn how to develop two robust MFC Windows applications that will use some very interesting STL code. One project, named `BarChart`, will draw a presentation-quality bar chart in the client area. The second project, named `LineChart`, will allow the user to specify points on a graph, draw the points, and connect the points with lines. Each of the projects will call upon skills you have developed over the past chapters.

Common AppWizard Code

For each of the projects in this chapter, you will need to generate the same base code with the AppWizard. Name the first workspace `BarChart`. Use the following steps to complete the project files with the AppWizard.

- Enter the Microsoft Visual Studio (Visual C++ compiler).
- Choose the `File` menu and select the `New` menu item.
- Select `Project Workspace` from the New dialog box.
- From the `New Project Workspace` dialog box:
  - Name the workspace `BarChart`.
  - Set the location of the workspace (for example, `C:\BarChart`).
  - Select `MFC AppWizard (exe)` from the list box.
- Step 1—Select a `Single document` application type.
- Step 2—Select no database support.
- Step 3—Select `None` for OLE compound document support.
- Step 4—Select no extra features.

- Step 5—Do not select comments. Select a statically linked library.
- Step 6—Examine and accept the base class.
- Select Finish to complete the AppWizard process.
- If the information in the New Project Information dialog box is correct, select OK.

These are the same steps you have used since Chapter 8. You can refer to Chapter 8 for more details on the various project creation steps. When you have completed the final step, shown above, the AppWizard will generate all of the basic files needed for the BarChart project.

Now, repeat the entire process for a workspace named LineChart. Save the LineChart files for the second application in this chapter.

The Bar Chart Application

The BarChart project will draw a presentation-quality bar chart in the client area of the window. This application also uses a menu and a data entry dialog box. This bar chart allows up to twelve bars to be drawn in the client area and uses a parser routine for entering data and labels as strings of characters. You will find that this data entry approach will reduce the overall size of the dialog box and also teach you some important STL coding techniques.

The complete application is built with the default AppWizard files you created earlier in this chapter. These files were created in the BarChart workspace. In addition to the original group of files, a new data entry dialog box resource must be added to the project.

Let's examine the modifications that are necessary to complete this project.

Modifying the String Table

To give the application a unique title in the title bar portion of the window, open the String Table resource, as shown in Figure 15.1.

Double-click the IDR_MAINFRAME string to open the dialog box shown in Figure 15.2.

Modify the contents of the string so they appear similar to the string shown in Figure 15.3.

Close the current dialog box to accept the changes. You will see this modification in the upper left corner of the project's window each time it is run.

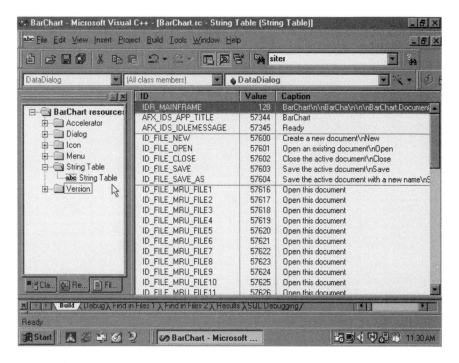

Figure 15.1   Open the String Table resource.

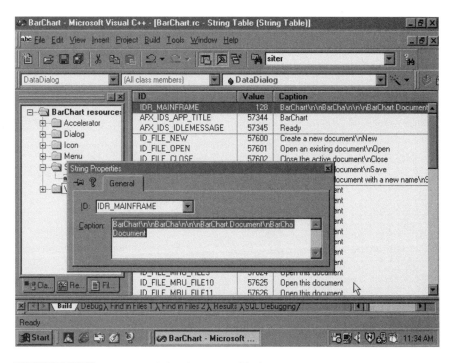

Figure 15.2   Open a dialog box to modify the IDR_MAINFRAME string resource.

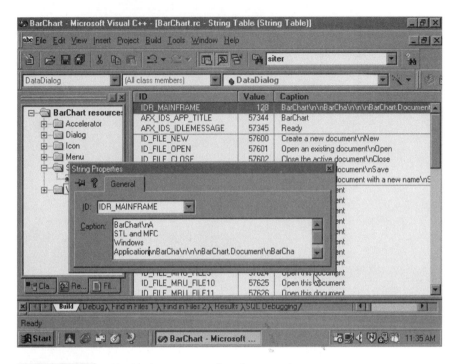

Figure 15.3   *Modify the string to reflect the new title.*

Modifying the Menu

The AppWizard generated a default menu as part of the base code, so it will be necessary to edit that menu and add a new Menu entry. Open the menu resource, as shown in Figure 15.4.

The Edit menu entry can be eliminated by selecting the entry with the mouse and pressing the Delete key. Replace this entry with a menu named Input and a menu item named Data Entry..., as shown in Figure 15.5.

When you add the Data Entry...menu item, change the ID value to IDM_DATAENTRY. Remember, this value can be altered by right-clicking the mouse on the menu item and selecting the Properties option.

Click on the File menu to display all File menu items. Eliminate all of the File menu items except the Exit item by clicking on each item and pressing the Delete key.

The modifications to the menu resource are now completed for the project.

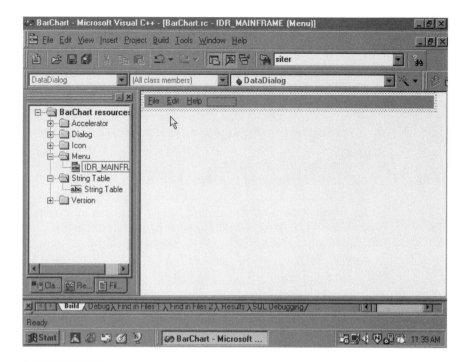

Figure 15.4   *The project's default* Menu *resource.*

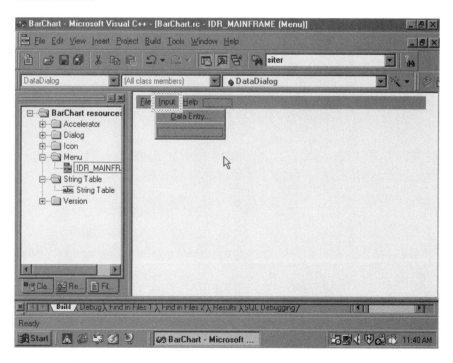

Figure 15.5   *The modified menu and menu items for the project.*

389

Creating a New Dialog Box

A new dialog box resource for data entry must be added to the application. From the Insert menu, select the Resource menu item. From the list of resources, select the Dialog option. Now, create a dialog box similar to the one shown in Figure 15.6.

The figure shows three of the five edit boxes that will eventually be used for user input. Each edit box has a unique ID value. From top to bottom, the ID values are IDC_EDIT1....IDC_EDIT5. You can right-click on an edit box and use the Properties option to alter these values. The dialog box, by default, is given an ID of IDD_DIALOG1. A new class will have to be added for the new dialog box to communicate with the other files in the project.

From the View menu, select the ClassWizard option to open the MFC ClassWizard dialog box. Select the Add Class...button to open the New Class dialog box, as shown in Figure 15.7.

The default base class for a dialog box is CDialog. Our unique class name is DataDialog. The only item not entered at this point is the dialog ID. Recall that the ID for the Dialog resource is IDD_DIALOG1, for this project. We accepted the suggested filename, DataDialog.cpp. Choose Cre-

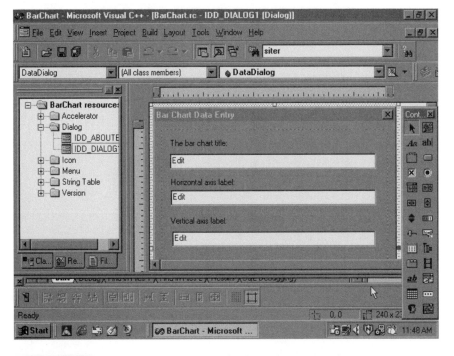

Figure 15.6   *A data entry dialog box for the* BarChart *application.*

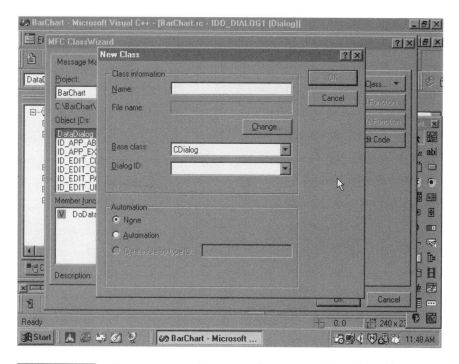

Figure 15.7   *The* New Class *dialog box allows a new class to be added to a project.*

ate to generate this new class and file. When you choose Create, a new class and file will be generated and you will be returned to the MFC Class-Wizard dialog box, as shown in Figure 15.8.

Figure 15.8 shows the MFC ClassWizard dialog box after a member function has been added: DoDataExchange(). This member function provides the functionality for communicating between the dialog box and the application.

To pass information to or from a dialog box, the member functions rely on member variables. Each edit box in this example will pass information to the application through a unique member variable.

Select the Member Variables tab, as shown in Figure 15.9.

Figure 15.9 shows three edit box IDs and a member variable associated with each. To add member variables, just use the Add Variable...button. When a control ID is selected, the Add Variable...button opens the Add Member Variable dialog box. This dialog box will permit you to name the member variable and set its category and type. Most member variables start with m_ (to denote member variable). All of the edit boxes in this project return strings. Yes, even the data points for the bar heights are returned in a string that will later be parsed.

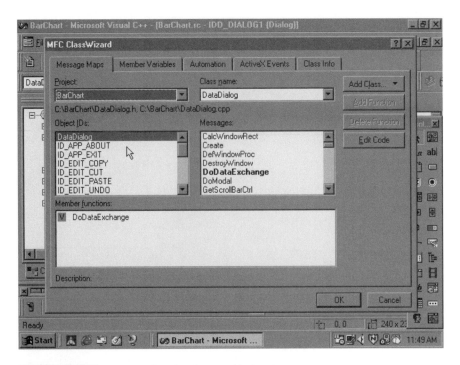

Figure 15.8   *A new class has been added to the* BarChart *project.*

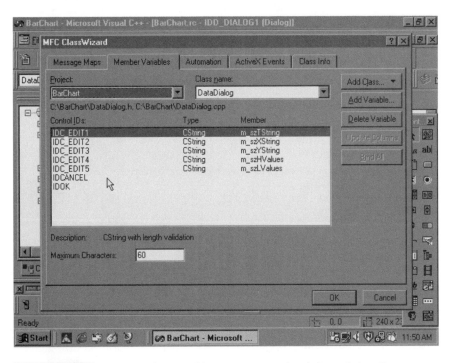

Figure 15.9   *Five member variables are associated with five edit box IDs.*

392

When you are satisfied with the member variable names, select OK to close the MFC ClassWizard dialog box.

The following listing is the complete listing for the DataDialog.cpp file generated by the ClassWizard. We did not, directly, add a single line of code to this file.

```cpp
// DataDialog.cpp : implementation file
//

#include "stdafx.h"
#include "BarChart.h"
#include "DataDialog.h"

#ifdef _DEBUG
#define new DEBUG_NEW
#undef THIS_FILE
static char THIS_FILE[] = __FILE__;
#endif

/////////////////////////////////////////////////////////////////
// DataDialog dialog

DataDialog::DataDialog(CWnd* pParent /*=NULL*/)
    : CDialog(DataDialog::IDD, pParent)
{
    //{{AFX_DATA_INIT(DataDialog)
    m_szTString = _T("");
    m_szXString = _T("");
    m_szYString = _T("");
    m_szHValues = _T("");
    m_szLValues = _T("");
    //}}AFX_DATA_INIT
}

void DataDialog::DoDataExchange(CDataExchange* pDX)
{
    CDialog::DoDataExchange(pDX);
    //{{AFX_DATA_MAP(DataDialog)
    DDX_Text(pDX, IDC_EDIT1, m_szTString);
    DDV_MaxChars(pDX, m_szTString, 60);
    DDX_Text(pDX, IDC_EDIT2, m_szXString);
    DDV_MaxChars(pDX, m_szXString, 60);
    DDX_Text(pDX, IDC_EDIT3, m_szYString);
    DDV_MaxChars(pDX, m_szYString, 60);
    DDX_Text(pDX, IDC_EDIT4, m_szHValues);
    DDV_MaxChars(pDX, m_szHValues, 120);
    DDX_Text(pDX, IDC_EDIT5, m_szLValues);
    DDV_MaxChars(pDX, m_szLValues, 120);
    //}}AFX_DATA_MAP
}
```

```
BEGIN_MESSAGE_MAP(DataDialog, Cdialog)
    //{{AFX_MSG_MAP(DataDialog)
        // NOTE: the ClassWizard will add message map macros
    //}}AFX_MSG_MAP
END_MESSAGE_MAP()

/////////////////////////////////////////////////////////////
// DataDialog message handlers
```

As you examine the previous file listing, can you see where the Class-Wizard used member functions, message handlers, and member variables?

The constructor is a wonderful place to initialize member variables. The following portion of this file is modified to reflect initial chart values:

```
DataDialog::DataDialog(CWnd* pParent /*=NULL*/)
    : CDialog(DataDialog::IDD, pParent)
{
    //{{AFX_DATA_INIT(DataDialog)
    m_szTString = _T("Bar Chart Title");
    m_szXString = _T("x-axis label");
    m_szYString = _T("y-axis label");
    m_szHValues = _T("40,10,30,20");
    m_szLValues = _T("#1,#2,#3,#4");
    //}}AFX_DATA_INIT
}
```

The `DoDataExchange()` member function is called by the framework to exchange and validate dialog data. This member function is never called directly. The `UpdateData()` member function is called, instead, to initialize the various dialog box controls or retrieve data. The ClassWizard writes an overridden version of this member function. This member function contains the data map of dialog data exchange (DDX) and validation (DDV) global function calls. The code between the delimiters is automatically maintained by the ClassWizard and should not be modified directly.

```
void DataDialog::DoDataExchange(CDataExchange* pDX)
{
    CDialog::DoDataExchange(pDX);
    //{{AFX_DATA_MAP(DataDialog)
    DDX_Text(pDX, IDC_EDIT1, m_szTString);
    DDV_MaxChars(pDX, m_szTString, 60);
    DDX_Text(pDX, IDC_EDIT2, m_szXString);
    DDV_MaxChars(pDX, m_szXString, 60);
    DDX_Text(pDX, IDC_EDIT3, m_szYString);
    DDV_MaxChars(pDX, m_szYString, 60);
    DDX_Text(pDX, IDC_EDIT4, m_szHValues);
    DDV_MaxChars(pDX, m_szHValues, 120);
    DDX_Text(pDX, IDC_EDIT5, m_szLValues);
    DDV_MaxChars(pDX, m_szLValues, 120);
```

```
          //}}}AFX_DATA_MAP
     }
```

Exchanging data between dialog box controls and the application has been greatly simplified with MFC's DDX and DDV capabilities. DDX encapsulates macros for the purpose of exchanging data. DDV functions allow you to make sure valid data has been entered in your dialog box controls. As you can see from the previous listing, DoDataExchange() uses a pointer, pDX, to the CDataExchange object.

Each data exchange function call is of type DDX_Text, since we are exchanging string information from each edit box control. DDX_Text is an overloaded member function and can actually accept the following types: BYTE, CString, double, DWORD, float, int, LONG, and UINT.

This project includes data validation for each edit box entry. In other words, the dialog box control will limit string lengths directly to 60 or 120 characters, respectively. These can be seen within the DDV_ functions of DoDataExchange().

The data entry dialog box is ready to exchange data with the project. Now we'll have to create the bar chart code. The bar chart code is completely contained in the BarChartView.cpp file.

The BarChartView.cpp File

The BarChartView.cpp file is the standard view file created by the App-Wizard. As you examine the following listing, you might wonder what has happened. Well, the bar chart application requires a little code!

Examine this code carefully and pay particular attention to the lines set in bold. These are the lines we had to write and insert ourselves.

```
// BarChartView.cpp : implementation of the CBarChartView class
//

#include "stdafx.h"
#include "BarChart.h"

#include "BarChartDoc.h"
#include "BarChartView.h"
#include "DataDialog.h"

#pragma warning (disable:4786)

// STL header files
#include <list>
#include <vector>

using namespace std;
```

```
typedef vector <int> pointarray;
typedef vector <int> scaledpointarray;
typedef list <string> stringlist;

DataDialog dlg;

#define maxnumber 12

#ifdef _DEBUG
#define new DEBUG_NEW
#undef THIS_FILE
static char THIS_FILE[] = __FILE__;
#endif

///////////////////////////////////////////////////////////////
// CBarChartView

IMPLEMENT_DYNCREATE(CBarChartView, Cview)

BEGIN_MESSAGE_MAP(CBarChartView, Cview)
    //{{AFX_MSG_MAP(CBarChartView)
    ON_WM_SIZE()
    ON_COMMAND(IDM_DATAENTRY, OnDataentry)
    //}}AFX_MSG_MAP
END_MESSAGE_MAP()

///////////////////////////////////////////////////////////////
// CBarChartView construction/destruction

CBarChartView::CBarChartView()
{
}

CBarChartView::~CBarChartView()
{
}

BOOL CBarChartView::PreCreateWindow(CREATESTRUCT& cs)
{
    return CView::PreCreateWindow(cs);
}

///////////////////////////////////////////////////////////////
// CBarChartView drawing

void CBarChartView::OnDraw(CDC* pDC)
{
    CBarChartDoc* pDoc = GetDocument();
    ASSERT_VALID(pDoc);

    pointarray rgIA;
    pointarray::iterator pai;
```

```
scaledpointarray rgsIA;
scaledpointarray::iterator spai;

stringlist rgSL;
stringlist::iterator sli;

static DWORD dwColor[12]={RGB(128,128,128),   //gray
                         RGB(255,0,0),        //red
                         RGB(0,255,0),        //green
                         RGB(0,0,255),        //blue
                         RGB(255,255,0),      //yellow
                         RGB(255,0,255),      //magenta
                         RGB(0,255,255),      //cyan
                         RGB(255,128,0),      //orange
                         RGB(0,128,64),       //dark green
                         RGB(255,128,182),    //pink
                         RGB(0,0,160),        //dark blue
                         RGB(128,255,6)};     //lite green

CFont newfont;
CFont* oldfont;
CBrush newbrush;
CBrush* oldbrush;

int i,iNBars,iBarWidth,iBarMax;
int ilenMaxLabel;
int x1,x2,y1,y2,z1,z2;
static char szLValues[60];
static char szHValues[60];
char sbuffer[10],*strptr;
static char *n,*p;

// make copies of data for re-drawing
strcpy(szHValues,dlg.m_szHValues);
strcpy(szLValues,dlg.m_szLValues);

// parse string to get bar heights
i = 0;
iNBars=0;
n=szHValues;
p=strtok(n,",");
while ((n!=NULL)) {
  rgIA.push_back(atoi(n));
  p=strtok(NULL,",");
  n=p;
  iNBars++;
  I++;
  if (i >= maxnumber) break;
}
```

```
// parse string to get bar labels
i = 0;
n=szLValues;
p=strtok(n,",");
while ((n!=NULL)) {
  rgSL.push_back(n);
  p=strtok(NULL,",");
  n=p;
  I++;
  if (i >= maxnumber) break;
}

iBarWidth=400/iNBars;

// Find bar with maximum height and scale
for (pai=rgIA.begin(); pai<rgIA.end(); pai++)
  if (iBarMax < *pai) iBarMax = *pai;

// Convert maximum y value to a string
strptr=_itoa(iBarMax,sbuffer,10);
ilenMaxLabel=strlen(sbuffer);

// Scale bars in array.  Hnighest bar = 270
for (pai=rgIA.begin(); pai<rgIA.end(); pai++)
  rgsIA.push_back((*pai * 270)/iBarMax);

// Create custom viewport and map mode
pDC->SetMapMode(MM_ISOTROPIC);
pDC->SetWindowExt(640,480);
pDC->SetViewportExt(cxClient,cyClient);
pDC->SetViewportOrg(0,0);

// Draw text if window is large enough
if ((cxClient>300)&&(cyClient>200)) {
  newfont.CreateFont(20,12,900,900,FW_NORMAL,
                     FALSE,FALSE,FALSE,
                     OEM_CHARSET,OUT_DEFAULT_PRECIS,
                     CLIP_DEFAULT_PRECIS,
                     DEFAULT_QUALITY,
                     34,
                     "Arial");
  oldfont=pDC->SelectObject(&newfont);
  pDC->TextOut(50,200+(strlen(dlg.m_szYString)*10/2),
               dlg.m_szYString,strlen(dlg.m_szYString));
  pDC->SelectObject(oldfoNt);
  newfont.DeleteObject();

  newfont.CreateFont(20,12,0,0,FW_NORMAL,
                     FALSE,FALSE,FALSE,OEM_CHARSET,
                     OUT_DEFAULT_PRECIS,
                     CLIP_DEFAULT_PRECIS,
```

```
                        DEFAULT_QUALITY,
                        34,
                        "Arial");
  oldfont=pDC->SelectObject(&newfont);
  pDC->TextOut((300-(strlen(dlg.m_szTString)*10/2)),
               15,dlg.m_szTString,strlen(dlg.m_szTString));
  pDC->TextOut((300-(strlen(dlg.m_szXString)*10/2)),
               365,dlg.m_szXString,strlen(dlg.m_szXString));
  pDC->TextOut((90-ilenMaxLabel*12),70,strptr,ilenMaxLabel);
  pDC->SelectObject(oldfont);
  newfont.DeleteObject();
}

// Draw coordinate axis
pDC->MoveTo(99,49);
pDC->LineTo(99,350);
pDC->LineTo(500,350);
pDC->MoveTo(99,350);

// Initial values
x1=100;
y1=350;
z1=50;
z2=z1+15;
x2=x1+iBarWidth;

// Draw each bar
I=0
for(spai=rgsIA.begin(); spai<rgsIA.end(); spai++) {
  newbrush.CreateSolidBrush(dwColor[i]);
  oldbrush=pDC->SelectObject(&newbrush);
  y2=350-*spai;
  pDC->Rectangle(x1,y1,x2,y2);
  x1=x2;
  x2+=iBarWidth;
  I++;
  pDC->SelectObject(&newbrush);
  newbrush.DeleteObject();
}

// Draw bar labels
I=0;
for(sli=rgSL.begin(); sli!=rgSL.end(); sli++) {
  if ((cxClient>300)&&(cyClient>200)) {
    newbrush.CreateSolidBrush(dwColor[i]);
    oldbrush=pDC->SelectObject(&newbrush);
    pDC->Rectangle(545,z1,560,z2);
    pDC->TextOut(565,z1, sli->c_str());
    z1=z2+15;
    z2+=30;
    I++;
```

```
        pDC->SelectObject(&newbrush);
        newbrush.DeleteObject();
      }
    }
}

/////////////////////////////////////////////////////////////////
// CBarChartView diagnostics

#ifdef _DEBUG
void CBarChartView::AssertValid() const
{
    CView::AssertValid();
}

void CBarChartView::Dump(CDumpContext& dc) const
{
    CView::Dump(dc);
}

CBarChartDoc* CBarChartView::GetDocument()
{
    ASSERT(m_pDocument->IsKindOf(RUNTIME_CLASS(CBarChartDoc)));
    return (CBarChartDoc*)m_pDocument;
}
#endif //_DEBUG

/////////////////////////////////////////////////////////////////
// CBarChartView message handlers

void CBarChartView::OnSize(UINT nType, int cx, int cy)
{
    CView::OnSize(nType, cx, cy);

    // TODO: Add your message handler code here
    cxClient = cx;
    cyClient = cy;
}

void CBarChartView::OnDataentry()
{
    // TODO: Add your command handler code here
    dlg.DoModal();
    InvalidateRect(NULL, TRUE);
    UpdateWindow();
}
```

The ClassWizard was used to add two member functions to the Bar-ChartView.cpp file. If you examine the previous listing, you will notice On-Dataentry() and OnSize(). If you are working along on your computer, use the ClassWizard to add these member functions to your project. You will also need to add the code contained within each member function.

Coding in the View File

The `BarChartView.cpp` application will allow the user to create a presentation-quality bar chart in the client area of a window. Our data entry dialog box is a modal dialog box that allows the user to specify a chart title, axis labels, and the heights of up to twelve bars. The bar chart will then be scaled to fit the current window. Individual bar colors are selected from an array of predefined values.

At the top of this file, you'll see the initial **#include statements** and **typedef** definitions for the STL components that will be used in the application.

```
// STL header files
#include <list>
#include <vector>

using namespace std;

typedef vector <int> pointarray;
typedef vector <int> scaledpointarray;
typedef list <string> stringlist;
```

As you can see, the application will use two STL vectors of type int along with an STL list of type string. There will be more on the STL portion of this project's code, shortly.

The following line of code is used to associate *dlg* with the `DataDialog` resource.

```
DataDialog dlg;
```

The maximum number of bars is set to twelve by *maxnumber* at the start of the application:

```
#define maxnumbar 12
```

The number of bars can be changed, but keep in mind that a good presentation won't crowd too many bars onto a single bar chart.

In the following sections, we'll examine the role of each member function to see how it contributes to the whole project.

THE ONSIZE() FUNCTION

The `OnSize()` member function is used to handle `WM_SIZE` messages. In this application, when the size of the window is changed by the user, the graphics are sized proportionally. The window size information obtained by On-Size() is placed in *cxClient* and *cyClient*. This information is then available to the OnDraw() member function for scaling.

THE ONDATAENTRY() FUNCTION

The OnDataentry() member function serves as our connection to the data entry dialog box.

```
     .
     .
     .
dlg.DoModal();
InvalidateRect(NULL,TRUE);
UpdateWindow();
     .
     .
     .
```

DoModal() is used to draw the modal dialog box. The function also returns the dialog box results. When the user selects the OK or Cancel push buttons, special message-handler member functions attempt to close the dialog box. Typically, the OnOK() member function will validate and update the dialog box data before closing the dialog box. The OnCancel() member function does not validate or update dialog box data before closing the dialog box.

Since there is always the potential of new bar chart data arriving when the dialog box is closed, the InvalidateRect() and UpdateWindow() functions are called to ensure the client area will be redrawn.

THE ONDRAW() FUNCTION

This member function handles most of the work for the BarChart application. Notice the following STL code at the start of the OnDraw() function:

```
pointarray rgIA;
pointarray::iterator pai;

scaledpointarray rgsIA;
scaledpointarray::iterator spai;

stringlist rgSL;
stringlist::iterator sli;
```

This application will use two STL vectors, an STL list, and associated iterators. The first, *pointarray*, is used for storing the original bar chart heights after they are parsed from the edit box data. The second, *scaledpointarray*, is used to scale the original data for plotting in the client area. Also notice the use of an STL list, *stringlist*, that will be used to store the parsed bar chart labels when they are retrieved from the appropriate edit box.

Next, notice that bar colors are picked from the *dwColor[]* array in a sequential manner. If the bar chart has five bars, they will always be gray, red, green, blue, and yellow. If the order of colors doesn't appeal to you, re-arrange the colors in the *dwColor[]* array.

CFont and CBrush are used to allow font and brush objects to be passed to any CDC (base class for display context) member functions. A change from the default font will be necessary to draw the chart title and axes labels. New brushes will be used to fill the rectangular bar chart bars. The syntax for creating new font and brush objects is simple:

```
CFont newfont;
CFont* oldfont;
CBrush newbrush;
CBrush* oldbrush;
```

The next block of interesting code involves the parsing of a string of data values being returned by the data entry dialog box. Before a bar chart can be drawn, it is necessary to obtain individual bar values. Thus, each bar chart bar's height will be determined by parsing the *szHValues* string. *szHValues* contains a copy of the string information returned by the *m_szHValues* member variable. The push_back method is used to push the integer data into a *pointarray* vector identified as *rgIA*. The number of bars retrieved will be held in *iNBars*.

The following portion of code shows how the parsing routine parses the string containing the heights of the bars:

```
// parse string to get bar heights
i = 0;
iNBars=0;
n=szHValues;
p=strtok(n,",");
while ((n!=NULL)) {
  rgIA.push_back(atoi(n));
  p=strtok(NULL,",");
  n=p;
  iNBars++;
  I++;
  if (i >= maxnumber) break;
}
```

In a similar manner, the next routine parses the string containing the individual bar labels:

```
// parse string to get bar labels
i = 0;
n=szLValues;
p=strtok(n,",");
while ((n!=NULL)) {
  rgSL.push_back(n);
```

```
    p=strtok(NULL,",");
    n=p;
    I++;
    if (i >= maxnumber) break;
}
```

Both parsing routines make use of the powerful `strtok()` function. In the second routine, each bar chart label is placed in a *stringlist* list identified as *rgSL*. This is achieved with the use of the push_back method.

The number of bars in the bar chart is determined by incrementing the variable *iNBars*, each time the parser finds a new bar value. This value will be used to determine the width of each bar chart bar. The bar width is calculated from the total number of bars. The bar chart is always drawn to the same screen width. So, the more bars contained in the bar chart, the narrower each individual bar becomes. Bar widths, *iBarWidth*, are calculated by using:

```
iBarWidth=400/iNBars;
```

The height of each bar is calculated in proportion to the tallest bar value. The tallest bar value is scaled and drawn to the same chart height regardless of its numeric value. The size of the tallest bar value is easy to find:

```
// Find bar with maximum height and scale
for (pai=rgIA.begin(); pai<rgIA.end(); pai++)
  if (iBarMax < *pai) iBarMax = *pai;
```

Here, the vector containing the original bar heights is traversed. If any value in the vector is greater than the value currently in *iBarMax*, the value in *iBarMax* is replaced with the new value.

The bar chart will print the numeric height of the tallest bar value on the vertical chart axis. This is the value found in *iBarMax*. The _itoa() macro is used to convert this numeric value to a string for later use:

```
// Convert maximum y value to a string
strptr=_itoa(iBarMax,sbuffer,10);
ilenMaxLabel=strlen(sbuffer);
```

Once the tallest bar has been scaled, the remaining bars in the array are scaled to its value:

```
// Scale bars in array.  Highest bar = 270
for (pai=rgIA.begin(); pai<rgIA.end(); pai++)
  rgsIA.push_back((*pai * 270)/iBarMax);
```

Again, the original vector is traversed with the use of the *pai* iterator. The scaled data values are placed in *scaledpointarray*, identified as *rgsIA*, with the use of the push_back method.

The mapping mode, window extent, viewport extent, and origin are set with the following four function calls:

```
// Create custom viewport and map mode
dc.SetMapMode(MM_ISOTROPIC);
dc.SetWindowExt(640,480);
dc.SetViewportExt(cx_Client,cy_Client);
dc.SetViewportOrg(0,0);
```

By setting the viewport and map mode values, the graphics can be scaled to remain proportional with the window size. Notice the use of *cx_Client* and *cy_Client* in the SetViewportExt() function call. They are obtained from the OnSize() member function.

Next, it is necessary to prepare several fonts for drawing titles and labels. The CreateFont() function uses a logical font that most closely matches the application's requirements from the GDI's pool of physical fonts. The syntax for the CreateFont() function is:

```
CreateFont(Height,Width,Escapement,Orientation,Weight,
          Italic,Underline,StrikeOut,CharSet,
          OutputPrecision,ClipPrecision,Quality,
          PitchAndFamily,Facename)
```

The first time the CreateFont() function is called, the parameters are set to the following values:

```
Height = 20
Width  = 12
Escapement = 900
Orientation = 900
Weight = FW_NORMAL
Italic = FALSE
Underline = FALSE
StrikeOut = FALSE
CharSet = OEM_CHARSET
OutputPrecision = OUT_DEFAULT_PRECIS
ClipPrecision = CLIP_DEFAULT_PRECIS
Quality = DEFAULT_QUALITY
PitchAndFamily = 34
Facename = "Arial"
```

Windows will attempt to find a font to match these specifications. This font will be used to print a vertical string of text in the window. Notice that *Escapement* and *Orientation* are set to 900. This value represents an angle of 90.0 degrees. The *Escapement* value rotates the line of text from horizontal to vertical. The *Orientation* value rotates each character by 90.0 degrees. This is the font that is used to draw the vertical axis label.

The CreateFont() function is called a second time. This time, the parameters are set to the following values:

```
Height = 20
Width  = 12
Escapement = 0
Orientation = 0
Weight = FW_NORMAL
Italic = FALSE
Underline = FALSE
StrikeOut = FALSE
CharSet = OEM_CHARSET
OutputPrecision = OUT_DEFAULT_PRECIS
ClipPrecision = CLIP_DEFAULT_PRECIS
Quality = DEFAULT_QUALITY
PitchAndFamily = 34
Facename = "Arial"
```

This is the font that will be used to draw all horizontal titles and labels.

Examine the following portion of code used to draw the vertical axis label:

```
// Draw text if window is large enough
if ((cx_Client>300)&&(cy_Client>200)) {
  newfont.CreateFont(20,12,900,900,FW_BOLD,
                     FALSE,FALSE,FALSE,
                     OEM_CHARSET,OUT_DEFAULT_PRECIS,
                     CLIP_DEFAULT_PRECIS,
                     DEFAULT_QUALITY,
                     34,
                     "Arial");
  oldfont=dc.SelectObject(&newfont);
  dc.TextOut(50,200+(strlen(dlg.m_szYString)*10/2),
             dlg.m_szYString,strlen(dlg.m_szYString));
      .
      .
      .
```

The window can be scaled and so can our graphics. It is important to eliminate the title and labels if the fonts become too small for the user to read. Thus, a check is made on the horizontal and vertical sizes before drawing the labels.

The x and y coordinate axes are drawn by using both the MoveTo() and LineTo() functions:

```
// Draw coordinate axis
dc.MoveTo(99,49);
dc.LineTo(99,350);
dc.LineTo(500,350);
dc.MoveTo(99,350);
```

In this application, the first bar chart bar is drawn at coordinate points 100,350 on the bar chart. These values are defined by *x1* and *y1*. The position of the first bar and its width along with all remaining bars are determined from the last drawing position and the width of each previous bar. Thus, the second x value is defined by *x2*.

```
// Initial values
x1=100;
y1=350;
z1=50;
z2=z1+15;
x2=x1+iBarWidth;
```

Bar chart heights are retrieved from *iBarSizeScaled[]*. This scaled value is modified and saved in *y2* for use by the Rectangle() function.

The closed rectangular shape is then filled with the current brush color. The brush color value changes with each pass through the loop. Here is the small portion of code that accomplishes this task:

```
// Draw each bar
I=0;
for(spai=rgsIA.begin(); spai<rgsIA.end(); spai++) {
  newbrush.CreateSolidBrush(dwColor[i]);
  oldbrush=pDC->SelectObject(&newbrush);
  y2=350-*spai;
  pDC->Rectangle(x1,y1,x2,y2);
  x1=x2;
  x2+=iBarWidth;
  I++;
  pDC->SelectObject(&newbrush);
  newbrush.DeleteObject();
}
```

A **for** loop is used to traverse the data contained in the STL vector *rgsIA*. With each pass, a new bar color is selected from the *dwColor[]* array. The Rectangle() function draws each bar of the bar chart. During each pass through the loop, *x1* and *x2* are updated to point to the next bar's initial position.

Bar chart bar labels are obtained in a similar manner:

```
// Draw bar labels
I=0;
for(sli=rgSL.begin(); sli!=rgSL.end(); sli++) {
  if ((cxClient>300)&&(cyClient>200)) {
    newbrush.CreateSolidBrush(dwColor[i]);
    oldbrush=pDC->SelectObject(&newbrush);
    pDC->Rectangle(545,z1,560,z2);
    pDC->TextOut(565,z1, sli->c_str());
    z1=z2+15;
    z2+=30;
    I++;
    pDC->SelectObject(&newbrush);
    newbrush.DeleteObject();
  }
```

Here, the *rgSL* STL list is traversed for label values. As long as the client area is large enough, a small graphics icon and label will be drawn to the window and form a legend.

The TextOut() function is used to draw the labels. This function requires that string data be returned in a specific manner. Thus, the syntax:

```
sli->c_str()
```

The *sli* iterator points to a c_str() function. The member function returns a pointer to a non-modifiable C string. This string is constructed by adding a terminating null element (E(0)) to the controlled sequence.

Running the BarChart Application

Build the BarChart application. You should initially see a default bar chart similar to Figure 15.10. Unique bar charts, similar to the example shown in Figure 15.11, can be drawn by entering new data in the bar chart's data dialog box.

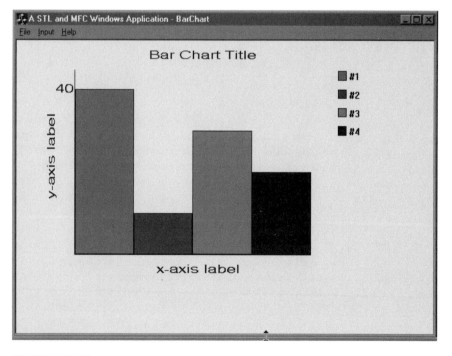

Figure 15.10   *The BarChart application's default bar chart.*

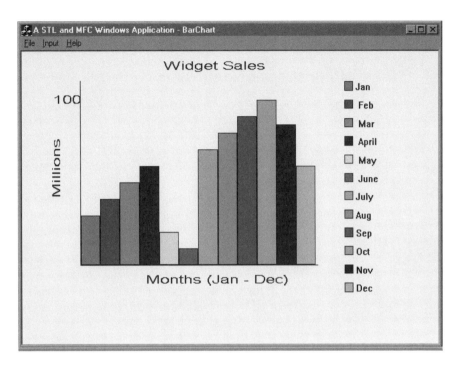

| Figure 15.11 | *A custom bar chart is created with the* BarChart *application.* |

Perhaps you would like to add additional features to the bar chart application, or change the sequence of bar colors. Now is the time to customize this application to suit your needs.

The Line Chart Application

The LineChart project will draw a presentation-quality line chart in the client area of a window. This application uses a menu and a data entry dialog box similar to those used by the BarChart application discussed in the previous sections. LineChart allows points to be specified by the user (x and y coordinates), then connects those points with lines. The data values for each point's x and y coordinates are obtained from separate edit box controls. Two parsing routines are used to obtain each point's coordinate pairs. Naturally, STL coding techniques play a very important role in the data retrieval process.

The complete application is built with the default AppWizard files you created earlier in this chapter. The project files were created in the LineChart workspace. In addition to the original group of files, a data entry dialog box resource must be added to the project.

Let's examine the modifications that are necessary to complete this project.

Modifying the String Table

To give the application a unique title in the title bar portion of the window, open the `String Table` resource, as shown in Figure 15.12.

Double-click on the `IDR_MAINFRAME` string to open the dialog box shown in Figure 15.13.

Modify the contents of this string so they appear similar to the string shown in Figure 15.14.

Close the current dialog box to accept the changes. You will see this modification in the upper left corner of the project's window each time it is run.

Modifying the Menu

The AppWizard generated a default menu as part of the base code, so it will be necessary to edit that menu and add a new menu entry. Open the `Menu` resource, as shown in Figure 15.15.

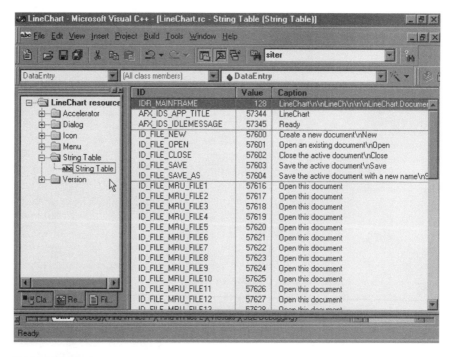

Figure 15.12   *Open the* `String Table` *resource.*

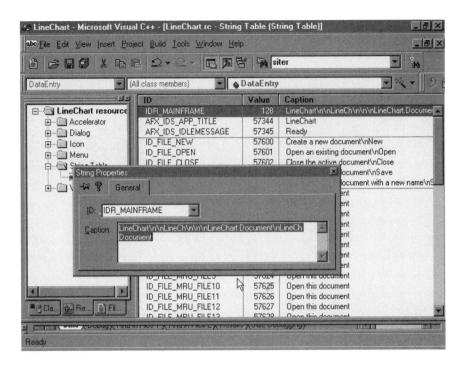

Figure 15.13 Open a dialog box in to modify the `IDR_MAINFRAME` string re-source.

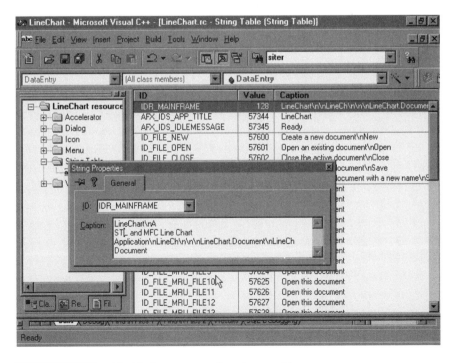

Figure 15.14 Modify the string to reflect the new title.

411

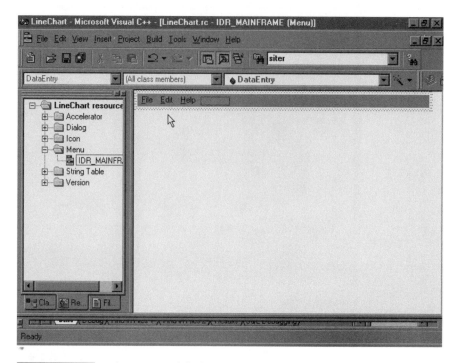

The project's default Menu *resource.*

The Edit menu entry can be eliminated by selecting the entry with the mouse and pressing the Delete key. Replace this entry with a menu named Input and a menu item named Data Entry..., as shown in Figure 15.16.

When you add the Data Entry...menu item, change the ID value to IDM_DATAENTRY. Remember, this value can be altered by right-clicking the mouse on the menu item and selecting the Properties option.

Click on the File menu to display all File menu items. Eliminate all of the File menu items except the Exit item by clicking on each item and pressing the Delete key.

The modifications to the menu resource are now completed for the project.

Creating a New Dialog Box

A new dialog box resource for data entry must be added to the application. From the Insert menu, select the Resource menu item. From the list of resources, select the Dialog option. Now, create a dialog box similar to the one shown in Figure 15.17.

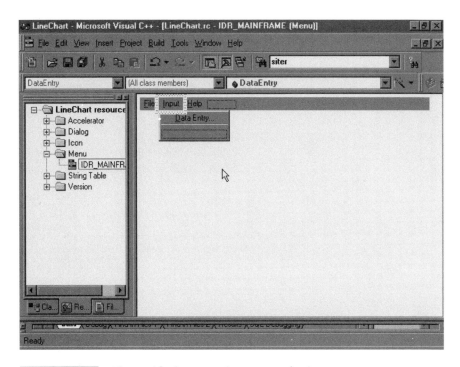

Figure 15.16   *The modified menu and menu items for the project.*

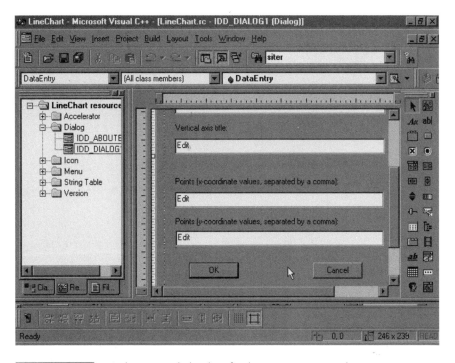

Figure 15.17   *A data entry dialog box for the* `LineChart` *application.*

413

As you can see the figure shows three of the five edit boxes that will eventually be used for user input. Each edit box has a unique ID value. From top to bottom, the ID values are IDC_EDIT1....IDC_EDIT5. You can right-click on an edit box and use the Properties option to alter these values. The dialog box, by default, is given an ID of IDD_DIALOG1. A new class will have to be added for the new dialog box to communicate with the other files in the project.

From the View menu, select the ClassWizard option, to open the MFC ClassWizard dialog box. Select the Add Class...button to open the New Class dialog box, as shown in Figure 15.18.

The default base class for a dialog box is CDialog. Our unique class name is DataEntry. The only item not entered at this point is the dialog ID. Recall that the ID for the Dialog resource is IDD_DIALOG1, for this project. We accepted the suggested filename, DataEntry.cpp. Choose Create to generate this new class and file. When you choose Create, a new class and file will be generated and you will be returned to the MFC ClassWizard dialog box, as shown in Figure 15.19.

Figure 15.19 shows the MFC ClassWizard dialog box after a member function has been added: DoDataExchange(). This member function pro-

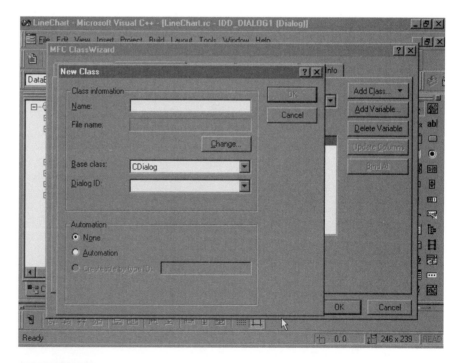

Figure 15.18   *The* New Class *dialog box allows a new class to be added to a project.*

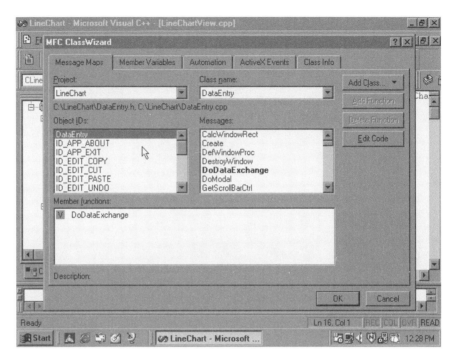

Figure 15.19   *A new class has been added to the* LineChart *project.*

vides the functionality for communicating between the dialog box and the application.

Remember, to pass information to or from a dialog box, the member functions rely on member variables. Each edit box in this example will pass information to the application through a unique member variable.

Select the Member Variables tab, as shown in Figure 15.20.

Figure 15.20 shows five edit box IDs and a member variable associated with each. To add member variables, just use the Add Variable...button. When a control ID is selected, the Add Variable...button opens the Add Member Variable dialog box. This dialog box will permit you to name the member variable, and set its category and type. Member variables start with m_ (to denote member variable). All of the edit boxes in this project return strings. The coordinate values for each point are returned in separate strings that will later be parsed.

When you are satisfied with the member variable names, select OK to close the MFC ClassWizard dialog box.

The following listing is the complete listing for the DataEntry.cpp file generated by the ClassWizard;

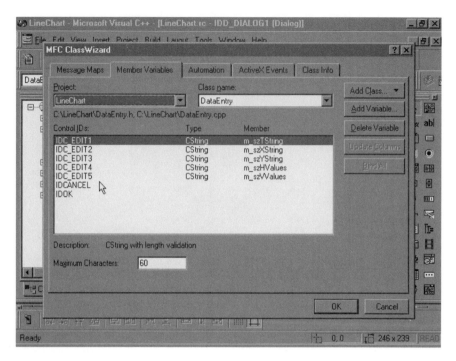

Figure 15.20   *Five member variables are associated with five edit box IDs.*

```cpp
// DataEntry.cpp : implementation file
//

#include "stdafx.h"
#include "LineChart.h"
#include "DataEntry.h"

#ifdef _DEBUG
#define new DEBUG_NEW
#undef THIS_FILE
static char THIS_FILE[] = __FILE__;
#endif

/////////////////////////////////////////////////////////////
// DataEntry dialog

DataEntry::DataEntry(CWnd* pParent /*=NULL*/)
    : CDialog(DataEntry::IDD, pParent)
{
    //{{AFX_DATA_INIT(DataEntry)
    m_szTString = _T("");
```

```
    m_szXString = _T("");
    m_szYString = _T("");
    m_szHValues = _T("");
    m_szVValues = _T("");
    //}}AFX_DATA_INIT
}

void DataEntry::DoDataExchange(CDataExchange* pDX)
{
    CDialog::DoDataExchange(pDX);
    //{{AFX_DATA_MAP(DataEntry)
    DDX_Text(pDX, IDC_EDIT1, m_szTString);
    DDV_MaxChars(pDX, m_szTString, 60);
    DDX_Text(pDX, IDC_EDIT2, m_szXString);
    DDV_MaxChars(pDX, m_szXString, 60);
    DDX_Text(pDX, IDC_EDIT3, m_szYString);
    DDV_MaxChars(pDX, m_szYString, 60);
    DDX_Text(pDX, IDC_EDIT4, m_szHValues);
    DDV_MaxChars(pDX, m_szHValues, 120);
    DDX_Text(pDX, IDC_EDIT5, m_szVValues);
    DDV_MaxChars(pDX, m_szVValues, 120);
    //}}AFX_DATA_MAP
}

BEGIN_MESSAGE_MAP(DataEntry, Cdialog)
    //{{AFX_MSG_MAP(DataEntry)
        // NOTE: the ClassWizard will add message map here
    //}}AFX_MSG_MAP
END_MESSAGE_MAP()
///////////////////////////////////////////////////////////
// DataEntry message handlers
```

Examine the previous file listing and find where the ClassWizard used member functions, message handlers, and member variables.

The constructor is used to initialize member variables. The following portion of this file is modified to reflect initial line chart values.

```
DataEntry::DataEntry(CWnd* pParent /*=NULL*/)
    : CDialog(DataEntry::IDD, pParent)
{
    //{{AFX_DATA_INIT(DataEntry)
    m_szTString = _T("Line Chart Title");
    m_szXString = _T("x-axis label");
    m_szYString = _T("y-axis label");
    m_szHValues = _T("50,70,150,200");
    m_szVValues = _T("10,70,35,90");
    //}}AFX_DATA_INIT
}
```

The DoDataExchange() member function is called by the framework to exchange and validate dialog data. This member function is never called directly. The UpdateData() member function is called, instead, to initialize the various dialog box controls or retrieve data. The ClassWizard writes an overridden version of this member function. This member function contains the data map of DDX and DDV global function calls. The code between the delimiters is automatically maintained by the ClassWizard and should not be modified directly.

```
void DataEntry::DoDataExchange(CDataExchange* pDX)
{
    CDialog::DoDataExchange(pDX)
    //{{AFX_DATA_MAP(DataEntry)
    DDX_Text(pDX, IDC_EDIT1, m_szTString);
    DDV_MaxChars(pDX, m_szTString, 60);
    DDX_Text(pDX, IDC_EDIT2, m_szXString);
    DDV_MaxChars(pDX, m_szXString, 60);
    DDX_Text(pDX, IDC_EDIT3, m_szYString);
    DDV_MaxChars(pDX, m_szYString, 60);
    DDX_Text(pDX, IDC_EDIT4, m_szHValues);
    DDV_MaxChars(pDX, m_szHValues, 120);
    DDX_Text(pDX, IDC_EDIT5, m_szVValues);
    DDV_MaxChars(pDX, m_szVValues, 120);
    //}}AFX_DATA_MAP
}
```

Exchanging data between dialog box controls and the application has been greatly simplified with MFC's DDX and DDV capabilities. DDX encapsulates macros for the purpose of exchanging data. DDV functions allow you to make sure valid data has been entered in your dialog box controls. As you can see from the previous listing, DoDataExchange() uses a pointer, pDX, to the CDataExchange object.

Each data exchange function call is of type DDX_Text, since we are exchanging string information from each edit box control. DDX_Text is an overloaded member function and can actually accept the following types: BYTE, CString, double, DWORD, float, int, LONG, and UINT.

This project includes data validation for each edit box entry. In other words, the dialog box control will limit string lengths directly to 60 or 120 characters, respectively. These can be seen within the DDV_ functions of DoDataExchange().

The data entry dialog box is ready to exchange data with the project. Now we'll have to create the line chart code. The line chart code is completely contained in the LineChartView.cpp file.

The `LineChartView.cpp` File

The `LineChartView.cpp` file is the standard view file created by the App-Wizard. As you examine the following listing you'll notice that this file contains numerous additional lines of code. Examine this code carefully and pay particular attention to the lines set in bold.

```cpp
// LineChartView.cpp : implementation of the CLineChartView class
//

#include "stdafx.h"
#include "LineChart.h"

#include "LineChartDoc.h"
#include "LineChartView.h"
#include "DataEntry.h"

// STL header
#include <vector>

using namespace std;
typedef struct pair<int,int> XY_PAIR;
typedef vector<XY_PAIR> dataarray;
typedef vector<XY_PAIR> scaleddataarray;

DataEntry dlg;

#ifdef _DEBUG
#define new DEBUG_NEW
#undef THIS_FILE
static char THIS_FILE[] = __FILE__;
#endif

/////////////////////////////////////////////////////////////////////
// CLineChartView

IMPLEMENT_DYNCREATE(CLineChartView, Cview)

BEGIN_MESSAGE_MAP(CLineChartView, Cview)
    //{{AFX_MSG_MAP(CLineChartView)
    ON_WM_SIZE()
    ON_COMMAND(IDM_DATAENTRY, OnDataentry)
    //}}AFX_MSG_MAP
END_MESSAGE_MAP()

/////////////////////////////////////////////////////////////////////
// CLineChartView construction/destruction

CLineChartView::CLineChartView()
{
```

```
}

CLineChartView::~CLineChartView()
{
}

BOOL CLineChartView::PreCreateWindow(CREATESTRUCT& cs)
{
    return CView::PreCreateWindow(cs);
}

/////////////////////////////////////////////////////////////
// CLineChartView drawing

void CLineChartView::OnDraw(CDC* pDC)
{
    CLineChartDoc* pDoc = GetDocument();
    ASSERT_VALID(pDoc);

    XY_PAIR datapair;
    XY_PAIR scaleddatapair;

    dataarray rgIPA;
    dataarray::iterator dai;

    scaleddataarray rgSIPA;
    scaleddataarray::iterator sdai;

    CFont newfont;
    CFont* oldfont;
    CPen newpen;
    CPen* oldpen;

    int i, x, y, iXMax, iYMax;
    int xtic, ytic;
    static char szHValues[60];

    static char szVValues[60];
    static char *s,*v;

    // make copies of data for redrawing
    // when WM_SIZE messages are received
    strcpy(szHValues,dlg.m_szHValues);
    strcpy(szVValues,dlg.m_szVValues);

    // parse szHValues to get x line points
    s=strtok(szHValues,",");
    while (s!=NULL) {
      datapair.first = atoi (s);
      rgIPA.push_back(datapair);
```

```
    s=strtok(NULL,",");
  }

  // parse szVValues to get y line points
  v=strtok(szVValues,",");
  for(dai=rgIPA.begin(); dai<rgIPA.end(); dai++) {
    dai->second = atoi (v);
    v=strtok(NULL,",");
  }

  // find maximum x and maximum y point
  for(dai=rgIPA.begin(); dai<rgIPA.end(); dai++) {
    if (iXMax<dai->first) iXMax=dai->first;
    if (iYMax<dai->second) iYMax=dai->second;
  }

  // scale x points in array.
  // max x value = 400, max y value is 300
  for(dai=rgIPA.begin(); dai<rgIPA.end(); dai++) {
    scaleddatapair.first=(dai->first * 400)/iXMax;
    scaleddatapair.second=(dai->second * 300)/iYMax;
    rgSIPA.push_back(scaleddatapair);
  }

  // create custom viewport and map mode
  pDC->SetMapMode(MM_ISOTROPIC);
  pDC->SetWindowExt(640,480);
  pDC->SetViewportExt(cxClient,cyClient);
  pDC->SetViewportOrg(0,0);

  // draw text when window is large enough
  if ((cxClient>300)&&(cyClient>200)) {
    newfont.CreateFont(20,12,900,900,FW_NORMAL,
                       FALSE,FALSE,FALSE,
                       OEM_CHARSET,OUT_DEFAULT_PRECIS,
                       CLIP_DEFAULT_PRECIS,
                       DEFAULT_QUALITY,
                       34,
                       "Arial");
    oldfont=pDC->SelectObject(&newfont);
    pDC->TextOut(50,200+(strlen(dlg.m_szYString)*10/2),
                 dlg.m_szYString,strlen(dlg.m_szYString));
    pDC->SelectObject(oldfont);
    newfont.DeleteObject();

    newfont.CreateFont(20,12,0,0,FW_NORMAL,
                       FALSE,FALSE,FALSE,OEM_CHARSET,
                       OUT_DEFAULT_PRECIS,
                       CLIP_DEFAULT_PRECIS,
                       DEFAULT_QUALITY,
```

```
                        34,
                        "Arial");
  oldfont=pDC->SelectObject(&newfont);
  pDC->TextOut((300-(strlen(dlg.m_szTString)*10/2)),
              15,dlg.m_szTString,strlen(dlg.m_szTString));
  pDC->TextOut((300-(strlen(dlg.m_szXString)*10/2)),
              365,dlg.m_szXString,strlen(dlg.m_szXString));
  pDC->SelectObject(oldfont);
  newfont.DeleteObject();
}


// draw coordinate axis
pDC->MoveTo(99,49);
pDC->LineTo(99,350);
pDC->LineTo(500,350);
pDC->MoveTo(99,350);


// draw x axis tic marks
xtic=140;
for (i=0;i<10;i++) {
  ytic=350;
  pDC->MoveTo(xtic,ytic);
  ytic=347;
  pDC->LineTo(xtic,ytic);
  xtic+=40;
}


// draw y axis tic marks
ytic=50;
for (i=0;i<10;i++) {
  xtic=100;
  pDC->MoveTo(xtic,ytic);
  xtic=103;
  pDC->LineTo(xtic,ytic);
  ytic+=30;
}


// Plot a + symbol for each point
newpen.CreatePen(PS_SOLID,1,PALETTERGB(0xFF,0x00,0x00));
oldpen=pDC->SelectObject(&newpen);
for(sdai=rgSIPA.begin(); sdai<rgSIPA.end(); sdai++) {
  x=100 + sdai->first;
  y=350—sdai->second;
  pDC->MoveTo(x-5,y);
  pDC->LineTo(x+5,y);
  pDC->MoveTo(x,y-5);
  pDC->LineTo(x,y+5);
}
pDC->SelectObject(&newpen);
newpen.DeleteObject();
```

```
    // Plot lines between points
    newpen.CreatePen(PS_SOLID,1,PALETTERGB(0x00,0x00,0xFF));
    oldpen=pDC->SelectObject(&newpen);
    sdai=rgSIPA.begin();
    x=100 + sdai->first;
    y=350-sdai->second;
    pDC->MoveTo(x,y);
    for(sdai=rgSIPA.begin(); sdai<rgSIPA.end(); sdai++) {
      x=100 + sdai->first;
      y=350-sdai->second;
      pDC->LineTo(x,y);
    }
    pDC->SelectObject(&newpen);
    newpen.DeleteObject();
}


/////////////////////////////////////////////////////////////////
// CLineChartView diagnostics

#ifdef _DEBUG
void CLineChartView::AssertValid() const
{
    CView::AssertValid();
}

void CLineChartView::Dump(CDumpContext& dc) const
{
    CView::Dump(dc);
}

CLineChartDoc* CLineChartView::GetDocument()
{
    ASSERT(m_pDocument->IsKindOf(RUNTIME_CLASS(CLineChartDoc)));
    return (CLineChartDoc*)m_pDocument;
}
#endif //_DEBUG


/////////////////////////////////////////////////////////////////
// CLineChartView message handlers

void CLineChartView::OnSize(UINT nType, int cx, int cy)
{
    CView::OnSize(nType, cx, cy);

    // TODO: Add your message handler code here
    cxClient = cx;
    cyClient = cy;
}

void CLineChartView::OnDataentry()
```

```
{
    // TODO: Add your command handler code here
    dlg.DoModal();
    InvalidateRect(NULL, TRUE);
    UpdateWindow();
}
```

The ClassWizard was used to add two member functions to the
LineChartView.cpp file. If you examine the previous listing, you will notice OnDataentry() and OnSize(). You'll need to use the ClassWizard to
add these member functions to your project. Then you will also need to add
the code contained within each member function.

Coding in the View File

The LineChartView.cpp application will allow the user to create a presentation-quality line chart in the client area of a window. The data entry dialog
box is a modal dialog box that allows the user to specify a chart title, axis labels, and the x and y coordinates of multiple data points. The line chart will
then be scaled to fit the current window.

At the top of this file, you'll see an initial **#include** statement and **typedef** definitions for the STL components that will be used in the application.

```
// STL header
#include <vector>

using namespace std;

typedef struct pair<int,int> XY_PAIR;
typedef vector<XY_PAIR> dataarray;
typedef vector<XY_PAIR> scaleddataarray;
```

As you can see, the application will use two STL vectors of type
XY_PAIR. These vectors have already been defined as an STL pair. There
will be more on the STL portion of this project's code, shortly.

The following line of code is used to associate *dlg* with the DataEntry resource.

```
DataEntry dlg;
```

In the following sections, we'll examine the role of each member function to see how it contributes to the whole project.

THE ONSIZE() FUNCTION

The OnSize() member function is used to handle WM_SIZE messages. In this
application, when the size of the window is changed by the user, the graphics are sized proportionally. The window size information obtained by On-

Size() is placed in *cxClient* and *cyClient*. This information is then available to the OnDraw() member function for scaling.

THE ONDATAENTRY() FUNCTION

The OnDataentry() member function serves as our connection to the data entry dialog box.

```
    .
    .
    .
  dlg.DoModal();
  InvalidateRect(NULL,TRUE);
  UpdateWindow();
    .
    .
    .
```

DoModal() is used to draw the modal dialog box. The function also returns the dialog box results. When the user selects the OK or Cancel push buttons, a special message-handler member functions attempt to close the dialog box. Usually, the OnOK() member function will validate and update the dialog box data before closing the dialog box. The OnCancel() member function does not validate or update dialog box data before closing the dialog box.

There is always the potential of new line chart data arriving when the dialog box is closed, so the InvalidateRect() and UpdateWindow() functions are called to ensure the client area will be redrawn.

THE ONDRAW() FUNCTION

This member function, handles most of the work for the LineChart application. The OnDraw() function initializes some interesting STL code at its start:

```
XY_PAIR datapair;
XY_PAIR scaleddatapair;

dataarray rgIPA;
dataarray::iterator dai;

scaleddataarray rgSIPA;
scaleddataarray::iterator sdai;
```

This application will use two STL vectors. The first, *dataarray*, is used for storing the original pairs of coordinate values for each point on the chart. The pairs are formed by using two separate parsing routines and extracting the data from two separate edit box controls. The second, *scaleddataarray*, is used to scale the original data pairs for plotting in the client area.

CFont and CPen are used to allow font and pen objects to be passed to any CDC (base class for display context) member functions. A change from the default font will be necessary to draw the chart title and axes labels. New pens will be used to draw the data point and connecting lines in the line chart. The syntax for creating new font and pen objects is simple:

```
CFont newfont;
CFont* oldfont;
CPen newpen;
CPen* oldpen;
```

The next block of interesting code involves the parsing of two strings of data values being returned by the data entry dialog box. Before a line chart can be drawn, it is necessary to obtain x and y coordinates for each data point on the chart. The x coordinate points are contained in *sxHValues*, while the y coordinate points are in *sxYValues*.

The following portion of code shows how the parsing routine parses the string containing the x and y coordinate points:

```
// parse szHValues to get x line points
s=strtok(szHValues,",");
while (s!=NULL) {
  datapair.first = atoi (s);
  rgIPA.push_back(datapair);
  s=strtok(NULL,",");
}

// parse szVValues to get y line points
v=strtok(szVValues,",");
for(dai=rgIPA.begin(); dai<rgIPA.end(); dai++) {
  dai->second = atoi (v);
  v=strtok(NULL,",");
}
```

Two separate parsing routines are needed because the strtok() function can only parse one string at a time. So, the first parsing routine uses the push_back method to load the x coordinate data members of the pair onto the *rgIPA* vector. The second parsing routine uses the push_back method to load the y coordinate data members of the pair onto the *rgIPA* vector.

The maximum x and y points are needed by the application to scale the graphics to the full size of the line chart. This is achieved by traversing the *rgIPA* vector pairs and saving the largest point values in *iXMax* and *iYMax*, respectively.

```
// find maximum x and maximum y point
for(dai=rgIPA.begin(); dai<rgIPA.end(); dai++) {
  if (iXMax<dai->first) iXMax=dai->first;
  if (iYMax<dai->second) iYMax=dai->second;
}
```

Next, the x and y coordinate pairs are scaled to fit the client drawing area of the window.

```
// scale x points in array.
// max x value = 400, max y value is 300
for(dai=rgIPA.begin(); dai<rgIPA.end(); dai++) {
  scaleddatapair.first=(dai->first * 400)/iXMax;
  scaleddatapair.second=(dai->second * 300)/iYMax;
  rgSIPA.push_back(scaleddatapair);
}
```

The *rgIPA* vector is traversed scaling the x and y data pairs. The x values are scaled by a factor of 400/iXMax and the y values by 300/iYMax. This will ensure that the largest x value is plotted to the extreme right on the chart and that the largest y value is plotted on the top of the chart. Traversing is achieved with the use of the *dai* iterator.

The mapping mode, window extent, viewport extent, and origin are set with the following four function calls:

```
// create custom viewport and map mode
dc.SetMapMode(MM_ISOTROPIC);
dc.SetWindowExt(640,480);
dc.SetViewportExt(cx_Client,cy_Client);
dc.SetViewportOrg(0,0);
```

By setting the viewport and map mode values, the graphics can be scaled to remain proportional with the window size. Notice the use of *cx_Client* and *cy_Client* in the SetViewportExt() function call. They are obtained from the OnSize() member function.

The next portion of code prepares several fonts for drawing titles and labels. The CreateFont() function uses the logical font that most closely matches the application's requirements from the GDI's pool of physical fonts. Since this code is so similar to the previous example, it will not be discussed in this section.

The coordinate axes for the line chart are drawn with simple MoveTo() and LineTo() function calls:

```
// draw coordinate axis
    pDC->MoveTo(99,49);
    pDC->LineTo(99,350);
    pDC->LineTo(500,350);
    pDC->MoveTo(99,350);
```

Tic marks are placed on both the x and y coordinate lines with the following code:

```
// draw x axis tic marks
xtic=140;
for (i=0;i<10;i++) {
```

```
    ytic=350;
    pDC->MoveTo(xtic,ytic);
    ytic=347;
    pDC->LineTo(xtic,ytic);
    xtic+=40;
}

// draw y axis tic marks
ytic=50;
for (i=0;i<10;i++) {
    xtic=100;
    pDC->MoveTo(xtic,ytic);
    xtic=103;
    pDC->LineTo(xtic,ytic);
    ytic+=30;
}
```

Next, the individual data points are plotted on the line chart. Since these will be tiny, a small red "+" symbol is created for each point.

```
// Plot a + symbol for each point
newpen.CreatePen(PS_SOLID,1,PALETTERGB(0xFF,0x00,0x00));
oldpen=pDC->SelectObject(&newpen);
for(sdai=rgSIPA.begin(); sdai<rgSIPA.end(); sdai++) {
    x=100 + sdai->first;
    y=350—sdai->second;
    pDC->MoveTo(x-5,y);
    pDC->LineTo(x+5,y);
    pDC->MoveTo(x,y-5);
    pDC->LineTo(x,y+5);
}
pDC->SelectObject(&newpen);
newpen.DeleteObject();
```

The *rgSIPA* vector is traversed with the *sdai* iterator and returns the scaled x and y coordinate points. These points are offset by either 100 or 350 to plot them on the chart, since the origin for this application wasn't changed.

Now, a blue line will be drawn between each pair of points using the following portion of code:

```
// Plot lines between points
newpen.CreatePen(PS_SOLID,1,PALETTERGB(0x00,0x00,0xFF));
oldpen=pDC->SelectObject(&newpen);
sdai=rgSIPA.begin();
x=100 + sdai->first;
y=350—sdai->second;
pDC->MoveTo(x,y);
for(sdai=rgSIPA.begin(); sdai<rgSIPA.end(); sdai++) {
    x=100 + sdai->first;
    y=350—sdai->second;
    pDC->LineTo(x,y);
```

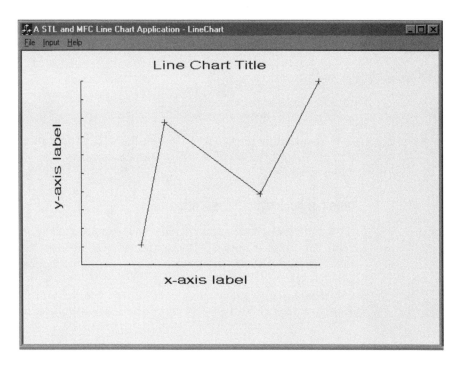

Figure 15.21   The LineChart *application's default line chart.*

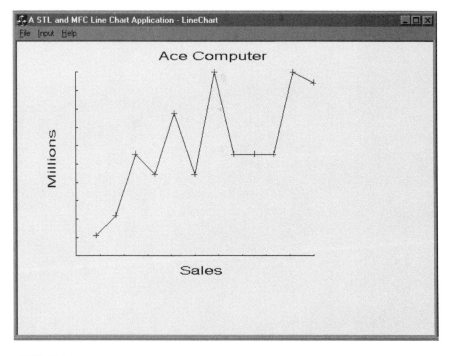

Figure 15.22   *A custom line chart created with the* LineChart *application.*

```
}
pDC->SelectObject(&newpen);
newpen.DeleteObject();
```

That's all there is to it. Presto—a line chart application using the power of the STL and the MFC! If you resize the window, the graphics will resize automatically.

Running theLineChart Application

Build the LineChart application. You should initially see a default line chart, similar to Figure 15.21. Unique line charts, similar to the example shown in Figure 15.22, can be drawn by entering new data in the line chart's data dialog box.

If you want to take this project a step further, you might want to add numeric values to both vertical and horizontal coordinate lines.

An MFC Screen Saver

Screen savers were originally created to protect your monitor from burning the phosphor dots on the screen. The earliest screen savers simply blanked the screen after a pre-determined amount of time. In recent years, however, we've come to expect more from screen saver applications: moving fish, trains, stars, scrolling marquees, and so on have become favorites. Some screen savers even contain advanced features, such as password protection. However, all Windows screen savers have a minimal set of features. These features include:

- A top-most window.
- A window without a border or a system menu that occupies the whole screen.
- A window without a cursor.
- Detect mouse movement or button pushes and any keyboard actions.
- Draw and move an image about on the screen.

All actions, such as deleting the acceptable period of inactivity or the restoration of the screen, are handled by Windows, not the screen saver.

The screen saver application developed in this chapter will blank the screen and start a little flying saucer and creature on a journey about your screen. The colorful saucer was created as a bitmapped image. The saucer will fly about your screen in a two-dimensional journey that will last until there is either mouse or keyboard activity on your system.

This application does not make use of the STL, but it does illustrate the fundamentals required of all screen saver applications.

Screen Saver Files

Design and build the basic code for the screen saver application with the AppWizard, as you have done with applications in previous chapters. Name this project `Saucer`.

This application will use four source code files: `Saucer.cpp`, `Saucerwnd.cpp`, `Drawwnd.cpp` and `stdafx.cpp`. There are also four header files associated with these source code files. The `Drawwnd.cpp` file is most closely associated with the view file. The `Saucerwnd.cpp` file corresponds to a file created for an additional class. The document file (doc) is not needed. Additionally, you'll need to create a bitmapped image of an object, like the saucer we drew. Let's look at each of the files in more detail.

The `Saucer.h` and `Saucer.cpp` Files

The `Saucer.h` header file is used for the declaration of the `CsaucerApp` class. Note in this case that the `CsaucerApp` class is derived from the `CWinApp` class, not the `CFrameWnd` class as in past examples. This is because our application's window will not use a standard window frame.

```
// saucer.h : main header file for the saucer application
//

#ifndef __AFXWIN_H__
  #error include 'stdafx.h' before this file for PCH
#endif

#include "resource.h"    // main symbols

// CsaucerApp:
// See saucer.cpp for the implementation of this class
//

class CsaucerApp : public CWinApp
{
public:
        CsaucerApp ;

// Overrides
  // ClassWizard generated virtual function overrides
        //{{AFX_VIRTUAL(CsaucerApp)
  public:
  virtual BOOL InitInstance ;
  //}}AFX_VIRTUAL


        //{{AFX_MSG(CsaucerApp)
```

```
            // NOTE—ClassWizard will add/remove member functions.
            //    DO NOT EDIT these blocks of generated code !
          //}}AFX_MSG
          DECLARE_MESSAGE_MAP()
        };
```

The Saucer.cpp file provides the implementation for the CsaucerApp class. You'll notice, in the following listing, that no additional code is added to the class constructor:

```
// saucer.cpp : Defines class behaviors for the application.
//

#include "stdafx.h"
#include "saucer.h"
#include "drawwnd.h"
#include "saucerwnd.h"

#ifdef _DEBUG
#undef THIS_FILE
static char BASED_CODE THIS_FILE[] = __FILE__;
#endif

// CsaucerApp

BEGIN_MESSAGE_MAP(CsaucerApp, CWinApp)
        //{{AFX_MSG_MAP(CsaucerApp)
    // NOTE—ClassWizard will add/remove mapping macros.
    //    DO NOT EDIT these blocks of generated code!
  //}}AFX_MSG
  ON_COMMAND(ID_HELP, CWinApp::OnHelp)
END_MESSAGE_MAP()

// CsaucerApp construction

CsaucerApp::CsaucerApp()
{
  // TODO: add construction code here,
  // Place all significant initialization in InitInstance
}

// The one and only CsaucerApp object

CsaucerApp theApp;

// CsaucerApp initialization

BOOL CsaucerApp::InitInstance()
{
  // Standard initialization
```

```
SetRegistryKey(_T("Flying Saucer"));

CsaucerWnd* pWnd = new CsaucerWnd;
pWnd->Create();
    m_pMainWnd = pWnd;
    return TRUE;
}
```

In this listing, notice that the InitInstance() member function is used to set the Registry key.

The Saucerwnd.h and Saucerwnd.cpp Files

The saucerwnd.h header file is used for the declaration of the CsaucerWnd class. The CsaucerWnd class is derived from the CDrawWnd class. The CDrawWnd class is described in the Drawwnd.h header file.

```
// saucerwnd.h : header file
//

// CsaucerWnd window

class CsaucerWnd : public CDrawWnd
{
// Construction
public:
        CsaucerWnd();

// Attributes
public:
  CPoint m_ptLast;

// Operations
public:
  BOOL Create();

// Overrides
  // ClassWizard generated virtual function overrides
        //{{AFX_VIRTUAL(CsaucerWnd)
  //}}AFX_VIRTUAL

// Implementation
public:
        virtual ~CsaucerWnd();

// Generated message map functions
protected:
        //{{AFX_MSG(CsaucerWnd)
```

```
afx_msg void OnSysCommand(UINT nID, LPARAM lParam);
afx_msg void OnDestroy();
afx_msg BOOL OnSetCursor(CWnd* pWnd, UINT nHitTest,
                         UINT message);
afx_msg BOOL OnNcActivate(BOOL bActive);
afx_msg void OnActivate(UINT nState, CWnd* pWndOther,
                        BOOL bMinimized);
afx_msg void OnActivateApp(BOOL bActive, HTASK hTask);
afx_msg void OnMouseMove(UINT nFlags, CPoint point);
afx_msg void OnLButtonDown(UINT nFlags, CPoint point);
afx_msg void OnRButtonDown(UINT nFlags, CPoint point);
afx_msg void OnKeyDown(UINT nChar, UINT nRepCnt,
                       UINT nFlags);
afx_msg void OnSysKeyDown(UINT nChar, UINT nRepCnt,
                          UINT nFlags);
//}}AFX_MSG
DECLARE_MESSAGE_MAP()
};
```

The message map declaration in the header file indicates which events will be used to trigger the return to the normal window. As you can see from the bolded lines of code, events such as system activities, key presses, mouse movements, and mouse button activations will be used to terminate the screen saver session.

The saucerwnd.cpp file implements the CsaucerWnd class and initializes several variables within the constructor. For example, the initial bitmap position is defined here:

```
// saucerwnd.cpp : implementation file
//

#include "stdafx.h"
#include "saucer.h"
#include "drawwnd.h"
#include "saucerwnd.h"

#ifdef _DEBUG
#undef THIS_FILE
static char BASED_CODE THIS_FILE[] = __FILE__;
#endif
// CsaucerWnd

CsaucerWnd::CsaucerWnd()
{
  m_ptLast = CPoint(-1, -1);
  m_nXPos = 320;
  m_nYPos = 240;
  m_nStep = 1;
}
```

```
CsaucerWnd::~CsaucerWnd()
{
}


BEGIN_MESSAGE_MAP(CsaucerWnd, CDrawWnd)
        //{{AFX_MSG_MAP(CsaucerWnd)
  ON_WM_SYSCOMMAND()
  ON_WM_DESTROY()
  ON_WM_SETCURSOR()
  ON_WM_NCACTIVATE()
  ON_WM_ACTIVATE()
  ON_WM_ACTIVATEAPP()
  ON_WM_MOUSEMOVE()
  ON_WM_LBUTTONDOWN()
  ON_WM_RBUTTONDOWN()
  ON_WM_KEYDOWN()
  ON_WM_SYSKEYDOWN()
  //}}AFX_MSG_MAP
END_MESSAGE_MAP()

// CsaucerWnd message handlers

BOOL CsaucerWnd::Create()
{
  CRect rect(0, 0, ::GetSystemMetrics(SM_CXSCREEN),
    ::GetSystemMetrics(SM_CYSCREEN));

  return CDrawWnd::Create(WS_EX_TOPMOST,
WS_VISIBLE|WS_POPUP,
                        rect, NULL, 0, NULL);
}

void CsaucerWnd::OnSysCommand(UINT nID, LPARAM lParam)
{
  if ((nID == SC_SCREENSAVE) || (nID == SC_CLOSE))
    return;
  CDrawWnd::OnSysCommand(nID, lParam);
}

void CsaucerWnd::OnDestroy()
{
  PostQuitMessage(0);
  CDrawWnd::OnDestroy();
}

BOOL CsaucerWnd::OnSetCursor(CWnd* pWnd, UINT nHitTest,
                                UINT message)
{
  SetCursor(NULL);
```

```
  return TRUE;
}

BOOL CsaucerWnd::OnNcActivate(BOOL bActive)
{
  if (!bActive)
    return FALSE;
  return CDrawWnd::OnNcActivate(bActive);
}

void CsaucerWnd::OnActivate(UINT nState, CWnd* pWndOther,
                            BOOL bMinimized)
{

  if (nState == WA_INACTIVE)
    PostMessage(WM_CLOSE);
  CDrawWnd::OnActivate(nState, pWndOther, bMinimized);
}

void CsaucerWnd::OnActivateApp(BOOL bActive, HTASK hTask)
{
  if (!bActive)
    PostMessage(WM_CLOSE);
  CDrawWnd::OnActivateApp(bActive, hTask);
}

void CsaucerWnd::OnMouseMove(UINT nFlags, CPoint point)
{
  if (m_ptLast == Cpoint(-1,-1))
    m_ptLast = point;
  else if (m_ptLast != point)
    PostMessage(WM_CLOSE);
  CDrawWnd::OnMouseMove(nFlags, point);
}

void CsaucerWnd::OnLButtonDown(UINT nFlags, CPoint point)
{
  PostMessage(WM_CLOSE);
  CDrawWnd::OnLButtonDown(nFlags, point);
}

void CsaucerWnd::OnRButtonDown(UINT nFlags, CPoint point)
{
  PostMessage(WM_CLOSE);
  CDrawWnd::OnRButtonDown(nFlags, point);
}

void CsaucerWnd::OnKeyDown(UINT nChar, UINT nRepCnt,
                           UINT nFlags)
{
```

```
    PostMessage(WM_CLOSE);
    CDrawWnd::OnKeyDown(nChar, nRepCnt, nFlags);
}

void CsaucerWnd::OnSysKeyDown(UINT nChar, UINT nRepCnt,
                             UINT nFlags)
{
    PostMessage(WM_CLOSE);
    CDrawWnd::OnSysKeyDown(nChar, nRepCnt, nFlags);
}
```

As you study the previous listing, you should notice that this window is designed to be a top-most window using a NULL value when calling the SetCursor() function.

All of the member functions used for terminating the screen saver use essentially the same code. They post a WM_CLOSE window message. When the message is sent, the screen saver application will terminate until Windows, once again, initiates it.

The Drawwnd.h and Drawwnd.cpp Files

The drawwnd.h header file is used for the declaration of the CDrawWnd class. You'll notice that the CDrawWnd class is derived from the CWnd class, too. A number of variables are declared in the public portion of this class. These variables will be used to set colors, step sizes, positions, and so on.

```
// drawwnd.h : header file
//

// CDrawWnd window

class CDrawWnd : public Cwnd
{
// Construction
public:
    CDrawWnd(BOOL bAutoDelete = TRUE);

// Attributes
public:
    CRgn m_rgnLast;
    int m_nXSteps, m_nYSteps;
    int m_nXPos, m_nYPos;
    int m_nStep;
    LOGBRUSH m_logbrush;
    LOGBRUSH m_logbrushBlack;
    static LPCTSTR m_lpszClassName;
    void SetSpeed();
    void SetColor(COLORREF cr);
```

```
// Operations
public:

// Overrides
    // ClassWizard generated virtual function overrides
    //{{AFX_VIRTUAL(CDrawWnd)
    public:
    virtual BOOL Create(DWORD dwExStyle, DWORD dwStyle,
                        const RECT& rect, CWnd* pParentWnd,
                        UINT nID,
                        CCreateContext* pContext = NULL);
    protected:
    virtual void PostNcDestroy();
    //}}AFX_VIRTUAL

// Implementation
public:
    virtual ~CDrawWnd();

protected:
    BOOL m_bAutoDelete;

    // Generated message map functions
protected:
    //{{AFX_MSG(CDrawWnd)
    afx_msg void OnTimer(UINT nIDEvent);
    afx_msg void OnPaint();
    afx_msg int OnCreate(LPCREATESTRUCT lpCreateStruct);
    //}}AFX_MSG
    DECLARE_MESSAGE_MAP()
};
```

The drawwnd.cpp file implements the CDrawWnd class. The class constructor is used to initialize several variables, including the step size (1 unit) for the graphics, background color (black), and so on.

```
// drawwnd.cpp : implementation file
//

#include "stdafx.h"
#include "saucer.h"
#include "drawwnd.h"

#ifdef _DEBUG
#undef THIS_FILE
static char BASED_CODE THIS_FILE[] = __FILE__;
#endif

LPCTSTR CDrawWnd::m_lpszClassName = NULL;

// CDrawWnd
```

```cpp
CDrawWnd::CDrawWnd(BOOL bAutoDelete)
{
  m_bAutoDelete = bAutoDelete;
  m_nXPos = 320;
  m_nYPos = 240;
  m_rgnLast.CreateRectRgn(0,0,0,0);

  m_nXSteps = 1;
  m_nYSteps = 1;
  m_logbrush.lbStyle = m_logbrushBlack.lbStyle = BS_SOLID;
  m_logbrush.lbHatch = m_logbrushBlack.lbHatch = 0;
  m_logbrushBlack.lbColor = RGB(0, 0, 0);
}

CDrawWnd::~CDrawWnd()
{
}


BEGIN_MESSAGE_MAP(CDrawWnd, Cwnd)
  //{{AFX_MSG_MAP(CDrawWnd)
  ON_WM_TIMER()
  ON_WM_PAINT()
  ON_WM_CREATE()
  //}}AFX_MSG_MAP
END_MESSAGE_MAP()

void CDrawWnd::SetSpeed()
{
  KillTimer(1);
  VERIFY(SetTimer(1, 30, NULL) != 0);
}

void CDrawWnd::SetColor(COLORREF cr)
{
  m_logbrush.lbColor = cr;
}

// CDrawWnd message handlers

void CDrawWnd::OnTimer(UINT nIDEvent)
{
  if (nIDEvent == 1)
  {
    CClientDC dc(this);
    CRect rect;
    CBitmap m_bitmap;
    CDC dcMem;
    BITMAP bm;

    GetClientRect(&rect);
```

```
    m_bitmap.LoadBitmap(IDB_SAUCER1);
    m_bitmap.GetObject(sizeof(bm),&bm);
    m_nXPos += m_nXSteps;
    m_nYPos += m_nYSteps;

    if (!dcMem.CreateCompatibleDC(&dc))
      return;
    CBitmap* pBitmapOld = dcMem.SelectObject(&m_bitmap);
    if (pBitmapOld == NULL)
      return;

    dc.BitBlt(m_nXPos,m_nYPos,bm.bmWidth,bm.bmHeight,
              &dcMem,0,0,SRCCOPY);

    if((m_nXPos+bm.bmWidth > rect.right) ||
        (m_nXPos < rect.left))
      m_nXSteps=-m_nXSteps;

    if((m_nYPos+bm.bmHeight > rect.bottom) ||
        (m_nYPos < rect.top))
      m_nYSteps=-m_nYSteps;

    dcMem.SelectObject(pBitmapOld);
  }
  else
    CWnd::OnTimer(nIDEvent);
}

void CDrawWnd::OnPaint()
{
  CPaintDC dc(this); // device context for painting
  CRect rect;
  CBrush brush(RGB(0,0,0));

  m_rgnLast.DeleteObject();
  m_rgnLast.CreateRectRgn(0,0,0,0);
  GetClientRect(rect);
  dc.FillRect(&rect, &brush);
  // Do not call CWnd::OnPaint() for painting messages
}

int CDrawWnd::OnCreate(LPCREATESTRUCT lpCreateStruct)
{
  if (CWnd::OnCreate(lpCreateStruct) == -1)
    return -1;

  SetSpeed();

  return 0;
}
```

```
BOOL CDrawWnd::Create(DWORD dwExStyle, DWORD dwStyle,
                      const RECT& rect,
                      CWnd* pParentWnd, UINT nID,
                      CCreateContext* pContext)
{
    // Register a class with no cursor
  if (m_lpszClassName == NULL)
  {
      m_lpszClassName = AfxRegisterWndClass(CS_HREDRAW|CS_VREDRAW,
      ::LoadCursor(AfxGetResourceHandle(),
      MAKEINTRESOURCE(IDC_NULLCURSOR)));
  }

    // TODO: Add specialized code here and/or call base class
  return CreateEx(dwExStyle, m_lpszClassName, _T(""),
                  dwStyle, rect.left, rect.top,
                  rect.right-rect.left,
                  rect.bottom-rect.top,
                  pParentWnd->GetSafeHwnd(), NULL, NULL );
}

void CDrawWnd::PostNcDestroy()
{
  if (m_bAutoDelete)
    delete this;
}
```

The number of timer ticks controls the animation speed. Thus, the speed of the animation is set with the SetTimer() function. In this case, Timer 1 is set to "tick" once every 30/1000 of a second. This value seemed just about right for this application, but it can be changed to speed up or slow down the movement of the bitmap.

The OnTimer() member function controls the movement of the bitmap image. The same basic code is used here, as in earlier chapters, for drawing bitmapped images to the screen. The real difference is in the fact that the image is being moved. Each time the OnTimer() function is called, the *m_nXPos* and *m_nYPos* variables are incremented by *m_nXSteps* and *m_nYSteps*, respectively.

```
m_nXPos += m_nXSteps;
m_nYPos += m_nYSteps;
```

Thus, with each timer tick, new X and Y positions are generated. The BitBlt() function moves the bitmap image to the new position.

```
dc.BitBlt(m_nXPos,m_nYPos,bm.bmWidth,bm.bmHeight,
          &dcMem,0,0,SRCCOPY);
```

When a collision occurs between the bitmap and any edge of the screen, the movement of the bitmap must be reversed. This reversal action is handled with the following portion of code:

```
if((m_nXPos+bm.bmWidth > rect.right) ||
    (m_nXPos < rect.left))
  m_nXSteps=-m_nXSteps;

if((m_nYPos+bm.bmHeight > rect.bottom) ||

    (m_nYPos < rect.top))
  m_nYSteps=-m_nYSteps;
```

The `OnPaint()` member function handles the background painting, while the `Create()` member function installs the NULL cursor.

Notice that the return value for this class returns the `CreateEx()` values, giving the extents of the rectangle used as the window.

```
return CreateEx(dwExStyle, m_lpszClassName, _T(""),
                dwStyle, rect.left, rect.top,
                rect.right-rect.left,
                rect.bottom-rect.top,
                pParentWnd->GetSafeHwnd(), NULL, NULL );
```

The *rect.left* variable represents the initial x-position and the *rect.top* variable the initial y-position of the CWnd window. The values obtained form *rect.right-rect.left* give the width of the CWnd in device units. Likewise, the *rect.bottom-rect.top* values give the height of the CWnd in device units.

The Build Operation

The project settings for this application will differ from those used in other chapters. Select the `Settings...` menu item from the `Build` menu. Use the Project Settings dialog box to set the Microsoft Foundation Classes to use a shared DLL, as shown in Figure 16.1.

From the same dialog box, select the C/C++ tab and make sure the preprocessor and project options include the following:

```
/nologo /MDd /W3 /Gm /GX /ZI /Od /D "WIN32" /D "_DEBUG" /D "_WINDOWS"
/D "_AFXDLL" /D "_MBCS" /Fp".\Debug/saucer.pch" /Yu"Stdafx.h"
/Fo".\Debug/" /Fd".\Debug/" /FD /c
```

These settings are partially shown in Figure 16.2.

Finally, select the `Link` tab to set the final format for a screen saver file with an `.scr` file extension, as shown in Figure 16.3.

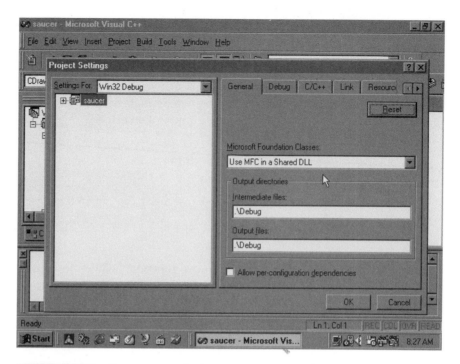

Figure 16.1   *Project settings for the* Saucer *project.*

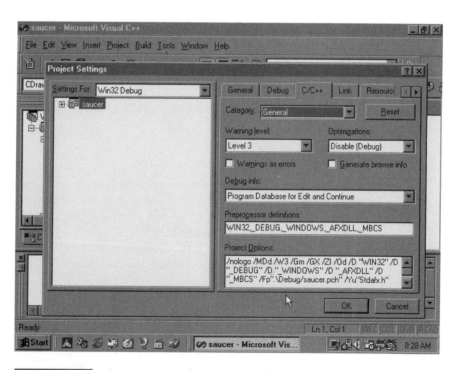

Figure 16.2   *Preprocessor and project options for the compiler.*

444

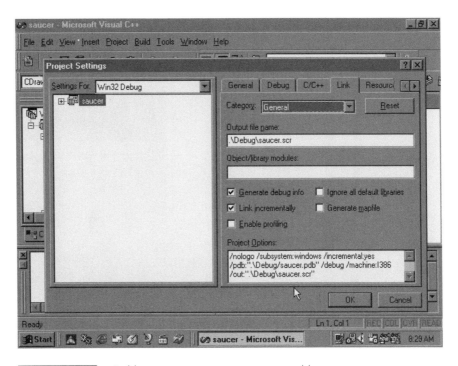

Figure 16.3   *Building an .scr screen saver executable.*

The linker's project options include:

```
/nologo /subsystem:windows /incremental:yes
/pdb:".\Debug/saucer.pdb" /debug /machine:I386
/out:".\Debug\saucer.scr"
```

Build the screen saver application by selecting the Rebuild All... menu item from the Build menu.

When a successful build occurs, you will have to move the saucer.scr file to the proper Windows subdirectory. Typically, for Windows 98 and Windows 2000, this will be C:\Windows\System.

Testing The Screen Saver

When the screen saver is run, you'll see a little saucer float about the screen. Figure 16.4 shows the bitmapped image while it was being created in the resource editor.

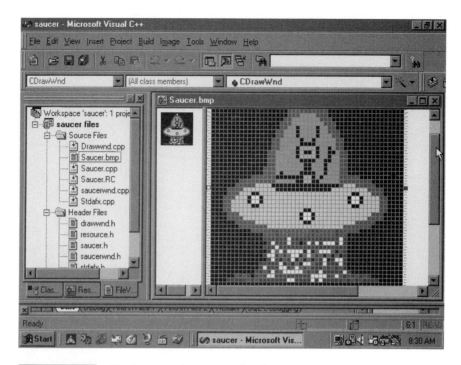

Figure 16.4   The bitmapped image used in the project.

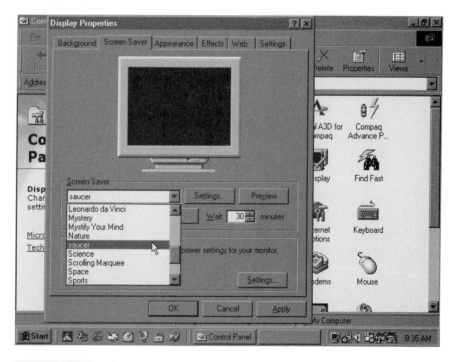

Figure 16.5   The saucer screen saver is installed from the `Display Properties` dialog box.

The screen saver is installed by choosing the Settings\Control Panel from the Windows 98 or Windows 2000 Start menu and selecting the Display option. Then, from the Display Properties dialog box shown in Figure 16.5, the saucer screen saver is selected in the Screen Saver dialog box.

While the screen saver application does not provide all of the robust abilities that can be built into a screen saver, such as password protection and an initial settings dialog box, it does provide you with all of the fundamentals for building great screen savers.

What's Next?

You now have the basic program for moving any bitmapped image two-dimensionally about on the screen. Why not create your own custom bitmap and use this application, as-is, as your own personal screen saver.

Perhaps you'll want to take a further step and include an STL application from a previous chapter in your screen saver design.